RESPONSIBLE BUSINESS

With the globalisation of markets, the phenomenon of market failure has also been globalised. Against the backdrop of the territoriality of nation state jurisdictions and the slow progress of international law based on the principle of sovereignty this poses a serious challenge. However while the legal infrastructure of globalised markets has a firm basis in formal national and international law, the side effects of economic transactions on public goods such as the environment, human health and consumer interests often escape state-based regulation. Therefore, attention is drawn to the potential of self-regulation by transnational industry. While hypotheses abound which try to grasp this phenomenon in conceptual terms, both empirical and legal research is still underdeveloped. This volume helps to fill this gap, in two ways: firstly by reconstructing self-regulatory settings such as multinational corporations, transnational production networks and industry-NGO partnerships in terms of organisation, problem-solving and legitimation, and secondly, by linking their empirical findings to formal law by examining how legal concepts are reflected in self-regulation, how the law builds on self-regulatory solutions, and how it helps to establish favorable conditions for private governance.

Oñati International Series in Law and Society

A SERIES PUBLISHED FOR THE OÑATI INSTITUTE FOR THE SOCIOLOGY OF LAW

Titles in this Series

Social Dynamics of Crime and Control: New Theories for a World in Transition edited by Susannah Karstedt and Kai Bussmann

Criminal Policy in Transition edited by Andrew Rutherford and Penny Green

Making Law for Families edited by Mavis Maclean

Poverty and the Law edited by Peter Robson and Asbjørn Kjønstad

Adapting Legal Cultures edited by Johannes Feest and David Nelken

Rethinking Law Society and Governance: Foucault's Bequest edited by Gary Wickham and George Pavlich

Rules and Networks edited by Richard Appelbaum, Bill Felstiner and Volkmar Gessner

Women in the World's Legal Professions edited by Ulrike Schultz and Gisela Shaw

Healing the Wounds edited by Marie-Claire Foblets and Trutz von Trotha

Imaginary Boundaries of Justice edited by Ronnie Lippens

Family Law and Family Values edited by Mavis Maclean

Contemporary Issues in the Semiotics of Law edited by Anne Wagner, Tracey Summerfield and Farid Benavides Vanegas

The Geography of Law: Landscapes, Identity and Regulation edited by Bill Taylor

Theory and Method in Socio-Legal Research edited by Reza Banakar and Max Travers

Luhmann on Law and Politics edited by Michael King and Chris Thornhill

Precarious Work, Women and the New Economy: The Challenge to Legal Norms edited by Judy Fudge and Rosemary Owens

Juvenile Law Violators, Human Rights, and the Development of New Juvenile Justice Systems edited by Eric L Jensen and Jørgen Jepsen

The Language Question in Europe and Diverse Societies: Political, Legal and Social Perspectives edited by Dario Castiglione and Chris Longman

European Ways of Law: Towards A European Sociology of Law edited by Volkmar Gessner and David Nelken

Crafting Transnational Policing: Police Capacity-Building and Global Policing Reform edited by Andrew Goldsmith and James Sheptycki

Constitutional Politics in the Middle East: With special reference to Turkey, Iraq, Iran and Afghanistan edited by Saïd Amir Arjomand

Parenting after Partnering: Containing Conflict after Separation edited by Mavis Maclean

Responsible Business

Self-Governance and Law in Transnational Economic Transactions

Edited by
Olaf Dilling
Martin Herberg
and
Gerd Winter

Oñati International Series in Law and Society

A SERIES PUBLISHED FOR THE OÑATI INSTITUTE FOR THE SOCIOLOGY OF LAW

• HART •
PUBLISHING

OXFORD AND PORTLAND OREGON
2008

Published in North America (US and Canada)
by Hart Publishing
c/o International Specialized Book Services
920 NE 58th Avenue, Suite 300
Portland, OR 97213-3786
USA
Tel: +1 503 287 3093 or toll-free: (1) 800 944 6190
Fax: +1 503 280 8832
E-mail: orders@isbs.com
Website: www.isbs.com

Hart Publishing, 16c Worcester Place, Oxford, OX1 2JW
Telephone: +44 (0)1865 517530 Fax: +44 (0)1865 510710
E-mail: mail@hartpub.co.uk
Website: http://www.hartpub.co.uk

British Library Cataloguing in Publication Data
Data Available

ISBN: 978-1-84113-779-7 (hardback)
ISBN: 978-1-84113-780-3 (paperback)

Typeset by Compuscript, Shannon
Printed and bound in Great Britain by
CPI Antony Rowe, Chippenham

Preface

Due to the principle of territoriality, states and their law cannot adequately deal with a growing number of transnational business transactions. For various reasons international law and organisations do not fill the regulatory gap. However, the absence of state-based law in cross-border relations does not result in anomy. Instead, self-governance of the private sector has emerged with the intention of both enabling transactions and regulating them.

This book strives to look more closely at the structures generating self-governance, and the nature of the informal law associated with it. It focuses on self-governance taking a 'public role', such as in transnational environmental, consumer and worker protection. It explores the self-governing potential of multinational corporations, production and marketing networks, creditor-debtor relations, international standardisation associations, transnational stewardship councils and communication networks. In addition, causes and factors driving self-governance, such as economic incentives, technical professionality and the transnational public are identified. The problem-solving capacity of self-governance is also assessed.

Besides explaining transnational self-governance, the authors look at the bridges that exist between the informal law of the private sector and the formal law of states and international regimes. Informal law is often reimbedded into formal law, for example where state regulation makes reference to and builds upon self-generated rules. Sometimes, formal law encourages self-governance to emerge, or even strives for control in order to exclude deviant variants. International law has also opened itself to address private actors. Moreover, transnational self-governance may be understood as a precursor to or an element of a new layer of transnational customary law.

The overall thrust of the book is twofold: to contribute to the theory of legal pluralism and interlegality, and to provide answers to the more practical question whether self-governance can be relied on as a source of benign global governance.

The contributions to this volume are based on papers presented at a workshop held at the Oñati International Institute for the Sociology of Law in 2005. The editors are thankful to the staff of the Institute for their friendly and effective way of organising the workshop. Several of the contributions were elaborated in the framework of the Collaborative Research Centre 'Transformations of the State' of the University of Bremen whose joint financing of the workshop is gratefully acknowledged. Finally, we wish to express our gratitude to the team of Hart Publishing for its careful copy-editing and smooth processing of the book.

Olaf Dilling, Martin Herberg, and Gerd Winter
Bremen, March 2008

Contents

List of Contributors

RALF BENDRATH is a researcher at the Collaborative Research Centre 'Transformations of the State', University of Bremen. His research interests include internet governance, privacy and data protection, security policy and the role of civil society in global governance. Recent publications include 'The Return of the State in Cyberspace. The Hybrid Regulation of Global Data Protection', in Myriam Dunn, Sai Felicia Krishna-Hensel and Victor Mauer (eds) *The Resurgence of the State: Trends and Processes in Cyberspace Governance* (Aldershot, Ashgate, 2007).

GRALF-PETER CALLIESS is Professor of Private and International Commercial Law at the University of Bremen Department of Law. He directs a research project on 'Legal Certainty and Fairness in International Commerce' at the Collaborative Research Centre 'Transformations of the State' at the same university. His present research is concerned with international and European private and commercial law and legal theory. He has published a book on cross-border consumer contracts in global electronic commerce (Mohr Siebeck, 2006).

JOSÉ AUGUSTO FONTOURA COSTA is Professor of Environmental Law and Economic Law at the University of Santos and University of the State of Amazonas, Department of Law. He co-directs a research project entitled 'International Environmental Regimes, especially their Influence on International Economic law'. His present research is concerned with International Law of Foreign Investment and Environmental Regimes.

CRISTIANE DERANI is Professor of Environmental Law and Economic Law at the University of Santos and University of the State of Amazonas, Department of Law. She co-directs a research project entitled 'International Environmental Regimes, especially their Influence on International Economic law'. Her present research is concerned with traditional knowledge and biodiversity in the framework of international trade and biotechnology development. She has published a book on Environmental and Economic Law (3rd edition, Saraiva, 2008).

OLAF DILLING is research associate at the Collaborative Research Center 'Transformations of the State' at the University of Bremen, Germany, where he is working on a project about transnational environmental governance and interlegality. He is currently writing his PhD thesis on product responsibility in international corporate networks. In 2005 he published 'Die Produktionsbedingung als Produkteigenschaft' in G Winter (ed) *Die Umweltverantwortung multinationaler Unternehmen* (Baden-Baden, Nomos-Verlagsgesellschaft).

CAROLA GLINSKI is a lawyer and a research fellow at the Centre for European Environmental Law at the University of Bremen, Germany. Her present research focuses on private regulation in global environmental governance. Recent publications include contributions to G Winter (ed), *Die Umweltverantwortung multinationaler Unternehmen*, (Baden-Baden, Nomos, 2005), S MacLeod (ed), *Global Governance and the Quest for Justice—Corporate Governance* (Oxford, Hart, 2006) and D McBarnet, A. Voiculescu and T Campbell (eds), *The New Corporate Accountability: Corporate Social Responsibility and the Law* (Cambridge, Cambridge University Press, 2007).

MARTIN HERBERG, Dipl Soz, Dr rer pol, is senior research fellow at the Collaborative Research Centre 'Transformations of the State', University of Bremen, Germany. His work concentrates on globalisation, socio-legal research and qualitative methodology. For further reading see 'From Diffusion to Interplay. The Constitutional State in the Age of Global Legal Pluralism', in A Hurrelmann, S Leibfried and P Mayer (eds), *Transforming the Golden Age State* (Houndmills, Palgrave, 2007).

EVA KOCHER is a university lecturer in civil law, labour law and comparative law, as well as a lawyer in Hamburg. She directed the German team in the context of the European research project 'Social standards in European transnational enterprises' (ESTER) at the University of Hamburg, Department of Economics and Politics. She has published several articles on legal aspects of self-regulation in transnational business activities, among them 'Unternehmerische Selbstverpflichtungen im Wettbewerb', (2005) *Gewerblicher Gechtsschutz und Urheberrecht* 647–52 and 'Private Standards between Soft Law and Hard Law' (2002) 3 *International Journal of Comparative Labour Law and Industrial Relations* 265–80.

ALEXANDRA LINDENTHAL is research associate at the Collaborative Research Centre 'Transformations of the State' at the University of Bremen, Germany. In 2007, she finished her PhD thesis concerning the Leadership of the European Union in the international regime on climate change. Currently, her research focuses on norm-setting processes of private actors in the transnational sphere. She co-edited *Institutionalisierung von Nachhaltigkeit* together with Thomas Beschorner, Torsten Behrens, Esther Hoffmann, Maria Hage, Barbara Thierfelder and Bernd Siebenhüner (Marburg, Metropolis, 2005).

ERROL MEIDINGER is Professor and Vice Dean of Law for Research and Faculty Development at the State University of New York in Buffalo and also an Honorary Professor at the University of Freiburg, Germany. His current research focuses on innovative institutional arrangements for promoting environmental conservation and social justice. These include supra-governmental regulatory initiatives such as forest certification and fair labour standards programmes, reconstructed property rights systems incorporating customary relationships and indigenous rights, and public-interest oriented intellectual property rights. Much of his work can be found at http://www.law.buffalo.edu/eemeid.

OREN PEREZ is a Professor at Bar Ilan University Faculty of Law. His main research areas are environmental law, international trade law and legal theory. Among his recent publications are *Ecological Sensitivity and Global Legal Pluralism: Rethinking the Trade and Environment Conflict* (Oxford, Hart Publishing, 2004) and *Paradoxes and Inconsistencies in the Law* (Oxford, Hart Publishing, 2006) co-edited with Gunther Teubner.

SOL PICCIOTTO is Professor Emeritus at Lancaster University Law School, UK, where he taught and was Head for several years from 1992. He previously taught at the Universities of Dar es Salaam and Warwick. He has researched and published widely on international business law and regulation, and has been conducting a personal research programme on regulatory networks and global governance under a research fellowship from the Economic and Social Research Council, from which the chapter in this volume results.

GERD WINTER is Professor of Public Law and the Sociology of Law at the University of Bremen Department of Law, Germany. He directs the Research Centre for European Environmental Law as well as a section of the Collaborative Research Centre 'Transformations of the State' at the same university. His present research is concerned with legal instruments of environmental protection, including business self-regulation, as addressed in this volume. He edited *Multilevel Governance of Global Environmental Change* (Cambridge, Cambridge University Press, 2006).

Introduction: Private Accountability in a Globalising World

OLAF DILLING, MARTIN HERBERG, AND GERD WINTER*

I. GLOBALISATION AND PRIVATE LAW-MAKING: LEGAL PLURALISM IN THE TRANSNATIONAL AGE

'UBI SOCIETAS IBI ius' (Grotius). Wherever social actors engage with each other for long periods of time, common norms and binding standards of behaviour emerge. At the level of world society, current developments appear to confirm this claim. Evidently, global players and other transnational actors do not approve of a state of anomy; rather, they prefer relatively clear and calculable standards and guidelines of behaviour, and often these actors are even eager to develop such standards themselves.

In many cases, these emerging norm structures do not simply represent an incoherent pool of social norms; in some respects, they represent a kind of a 'living law' of commerce and industry, a 'global law without a state' (Teubner, 1997). These norms are based on their own grounds for validity, they are of lasting character and they often entail their own mechanisms for implementation and control. This development questions many categories of classical legal thinking, among others the unity of law and the idea of the nation state's monopoly on law-making.

The existence of a plurality of norm structures is not new, however. A number of phenomena, discussed in legal sociology since its very beginning, have persistently challenged the state-centered concept of law: just think of different forms of industrial voluntary commitments on the national level, or the increasing relevance of technical standardisation by expert committees (Schepel, 2005). Yet, by introducing procedural safeguards and material opening clauses, state law was able to retain control of these other sources of law. Thus, the state-centric conception of law was maintained. By contrast, today a new level of informality has been reached due to the globalisation

* We wish to thank Harry Bauer for his help in translating substantial parts of this introduction into the English language.

of social spheres. While at the national level activities like private technical standardisation remain embedded in institutional regulatory arrangements, on the transnational level norm generation often appears to be untamed and rampant.

Partly, these private initiatives simply represent a transfer of national standards into the global context. As states cannot extend their law to other continents, private actors can lend global reach to the rules of their home country merely as a result of their private autonomy and their transnational organisational capability. Here, the actors of world society function as transfer managers conveying legal achievements from particular national contexts to the global level.

Often, norms and rules are also generated by private actors themselves; this mostly becomes manifest both in the emergence of new, creative and unconventional types of norms, and in the nature of these norms as highly problem-oriented and practical. Private actors seem unconcerned that such developments can hardly be reconciled with the formal qualities of (modern) law and the criteria of democratic legislation in its classical shape. To the contrary, often the informality and flexibility of these arrangements are seen as the particular advantage of this kind of law-making (Herberg, 2006).

Yet, these processes do not cut off state law from the informal law of world society. Due to their practical relevance, the emerging informal norms cannot easily be ignored from a legal perspective. Although most of the new normative formations lack a classical legal form—for example, as a contract with all its necessary requirements—they nevertheless encompass lawyers' professional concerns as to how the emergent norms can be brought into accordance with generalisable values and legitimated procedures, and thus with formal law. If actors trust in the compliance with a particular norm, if legal interests of a third party are affected, if rights and obligations are allocated in a particular way, this issue is always at stake.

Here lies the first aim of this volume: it is about the interface between the emerging para-legal systems and national as well as international law. As it turns out, dealing with the informal norms of the transnational sphere entails manifold challenges to interdisciplinarity. To bring the interface into focus, social sciences and jurisprudence must be employed both to provide disciplinary analysis and to develop new tools for interlinkage.

II. VARIETIES OF LAW: TOWARDS A TYPOLOGY OF PRIVATE GOVERNANCE

Thus far, the emerging law of world society has mainly found attention in the form of a new 'lex mercatoria'. Industries with a high level of cross-border transactions develop their own practices and, hence, solve different coordination problems of transnational business that otherwise would remain untouched due to a lack of convincing mechanisms in state law (Appelbaum *et al*, 2001).

The evidence for such internal business norms is hardly surprising as far as it serves to coordinate the actors' private interests. Yet, the real challenge for private self-regulation arises in the field of public interest. Arguably, there is a stark contrast between, on the one side, organising one's own company and arranging credit security and liability for defects among equals and, on the other side, achieving recognition for fair wages, good working conditions, the protection of natural resources and consumer interests among unequals (Winter, 2005).

It is this volume's second aim to look deeper into this matter by contrasting the emergent private sector regimes, evaluating their problem-solving potential and detecting the driving forces behind them. Many of the abovementioned developments are currently discussed under the heading of 'global governance', focusing on how the common goods can be handled beyond classical hierarchical and formal procedures (see Rosenau and Czempiel, 1992). The concept highlights the increasing relevance of private actors as norm-makers and draws attention to processes of experimentation and creative and unconventional strategies in the provision of public goods.

These aspects gain additional relevance in the global context where a plethora of steering mechanisms of non-state origin exists. The role of private actors is not limited to influencing the ongoing political processes of law-making. Instead, without recognition by state actors they generate their 'own' law.

For a provisional taxonomy, it might be helpful to distinguish three actor constellations from which the para-legal systems of the business world emerge.

(1) In some respect, the first constellation—corporate self-responsibility—is the simplest case. Often based on existing societal demands and expectations, single multinational corporations independently define binding rules for conduct, concerning affairs in their own subsidiaries. Frequently, internal norms and rules are made public by announcing some kind of self-commitment; often compliance is guaranteed by internal monitoring and control mechanisms. Thus, a kind of 'inner law' of multinational corporations emerges. The parent company proactively accepts responsibility for behaviour in different countries of investment, although its subsidiaries are legally independent entities. Apart from single enterprises, corporate associations and standardisation organisations present a second kind of corporate self-responsibility.

(2) The second constellation—the law of transnational corporate networks—shows a higher level of complexity. The reach of networks by far exceeds that of single corporate groups; they encompass regions of very different development and firms from very different industries. As the concept of networks implies, different companies acknowledge that the prevailing issues cannot be resolved single-handedly.

Accordingly, different stocks of knowledge and resources have to be pooled. Transcending single companies, a division of tasks and responsibilities exists on the basis of shared norms and values. Common rules are developed and often new forms of control emerge, especially more generalised control procedures as an alternative to checking and testing on a case-to-case basis.

(3) The third constellation—non-governmental organisation (NGO)–business partnerships—mobilise the power of civil society, particularly by organising consumer interests. Increasingly, NGOs address corporations directly with their demands instead of choosing to go through state institutions. Frequently, this leads to the mutual development of standards which are ambitious in substance and achievable in practice. In such hybrid arrangements, NGOs guarantee some objectivity and neutrality, especially concerning the monitoring of compliance. The use of market mechanisms, especially the award of quality marks and certificates, provides corporations with an economic incentive for cooperation. The procedures of norm creation are highly institutionalised—frequently granting all parties equal opportunities to influence proceedings—and often institutions for dispute resolution and for further norm development exist.

These three actor constellations—single enterprises,[1] networks, and partnerships—are those which will more fully be explored in this volume. Even though they are not meant to cover the entire spectrum of non-state governance structures, they are widespread and particularly pertinent for closer examination. All of them show characteristics which are normally attributed to classical state law. Insofar as they establish a clear distinction between acceptable and non-acceptable practices and create trust in the binding character of rules, one can speak of 'soft law' (Kirton and Trebilcock, 2004). In some respects, the para-legal systems under research show a transition from soft to hard law, since bodies for norm implementation are set up and powers are created to impose sanctions in cases of violation.

The degree of consolidation can only be identified from case to case, in general, however, the resemblance to law is striking. Yet, concerning the reach of these norms one has to tame expectations. Private actors might not be able to generate a comprehensive and universal conception of justice for the entire world society, even if it is the rule that within certain business segments the relevant norms are widely dispersed. Nevertheless, without a central regulatory authority superior to individual firms and corporate

[1] Corporate associations and standardisation organisations are not dealt with in depth in this volume. However, some of the chapters do include some initiatives of industry associations as an additional source of transnational standards.

networks, collectively shared standards do emerge out of mutual learning and the horizontal exchange of experience.

Under aspects of democracy and the rule of law, equivalent procedures to state law can rarely be found (perhaps the pluralistic arrangements between business actors and NGOs show the most advanced mechanisms of democratic legitimation). However, the creation of norms is always oriented towards convincing solutions, which find maximum recognition by all relevant groups and stakeholders.

Regarding aspects of implementation, world society cannot draw on an executive body comparable to national administrative systems, yet there exists a tight net of norm control. Frequently, specially trained actors take on auditing and monitoring functions, leading to in-depth enquiries and the systematic search for violations. In order to enforce compliance, private actors possess numerous sanctioning mechanisms: from measures in staff management (especially within the type of 'inner law' of corporate groups), through the cancellation of business dealings (within networks), to the withdrawal of certificates or quality marks (especially relevant in the context of NGO–business partnerships). Frequently, in the case of disputes, an appeal to court-like institutions is possible.

To summarise: in the era of globalisation, the institutions of the constitutional state seem to be increasingly bypassed by informal law-making. As soon as one abandons the common equation of law as state law, numerous new issues demand attention, raising questions about the origins of the emergent norms, about their efficacy and about the future of state law in a situation of global legal pluralism.

III. TOWARDS A THEORY AND APPRAISAL: PERFORMANCE AND LEGITIMACY OF THE NEW MODES OF GOVERNANCE

At the current moment, a comprehensive theory explaining and appraising global norm emergence does not exist; yet, there are numerous approaches, middle-range concepts and also a number of methodological principles that are commonly employed by research in the field.

To develop these approaches further towards an empirically informed general theory is the third major aim of this volume. The main challenge is to portray the new governance mechanisms not as a deficiency but to define them in their positivity, their inherent rationality and their productive potential. This touches upon the point that globalisation does not per se dissolve order. On the other hand, the emerging norms in their actual shape rather resemble a patchwork of sectoral regimes, instead of a comprehensive and consistent system.

In some regards, the volume's focus on private governance is a somewhat narrow frame of reference. That is to say, certain phenomena such as the unscrupulous abuse of power are left out. Nevertheless, in terms of the existing problem-solving capacities of the corporate world, the contributions to this volume can claim to be based on a realistic perspective. The widely held anti-globalisation positions are replaced by a perspective stressing the double character of economic globalisation: on the one hand, globalisation is the source of numerous problems (from the global transfer of ecologic risks through the exploitation of cheap labour to human rights violations), on the other hand, it may provide various mechanisms for resolving or at least cushioning these problems.

Concerning industry's scope for engaging in public or long-term concerns, it should be clearly stressed that economic rationality cannot be equated with a one-dimensional logic of cost reduction. Often, global players are market leaders in their business segment, and the exploitation of price differences is not always the most important motive for transnationalisation. Numerous other aspects like reputation, brand image, trust and issues of staff recruitment are also important prerequisites for a firm's success. Research into the global emergence of norms requires a 'praxeological' approach (Bourdieu, 1977), an approach that focuses on a concept of praxis as a source of innovation. The bases for norm formation from below are processes of organisational and inter-organisational learning, which can be defined as the reconceptualisation of existing frames and concepts in the confrontation with new circumstances, occurring scandals, and failures.

All this does not, however, imply that the attributes of creativity, innovation and learning capacity could be ascribed to the initiatives at stake without the precise reconstruction of their actual shape and operational mode. Certainly, the concept of governance is coined in opposition to governmental inefficacy and gridlock. Yet, neither can it be claimed that emerging steering mechanisms are free of such deficiencies, nor can it reasonably be argued that they are always founded on an unbiased perception of the prevailing problems.

The effort to come to, as far as possible, a differentiated perspective also implies evaluating private regulatory structures with respect to their transparency and accessibility for third parties, as well as their compliance with fundamental rights. Quite often, the success of private initiatives is gained at the cost of classical constitutional values: for instance, when the demands of weaker groups are insufficiently taken into account in the process of norm formulation, when the para-legal systems mainly consist of internal, non-published (or even implicit) norms and standards, or when the voluntary character of rules is given as an excuse for violations.

From a more minimalist perspective, one can perceive the legitimacy of the emerging norms simply in the fact that they exceed the legal requirements in some countries (as a higher level of protection is perceived to be better than a lower one). Yet, if one takes into account that private actors de facto work as global norm makers, one could raise more ambitious standards of legitimation, for instance, the possibility to revise norms in case of a better cognitive basis, a certain pluralism in decision-making, a consistent separation of norm creation and norm implementation in order to guarantee the necessary neutrality, and a fair procedure for dispute resolution in case of norm violation.

IV. RETHINKING FORMAL LAW

Exactly here is the systematic place where formal law comes back into the game. By including the informal structures within its area of responsibility, formal law can enhance their degree of publicity, reliability and substantial consistency and, therefore, their legitimacy. In doing this, formal law will itself become subject to numerous changes and processes of self-transformation.

To examine such internal readjustment of formal law to transnational private governance is the fourth aim of this volume. Changes in this respect can be expected at three levels: that of state law, that of international law, and that of self-constitutionalisation of transnational law.

(1) Traditionally, informal norms are touched upon by state law via explicit reference or via opening clauses relating to negligence, good customs, or state of the art, for example. From the vantage point of parliamentary legitimation, this has always been problematic yet it has been accepted since the processes of norm creation are embedded into a reliable procedural arrangement and are overseen by a national public. The transnationalisation of norm creation raises the question whether reference and hinge conceptions have to be constituted anew, that is, under what circumstances and criteria the transnational norms are to be legally recognised. Instead of merely reacting to informal norms, state law can also proactively attempt to foster and shape their creation. Also in this respect, transnationalisation requires a new approach. Although a single state does not hold competence for law-making in the transnational realm, it nevertheless can indirectly impact on transnationally active corporations, eg, via setting conditions for access to its market.

(2) Such state adaptations and proactive undertakings run the risk of increasing the divergence between the practices of single states. This demands international harmonisation of opening clauses and proactive instruments. A prominent example is the World Trade Organization (WTO) Agreement on Technical Barriers to Trade, which requires contracting states to base national trade restrictions on the standards of transnational standardisation bodies. Yet, requirements of international law as to how such standardisation shall be organised are still insufficient. More advanced forms of constitutionalisation are

necessary in order to do justice to the particularities of the respective processes of norm formation.

(3) In some respects, the quasi-legal orders of world society themselves show constitutional characteristics. In addition to different social and ecological standards and to existing mechanisms of control and implementation, superior norms develop that define where the decision-making power should be located, how violations should be handled, and how third parties should be included. By analogy to state constitutions, private regulations embody mechanisms of self-restraint to reduce intrusions on other actors and other domains (see Teubner, 2003). Is world society thus about to develop functional equivalents to the classical constitutional state, and will the latter gradually become marginal?

Here, again, one has to take into account the relevance of the new phenomena, but at the same time we should avoid relinquishing state achievements in a rush. The emerging norms do not possess the basic, framing nature of a state constitution, they rather mark the focal point for order, representing dynamic systems which emerge out of single fields of praxis and spread by mutual learning and the exchange of experiences. Instead of modelling para-legal systems as an autonomous, self-sufficient legal realm, the focus is on mapping an intermediate zone between the transnational arena and the state-centric world (Sassen, 2002: 107).

Learning processes of this kind could well coagulate into binding principles of transnational law. Although not forming an outright constitution, the existence of such principles could nevertheless encourage state constitutions and international quasi-constitutional frameworks to balance the conflicting normative orders that emerge outside their realm.

V. SUMMARY OF THE CONTRIBUTIONS

The first chapters of the book, assembled in Part I ('Corporate Responsibility and the Law'), deal with the emergent 'inner law' of multinational corporations in different branches and different policy fields.

Martin Herberg's chapter focuses on the global players of the German chemical sector, empirically reconstructing the emergence of environmental standards concerning the behaviour of subsidiaries in the different countries of investment. The existing governance mechanisms are reconstructed in a passage from the published codes and guidelines further to the micro-processes on the shop floor. The analysis is conducted from a socio-legal viewpoint, scrutinising the emergent governance mechanisms under aspects of effectiveness as well as under the aspect of possible legal references—and thus evaluating the chances of re-embedding them into the institutional system. For Herberg, even in a situation of global legal pluralism, the organs of formal and state law remain an important point of reference, at least in the case of disputes and conflicts of expectations. In its search for useful steering mechanisms, the nation state has to make intensive use of the intelligence and practical knowledge of societal actors. In this context, the supportive function of empirical social research is of great significance, since this societal intelligence, in order to be utilised, first of all has to be thoroughly analysed.

In the second chapter, *Carola Glinski* goes deeper into the legal details of corporate governance. The legal effects are analysed, considering the legitimacy of private rule-making, in particular where weaker contract parties or third parties are concerned. The chapter covers the effects in sales law, the law of misleading advertising, the law of unfair competition and tort law. Glinski concludes that private regulation has legal effects in private law, although these effects may not always, or may rarely, be intended. However, it is only beyond a certain degree of consolidation that those norms constitute legal effects. First of all, private regulation can trigger immediate obligations for those who establish or adopt the rules. Furthermore, private regulation is capable of setting minimum standards for a whole group of corporations, if the authors of the rules are sufficiently representative. This applies both with regard to fair business conduct as well as due diligence in tort law. Thus, private regulation can have a transnational regulatory effect based on private law mechanisms, where public law mechanisms are not available.

The third chapter by *Eva Kocher* focuses on industrial relations. The chapter deals with corporate social responsibility programmes as a possible universal way to enforce workers' rights in transnational business relations. Presenting the results from an empirical study on German firms acting abroad, Kocher shows that the firms often do not enforce their own social standards because of conflicts with national norms or local practices. Considering the legal value of corporate codes of conduct, Kocher analyses how German or European law could sanction violations of voluntary commitments. She concludes that there is no general answer to such legal effects. Kocher then explores to what extent industrial minimum standards can become relevant in the law of unfair competition. Unlike Glinski, who puts the same question in relation to the self-commitment of business, Kocher focuses on the soft law of international organisations, such as the OECD guidelines and the ILO core labour standards.

Part II ('Private Standards in Transnational Business Relations') deals with self-regulation in business networks. The chapters assembled in this part take production chains and the finance sector as case studies.

In his chapter *Olaf Dilling* illustrates the links between private self-regulation and the law by analysing the management of chemical substances in the electric and electronic equipment industry. National product regulation (and to some extent also the regulation of production processes) influences product standards employed by leading corporations within their transnational supplier networks. It turns out that the diffusion of regulatory standards within transnational business networks is not a linear process: to some extent corporate actors selectively adopt legal standards and proactively self-regulate substances of concern. In the analysed corporate standards, various mixed forms of generalisation, proactive adoption and anticipation of national laws can be found. Thus, the distinction between regulatory compliance and self-regulation is blurred. The relationship between national law and self-regulatory corporate standards is thus symptomatic of a changed relationship between the state and the private sector, especially multinational corporations: it could be characterised by the mutual reliance of national legislators and globally operating corporations, rather than by classic hierarchic patterns of linear determination.

Alexandra Lindenthal's chapter deals with a similar case, namely the management of hazardous chemicals in a transnational network composed of suppliers to the automotive sector. Basing her chapter on an empirical analysis, Lindenthal describes some common efforts of the actors involved to handle chemicals safely in a concerted way. Several elements of self-regulation are reconstructed from these cases, integrating the economic interests of the participating firms and the public interest. Networks are not necessarily based on equal participation. Often, as in the automotive and the chemical industries, powerful lead firms play a decisive role in influencing other firms to establish the safe transnational management of chemical substances. Conditions motivating firms to handle chemical substances in a safe way include: that unsafe handling could endanger smooth production, that the firm perceives itself as a socially embedded actor with a good reputation, and that the firm's staff show increased awareness of risks and management techniques of dangerous chemicals. Lindenthal concludes by highlighting several mechanisms of how the chemical industry's self-regulation is integrated into the new concept of EC chemicals regulation.

Oren Perez examines in his chapter environmental self-regulation in the finance sector. He outlines how 'green finance' was transformed from a field governed by multiple, stand-alone organisational-contractual instruments, to a field governed by a relatively small number of transnational codes. This transformation has also taken place in ethical investment and environmental reporting. Against the recurrent accusation that these so-called 'soft' legal instruments are nothing but 'greenwash', he provides evidence that the new global legal apparatus has triggered discernible changes in the practices and organisational routines of financial institutions and transnational corporations. However, Perez admits that to ascertain to what extent these changes had a meaningful ecological impact would require methodologically more sophisticated studies. He proceeds by asking how the emerging informal regimes are received by state and international law. He predicts that after the current phase of patchy links more systematic bridges will be built, including the legal establishment of rules on transparency, on finance, investment and reporting, as well as on liability in cases of violation of such rules even in cases where no economic damage has been caused to the concerned individual.

Part III ('Consumer-based Private Governance and the Law') concentrates on the regulatory potential of responsible organised consumerism.

Ralf Bendrath's chapter deals with issues of privacy and data protection, providing an overview of different self-governance mechanisms. Although early data protection started out as law-based regulation by nation states, on a global scale, self-governance mechanisms have become more important due to the rise of worldwide telecommunications and the internet. Examples are codes of conduct developed within the private sector with limited participation by public actors or NGOs, and software tools—'technical codes'—for online privacy protection. Even if these private codes and standards are—due to their uncontrolled growth—extremely diverse, there are also certain tendencies towards harmonisation. In this context, the case of an EU directive requiring adequate protection is analysed, resulting in private standardisation processes in the United States. The chapter shows that, in recent developments, a stronger, but transformed role of the state can often be found. Instead of regulating data processors directly, governments and supervisory agencies now focus more on the intermediaries, such as developers of standards, large software companies, or industry associations. And, in place of prescribing and penalising, they rely more on incentive structures like certifications or public funding for social and technical self-governance instruments.

In his chapter *Gralf-Peter Calliess* addresses the issue of transnational consumer contracts, a topic of renewed relevance since the development of online shopping over the internet. This leads him to the question if private ordering can sufficiently fulfil a regulatory function in protecting consumers' rights—and not only a coordinative function as known from the 'lex mercatoria'. He discusses four different mechanisms of private ordering which have become important for business-to-consumer e-commerce: reputation, quality marks with associated codes of conduct, online dispute resolution, and the role of intermediaries as trusted third parties. Calliess shows that these mechanisms are integrated into transnational civil consumer protection regimes by operators of virtual market-places such as 'eBay'. This can help to enhance consumers' trust and to exclude opportunistic behaviour. The protection regimes can develop a fairly high degree of autonomy. Sometimes they even circumvent interventions of state law which do not conform to the rationale of the virtual market-place. According to Calliess, national law can no longer play its traditional role to grant fairness of these regimes, instead, they require to be embedded in a procedural constitution of freedom on a global level. To substantiate this thesis, he outlines the emergence of reflexive standards of private ordering and co-regulatory initiatives to develop criteria for fair transnational civil regimes.

Errol Meidinger examines in his chapter transnational certification systems. In the forestry and other sectors, environmental and social justice organisations used the marketing interests of large transnational corporations to force the issue of global standards. Meidinger describes the structure and practice of the certification institutions such as the Forest Stewardship Council and compares and contrasts some of the institutional arrangements that have emerged in different sectors. He points out that by ensuring transparency and procedural fairness the certification programmes have elaborated a genuine kind of administrative law. He then examines the relationships and compatibility between the emergent certification institutions and state-based legal systems, with primary reference to the US legal system and the international trading regime. The possibilities, he says, are nearly infinite, since states can choose to react or not to react, to incorporate, repudiate, or regulate certification standards, and to do so either immediately through direct action or from a distance through general legal standards. In conclusion, Meidinger raises the more fundamental question of how effective the certification systems are, whose interests they serve, and if they can provide legitimacy.

These questions are also addressed in the chapter by *Cristiane Derani* and *José Augusto Costa*. Taking the Brazilian rainforests as a case of resource depletion they describe the certification schemes practised in the country. They include both the voluntary Forest Stewardship Council scheme and a semi-binding national scheme of certification. Derani and Costa explain the emergence of certification by the incapacity of the official legal system to implement forest protection policies. Although forest legislation and administration is well developed on the textual level, due to corruption and other causes, enforcement is deplorably deficient. Certification is therefore a replacement structure for ineffective state law. The law even recognises certification by alleviating the preconditions for logging concessions. However, they warn that in spite of some progress certification of the wood cutting, processing, and marketing chain covers only a tiny part of the whole wood industry. This is, they say, due to a number of factors, including in particular the higher costs of certified production and the lack of environmental awareness among internal Brazilian consumers. Theorising about their findings the authors stress that in the long run a viable regime of sustainable management of tropical forests will have to rely on a parallel structure of private regulation and a somewhat more sophisticated state regulation.

In Part IV ('Transnational Self-governance in Perspective') *Sol Picciotto* puts the issue of private self-regulation into the broad context of networked governance. On the basis of various recent developments, Picciotto shows the restrictions of the classical state-centred and formalistic concept of law. Accordingly, he develops a multi-dimensional model of the different types of governance in the post-national age. One dimension is processes of privatisation and deregulation on the national level, illustrated against the background of the radical reforms in Great Britain of the 1980s. Another dimension is the delegation of decision power to technical committees and epistemic communities on the European level. Furthermore, a layer of soft law is emerging in the international arena, often involving non-state actors, which additionally challenges classical statehood. In a rich panorama of these different dimensions, cases like the privatisation of public transport on the national level, and the regulation of financial services on the international level are discussed. Focusing on destabilising effects for democracy and the rule of law, Picciotto also shows to what enormous extent the shift towards network governance is driven by formal legal structures. Therefore, formal law can play an important role in democratising these processes, since the specific strength of law is based on its flexibility rather than precision.

REFERENCES

Appelbaum, RP, Felstiner, WLF, and Gessner, V (eds) (2001) *Rules and Networks. The Legal Culture of Global Business Transactions* (Oxford, Hart Publishing).

Bourdieu, P (1977) *Outline of a Theory of Practice* (Cambridge, Cambridge University Press).

Herberg, M (2006) *Private Regulative in den Lücken der Staatenwelt. Umweltschutz im multinationalen Konzern zwischen staatlicher Steuerung und gesellschaftlicher Selbstregulierung* (Frankfurt, Campus).

Kirton, J and Trebilcock, M (eds) (2004) *Hard Choices, Soft Law: Voluntary Standards in Global Trade, Environment and Social Governance* (Burlington, Ashgate).

Sassen, S (2002) 'The State and Globalization' in R Hall and T Biersteker (eds), *The Emergence of Private Authority in Global Governance* (Cambridge, Cambridge University Press) 91–114.

Schepel, H (2005) *The Constitution of Private Governance. Product Standards in the Regulation of Integration Markets* (Oxford, Hart Publishing).

Teubner, G (1997) *Global Law without a State* (Dartmouth, Aldershot).

—— (2003) 'Globale Zivilverfassungen. Alternativen zur staatszentrierten Verfassungstheorie' in 63 *Zeitschrift für ausländisches öffentliches Recht und Völkerrecht* 1–28.

Winter, G (2005) 'Einführung' in G Winter (ed) *Die Umweltverantwortung multinationaler Unternehmen. Selbststeuerung und Recht bei Auslandsinvestitionen* (Baden-Baden: Nomos).

Part I

Corporate Responsibility and the Law

1

Global Legal Pluralism and Interlegality: Environmental Self-Regulation in Multinational Enterprises as Global Law-Making

MARTIN HERBERG

I. GLOBAL LEGAL PLURALISM, PRIVATE GOVERNANCE, AND THE CONCEPT OF INTERLEGALITY[1]

THE PROCESS OF globalisation leads to numerous changes in the balance of societal forces and powers, including a diffusion of public functions from the state-centric to the corporate world. While the nation state increasingly fails to control effectively the chains of action in the transnational arena, there is evidence of a large number of non-state initiatives capable of filling the gaps of the prevailing institutional order. Due to their informality, the emerging norms of the transnational sphere often bear a considerable problem-solving capacity, but at the same time, they seriously challenge the state's constitutional prerogatives, including its operational responsibilities for social and environmental regulation.

Multinational enterprises, insurance companies, banking corporations, and providers of internet services are all engaged in the establishment and enforcement of standards tightly connected with the field of problems they are acting in. Often enough, transnational actors adopt the envisaged regulatory tasks without any mandate from the official institutions. Instead of applying for an authorisation from 'above', they seem to authorise themselves. The result is the emergence of transnational governance

[1] This chapter presents some of the results of two partly overlapping research projects: the completed project 'The Double Standard in Foreign Direct Investments' (conducted by the FEU Bremen Research Centre for European Environmental Law), and the current project 'Transnational Governance' in the context of the Collaborative Research Centre 597, 'Statehood in Transition' (Bremen University). I am indebted to Olaf Dilling, Prof Dr Virginia Haufler, Prof Dr Christian Joerges, Prof Dr Beate Kohler-Koch, Prof Dr Stephan Leibfried, Prof Dr Erol Meidinger, Prof Dr Eva Senghaas-Knobloch, and Prof Dr Gerd Winter for valuable commentaries and suggestions.

mechanisms of an extra-legal character which, nonetheless, share many features with classical law as defined by the state: 'It is neither an essential part of the concept of law that it originates from the state, nor that it is the basis for the decisions of courts and other institutions' (Ehrlich, 1989: 17). Apparently, this insight from the early stage of the sociology of law gains new topicality through the occurrence of an emerging 'Global Law without a State' (*cf* Günter and Randeria, 2000; Teubner, 2000).

It is one of the characteristics of these quasi-legal structures that they consist of several, closely interlocked norms and regulations on different levels, which are sufficiently specific to establish clear-cut demarcations between admissible and inadmissible practices. Compliance with the rules often cannot be just left to voluntary action; instead, it is necessary, in most cases, to institute specialised organs of surveillance and enforcement. Furthermore, there is the aspect of normative anchoring, which means that the steering arrangements typically have their own footing in a layer of deeper foundations and sources of normative validity. The binding character partly results from experiences of crisis in the past and the learning processes which have taken place; partly it is the compliance with the existing rules over longer time-spans, from which these rules derive their validity; and partly the binding power becomes enhanced by an act of public commitment, whereby an actor brings his own credibility into play as an additional foundation of normative obligation.

Over the last few years, the emergence of private regulations in global governance has become a fruitful research field for many disciplines, among them, the theory of international relations, as well as socio-legal studies and the juridical debate on the future of law in an age of globalisation. But, at the same time, the emerging structures of self-regulation are precarious and difficult to handle, as they permanently confront the researcher with the state-centric burdens of his own discipline—be it the sociological model of society as kept 'enclosed' by the nation state (for a critique see Beck, 1997: 48), or the positivistic bias in juridical discourse (see Lampe, 1995).

That is to say, research into the global emergence of norms requires a bottom-up approach, an approach that focuses on processes of self-regulation that cut across the political geography of sovereign states. In addition, the challenge is to portray the new governance mechanisms not in terms of possible deficiencies, but to define them in their inherent rationality and their productive potential. Indeed, the emergent regulatory systems are precarious because of their limited transparency, their weakly developed possibilities for third party participation, and their problematic backward linkage to the norms of national and international law: 'The attribution of public functions to private actors directly challenges democratic and liberal theories of governance and law' (Cutler, 2002: 33). For many authors, the emergence of private governance signalises a loss of the state's steering capacity—authority will be withdrawn from the state and gradually taken over by private actors (Pauly, 2002: 76), with the state slipping into a rather passive and marginalised role. However, first of all, a realistic evaluation of the new constellation requires a differentiated and empirically grounded reconstruction.

Much of the predominant reservation against private governance is highlighted in the catchphrase of a new 'Nobody's Rule' (in German, *Niemandsherrschaft*: Beck, 2002: 102). The fact that many relevant decisions are made behind closed doors, the unsettled juridical enforceability, and the distinct lack of publicity of most existing standards seem to weaken the position of societal actors *vis-à-vis* the corporate world. The emergence of private authority goes together with an increased amount of uncertainty and, for many members of society, an erosion of their civil rights—even if the quasi-legal systems fulfil the function of protecting these rights in some other ways. This peculiar double-edged character of private norm-setting poses the question whether states' formal law could contribute to the integration and configuration of the new responsibilities, providing them with a new degree of transparency and accessibility.

According to a widespread view, the chances for this integration are rather poor: the corporate and state-centric worlds have already drifted apart from each other to such an extent that the creation of new steering mechanisms at the intersection of both could hardly be expected. In political science, it is mainly the so-called dualistic model of Rosenau (1992) which sets the tone of the debate—in today's world many institutions of the state merely exist as an empty shell, while the actors in the non-governmental sphere have learned to withdraw from the state's influence.

So, on the one hand, the transnational sphere is seen as the workspace of numerous problem-solving mechanisms of the most diverse provenance—the number of which figures in the millions—while a useful set of instruments for the coordination of these mechanisms, on the other hand, seems out of reach. Tendencies to conceptualise the relationship between the two spheres as incommensurable can also be found in jurisprudence—the practised informal law of world society represents a system of norms 'the legal source of which is not only independent of national legal systems but, in fact, is directed against practices of the nation states' (Teubner, 2000: 250). According to this reading, the categories of positive law have their limits where the sphere of transnational norm structures begins; being 'highly rational in itself, but irrational with respect to society as a whole' (*ibid*: 270), state law is much too fixated on its own code to open itself up to the emerging structures.

However, it does not appear that this characterisation will be the last word on the relationship between the two spheres. Even as early as the beginning of the twentieth century, Max Weber had predicted that, together with the growth of world trade, there would be an increase in informal norm-making, leading to various new challenges for legal practice (1980: 506).

That informal regulations can, in principle, be linked back to existing law can also be seen in the lessons learned on the national level in recent decades—one only has to think of the new steering instruments being discussed under the concepts of 'regulated self-regulation' and 'reflexive law' (*cf* Schmidt-Preuß, 1998). Although a linear transfer of such forms of regulation to the transnational level would certainly be too hasty, it is possible, however, to transfer many of the arguments about the flexibility and openness of formal law to the up-to-date constellation.

As Weber pointed out (1980: 397), the concept of modern law is unavoidably bound to its ability to re-adjust the demarcations between legally relevant and irrelevant facts over and over again, according to its own rationality and mode of operation. Concerning the quality of legal decisions, formal criteria and aspects of legal certainty are only one dimension—equally important are aspects of a more substantive character, among them the need for a realistic definition of the cases under examination, as well as questions of problem adequacy. The unity of law is neither a pre-established harmony nor is it an illusion, but instead it is a practical accomplishment on all levels and in all stages of the law-making process.[2]

More appropriate, therefore, than the assumption of a bifurcation between the different norm structures, is the idea of manifold interactions: a view emphasised by some authors through the use of the term 'interlegality' (Günter and Randeria, 2001: 31), representing the starting point of a most promising research programme. The aims of this approach are as follows: a reconstruction of the functioning of private steering mechanisms and an exploration into to the extent to which they trigger off links with state-defined law; an assessment of the fields of law in which such links can be found; and an identification of the patterns which cause the law to exceed its original scope at some points. Examining this set of issues necessitates an interdisciplinary, juridical–sociological approach, and it is the methods of reconstructive social research which play a key role in the integration of both disciplines.

Authors of many previous contributions have contented themselves with giving a rather cursory overview of the different self-regulatory elements. Compared with this line of work, however, it appears necessary to explore systematically the core of the steering arrangements and to determine precisely how the responsibilities between the different actors or acting units are in fact distributed. The successful completion of this task does not only represent important groundwork for the subsequent analyses of the various interlegal linkages between the two spheres

[2] Until now, the above-mentioned sections in Max Weber's opus have been overlooked by most socio-legal theorists. Ironically enough, it is the very erosion of the classical, positivistic conception of law—often labelled as the 'traditional Weberian approach'—which provides Weber's thoughts with new relevance.

(a step which also requires an empirical approach, since many innovations, before they reach the level of official norm-making, are prepared at the level of administration and jurisdiction). The detailed reconstruction of the private steering systems can also supply the legal practitioner with the urgently needed empirical expertise and, thus, increase the problem adequacy of legal decisions.

Broken down into a simple formula, the outlined approach represents a 'socio-legal analysis *of* the emergent law as a socio-legal analysis *for* the existing state law' (see Herberg, 2005a: 401), and we can dare to predict that the role of this approach will continue to grow further under the circumstances of today's global legal pluralism. In the following sections, the sketched approach shall be applied to a specific case, namely, the emergence of transnational private self-regulatory systems in the field of environmental protection and safety in multinational enterprises, based on a survey of the eight largest corporations in the German chemical industry.[3]

II. ENVIRONMENTAL PROTECTION IN MULTINATIONAL ENTERPRISES: NEW GOVERNANCE MECHANISMS AS A RESULT OF COLLECTIVE LEARNING

While globalisation used to be equated for a long time with the tendency of different countries to move towards convergence, the emphasis today is more on aspects of fragmentation (see, for example, Robertson 1998)—the recent changes in world society represent an increasing porosity of the old borders, combined with the emergence of new borders, demarcations, and inequalities.

This co-existence of homogenisation and fragmentation also coins many of the problems discussed with respect to the growing role of multinational enterprises. Certainly, the activities of the 'global players' contribute to an ever-strengthening involvement of the less developed countries in the world-market, but, at the same time, a basic asymmetry is documented by the fact that almost all of these enterprises are from the western world. Apart from a few exceptions, the technologies transferred are developed in the home countries, and the ability to come up with something of equal quality remains a long way off for many of the receiving countries. Also difficult to achieve, and only possible to build up through lengthy follow-up processes, is the framework of structures for an institutional re-embedding of these production processes. In the 'old' industrial nations this framework has

[3] The sample consists of the companies BASF, Bayer, Beiersdorf, Degussa, Henkel, Merck, Wacker, and Celanese (the German successor company to Hoechst). For the research design, see Herberg, 2001, 2003, and 2005.

evolved parallel to technological progress, while in most of the developing countries, it is clearly still in its early stages.

Accordingly, the systems of environmental law of many developing countries are showing numerous regulatory gaps and steering deficits. In Africa, the legal situation is marked by a dominance of outdated laws which concentrate on aspects of the distribution of natural resources and hardly take into account the problems of industrial environmental pollution (*cf* Areola, 1998; Kaniaru *et al*, 1995; WHO/UNEP, 1992). While many countries of Asia, Latin America, and Eastern Europe have specific laws for individual problems such as water and air pollution, legislation is often missing for other problems such as the disposal of (toxic) waste or soil conservation (*cf* Banister, 2000; Bowman and Hunter, 1992; Bowonder *et al*, 1994; El-Bahay, 1998). But even countries with a variety of environmental law Acts often lack the necessary substructure of norm-specifying standards (*cf* Gündling, 1998). On top of that, there are the often-mentioned deficits in enforcement due to corruption and lack of capacity of the administrative authorities (Kamau, 2005). Regarding the existing legal gaps, it is difficult to understand how some authors can speak of a worldwide diffusion of Western environmental laws and standards as the 'bright side' of globalisation (Weidner and Jänicke, 2001: 294).

According to a popular view, both aspects, the internationalisation of production and the regulatory gaps in the developing countries, are closely connected. While corporations prefer to operate in countries with low environmental standards for economic reasons, the latter see themselves forced either to refrain from putting forward their demands or even to reduce them further and further (*cf* Leonard, 1988; with further references). It is certainly true that the damages resulting from the activities of multinational enterprises have in the past reached an extent which would have hardly been conceivable on the companies' home territory. To attribute this to a deliberately planned strategy of taking advantage of the lower standards, however, would, in many cases, be missing the point.

In many sectors, firms are primarily interested in long-term and scandal-free business, especially in the case of capital- and knowledge-intensive investments, and the industrial plants are fitted out with equipment which, if not at the cutting edge of technology in every respect, nevertheless provides a reasonable level of protection. The reasons for the above-mentioned problems are to be viewed less as the particularly unscrupulous conduct of corporate management, but rather as a broad range of wrong decisions and operating errors at local level which are more likely to point to a certain loss of control on the part of the companies' head offices.

In the parent firms, it was believed for a long time that for a safe, environment-friendly operation on foreign production sites, it would be sufficient merely to provide the necessary basic equipment and all relevant operating instructions. However, due to an increase in unexpected mismanagement, this view has gotten into a crisis. The Bhopal catastrophe of 1984 played a key role in the revision of the old model of a decentralised corporation. At least of similar importance was the wide range of 'small-scale' negligence and erroneous operational practices occurring over the years, which made it ever more evident that head offices, in order to maintain a minimum of normality, have to integrate local operations into a tight net of controls. The concept of normality might be confusing to some readers here, but it is important to see that occurrences such as the total disregard of matters of maintenance, or the dumping of biocide pollutants (so-called 'killing agents') into a sewage plant so that it can no longer work are not only problematic in ethical and ecological terms, instead, occurrences like these are also apt to fundamentally undermine trust in the functioning of a corporation's entire organisation.

The lack of appropriate institutional structures in countries of operation thus urges the management to establish appropriate steering mechanisms themselves, in order to maintain control, and, at the same time, the types of mismanagement referred to above lead to problems in the corporations' relationship with the public. The result is a situation in which issues of legitimacy become more and more separated from criteria of mere legal conformity. Sheer compliance with all formal legal demands increasingly proves to be insufficient for economic activity to be legitimate and acceptable (or, more precisely, '*akzeptanzfähig*', as Jürgen Habermas puts it).[4] Thus, corporations see themselves confronted with the expectation to exceed the level of what is legally required in many different respects. How both factors—the influence of a critical public and intra-organisational learning processes on account of new experiences—are to be assessed in relation to one another is difficult to answer empirically. It is fundamentally true that a corporation's self-image cannot be shaken by just any criticism, but public pressure can nonetheless cause changes in the attitudes and policies of enterprises, especially where mismanagement has reached a degree which the practitioners within the company themselves perceive as alarming. Public opinion then functions as an additional incentive to take seriously internal anomalies and to counter these with particular organisational and restructuring measures.

As a result, the described problems of steering and legitimacy constitute for the personnel at the corporations' headquarters, what might be called a 'collective field of experience' (in German, '*Erfahrungsraum*': Mannheim,

[4] The political relevance of the problem also shows itself in the development of different codes of conduct by international organisations such as the UNO, the International Labour Organization (ILO), and the OECD. Just recently, the guidelines of the OECD were updated to a very demanding standard from an environmental point of view (*cf* Böttger, 2002: 133*ff*). Certainly, as they are lacking any binding force, these initiatives are rather irrelevant as steering instruments, but they nevertheless aptly express the normative expectations of the international community towards the global players.

1980: 272)—a constellation of problems that several actors see themselves confronted with in a similar way, and which is liable to trigger off processes of mutual learning and steering initiatives of a similar basic structure, even if a centralised regulatory body above the individual corporations does not exist. Instead of only emerging in single, particularly progressive firms, the steering systems under examination determine the standard of conduct for entire fields of practice—an observation which can have far-reaching consequences also for the legal treatment of these self-regulatory systems.

In the empirical reconstruction described here, this aspect was taken into account by limiting the sample to a relatively homogenous set of actors and through systematic comparisons between the individual firms. The aim is to explore those structures which constitute the common standard of conduct, the state of the art, so to speak, of the range of actors concerned.

III. CODES OF CONDUCT, AUDITS, AND STANDARDS: THE ANATOMY OF PRIVATE GOVERNANCE

The corporations' steering systems consist of several closely related components with differing functions. The outer layer, as it were, is made up of those elements which were specifically created for contact with the outside world. Each firm in the sample publishes its own environmental guidelines, which were submitted to a careful qualitative-sociological analysis.

Many other components, including the internal organisational structure, control systems, and operative standards, are largely hidden from the public's attention and can only be identified when one successively acquaints oneself with the processes within the corporations. Each firm has its own special departments, mostly under the label of 'corporate representatives for environmental protection and safety' (in German: *Konzernbeauftragte für Sicherheit und Umweltschutz*) with the task of controlling the individual parts of the corporate group. The members of these task forces were the interview partners in 12 in-depth interviews. In each of the firms there exists a tight mesh of organisational and technical standards, which are only partly laid down in internal documents, since the process of formalisation is still at an early stage, and which therefore have to be derived from the interviews with the practitioners.

For the empirical analysis, it appears advisable, so to speak, to reconstruct the steering arrangements working from the 'outside' to the 'inside', starting off with the companies' documents addressed to the public.

A. Corporate Guidelines

For the interpretation of the environmental and safety guidelines, it is important to bear in mind that they represent self-binding (speech) acts, even if this is not always explicitly stated. The documents carry headlines such as 'Principles of Environmental Protection and Safety', 'Worldwide Standards', or, as in one case, 'Environmental Guidelines: our "Constitution"' (in German: *Unser 'Grundgesetz'*), an analogy with which the authors emphasise the documents' similarity to written law in an almost provocative manner. The length of the texts usually is one to three pages. The actual guidelines are mostly preceded by a preliminary remark in which the regulations are placed in a broader societal context, and in which connections between environmental protection and economic success are highlighted. The actual guidelines themselves are mostly kept very brief. Besides aspects of the prevention of outright dangerous effects, the regulations advocate precautionary measures of emission minimisation. Frequently, they contain the principle of continuous instruction and training of all employees; in some of the documents, the establishment of transcorporational management systems is propagated, and, in many cases, additional to the duty of an environmentally friendly configuration of all internal operations, there is also the duty to supervise external business partners.

The corporate codes are an almost paradigmatic example of how private actors, by their own means, manage to establish norm systems of considerable binding effect. By presenting their codes of conduct to the public, the corporations put behind them the failures of the past; the texts claim credibility, and they do so (only seemingly paradoxically) by publicly mortgaging the corporations' integrity and credibility with the burden of compliance with the stated duties. Through publication of the guidelines, normative facts are created, as with any speech act of the type of a self-obligation (*cf* Austin, 2002; Rolf, 1997). Later deviations from the norms cannot just be presented as a simple shift of the firm's policy; they rather take on the quality of a violation of justified normative expectations. Three aspects are relevant for a more detailed discussion of the documents' structure: first, the way in which the authors relate to the sphere of existing state law; second, the question of the problem adequacy of the regulations and their applicability in specific cases; and, third, the arrangement of power in the relationship between parent and subsidiary company.

In regard to the links with existing law, it must be noted that, for the normative anchoring of self-obligations, apparently no use is made of existing juridical formats such as contract or statute. Thus, their foundations of validity are quite autonomous—a form of creating order by anchoring normative expectations in the common structures of the life-world. Through their self-binding acts, the actors turn 'from potential to manifest subjects' (Oevermann, 1983: 237); it becomes possible for others to anticipate future behaviour and—on the assumption of a certain degree of trustworthiness—make it the basis of their own behaviour. This is not to be equated with an erosion of the state's authority, as the guidelines logically can only claim to attain a level above what is legally demanded. This is adequately expressed through wordings such as 'We tackle what is perceived as necessary, even if there are no legal obligations or official requirements' (BASF). If in the texts the intention was expressed to lower or disregard the legal standards in particular cases, then the guidelines would obviously have failed as a means of building up trust—presenting themselves as self-obligations, they were in fact, a speech act of the type of thread.[5]

The attempt to (re)gain public trust furthermore necessitates the provision of the addressee with a rough idea of what he actually is to build his trust on. So the guidelines, despite their programmatic character, have to contain specific information about the problems at hand and their respective solutions. As critics have often claimed, the corporations' codes of conduct mostly show a very high level of abstraction (accusation of 'eco-rhetoric': *cf* Fuchs, 1997; Greer and Bruno, 1996); as soon as the texts are analysed more thoroughly confronting them with different cases and possible forms of behaviour, however, it quickly becomes clear that their content is sufficiently precise to identify certain practices as inadmissible, at least in instances of very damaging practices.

For instance, the statement 'We create products which are safe to make, safe to use, and safe to dispose of' in the context of a self-binding act can mean nothing else but '*All* our products are safe to make, safe to use, and safe to dispose of' (the reading 'we manufacture such products *among others*' is unthinkable, as it would confront the reader with the imposition to view something which is part of everyday business anyway as a special service). One implication of this statement is that, within the corporation, there must be effective forms of information management, so that new experiences with the harmful potential of certain substances at one site can immediately be communicated to all other sites, in order that the necessary countermeasures are also taken in those parts of the company.

As regards the third point, the question of corporations' internal steering capacity, it is important to see that usually, in the case of promises made to one another by individuals in everyday life, there is no question concerning their ability to control their own action, whereas in the case of self-binding acts of corporate actors, who are scattered across several continents, there definitely is. It is an important implication of the guidelines that the corporate management, as author of the texts, must be able to take responsibility that the promises are kept, and to influence the processes in the different parts of the corporation. This implication does not appear unrealistic, as the headquarters normally hold all, or a majority of, the

[5] That also the opposite case, the explicit promise of compliance with existing law, in the end leads to a distortion of a document's meaning structure, is only mentioned here for the sake of completeness (*cf*, in detail, Herberg, 2001). There are single guidelines in which promises of legal compliance of this kind are in fact found—a proof of the difficulties in reaching a balance between public governance and private governance under today's circumstances.

shares of subsidiaries (at least in the chemical industry). In order to achieve the effect of a trustworthy self-binding act, the texts must not contain any indications that compliance with them is left to the employees' discretion. If this were the case, then the guidelines could at best be used for internal circulation, but not as promotional material and a trust-building measure in external relations.

It is important to see that this does not necessarily lead to a situation, where all decisions are concentrated at the corporation's headquarters. But, to meet the standard, the corporation must ensure that if severe mismanagement were to occur in one of its subsidiaries, it has a certain likelihood of being discovered in order to trigger the appropriate countermeasures.

B. Auditing

For the analysis of internal control systems, it is once more advisable first to clarify their relationship with the existing law, then to consider the aspects of problem adequacy, and finally to delineate the relationship between parent and subsidiary company, as it is documented in the statements of the interviewees. Concerning the competencies of environmental departments at the level of corporate management, the companies researched seek to ensure an outfitting of the plants with all necessary technical devices from the beginning of the construction phase, something which is institutionally anchored in a certain veto power of the environmental departments vis-à-vis the other divisions of the enterprise. Another task is the instruction of the companies abroad with respect to all occurring problems of plant operation and maintenance, which, in particularly severe cases, takes the form of on-site counselling and can be demanded by the subsidiaries at any time.[6]

While this still largely corresponds to the old, rather decentralised model of the corporation—the head offices as provider of technology and expertise—, a decisive shift of emphasis is expressed in the new tasks and competencies of the environmental departments: All environmentally relevant installations and processes are thoroughly checked at regular intervals of about every two to three years at all locations. The results of these checks are put down in a detailed report and will be combined with specific proposals and demands for repairs.

As for the links with existing law, the corporate liability law of the different countries of the world is far from stipulating steering activities such as these in a binding fashion. The subsidiaries are legally independent units, and the parent company is only liable for their omissions where the

[6] One of the interviewees stated the following: 'If there is a factory somewhere and they say, "folks, we won't continue production, we want an immediate check", then we are there on the spot the next day' (interview, 13 December 2000).

subsidiaries' autonomy was restricted to such a degree that a reasonable fulfilment of their duties was no longer possible. Regulatory devices such as the US Foreign Environmental Practices Act, which was intended to subject to minimum standards the foreign activities of all US enterprises (*cf* Neff, 1990), have proved to be 'nine-day wonders'—probably not least because of the impossibility of ensuring the establishment of administrative, transnational implementation systems as the necessary substructure. Now, when the corporations begin to establish respective control structures themselves, they take on the role of a global executive organ, which can partly involve quasi-policing and quasi-criminological elements, too—especially if hidden deficiencies are also detected, and if the controllers have effective means of intervention at their disposal.

In fact, the database contains numerous indications that during the on-site controls ('audits'), one can also get to the bottom of these 'hidden' problems. The representatives of the corporations act as 'specialists for the discovery of what is difficult to discover' (Oevermann *et al*, 1985: 135), with the task of revealing the real condition of machinery, however well looked-after it may appear at first glance. In this, the auditors rely on their own technical expertise (most of them have many years of experience as plant managers) as well as on their knowledge of particular omissions and operation errors that often occur. In the majority of instances, the starting point of the audits is an examination of the internal handbooks, processes, and maintenance plans. By doing this, detailed inquiries, in the form of a tour of the plant, do not become obsolete; on the contrary: it seems that the on-site inspections are used to concentrate on those aspects which in the context of the document analysis appear to be unproblematic at first.[7] Certainly, the conducted audits do not allow a complete analysis of deficits, but through a skilful choice of items to be observed, it seems possible to identify at least those deficits which represent symptoms of more far-reaching dysfunctions.

While a certain hierarchical factor is already manifest in the ability of the corporations' representatives to define individual problems as breaches of corporation-wide norms and rules, this becomes underpinned, in addition, through the existing competencies to intervene, and to issue directives. In fact, these authoritative elements are only very discretely raised in the corporations' public self-presentation, which may be due to a variety

[7] It is an indication of the auditors' interest in evidence-oriented investigations that a perfectly designed handbook with highly detailed operating instructions is not nearly considered proof of proper operations according to the rules. Colleagues in the field who attach too much relevance to the formal systems, especially those in the consulting and certification branch, constitute the 'negative point of comparison' (in German: *negativer Gegenhorizont*; Bohnsack, 1993: 41), of their own approach; the criticism refers to auditors 'who do something which is only theoretical', and whose overemphasis on formal organisational aspects has long since 'abandoned the grip on the ground' (interview, 15 January 2001).

of reasons, ranging from the fear of new juridical risks, to the efforts to present the company as a well-integrated, conflict-free enterprise to the outside world. In practice, however, the auditors' rights to take action play an important role, and, in particularly serious cases, they can reach as far as the imposition of a shutdown with immediate effect: 'When we get some place where danger is looming, we say, please stop this at once' (interview, 13 December 2000). Similar statements can also be found throughout all of the other interviews, and the small word 'please' here expresses a certain 'role distance' (Goffman, 1972: 75), which again is due to the tension between the autonomy of the parts of the corporation, and headquarters' claim to be responsible for corporate governance.

It is not inconsistent with the existence of those hierarchical elements that the auditors largely take care to use their executive authority in as cooperative and peaceful a manner as possible. 'We want to convince people of the sensefullness of things. That's how we make sure things run smoothly' (interview, 13 March 2001). The criticisms and orders of the auditors are normally so convincing that they immediately exert influence on those locally responsible—not least because mismanagement, in many cases, points less to an exaggerated interest in cost reduction, but rather to organisational failure and problems of communication in the transfer of technology (for example, if protection devices, for simple reasons such as wrong installation, are increasing the amount of damage, rather than reducing it).

It should be added that the authority to issue directives not only represents a general authorisation, which can be used by the implementers in a flexible manner. Their authority to intervene does not provide them with full discretion as to whether and how to take measures. Rather, if deficits above a certain level occur, the auditors are obliged to take the necessary steps with all necessary insistence so that things are put right, or, in cases of blunt disobedience, to alert the top management. Summing up, the integration of the various environmental and safety issues into the activities of the multinationals is accompanied by a basic transformation of their structure. Instead of solely dealing with strategic aspects of general business policy, the parent company is highly involved in the on-site operative processes. The distribution of responsibility between the parent and subsidiary, as it can be reconstructed from the database, assigns to the individual company a new position—which one would not have necessarily expected, judging as an outsider and on the basis of the literature on the 'heterarchic', 'polycentric', or 'postmodern' corporation (Chandler, 1966; Bartlett and Goshal, 1999; Teubner, 1991): Certainly, the subsidiaries are still independent, but independent in a clearly qualified sense. One may characterise this as 'independence under reservation', an independence with provisions made for intervention by the parent company.

C. Internal Standards

While the empirical analysis of internal auditing informs us about how implementation takes place, a more detailed examination of the criteria on which this is based is still missing. In each of the firms, there is a close-meshed net of norms and rules for each source of potential problems, such as safety of machinery, air pollution control, sewage treatment, and waste management, all functioning to ensure that the processes are controllable and effectively prevent the shift of negative effects onto society at large. For the sociological analysis of the emerging structures of societal law, the reconstruction of these standards is particularly important, as they provide insights into the level of risk prevention which can actually be expected of the 'global players' according to the state of common practice today.

Here, too, the focus is on the criteria of care which are marked by a high degree of uniformity across the firms compared. This uniformity may result from the similarities of the prevailing problems, from the corporations being culturally rooted in the same country of origin, or from the horizontal exchange of experiences between the firms. In the context of a sociological survey, an exhaustive stocktake of the prevailing norms and rules is not possible, of course, but through appropriate interviewing, it can be ensured that those standards which apply to typical regularly occurring dysfunctions and, from that point of view, play a central role in practice, will be identified.

Basically, the internal norms and rules to a certain extent lean on the specifications of German environmental and technology law, but at the same time, the corporations are not heading towards a detailed transfer of German standards. The law of the country of origin plays an important role as a source of stimulation in the attempt to establish a uniform level of protection, filling the legal lacunae in the host countries, but the adoption of certain norms is always based on the risk assessment made in the corporations' head offices: 'We try to neutralise what we think is good in German environmental law in such a way that it can be transferred abroad. We will not say, however, you have to have paragraph 20 merely because we have it in Germany' (interview, 13 December 2000).

Differences between corporations' worldwide norms and the legal standards in their country of origin are due to the fact, first, that some of the legal regulations are considered to be carried too far, even for German conditions. In addition to this, the state of affairs in the local industry in many of the countries abroad makes the use of particularly elaborate technologies appear to be a luxury—a luxury which may seem unaffordable considering the strong pressure of competition.

The existing rules first concern the technical equipment of the production sites. When a new plant is built, the most important decisions are made by the parent companies. However, modification, enlargement, and repair of existing installations come within the responsibility of the individual foreign subsidiaries, something that can turn out to be the source of numerous deficits. This not only applies to cases in which necessary measures are delayed on account of costs. Among the instances of mismanagement, there is also the neglect of maintenance activities which could have been conducted with little effort and at low cost, or occurrences of constructions being paradoxical in themselves, that is, cases in which an installation fails to meet its initial purpose because of installation errors. The following rules represent an analytical abstraction derived from the statements of and examples given by the interviewees, and are accepted in all corporations as a minimum level of diligence:

— In dealing with technical equipment, matters of abrasion must always be taken into consideration. Leaks in the sealing of sewage plant basins, containers, and pipes have to be quickly repaired (in this, technological developments have to be taken into account: 'In the past, the basins were tiled. This is no longer state of the art today': interview, 7 January 2002).
— Subterranean tanks containing substances harmful to the soil must be double-walled and must have sensory leak control devices.
— When chemicals are stored, safe distances must be kept between certain substances (for example, substances which violently react with others).

The impact of the steering arrangements reaches all the way down to the 'micro' level of the operations inside a plant, which is an important adaptation to the vast destructive potential of even minor deviations. An interpretation in terms of 'corporate ethics' or 'corporate philosophy' (as detailed in many contributions from the management literature: see Stöckl, 1996; Scherer, 2003), here turns out to be inadequate, since many of the regulations refer to underlying necessities and 'basic rules' (Cicourel, 1973), which are anchored in the basic layers of technical rationality. This is also emphasised by the interviewees themselves (for example, 'The whole thing has its foundations in natural sciences': interview, 15 April 2002). The above-mentioned rules do not exist as written guidelines,[8] but this, however, does not reduce their binding force. Admittedly, their implementation could be heavily optimised through a comprehensive set of written instructions, and efforts of this kind can, indeed, be observed in all the corporations examined.

While the standards listed above serve as examples for the regulation of plant installation, the internal norm systems also consist of standards for the conduct of organisational and operational procedures, characterised by

[8] The standards for the safe storage of chemicals are an exception. Here, corporations make use of a recommendation by the Association of the Chemicals Industry (VCI) which internally is given the status of an instruction to be observed throughout the corporation—with numerous criteria for classification, and quantitative data about necessary safety distances.

a high degree of relatedness to the practical problems encountered on the ground:

- — For particular tasks, such as disposal of sewage or waste, specialised responsibilities have to be set up, analogous to the function of the *Betriebsbeauftragter* (representative of environmental affairs) in German environmental law.
- — Such units have to be vested with the authority to issue directives: 'They also have to be in a position to tell the factory management, I don't accept anything beyond this range, since a water treatment plant is not a general dogsbody' (interview, 5 December 2001).
- — For certain dangerous activities, for example activities inside the tanks, a so-called 'permission system' has to be introduced, in order to eliminate all sources of danger as they approach.
- — Waste disposal companies which purchase hazardous waste have to be regularly checked for their reliability: 'It is something we first had to learn, that it is crucial to check the end users. And I must say, it is not yet known everywhere that this is crucial' (interview, 15 April 2002).

Just as it makes good sociological sense to classify certain rules as basic criteria of technical rationality (the necessity, for example, to watch the abrasion factor when dealing with technique), so in the empirical reconstruction one also comes across some basic criteria of organisational rationality, such as the rule to minimise the degree of carelessness through appropriately structured procedures, or the principle to avoid dangerous solo attempts of individuals. The specifications closely match the problems at the operational level, which characterises the emerging governance mechanisms as pragmatic arrangements.

Unlike some decades ago, when it was still considered sufficient to equip subsidiaries with the necessary machinery and handbooks, companies have learned that they must also make the entire background of (once tacit) technical and organisational basic rules the focal point of their internal communications. Even where, from the perspective of an outsider, production processes have not changed, this represents a different constellation to the old situation—it represents nothing less than the overcoming of the almost ethnocentric idea that the practical meaning and use of the technologies transferred would stay the same in every country of the world.

IV. DISEMBEDDED LAW? THE INTEGRATION OF SELF-REGULATORY SYSTEMS INTO THE INSTITUTIONAL ORDER

The empirical reconstruction has provided numerous insights into the development of an emerging transnational law, which can be found in a similar fashion in many other problem areas of the corporate world. The specifications are sufficiently concrete to establish clear-cut demarcations between what is admissible and what is not, and, at the same time, they are of a generality which makes them relevant to the entire field of actors, notwithstanding the fact that these fields extend across transnational boundaries. As mentioned above, the emergence of law-making competencies beyond the national state, which are exercised by transnational actors, should not be perceived as a zero-sum game. Moreover, by interlocking its actions with the informal governance mechanisms of the transnational sphere, the state not only provides the informal norms and rules with a higher degree of reliability, transparency, and legitimacy, but also increases its own problem-solving capabilities.

Thus, despite the informal character of the governance mechanisms, numerous different cases can be identified in which they interact with formal, state-defined law. Partly, it can be observed that the local authorities inform themselves about the existing standards and incorporate these into their decisions (Böhm, 2002: 184). A further linkage can be found, where the internal governance mechanisms anchored in common practice give rise to new forms of corporate liability, inspired by the logic of tort law (*cf* Herberg, 2006; Glinski, chapter two, this volume; Kocher, chapter three, this volume). In some cases, those self-binding acts addressed to the outside world, too, can become the basis of claims for compensation, namely if the claimants can prove their expectations to be justified expectations, based on promises made in the corporate codes.

Some authors use the notion of a growing 'legal porosity' (Santos, 1995: 473) to emphasise the numerous legal irritations resulting from today's norm-pluralistic constellation for the legal practitioner. Both at the level of defining facts, and at the level of interpreting the law, difficulties in precisely differentiating between law and non-law are on the increase. In view of basic juridical categories such as common practice or the principle of protection of trust, the practitioner of law will often feel compelled to examine the informal structures more carefully. The difficulties, however, begin with the identification of the existing norms and the reach of their contents. In many cases, the existence of identical regulations in a greater number of other, comparable, companies will be the decisive argument in determining whether they are legally relevant; but how is the lawyer to gain the necessary insider knowledge? Where there is a lack of usable empirical expertise, legal practitioners find themselves faced with considerable cognitive problems, including the difficulty of conducting the necessary reconstruction by themselves.

In Weberian terms, the problem mainly lies in the danger of a disintegration of the formal-rational and the substantive-rational components of modern law (*cf* Weber, 1980: 397). The legal-positivistic theorem that everything not explicitly forbidden is thus permitted, again and again reaches its limits under today's conditions. At the same time, however, it would equate to sacrificing the reliability, precision, and systematic nature of law if one imported into the legal discourse each and every standard appearing to be practically or politically desirable. While the previous considerations have been restricted to a reconstruction of emerging (para-) legal structures, it must now be asked which forms of legal re-embedding can be observed—so to speak, as the other side of interlegal analysis. This, however, can only be roughly outlined in the following paragraphs.

There is much indication that the actors in developing countries have learned that their attractiveness to multinational firms and a reasonable level of environmental protection are not mutually exclusive. In some cases, the authorities even impose much stricter standards on the multinationals than they would do on domestic firms: 'The USB (Chinese Environment Bureau) often demands of foreign companies to install the latest environmental protection technology, even if such measures exceed the Chinese standard' (Böhm, 2000: 184). Seen from the point of view of law's substantive rationality, a stricter treatment of multinationals seems to have its legitimacy in the above average financial power of these firms, their steering capacity, and their privileged access to modern technologies; in the pure legal sense, this treatment, of course, is in a certain tension with the principle of non-discrimination in existing international economic law.

An important question is to what extent the authorities in their decisions make use of the norms instituted by the corporate world itself, since such a 'reflexive' mode of steering would avoid the problems of a pure mechanical execution of law identical for all types of enterprises, as well as the problem of voluntary discrimination against individual firms on account of their foreign origin. Here, the legal principle of equality, one might say, becomes the battlefield of the antagonism between formal and substantive rationality, and it is this principle which in some ways drives the law beyond its own limits in various fields, and prompts it to look at the differences between the actors and their respective capacities—according to the requirement to treat as equal what is equal and as unequal what is unequal (*cf* Hirschberg, 1981).

Also the new responsibilities of multinationals' headquarters are causing resonances within state-defined law, and here also, one finds mechanisms worthy of being reconstructed in more detail—not least because they can become a model for institutional adaptations on a larger scale. From a formal point of view, the subsidiaries of the multinationals are legally independent enterprises which normally have to meet their liabilities themselves. According to popular opinion, laying claim against the parent company for liability is permissible only where the latter has drastically reduced the autonomy of the subsidiary or has enacted a particular decision against the subsidiary's will. The legal innovation, which has become apparent in only a small number of decisions thus far, now is to regard the opposite constellation also as a form of culpable conduct: from this point of view, cases of an atypical reserve towards steering on the part of the headquarters, in the sense of a neglect of existing duties of diligence and supervision are also unacceptable.[9]

The corresponding concept of liability can be broken down to the following formula: parent companies which have neglected to implement steering systems of the kind that are in common use, or which have detected serious deficiencies during their internal checks and audits, but have not put an end to them, are liable on account of an offence against their organisational duties. That this legal mechanism has been scarcely used above all seems to stem from the traditional idea that the less headquarters interfered with processes on site, the more easily a problem-free integration of the subsidiary into the context of the host country could be achieved—a view which, according to the incidents of the past, can in fact be considered disproved. The driving force further developing the law here is the principle of apportioning blame according to the existing potentials of power and influence ('respondeat superior': Fikentscher, 1976: 673). Certainly, this principle is put to a hard test through an ever more complex division of labour, but at the same time, it generates over and over again regulations that effectively limit the externalisation of costs and damages to third parties.

New demands on legal practices can also result from the corporate codes which, even if they are addressed to a very broad public, create concrete expectations on the part of concrete actors which interact with the particular enterprise, and, in doing so, trust in the firms' compliance with their promises. From the view of pure formal legal aspects, only such declarations which either exist in the form of a classical contract or at least express the intention to accept the legal effects of the statement (ie the so called *Rechtsbindungswille* in German civil law) will be considered as judiciable. In legal practice, however, there are numerous tendencies to push these criteria forward (*cf* Köndgen, 1981, with further references).

Historically, the principle of the protection of trust has always played a vivid role in overcoming too formalistic elements of juridical practice, be it in administrative law or in contract law. The key idea is the protection of legitimate expectations, which the trusting party derives from the promises of their interaction partners, and to some extent also from their advertisement and self-presentation, as well as from the customs and professional standards in the relevant field of practice. In all of these cases, the exclusion of informal obligations from the realm of formal law would surely lead to distorted or paradoxical legal results, and for this reason, the principle of confidence and trust has triggered a broad range of innovative legal

[9] The examples from the US jurisdiction mainly refer to the so-called 'Good Samaritan' doctrine, according to which even the headquarters' basic capability of control leads to far-reaching duties of surveillance and corrective intervention (*cf* Meier, 2000: 496*ff*).

concepts, among them litigation for breach of promises in certain contexts, and the successive juridification of professional standards.

As this overview shows, the potential linkages between formal law and the emerging para-legal systems of the transnational sphere are manifold. The utilisation of this potential for the further development of law, however, in many cases is still in its infancy, and several aspects so far, first of all, define themselves *ex negativo*, as a break with the paradigm of the unity and completeness of law. A blindness of law to the norm-making processes in (world) society is out of the question; to the contrary, not only with respect to substantive aspects, but also for the sustenance of the formal rationality and efficiency of modern law, many cases depend on an incorporation of the emerging societal norms and responsibilities into the law's own structures.

V. THE CONSTITUTIONAL STATE IN THE AGE OF GLOBAL LEGAL PLURALISM

In the debate on the chances of 'Governance without World Government' (Zürn, 1998), the important role of private companies' contributions to the steering architecture has often been emphasised, yet a systematic study of this field remains to be done. The findings concerning the environmental self-regulatory systems of the eight largest German multinationals in the chemical sector are a possible step towards this aim; other important cases to be studied might be chemicals corporations of a smaller size and/or from other countries, or enterprises in the mining and oil industries, the automobile, electrical, and engineering industries, and the food and textile industries (as to the latter, *cf* Bair and Gereffi, 2000).

The emerging steering arrangements of the economic world fill up spaces in which state control so far is present only to a small degree, and where possible solutions on the international level have been undermined through the struggle between different national interests. This does not mean, of course, that these spaces will be permanently blocked off from action on part of the state. As indicated by the concept of interlegality, the decoupling between state law and informal rule-making is paralleled by various processes leading in the converse direction: Due to the practical relevance of the informal mechanisms, there are numerous interactions with existing state-defined law. Often, the emerging governance systems are lacking in fair procedures for dispute resolution, and that is why, in cases of breaches, the judicial institutions of the state remain an important platform. The law sees itself confronted with new normativities from many directions, and is thereby starting to change its own identity.

In these processes, a transition in some ways can be observed from a nation state tied to a territory towards the nation state as a transmission belt (or, more precisely, as a plurality of transmission belts) between the transnational and the national spheres (Messner, 2002: 28). The authorities and courts of the different countries are increasingly worked into the steering processes of the transnational sphere, and in many cases, they see themselves prompted to extend their investigations and steering activities beyond the nation state's borders. The host countries of the corporations can take up the norms that the latter themselves have established, and thereby, create legal regimes which would not have been possible without knowledge of those standards. At the same time, the institutions of the state in the countries of origin are increasingly confronted with claims of extra-territorial origin, among them the complaints of parties injured on site, and these claims cannot be rejected out of hand, for example by arguing that the subsidiaries were legally independent entities, falling outside the influence of the parent companies just by definition.

Globalisation, therefore, should not rashly be equated with denationalisation. While forcing us to modify many of the old unitary and hierarchical notions of order, globalisation does not per se lead to a situation of anomy or amorphousness. Where the state manages adequately to adapt its institutions to the new challenges, it remains a relevant actor in the global steering process. The nation state partly acts as an important initiator of self-regulation, partly contributes to increasing the reliability of private self-regulatory systems through supporting measures, and, in many cases, represents an important clearing-house for claims and demands which emerge whenever self-regulation fails or reaches its limits.

In the long run, the manifold interconnections might very well add up to a new model of interlocked governance and statehood, with the state regaining its regulatory competence inside, and, to some extent also, outside its territory. Here, too, in principle, it is true what is being said about the different forms of indirect and 'reflexive' regulation within the national sphere: in its search for useful steering mechanisms, the nation state intensively has to make use of the intelligence and practical knowledge of societal actors (*cf* Mayntz and Scharpf, 1995). In this context, the supportive function of empirical social research is of great significance, since this intelligence, in order to be utilised, first of all has to be thoroughly analysed.

REFERENCES

Areola, O (1998) 'Comparative Environmental Issues and Politics in Nigeria' in U Desay, *Ecological Policy and Politics in Developing Countries* (New York, State University of New York Press) 229–66.

Austin, J (2002) *Zur Theorie der Sprechakte (How to do Things with Words)* (Stuttgart, Reclam).

Bair, J and Gereffi, G (2000) 'Industrielle Entwicklung, Netzwerke und Beschäftigung in der Bekleidungsindustrie' in C Dörrenbächer and D Plewe (eds), *Grenzenlose Kontrolle? Organisatorischer Wandel und politische Macht multinationaler Unternehmen* (Berlin, Edition Sigma), 195–215.

Banister, J (2000) 'Population, Public Health and the Environment in China', in RL Edmonds (ed), *Managing the Chinese Environment* (New York: Oxford University Press) 262–91.

Bartlett, C and Goshal, S (1999) *Managing across Borders: The Transnational Solution* (Boston, Harvard Business School Press).

Beck, U (1997) Was ist Globalisierung? Irrtümer des Globalismus—Antworten auf Globalisierung (Frankfurt/Main, Suhrkamp).

—— (2002) *Macht und Gegenmacht im globalen Zeitalter. Neue weltpolitische Ökonomie* (Frankfurt/Main, Suhrkamp).

Böhm, U (2000) *Umweltorientiertes Management multinationaler Unternehmen in der VR China* (Baden-Baden, Nomos).

Bohnsack, R (1993) Rekonstruktive Sozialforschung. Einführung in Methodologie und Praxis qualitativer Forschung (Opladen, Leske und Budrich).

Böttger, K (2002) *Die Umweltpflichtigkeit von Auslandsdirektinvestitionen im Völkerrecht* (Baden-Baden, Nomos).

Bowman, M and Hunter, D (1992) 'Environmental Reforms in Post-Communist Central Europe: From High to Hard Reality', in 13 *Michigan Journal of International Law* 921–80.

Bowonder, B, Kasperson, J and Kasperson, RE (1994) 'Industrial Risk Management in India since Bhopal' in S Jasanoff (ed), *Learning from Disaster. Risk Management After Bhopal* (Philadelphia, Pennsylvania Press) 66–90.

Chandler, A (1966) *Strategy and Structure* (Cambridge/London, MIT Press).

Cicourel, A (1973) 'Basisregeln und normative Regeln im Prozess des Aushandelns von Status und Rolle. In: Arbeitsgruppe Bielefelder Soziologen', in *Alltagswissen, Interaktion und gesellschaftliche Wirklichkeit* Bd I (Reinbek bei Hamburg, Rowohlt) 147–76.

Cutler, C (2002) 'Private International Regimes and Interfirm Cooperation' in R Hall and T Biersteker (eds) *The Emergence of Private Authority in Global Governance* (Cambridge, Cambridge University Press) 23–42.

Ehrlich, E (1989) *Grundlegung der Soziologie des Rechts* (Berlin, Duncker und Humblot).

El-Bahay, S (1998) Umweltschutz in Ägypten—realistische Forderung oder Utopie? Probleme und Chancen einer ökologisch orientierten Politik in einem Land der 'Dritten Welt' (Münster, Waxmann).

Fikentscher, W (1976) *Schuldrecht* (Berlin/New York, de Gruyter).

Fuchs, P (1997) Transnationale Konzerne als Akteure 'nachhaltiger' Entwicklung? In (2) *Nord-Süd aktuell* pp 284–300.

Goffman, E (1972) *Encounters. Two Studies in the Sociology of Interaction* (London, Penguin Press).

Greer, J and Bruno, K (1996) *Greenwash. The Reality Behind Corporate Environmentalism* (Third World Network, Penang).

Gündling, L (1998) *Umweltrechtsberatung und Institutionenentwicklung im Umweltbereich* (Wiesbaden, Universum Verlagsanstalt).

Günter, K and Randeria, S (2001) *Recht, Kultur und Gesellschaft im Prozess der Globalisierung* (Bad Homburg, Werner Reimers Stiftung).

Herberg, M (2001) 'Codes of Conduct und kommunikative Vernunft. Rechtssoziologische Überlegungen zu den Umweltleitlinien transnationaler Chemiekonzerne', in (22) Zeitschrift für Rechtssoziologie pp 25–50.

—— (2001a) *'Die Betriebe müssen ihre Hausaufgaben machen'. Auslandsaudits als Instrument der umweltbezogenen Selbstregulierung in transnationalen Chemiekonzernen,* Bremen, Arbeitspapiere der FEU Forschungsstelle für Europäisches Umweltrecht.

—— (2003) 'Kooperatives Regierungshandeln und Codes of Conduct im Politikfeld Umweltschutz bei Auslandsdirektinvestitionen', in B Hansjürgens and W Köck (eds), *Kooperative Umweltpolitik* (Baden-Baden, Nomos).

—— (2005) *Entkoppeltes Recht? Die Umweltstandards multinationaler Konzerne zwischen Informalität und Verrechtlichung*, Bremen, Transtate Working Papers.

—— (2005a) "Re-embedding the Disembedded". Die Umweltstandards multinationaler Konzerne in der globalen Steuerungsarchitektur, in (4) *Soziale Welt*, 399–416.

—— (2006) 'Private Authority, Global Governance, and the Law: The Case of Environmental Self-Regulation in Multinational Enterprises' in G Winter (ed), *Multilevel Governance of Global Environmental Change: Perspectives from Science, Sociology and the Law* (Cambridge, Cambridge University Press), 149–78.

Hirschberg, L (1981) *Der Grundsatz der Verhältnismäßigkeit* (Göttingen, Otto Schwarz).

Kamau, E (2005) 'Environmental Regimes and Direct Investment in Third World Countries' in Gerd Winter (ed), *Die Umweltverantwortung multinationaler Unternehmen. Selbststeuerung und Recht bei Auslandsdirektinvestitionen* (Baden-Baden, Nomos) 147–86.

Kaniaru, D, Manjit, I, Mrema, E and Chowdhury, S (1995) 'UNEP's Programme of Assistance on National Legislation and Institutions', in United Nations Environment Programme (ed), *UNEP's New Way Forward: Environmental Law and Sustainable Development* (Nairobi, Earthprint), 153–70.

Köndgen, J (1981) *Selbstbindung ohne Vertrag. Zur Haftung aus geschäftsbezogenem Handeln* (Tübingen, Mohr Siebeck).

Lampe, E-J (ed) (1995) *Rechtsgleichheit und Rechtspluralismus* (Baden-Baden, Nomos).

Leonard, J (1988) *Pollution and the Struggle for the World Product: Multinational Corporations, Environment and International Comparative Advantage* (Cambridge, Cambridge University Press).

Mannheim, K (1980) *Strukturen des Denkens* (Frankfurt am Main, Suhrkamp).

Mayntz, R and Scharpf, F (1995) *Gesellschaftliche Selbstregulierung und politische Steuerung* (Frankfurtam Main, Campus).

Meier, W (2000) *Grenzüberschreitender Durchgriff in der Unternehmensgruppe nach US-amerikanischem Recht* (Frankfurt am Main, Peter Lang).

Messner, D (2002) *Nationalstaaten in der Global Governance-Architektur*, INEF-Report (Duisburg).

Neff, A (1990) 'Not in Their Backyards Either. A Proposal for a Foreign Environmental Practices Act' (17) *Ecology Law Quarterly* 477–500.

Oevermann, U (1983) 'Zur Sache. Die Bedeutung von Adornos methodologischem Selbstverständnis für die Begründung einer materialen soziologischen Strukturanalyse' in J Habermas and L Friedeburg (eds), *Adorno-Konferenz* (Frankfurt am Main, Suhrkamp) 234–64.

Oevermann, U, Schuster, L and Simm, A (1985) *Zum Problem der Perseveranz in Delikttyp und modus operandi* (Wiesbaden, BKA-Reihe).

Pauly, LW (2002) 'Global Finance, Political Authority, and the Problem of Legitimation' in R Hall and T Biersteker, T (eds) (2002) *The Emergence of Private Authority in Global Governance* (Cambridge, Cambridge University Press) 76–90.

Robertson, R (1998) 'Globalisierung: Homogenität und Heterogenität in Raum und Zeit', in U Beck (ed), *Perspektiven der Weltgesellschaft* (Frankfurt am Main, Suhrkamp) 192–215.

Rolf, E (1997) *Illokutionäre Kräfte. Grundbegriffe der Illokutionslogik* (Opladen, Westdeutscher Verlag).

Rosenau, J (1992) 'Governance, Order and Change in World Politics' in J Rosenau and EO Czempiel (eds), *Governance without Government. Order and Change in World Politics* (Cambridge, Cambridge University Press) 3–17.

Santos, B de Sousa (1995) *Toward a New Common Sense. Law, Science and Politics in the Paradigmatic Transition* (New York/London, Butterworths).

Scherer, A (2003) *Multinationale Unternehmen und Globalisierung. Zur Neuorientierung der Theorie der multinationalen Unternehmung* (Heidelberg, Physica Verlag).

Schmidt-Preuß, M (1998) 'Verwaltung und Verwaltungsrecht zwischen gesellschaftlicher Selbstregulierung und staatlicher Steuerung' (56) Verhandlungen der Vereinigung deutscher Staatsrechtslehrer pp 160 *ff*.

Stöckl, W (1996) *Ökologieorientierte Führung multinationaler Unternehmen in Entwicklungsländern* (Wiesbaden, Deutscher Universitätsverlag).

Teubner, G (1991) 'Unitas Multiplex—Das Konzernrecht in der neuen Dezentralität der Unternehmensgruppe' 20(2) *Zeitschrift für Unternehmens- und Gesellschaftsrecht* 189–207.

—— (2000) 'Des Königs viele Leiber. Die Selbstdekonstruktion der Hierarchie des Rechts' in H Brunkhorst and M Kettner (eds), *Globalisierung und Demokratie* (Frankfurt/Main, Suhrkamp) 240–73.

Weber, M (1980) *Wirtschaft und Gesellschaft. Grundriss der verstehenden Soziologie* (Tübingen, Mohr).

Weidner, H and Jänicke, M (2001) 'Die umweltpolitischen Chancen der Globalisierung' in L Röller, and C Wey (eds), *Die soziale Marktwirtschaft in der neuen Weltwirtschaft* (Berlin, WZB-Jahrbuch), 293–300.

WHO/UNEP (1992) *Urban Air Pollution in Megacities of the World* (Oxford, Alden Press).

Zürn, M (1998) *Regieren jenseits des Nationalstaats. Globalisierung und Denationalisierung als Chance* (Frankfurt am Main, Suhrkamp).

2

Bridging the Gap: The Legal Potential of Private Regulation[1]

CAROLA GLINSKI

I. INTRODUCTION

THIS CHAPTER DEALS with the legal potential of corporate codes of conduct and other private regulatory instruments concerning aspects of public interest. The topics of environmental conduct, health and safety issues, and labour standards in transnational activities have been chosen because one can observe a regulatory gap with regard to the conduct of multinational corporations in developing countries. First, no international conventions have been adopted in this field. Second, countries pursuing high standards of protection do not have any direct regulatory power over the production standards in developing countries, due to the international law principle of sovereignty. This applies to the countries in which the parent companies are situated as well as to those countries in which products from low protection countries are marketed.[2] To a certain extent, private regulation is seen as a way to bridge the gap between the different national protection levels.

Indeed, there is a considerable number and variety of private regulatory instruments dealing with environmental conduct, health and safety issues, and labour standards in transnational activities. This paper focuses on those standards that are adopted by single enterprises, groups of enterprises, or business associations and explores the circumstances under which such private regulation can have legal effects.

The approach taken in the literature to the issue of the private regulation of global or transnational problems varies greatly. On the one hand, ideas

[1] Parts of this chapter are also incorporated in a chapter of mine entitled 'Corporate Self-Regulation: Moral or Legal Obligation?' in Doreen McBarnet, Aurora Voiculescu and Tom Campbell (eds), *The New Corporate Accountability: Corporate Social Responsibility and the Law* (Cambridge, Cambridge University Press, 2007).

[2] On foreign direct investment see the analysis by Böttger, 2002. On the relationship between international trade and the protection of the environment see, eg, Mavroidis, 2000.

of legal pluralism have developed which are based on systems theory (for example, Teubner, 1997, 2004a, 2004b), or on neoliberal or classical liberal, private law-oriented ideas of freedom and self-organisation of citizens and civil society (for example, Ladeur, 2000: 78*ff*). These ideas would, roughly speaking, lead to the recognition of private regulation of different social sectors as a source of law that is as valid as formal national or international law. They could even lead to the replacement of formal law, since the national state loses its capacity to regulate problems as they become transnational or international, and due to the lack of adequate international law-making institutions to address these problems. Frequently, these theories are only based on very general ideas about the legitimacy of private regulation. In contrast to this perspective, in the view of more traditional legal scholars private regulatory instruments are first of all social norms. Law is basically restricted to the classical, and therefore legitimate, sources of law.[3]

One field that has attracted much attention from lawyers is the standards established by semi-public or state-approved standards organisations or institutes. Broad debate has surrounded technical standards adopted by, for example, the Deutsches Institut für Normung eV (DIN), the Verband Deutscher Elektrotechniker eV (VDE), the British Standards Institution (BSI), the Comité Européen de Normalisation (CEN), the International Organization for Standardisation (ISO) (for example, Marburger, 1979: 429*ff*; Falke and Schepel, 2000: 321*ff*; Falke, 2000: 448*ff*; Finke, 2001). Purely private regulatory instruments do not appear to have been considered in this debate.

This chapter takes a differentiated approach. First, it distinguishes those legal effects that concern only the authors of private rules (section III). Second, it looks at the broader legal effects that are binding on a whole group of corporations, which means that they are also binding on outsiders who have not adhered to the private rules (section IV). Third, 'real standardisation', that is, the legal effects that are binding not only on authors and outsiders but also on third parties, including those who are negatively affected will be examined (section V).[4]

These three 'levels' of binding effects can be found in very different fields of law. They can, for example, be related to market effects or to liability for

[3] See, eg, the speech of Lord President Hope of Craighead in *Mumford and Smith v Bank of Scotland* (1996) SLT 392, at 398, concerning a bank's obligation to advise a spousal guarantor to take independent advice, a duty enshrined in the Banking Code: 'So far as the law of Scotland is concerned, however, we do not consider that the practice described in … the code … can be said to be a matter of legal obligation, or legal duty, so far as banks, building societies or any other creditors are concerned.'

[4] Another type of interaction between private regulation and the law could be discovered in the field of liability of multinational corporations for (environmental) damage caused by their subsidiaries, see Glinski, 2004; 2005b; 2007.

damages. Of course, important differences exist between the characteristics, requirements, and legal consequences of market-related legal effects on one hand, and tort law effects on the other. For example, private rules that aim at market effects are concerned with fairness and ethical conduct, whereas those rules relevant to tort law usually deal with technical requirements. Market effects at least necessitate communication of rules, whereas tort law effects could also be provoked by internal regulation that is based on know-how. Nevertheless, there are common features of private regulation in particular at the third level of binding effects, which can be related back to general prerequisites for the legitimacy of private regulation. These general prerequisites will be dealt with first (section II).

II. GENERAL PREREQUISITES FOR PRIVATE REGULATION IN PRIVATE LAW, AS DISTINGUISHED FROM PUBLIC LAW

In order to determine the requirements for the legitimacy of private regulation in private law, it might be helpful to distinguish private law from public law. This very general but nevertheless highly controversial distinction is not meant to relate strictly to the German legal system but more generally to the particularities and the purposes of the respective fields of law. Private law and public law essentially differ with regard to different actors (individual citizens in private law versus state actors in public law) and different responsibilities (individual interests in private law versus public interest in public law).

At its core, private law focuses on private autonomy and leaves to citizens the free choice of purposes and instruments of their (legal) engagements. Private law primarily deals with the individual interest that is institutionally secured by freedom of contract. However, private law can also be concerned with the public interest. Here, the idea is that the concurrence of the different individual interests pursued would, as a reflex, also promote the public interest (for example, Hoffmann-Riem, 1996: 268*ff*).

In contrast, public law is basically concerned with the public interest. As private regulation is not democratically anchored in the classical public law chain of legitimacy, democratic substitutes, in particular fair and pluralistic decision-making procedures, must be put in place in order to ensure that the public interest is served. Thus, private regulation in the field of public law must satisfy two elements of equal opportunity to participate in the decision-making process: equal input and dedication to the public interest (output).[5]

However, the right to self-organise under private law is not unlimited either. Legal effects of private regulation have legitimacy requirements not only in public law but also in private law, as private law does not refrain

[5] Further restrictions may stem from constitutional law or overarching principles of law, such as the rule of law (see, eg, Denninger, 1990: 117*ff*; Hoffmann-Riem, 1996; di Fabio, 1997; Lübbe-Wolf, 2001: 265*ff*).

completely from normative control. The prerequisites of the legal effects of private regulation depend on the extent to which private regulation (and the relevant field of law) merely safeguards the private autonomy of the actors, serves a group interest, accounts for third party interests, or aims at serving the public interest. Thus, private law effects may not only require consensus among those who participate in the decision-making process, but may also involve safeguarding the group interest, the interest of third parties, or the public interest to the extent they may be concerned (see also Bachmann, 2002).

III. LEGAL EFFECTS ON AUTHORS OR SIGNATORIES OF PRIVATE REGULATORY INSTRUMENTS

The idea that authors or signatories of private regulatory instruments could be bound to their content is not far-fetched. In the following paragraphs, two grounds of legal effects of private regulatory instruments on their authors will be discussed: (1) confidence in communications of private rules that are relevant for market relations, and (2) the expertise of the author that finds its expression in a regulatory instrument with relevance for tort law.

A. Confidence in Published Private Regulation

A number of private regulatory instruments, such as corporate codes of conduct, but also social or environmental reports or advertisements giving messages concerning self-imposed rules, are published. By doing so, corporations aim both to improve their reputation and increase their market share (see, for example, Howells and Weatherill, 2005: 73). By describing their own behaviour in more or less specific wording, corporations create confidence or expectations among consumers and trading partners, as such descriptions have the character of promises.[6] Otherwise they fail in their intention to gain or regain a positive reputation. This is particularly true of private regulation that refers to social and environmental standards pertaining to production in or trade with developing countries (see also Kocher, 2004). The related legal effects are based on the legal protection of legitimate expectations in the compliance with these promises in contract law, as well as in the law on misleading advertising, which forms part of competition law.

1. *Contract Law*

There is no doubt that a corporation is, in principle, allowed to make promises concerning its own behaviour either by establishing or signing

[6] On the promissory character of the language used see Herberg, 2001.

a (corporate) code of conduct, or simply by making certain guarantees when advertising, and that such promises can be introduced into a contract (Howells and Weatherill, 2005: 73). Contract law forms the core of private law. It is based on the principle of party autonomy, allowing contracting parties to regulate their relationship according to their own needs. On the whole, no further legitimacy requirements apply, and only a few restrictions exist, namely that the agreement must be neither illegal nor immoral. Within this framework the contracting parties can freely determine their mutual obligations. The only relevant requirement for the legal effect of such private regulation is that the parties consent. Consent in this case is to be assessed objectively. Although contracting parties usually pursue their own interest, altruistic intentions are, of course, not excluded.

Contract law must also safeguard the parties' private autonomy, particularly where there is a power imbalance between them. This is, for example, a key aim of consumer protection law. Therefore, contract law should protect the intentions and expectations of the contracting partners, even if they are of an altruistic nature, and these may well be shaped by a code of conduct to which the contracting partner is a signatory (see also Barron, 2007). For example, a company may have publicised a code of conduct that includes a promise not to use lumber harvested from a rainforest, and a purchaser who wishes to buy an environmentally sound product should be protected by contract law if the company breaches this promise.

Remaining problems for the enforcement of such contractual promises stem from specific limits set by national contract laws. For example, under the old German sales law, the courts hesitated to hold statements contractual that were made before the conclusion of the contract, and in particular statements made in advertising that were not expressly included in the contract. Second, courts refused to hold sellers liable for statements made by producers. Finally, the courts were extremely reluctant to include factors in the range of qualities relevant in sales law that are not physical characteristics of the goods per se such as their environmental quality or the way they were produced (for example, Peifer, 2001: 265*ff*).

In contrast, the EC Sales Law Directive of 1999 (and its national implementations) has included into the conformity requirement all the qualities that determine the value of a product. According to Article 2(2)(d) of the Consumer Sales Directive 1999/44/EC,[7] which sets the minimum standards for the consumer sales laws of Member States, the concept of conformity includes conformity with public statements on the specific characteristics made about the products not only by the seller, but also by the producer or his representative, particularly in advertising or on labelling. A code of conduct is an example of such a public statement. As a result, EC sales

[7] Directive 1999/44/EC on certain aspects of the sale of consumer goods and associated guarantees, 1999 OJ L 171/12.

law acknowledges that the producer's statements may have a far greater effect on a consumer's purchasing decisions than communications between the consumer and the seller (Staudenmayer, 2000: 551). Furthermore, the concept of conformity not only extends to the product-related characteristics of the goods in question (for example, their toxicity) but also to the circumstances under which they were produced. This is particularly true when the price of ethically produced goods is higher than the price of goods produced otherwise; the specific production methods are usually decisive for the purchase (for details, see Glinski, 2004; 2005b: 216*ff*; Glinski and Rott, 2003).

2. *Advertising Law*

The situation is similar in the law of misleading advertising. Insofar as the free decision of the average consumer may be influenced by a published code of conduct, or a particular product labelling (through which the signatories promise to apply ethical or environmentally sound production methods), the law protects the legitimate expectations of the consumer. Non-compliance is a violation of the law of misleading advertising. In principle, there are no further requirements. Remaining problems in fighting misleading advertising are, again, created through limitations in the law itself.

For example, the recent Directive 2005/29/EC pays much attention to the power of codes of conduct, although whether or not the Directive applies to advertising claims regarding ethical and environmentally sound production methods is unclear (for further details see Glinski, 2005a: 200*ff*; Kocher, 2005: 651*ff*). Under Article 6(2)(b) of the Directive, a trader who does not comply with 'commitments [in a code of conduct] that are firm and capable of being verified' is acting unfairly.[8] At the same time, so-called 'aspirational commitments'[9] included in codes of conduct do not appear to be caught under the law of misleading advertising as set out in the Directive. Furthermore, the Directive is concerned only with protecting consumers' economic interests, and not their taste, decency, and social responsibility unless the trader establishes a specific connection between its obligations in these areas and the marketing of its products.[10] Thus, statements made regarding the use of environmentally sound or ethical production methods

[8] This can be explained from the history of the Directive. Initially, the Commission had planned to introduce a co-regulation approach, with a framework rule that was to be fleshed out by the trade associations (Micklitz and Keßler, 2002: 895*ff*). This approach, however, was not followed in the end.

[9] The notion 'aspirational' refers to 'best efforts' as opposed to firm duties, see COM (2002) 289 final, at 11. For more details see Howells *et al*, 2006: 208.

[10] See the Commission's proposal for a Directive on unfair commercial practices: COM (2003) 356 final, at 11*ff*, and recital (7) of Directive 2005/29/EC.

may not even come under the Directive, instead remaining within the competence of the Member States.[11] For instance, a trader may make a general claim that it does not use lumber harvested from rainforests, without attributing this statement to a specific product. Whether or not such a general statement would be regarded as establishing a 'specific connection' is not entirely clear.

B. Expertise Expressed in Regulatory Instruments

While private regulatory instruments, in particular codes of conduct or ethical guidelines, are usually publicly accessible, private regulation can also take entirely different forms, such as *internal* regulation in contracts, management handbooks, or simply the internal environmental or safety management of multinational enterprises (see, in particular, Herberg, 2007). It is not required that such regulatory instruments be published. Such documents may simply aim at providing guidance to employees or subsidiaries in order to improve performance and to prevent losses. Both types of private regulation, published instruments as well as internal ones, provide an indication of what the author or signatory has recognised to be necessary to avoid causing damage. They may therefore play an important role in tort law.

Tort law liability usually requires conduct in breach of due diligence. Due diligence may be the core question where environmental damage and personal injury result from the operation of an industrial plant, particularly in developing countries. Under the recognised principles of tort law, corporations act in breach of due diligence and can be held liable if they violate their own (internal) technical norms or deviate from their normal course of conduct which they had previously recognised as necessary. This is true even where the requirements expressed in their private rules exceed what is otherwise legally required. Here, the law can impose higher standards of due diligence on a corporation by applying that corporation's own private rules or normal practices.

The reason for this legal effect of private regulatory instruments on their authors is not party autonomy but the expertise that the instruments give evidence of. Tort liability has traditionally been, and remains, principally based on individual fault. This has changed in so far as a more objective due diligence standard has evolved.[12] The purpose of such an objective

[11] The precise scope of the exclusion of matters of taste, decency, and social responsibility is unclear (see eg Henning-Bodewig, 2005: 633, fn 25).

[12] See generally (but with special focus to German and US tort law) Brüggemeier, 2004: *5ff*, *65ff*, and *76ff*. For objective standards in the different European legal orders see eg von Bar, 1999: 248*ff*; Wurmnest, 2003: 113*ff*. Typical notions are the standards of the 'reasonable man' (UK, US), or the 'bon père de famille' (France).

standard, however, is merely to introduce an applicable *minimum* standard, thereby raising the diligence required of those who lack certain abilities (see, for example, Deutsch and Ahrens, 2001: 62*ff*). This is consistent with the increasingly important purpose of prevention. In contrast, the introduction of an objective standard has not lowered the diligence requirements for those who possess special knowledge and abilities (see, for example, Mertens, 1994: §276, no 56). Thus, the standard to which an individual corporation is legally bound is defined by the level of expertise expressed in its own private regulation or practice.

IV. LEGAL EFFECTS ON OUTSIDERS THROUGH GENERALISATION

Furthermore, it is possible that the rules established by private actors could have a binding effect on others (that is, other corporations) who have not previously adhered to such rules. This generalising effect may actually be intended by those actors instituting private regulation, whose aim might be to civilise the market or to introduce higher safety standards by excluding unwanted conduct by 'black sheep'. A typical example of this is the guidelines set by professional bodies for their members. However, the generalisation of standards could even occur in cases where such a result was not intended (for example, internal regulation aiming to improve production processes).

To some extent, the law itself paves the way for generalisation, for instance, by taking into consideration commonly shared views or practices that exist in particular lines of business. This shall be illustrated taking the examples of 'reasonable consumer expectations' in market relations and of 'due diligence' under tort law. In these cases, the legitimacy of the creation of legal effects on outsiders must be paid special attention. These legitimacy requirements differ from one field of law to another, depending upon their particular aims and objectives.

A. Generalised Expectations

Generalised consumer expectations play a role in contract law, but also in advertisement law. For example, under the Consumer Sales Directive 1999/44/EC, consumer goods must, inter alia, 'show the quality and performance which are normal in goods of the same type and which the consumer can *reasonably* expect. …' Similarly, the Unfair Commercial Practices Directive 2005/29/EC prohibits misleading the 'average consumer', who is defined as being *reasonably* well informed and *reasonably* observant and circumspect.[13]

[13] See recital (18) of Directive 2005/29/EC.

Although 'reasonable' consumer expectations include a normative element, they nevertheless depend on the expectations of real consumers. Codes of conduct and other publicly accessible private regulation may have the effect of shaping consumer expectations, thereby setting standards that all traders in the same line of business are bound to. If traders want to avoid being bound to a new standard, they have to clarify this by explaining that they were acting differently. Consumer expectations, for example, regarding the environmental quality of a product, are not necessarily limited to the legally required minimum standard but could be higher (Wilhelmsson, 2002–2003: 97*ff*).

Whether or not a code of conduct has the effect of shaping consumer expectations is primarily a question of fact. Clearly, a code of conduct will only have this effect if the most important traders or the vast majority of traders adhere to it. Moreover, intensive publicising is necessary, since consumers must be aware of the code. Finally, the issue must be of some significance to consumers.

The most prominent example would be child labour, as the issue that attracts the highest degree of attention from consumers in industrialised countries (see Parkinson, 2006: 9). For example, it may be possible at some point in the future to expect that carpets have not been knotted by children, if the vast majority of carpet producers adhere to a specific code of conduct that is well known to consumers. As a consequence, a carpet that *has* been produced with child labour would not be in conformity with a sales contract unless the parties have agreed on this fact. Additionally, not to declare in the advertising of the carpet that it was produced with child labour would be considered a misleading omission, and therefore, an unlawful commercial practice under advertising law.[14] In both fields of law, information obligations would arise. Another possible example could be sustainable forestry.

'Outsiders' may be negatively affected by consumer expectations that have been influenced, for example, by a widely known code of conduct. This effect is, however, rather weak as those outsiders who do not comply with the code of conduct do not necessarily act unlawfully, since they may indicate their non-adherence to those rules. Apart from this, the objective criterion of consumer expectations was introduced by law with the aim of providing exactly this kind of legal certainty.

[14] This approach was rejected, in 1980, by the German Bundesgerichtshof, 9/5/1980, (1980) *Neue Juristische Wochenschrift* 2018 at 2020, in the *Asbestos* case: see below at V.A. The court basically argued that German consumers did not care about production methods in developing countries (see also Oppenhoff, 1980). This, however, is certainly not true any longer for at least a considerable segment of consumers.

B. Generalised Minimum Requirements

Private regulation by corporations could determine the minimum standard of care the breach of which constitutes liability under tort law. Private regulation here includes the common practice of producers as well as the measures recognised as necessary—regardless of whether they are based on an agreement between corporations or simply exercised or (internally) regulated in parallel. Outsiders, that is, producers who do not adhere to the relevant practice or rule, would also be bound by this minimum standard as defined by the practice or regulation of others.

The binding effect on outsiders essentially stems from the tort law requirement of due diligence, which stipulates that damage must be predictable and avoidable. Here, the individual ability to recognise and avoid damage is replaced by the specific abilities within a certain line of business or a category of producers. The binding effect on outsiders is a (legitimate) consequence of the legal decision in favour of objective standards and is reflected by the term 'duty of care' (see, for example, Brüggemeier, 2004: 109*ff*).

All measures taken to prevent damage that are usually applied in practice or are deemed adequate by the relevant category of producers must be regarded as measures that the members of the profession or business are able to recognise and adopt—even where lower institutionalised technical norms exist.[15] Notably, this determination of the minimum standard does not preclude producers from taking different measures as long as the same safety level is achieved. The burden of proof then falls on the producer (Marburger, 1979: 470; Falke, 2000: 453*ff*).

Interestingly, a similar result can be found in German literature as well as in legal writings from other European countries with respect to public law standards or semi-private technical norms adopted by standardisation organisations (Falke and Schepel, 2000: 233). Again, the main argument goes that the standards set out in public safety legislation or in institutionalised technical norms represent measures that the profession must be aware of and be capable of taking. Therefore, a strong presumption of negligence arises where there has been non-compliance with these (minimum) requirements, unless the tortfeasor can prove that measures taken were at least equivalent to those required (Falke, 2000: 453; Huth, 1992: 224).[16]

[15] See, eg, LG Berlin, 18/10/1996, (1997) *Neue Juristische Wochenschrift-Entscheidungsdienst Versicherungs- und Haftungsrecht* 94. This means that at least the standard of the actual practice has to be complied with.

[16] Even those academics who are generally reluctant to recognise the relevance of public law standards or institutionalised technical norms in tort law and/or who emphasise the possibility of alternative measures recognise that any alternative measures must minimally reach the same level of protection (Marburger, 1983: 602).

Courts have taken the same view. German courts, for example, have frequently held that non-compliance with DIN standards led to tort law liability,[17] and so have English courts.[18]

This legal effect of a minimum standard of due diligence does, however, have some prerequisites: First, the private rule or practice must be established or followed by a representative variety of corporations. In contrast, a large number of adhering corporations is not necessary since the relevant criterion is not consent but the ability of the relevant category of producers, or peer group (*Verkehrskreis*), to recognise and follow the rule.

Second, one must determine the correct peer group. In the domestic context of an industrialised country, the relevant peer group is those companies working in the respective line of business, which is also usually subject to the same public law requirements. This may be different in the context of a developing country where domestic producers with a low level of environmental and safety standards and subsidiaries of multinational corporations operate in the same line of business. Under such circumstances, other criteria such as technological know-how, (environmental) management abilities, access to technology, and financial resources must be considered when determining the relevant category of producers.[19] The consequence of this approach is that different standards are applied to corporations within the same line of business, such that sophisticated producers, particularly the subsidiaries of large multinational corporations, must meet the higher standard of their particular peer group.

With such a consideration of different peer groups that forms part of tort law, it is possible to compensate for the divergence of public law standards globally, at least with the legal consequences of tort law. The fact that different categories of producers in the same line of business face different

[17] See, eg, BGH, 4/4/1989, (1989) *Neue Juristische Wochenschrift—Rechtsprechungs-Report* 921; BGH, 12/11/1996, (1997) *Neue Juristische Wochenschrift* 582; BGH, 27/4/1999, (1999) *Neue Juristische Wochenschrift* 2593. Decisions deviating from this position have been made only in exceptional cases where, eg, the lack of attention by the injured party was the predominant cause of injury. See, eg, OLG Hamm, 5/5/1995, (1995) *Neue Zeitschrift für Verkehrsrecht* 484; OLG Hamm, 17/9/1996, (1997) *Neue Juristische Wochenschrift—Entscheidungsdienst Versicherungs- und Haftungsrecht* 71; OLG Hamm, 22/3/2004, (2004) *Neue Zeitschrift für Verkehrsrecht* 648. The courts did not argue that a standard set out in the respective technical norm was too high.

[18] An illustrative example is *Ward v The Ritz Hotel (London)* [1992] PIQR 315: The balustrade of the hotel's balcony was lower than the relevant British norm. A guest fell down and was injured. Although the judge in the first instance denied the relevance of a breach of an institutionalised EN norm for establishing negligence, the majority of the Court of Appeal held that the failure to comply with the relevant technical norm constituted negligence. See also Falke and Schepel, 2000: 234*ff*, with further references. In some other countries, in particular Ireland, Greece, Denmark, and Sweden, the civil courts have not given much regard to these technical standards, and therefore, they have not played a significant role in this respect (Falke and Schepel, 2000: 321).

[19] See also Herberg, 2005: 108*ff*.

requirements under tort law is likely not to be a violation of international law, in particular of the principle of national treatment that is usually enshrined in investment agreements, provided that the producer's nationality and its link with a foreign investor as such are not considered to be relevant criteria.[20]

If the establishment of a minimum standard can be called 'private regulation' at all and not merely an effect of the tort law decision in favour of objective standards, legitimacy considerations need only to take account of outsiders that may be negatively affected. In this respect, it is highly unlikely that a minimum standard established by private regulation will weigh the interests of potential victims and the general public over the economic interest of the producers, as it can be assumed that a representative variety of corporations will safeguard their own (economic) group interest and that stronger protection by tort law is not required. As long as outsiders belong to the same category of producers, there is no need to exempt them from the same requirements of due diligence. The interests of potential victims and the public interest in the protection of the environment cannot be negatively affected anyway since minimum standards do not deprive them of any rights and do not constitute a 'safe harbour' for producers.

V. LEGAL EFFECTS ON THIRD PARTIES: REAL STANDARDISATION ESTABLISHING A 'SAFE HARBOUR'?

Until now, only legal effects on outsiders like other traders or producers in the same field in the sense of minimum standards have been considered. Private regulation could, however, go even further and aim at defining a correct standard of lawful conduct that not only excludes black sheep from the market but establishes a legal safe harbour for those who comply with the private rules. Thus, compliance with such private rules would in effect amount to compliance with the law. Such establishment of a safe harbour would take effect on third parties, namely those that are negatively affected by particular corporate conduct, such as those addressed by marketing practices, customers in a privately regulated market, or accident victims or others who face certain consequences arising from production methods. If one accepted such a safe harbour effect, third parties could not take action against certain marketing practices, or claim compensation for damage suffered where traders or producers meet the standard of their own private rules.

The vehicle for the consideration of such private regulation would be general terms and other legal expressions that refer to societal norms. Private

[20] For the difficult relationship between investment agreements and environmental standards see, eg, Madalena, 2003: 70*ff*.

actors could try to make the law more concrete by defining examples of proper corporate conduct,[21] and thereby establishing an intermediate set of rules between the general provisions set out in the law and court rulings on individual cases. This would then define the 'normal' case in a certain context. The criteria for concretising general terms may differ across the various legal systems regarding whether a more empirical or more normative approach is taken. Under an empirical approach, which emphasises normal business practice, national and international business customs, but also the guidelines, recommendations, or standards established in codes of conduct by business associations or professional bodies, could gain considerable importance. However, it is difficult to imagine that a legal system would completely refrain from exercising normative control. For example, unfair competition laws usually refer to 'good faith', 'good morals', or 'good practices', which are expressions that refer at least partly to extra-legal 'norms', not merely business customs, as demonstrated by the use of the word 'good' (see Köhler, 2005: 796; Emmerich, 2004: 65*ff*). These extra-legal norms are subject to societal consent on values (for a detailed analysis see Teubner, 1971). Similarly, the tort law due diligence standard is normative, not empirical, and therefore does not simply depend on custom or common practice, which may be unacceptably lax (Brüggemeier, 2004: 66*ff*).[22] Where no general clause exists, such as under the United Kingdom's law of unfair competition before the implementation of the Unfair Commercial Practices Directive 2005/29/EC (Bodewig, 2004), there is no vehicle available for such external effects of private regulation.

Finally, in order to create this widespread binding effect, special legitimacy requirements must be met, which differ from one field of law to another. Whether or not such private regulation is possible will be discussed in the following sections by examining the fairness standards under the law of unfair competition, and technical standards under tort law.

A. Ethical or Fairness Standards

Notions of fairness, good faith, good practice, and good morals play a role in many fields of law, including the laws on unfair contract terms and on unfair competition. For example, the Unfair Commercial Practices Directive 2005/29/EC prohibits 'unfair' commercial practices, and under

[21] See, eg, the proposal for a Directive on Unfair Commercial Practices, COM(2003) 356 final, at 18.

[22] For the position taken under German law see Mertens, 1994: §276, no 60. For US tort law see, eg, *Texas and Pacific Ry Co v Beymer*, 189 US 468, 470 (1903, per Holmes, J); *'The TJ Hooper'*, 60 F 2d 737 (2d Cir 1932, per Learned Hand, CJ). For the English law stance see, eg, *Edward Wong Finance Co Ltd v Johnson Stokes and Master* [1984] AC 296. This was different in pre-industrialisation US case-law, where the legal requirement of due care was held never to exceed social custom (Schepel, 2005: 340*ff*).

the Unfair Contract Terms Directive 93/13/EEC,[23] 'unfair' terms used in a contract concluded with a consumer by a seller or supplier shall not be binding on the consumer. The relevant issues shall be discussed with a view to the law of unfair commercial practices, as illustrated by the *Asbestos* case decided by the German Bundesgerichtshof (BGH) in 1980.[24] This case concerned the application, or abuse, of different employee-protection standards across different countries. In this case, a company marketed certain asbestos products in Germany, which had been produced in South Korea under circumstances that would have been clearly illegal under German law and also under ILO Convention No 139[25] due to the fact that employees were in no way protected against inhaling toxic asbestos fibres. In contrast, Korean law did not prohibit this method of manufacture and Korea was not a signatory to the ILO Convention. As a result of this discrepancy between legal standards, the Korean products could be marketed at a much cheaper price than competing German products. Competitors complained that the advantage gained from the abuse of low employee protection standards in foreign states was unlawful under the German law on unfair competition.

In principle, the Bundesgerichtshof envisaged a case where production methods could deviate so grossly from the basic requirements of morality and public order that trade in such products would be unlawful, and it recognised that an ILO Convention could indicate global consensus on such basic requirements. In the absence of such global consensus, the Bundesgerichtshof recognised that laws differ between countries and that, in particular, developing countries must be allowed to maintain lower employee protection standards in order to be able to compete in the global market. In this particular case the court could not identify global consensus on employee protection standards, largely because the relevant ILO Convention (No 139) had been ratified by only a small number of states. Therefore, the German Bundesgerichtshof rejected the arguments advanced by the German competitors.

In a similar scenario, a rule which stipulates that asbestos products should not be produced without employee protection could be set out in a code of conduct, signed by a number of corporations. In the following section, the requirements will be discussed for such a code of conduct to determine in fact the fairness standard that has the impact of concretising a general fairness clause, and therefore, be binding on the relevant parties.

[23] OJ 1993 L 95/29.

[24] Bundesgerichtshof, 9/5/1980, (1980) *Neue Juristische Wochenschrift* 2018 ('*Asbestos*').

[25] Convention concerning Prevention and Control of Occupational Hazards caused by Carcinogenic Substances and Agents (Occupational Cancer Convention) of 24 June 1974, available at http://www.ilo.org/ilolex/cgi-lex/convde.pl?C139.

The law of unfair competition serves three purposes: the protection of competitors, the protection of competition as a public good, and the protection of consumers.[26] These interests would have to be accounted for if the private regulation of interests is to determine the required standard of fairness.

First of all, consensus among the competing corporations is essential. As a result, fairness standards would have to be based on a collective code of conduct or an agreement.[27] The relevant group for examination would include all players competing in a particular market, for example, the European market. While it is not necessary that all the members of the relevant group agree, the agreement certainly has to include the vast majority of traders (see also Kocher, 2005: 649). In addition, the consensus position must reflect the group interest of the competitors such that it is theoretically acceptable to all members of the group. This requires that the rule be adopted by a representative variety of the group members in order not to unfairly exclude certain parties. This would prevent the situation where a number of big companies effectively create the rules for their own benefit, to the disadvantage of small and medium-sized enterprises. Furthermore, companies from industrialised countries should not be able to establish rules that are equally valid for companies from the developing world where an entirely different idea of fairness may exist.

One can justify disregarding the views of a small number of corporations on the basis that the law itself calls for some objective standard that does not take account of each individual opinion. Furthermore, the standardisation of fairness increases legal certainty and, therefore, serves both the public and the group interest.

Regarding different social and environmental standards in industrialised and developing countries, two different 'norms' might be subject to consensus, with different groups of corporations concerned. First, there may be consensus on the unfairness of deliberately taking advantage of gross imbalances in the protection of public goods, such as the environment, by moving production into low protection countries (see also Knieper and Fromm, 1980: 2020; Oppenhoff, 1980: 862). The group of corporations concerned would be composed of multinational corporations, mainly, but not necessarily only, from industrialised countries. Thus, consensus would have to be reached between these multinational corporations.

Second, and even more far-reaching, would be a consensus to the effect that trade in products which have been produced using methods that grossly deviate from the basic requirements of good morals and public

[26] See, eg, the aims of the German *Gesetz gegen den unlauteren Wettbewerb* (Act against unfair competition—UWG) as laid down in §1 UWG.

[27] International certification systems may play an important role in indicating even a 'transnational' consensus (Kocher, 2005: 651).

order is unlawful under the law of unfair commercial practices. The group concerned here would all be producers that apply such production methods and compete, for example, in the European market, including corporations that are genuinely situated in the countries where production takes place. Thus, consensus would have to include a representative number of corporations from developing countries as well.

The requirement of a broad consensus also applies on the consumer side. Consumer interests may be affected, in particular, where higher fairness standards lead to increased purchase prices, since cheap prices are a main interest of less altruistic consumers. In principle, consumer representatives could ascertain consensus. In an Icelandic case concerning the law on sureties, the Icelandic Supreme Court held that the provisions of an agreement that had been negotiated between banking associations, consumers, and the competent ministry was determinative of the meaning of 'good faith'.[28] It would be more difficult to identify the relevant consumer representatives when it comes to protecting assets in developing countries. Environmental groups and NGOs working in the area of development do not represent the whole spectrum of consumers; rather, they only speak for those who are concerned with the protection of the environment and of people in developing countries. National consumer associations might be more representative, but they rarely cover this specific field and do not necessarily have a democratic mandate. It is not required that all consumers agree to specific minimum standards but, once again, the group must be representative. As in the case of corporate competitors, the views of the most unscrupulous consumers could be neglected.

The public good of fair and undistorted competition should normally not be negatively affected by the introduction of higher fairness standards unless competition is reduced by a cartel-type exclusion of certain competitors that do not adhere to the higher standards.

In principle, there are no further requirements for the transposition of private regulation into minimum requirements of lawful conduct in unfair competition law, although there may be limitations arising in other fields of law. In particular, competition lawyers might argue that competition law does not apply to issues that emerge prior to the actual competition in the market place and, in particular, not apply to environmental aspects of the production process. Rather, they might assert that these issues are subject to public law only. German case-law on this issue is not entirely consistent.[29] In 1992, the BGH held that a trader had gained an unfair advantage over his competitors, and thus had violated competition law, by paying his

[28] Icelandic Supreme Court HR (I) 17.5.2005, case no 163/2005, *Sparekassen i Havnefjord v Guðbergsson*, quoted in Fogt (2007).

[29] See Sack, 2005: *540ff*, who analyses BGH case-law and the situation under the new Act against Unfair Competition of 2004.

employees less than the minimum wage.[30] In contrast, in 2000, the BGH took a narrow view in a case in which a German producer of lumber had violated German environmental law and was selling lumber more cheaply than his competitors.[31] However, opinions like this are generally on the decline. In fact, even competition lawyers argue in favour of introducing social and environmental standards in World Trade Organization law to level out extensive differences in these areas. Consensus on the relevance for competition of grossly unequal production methods could overcome the courts' reluctance to recognise new standards under existing competition law.

In practice, the requirement of a broad consensus among producers and consumers will relate only to grossly unacceptable practices such as production that destroys the lives of indigenous peoples (for example, Texaco's oil production in Ecuador) or the cutting down of rainforests without employing 'modern' sustainable forestry techniques. Thus, to some extent, the law of unfair competition could fill the gap arising from the lack of global harmonisation of social and environmental standards. Producers from developing countries are protected by the fact that consensus is required; private regulation will not operate to their disadvantage unless they agree.

B. Technical Standards

Although private regulation of technical standards also aims at harmonisation in order to facilitate economic transactions or at informing the profession, another key purpose is the creation of a safe harbour in tort (see, for example, Hart, 1998: 12*ff* on medical guidelines). In the context of semi-private technical standardisation, the following two legal effects are discussed in the literature: (1) the strong presumption of negligence where the conduct of the tortfeasor has breached the relevant technical norm (see IV.B above); and, vice versa, (2) a presumption of due diligence whereby a tortfeasor will not be found liable where he acted in line with the relevant technical norm, even though damage was caused.[32]

Any standard where compliance with which exempts the producer who has caused damage from liability so that that the injured parties and/or

[30] BGH, 3/12/1992, (1993) *Gewerblicher Rechtsschutz und Urheberrecht* 980. For more details on this line of cases see Kocher, 2005: 648*ff*.

[31] BGH, 11/5/2000, (2000) *Neue Juristische Wochenschrift* 3351. Lower instance courts have recently held that the intentional breach of waste law comes under the law of unfair competition if the trader aims at gaining an unjustified advantage over his competitors, see LG Berlin, 6/6/2003, 102 O 82/03, unpublished; LG Duisburg, 13/5/2004, (2004) *Abfallrecht* 182, both on the refusal to accept the return of packaging waste.

[32] In detail, it is discussed controversially whether these presumptions form part of substantive law or merely impact on the burden of proof (see, in particular, Marburger, 1979: 445*ff*; Finke, 2001: 15*ff*).

the general public have to bear the costs of the damage would have to be higher than, or at least as high as, the minimum standard, but in principle, not necessarily the highest state of the art. Obviously, the interests of third parties (that is, the victims) and also the public interest (for example, in the areas of environmental protection, public safety, or the avoidance of public costs of remedying the damage) are directly affected by any regulation with regard to a 'safe harbour'.

Here, it is important to keep in mind that the general due diligence clause in tort law does not aim at enabling private autonomy—especially that of the tortfeasors (Brüggemeier, 2004: 68). Instead, its concretisation must theoretically lead to the correct determination of the legally required conduct in a particular situation, while taking account of the two main purposes of tort law (see also Brüggemeier, 2004: 66*ff*; Falke, 2000: 452). One key purpose is the compensation of the injured party, which involves, especially in the context of fault-based tort law, the allocation of damages. The other purpose of tort law is the prevention of damage, which has increasing importance, particularly concerning issues of environmental liability (see, for example, Wurmnest, 2003: 94*ff*; Brüggemeier, 2004: 3*ff*).[33]

For the prevention of damage, it is essential that the due diligence standard is technically or substantively correct with regard to damage minimisation, a question that can be answered best by experts. In contrast, the decision on the allocation of damages, which is included in the determination of the necessary conduct for an exemption from liability, must take into account the public interest. This is a question of societal values, such as an individual's freedom to act or the public's interest in economic development, versus the protection of health and safety or the environment.[34] It is for these reasons that tort lawyers have discussed the legal effect of standardising due diligence only in connection with semi-private norms adopted by recognised standardisation organisations that follow a certain pluralistic procedure, and not those arising from purely private corporate rules or practice. The starting point for most scholars is the standardisation of public safety requirements, drawing conclusions from public safety law for tort law. In contrast, the approach taken here is specific to tort law, although some of the traditional arguments may nevertheless still apply.

In order to guarantee the *substantive correctness* of the regulation with regard to the prevention of damages, the relevant technical standard must be based on expertise the quality of which has to be ensured by the selection of experts who are qualified, independent, and reliable. The technical and

[33] On the increasing purpose of prevention in environmental law see, in particular, Marburger, 1992: 28*ff*.

[34] For an overview of the societal changes which impacted upon tort law from the pre-industrialisation period to industrialisation see, eg, Brüggemeier, 2004: 3*ff*. For the position taken under German law see, eg, Deutsch and Ahrens, 2001: 2*ff*; Larenz and Canaris, 1994: 350*ff*.

scientific expertise must include and balance different opinions and perspectives from different scientific areas concerned. In addition, the decision procedure must be transparent, and the developed norms must be published and explained (and ideally, externally evaluated) and their application monitored (Hoffmann-Riem, 1996: 320*ff*; Hart, 1998, 12*ff*). Norms may also be regarded as reliable if there is empirical evidence indicating that adherence to them has effectively prevented damage (Marburger, 1983: 602), for example, in other countries.

For the *allocation of damages*, a representative variety of the interests concerned (including, for example, social and environmental interests) must be taken into account. As a result, the requirements of a fair procedure must be met: for example, interests have to be balanced to make sure that the less powerful (social and environmental) interests have an equal opportunity to have an input as the traditionally powerful economic interests or well-informed circles. This may include the guarantee that those representing these less powerful interests are actually able to participate in the decision-making procedure, that they obtain all relevant information in due time, and that certain key interests are not overridden. One possibility here would be a consensus requirement, which is already vaguely included in the DIN procedure (Falke, 2000: 146). It may even be necessary to provide special protection for certain interests such as life and health in order to reflect their human rights value (Hoffmann-Riem, 1996: 319*ff*).[35]

As an immediate consequence, norms adopted *unilaterally* by corporations or through corporate common practice (although they may be relevant for defining a minimum standard, see IV.B above) certainly lack the necessary legitimacy to define a 'safe harbour' in favour of producers but to the disadvantage of third persons or the general public, as there are no safeguards in place for their substantial correctness (although they may in fact reflect the state of the art) or for the reflection of the public interest.

However, a number of objections specific to tort law must be raised against *multilateral* private regulation as well. To start with, the existence of an 'ideal' committee that truly reflects the 'ideal expertise' and the public interest is not very likely. This is especially true in light of the oft-mentioned shortcomings of the ISO, CEN, and DIN, where, despite all precautions, the producers and users of technology dominate the standardisation process due to their superior knowledge and their resources (Krut and Gleckmann, 1998; Falke, 2000: 452).

More fundamentally, the requirements for substantially correct and representative private rule-making, which may be adequate for public law, do not really suit the purposes of tort law, as they guarantee neither the substantial adequacy nor the legitimacy of the results.

[35] See generally Denninger, 1990: 170*ff*, concerning standardisation of public law requirements.

Academic literature on semi-private technical norms already provides some arguments on why public, semi-public, or private standardisation is inadequate for defining a 'safe harbour' in tort law. First, standardisation aims at regulating the typical case, whereas additional or more specific safety measures may be necessary in the individual case, which is relevant in tort law (Falke, 2000: 452; Hoffmann-Riem, 1996: 286). Second, the regulatory procedure in such a committee is time-consuming and may lag behind more advanced knowledge or practice. Corporations should remain responsible for critically evaluating their own production patterns and improving them accordingly on the basis of newly discovered risks, instead of simply relying on established standards (Sach, 1994: 239; Falke, 2000: 451).[36]

These considerations can also be traced in case-law on the relevance under tort law of technical standards adopted by standardisation organisations and of public safety law. German courts have required the observance of higher standards of diligence than are set out in technical standards, where they regarded the technical standards as outdated, incomplete (that is, they did not address the relevant problem), or not applicable to the particular circumstances of the case.[37] Furthermore, the BGH held in 1952 that, although certain conduct complied with the standard set out under public safety law, it might not necessarily meet the tort law diligence standard even under normal circumstances and, furthermore, that the circumstances of the individual case were always decisive.[38] In the 'ice hockey' case of 1983, the BGH even regarded an institutionalised technical norm as being *generally* too low for the typical and normal case. The court held that

> to concretise the duty of care, one can indeed draw from the rules of technology as they are laid down in the relevant standards, and, as they are drafted by committees of experts, they often offer a useful measure of the care that may be required in a given case. However, they do not always determine the ultimate care that can be expected in a particular case and do not discharge the judge from his duty to take account of the safety interests of potential victims.[39]

[36] For further arguments against the general identity of public safety and tort law standards see Falke, 2000: 451*ff*, with further references.

[37] See, eg, BGH, 27/9/1994, (1994) *Neue Juristische Wochenschrift* 3349 (outdated standard); BGH, 13/3/2001, (2001) *Neue Juristische Wochenschrift* 2019 (incomplete standard); OLG Zweibrücken, 20/9/1976, (1977) *Neue Juristische Wochenschrift* 111 (unusual circumstances).

[38] BGH, 3/12/1952 (1953) *Versicherungsrecht* 82: A farmer made a fire on his land, which was located 120 m from a forest and which ultimately caused a forest fire. German public law prohibited the making of a fire within a distance of 100 m from a forest. The BGH denied any presumption of due diligence stemming from the mere fact that the farmer kept this distance of 100 m.

[39] BGH, 29/11/1983, (1984) *Neue Juristische Wochenschrift* 801; translation by Schepel, 2005: 346.

Finally, those civil courts that have in fact applied institutionalised technical norms on the basis that they constituted the correct diligence standard have always explicitly reserved their independence from any technical norm but stated that they had no reason to deviate from that standard in the individual case.[40]

The same result can be found in literature and case-law from other Member States of the EC. Falke and Schepel have observed that in judgments on cases of tort liability, 'non-compliance is of greater legal significance than compliance with standards' (Falke and Schepel, 2000: 235), and that compliance 'leads to scarcely more than a mere indication of fulfilling duties of care (at all)' (Falke and Schepel, 2000: 233, with further references).

There are other important reasons why a 'safe harbour' cannot be legitimately established by private regulation stemming from the particularities of environmental liability and from legitimacy considerations. First, in environmental liability law (that is, liability for damages caused by industrial installations), there is a worldwide trend towards strict liability. Therefore, fault-based liability in these circumstances is a relict anyway. In order to be in line with this tendency towards strict liability, the standard of due diligence required under fault-based tort law should reasonably reflect the highest state of the art that can be determined by the 'ideal expert'. Any 'safe harbour' below this standard appears inadequate.

Second, legitimacy considerations also prevent private regulation from establishing a 'safe harbour' in tort law; if a private committee, no matter how pluralistic, could determine a standard of due diligence below the highest state of the art, it would decide that, in a case of compliance with this lower standard, the victims had to bear their damage without any compensation. Thus, a private committee would be allowed to place a special burden on a group of persons (that is, the future injured parties) who cannot be identified in advance, and therefore, cannot be included in the decision-making process in proportion to their potential suffering. For tort law, this is a problem that cannot be resolved through fair procedural requirements.[41] It is important to note that future victims of industrial accidents usually have no control over their exposure to the risk of uncompensated damage.[42] Moreover, a private committee has no alternative compensatory mechanisms available.

As a result, the general exclusion of liability for certain conduct below the highest state of the art can only be decided by a democratically

[40] A leading case is BGH, 1/3/1988, (1989) *Neue Juristische Wochenschrift* 2667.

[41] In contrast, the contractual limitation of liability between a producer and members of a local community would seem possible but this is not a matter of standardisation of due diligence.

[42] This may be different in product liability cases.

legitimated legislator, for example, through specific tort law legislation (see also Sach, 1994: 236). Such legislation should then by accompanied by a compensatory scheme, such as insurance for victims who would otherwise remain uncompensated.[43] Political reasons for such a decision may be the desire to attract (risk) technology, or to offer an incentive to establish some reasonable standard in the first place, in particular, in instances where there is no adequate public law regulation of the subject matter, as it occurs in developing countries.

In this context, there is an important distinction to be made between tort law and public law. In public law, the risk of placing a special burden on potential victims through a general decision favouring high-risk technology may be acceptable just because it can be balanced by tort law compensation in the individual case. This compensatory function vis-à-vis public law is indeed one of the important functions of tort law (see also Gerlach, 1988: 164*ff*; Sach, 1994: 242*ff*). As an illustration, one may point to high-risk technologies permissible under public law (such as nuclear power or genetically modified organisms) that are accompanied by (strict) liability regimes so that potential victims may be compensated in cases where damage occurs. This compensatory function of tort law could not be met if (private) standardisation in tort law and in public law followed the same criteria.[44] A further important argument in this context is that, despite the many precautions taken, the domination by producers and users of the technology of the (semi-)private regulative process, which might lead to an insufficient level of safety in public law, should not impact on tort law as well. Rather, tort law should be able to compensate for such potential shortcomings (Falke, 2000: 452).

It can thus be concluded that tort law does not really allow for the determination of a 'safe harbour', whether by a corporate code of conduct, an 'ideal' pluralistic committee, or through the establishment of semi-private institutionalised norms. In principle, due diligence in environmental liability requires diligence at the highest state of the art. A general decision favouring the exclusion of liability for conduct below the highest state of the art may be made only by a democratically legitimated legislator. Apart

[43] See Brüggemeier, 2004: 3*ff*, on the introduction of insurance to balance shortcomings in protection by tort law during industrial development in Germany and in the United States.

[44] The 'unity of the legal order', also with a view to standards of lawful conduct under public safety law and under tort law, has occasionally been claimed (see in particular Engisch, 1987: 58) but was rejected by the majority of academic writers for the above-mentioned reasons. For the relationship between public law and private law see generally Hoffmann-Riem, 1996. See in contrast Marburger, 1983: 602, who sees the tort law relevance of technical norms in parallel to their relevance under public law, arguing that both serve the purpose of protecting individual rights. In this context, Marburger distinguishes strict liability regimes from fault-based tort law and only accepts the compensatory function of the first. Thus, technical norms should also contribute to the establishment of a 'safe harbour' in tort law as well as in public law provided that the respective norm is not outdated, actually considers the problem at hand, and that the individual case is not untypical.

from this, the justification for not meeting the highest state of the art in the individual case can only be decided by the civil courts. In exceptional cases, it may, for example, be acceptable not to apply the highest safety standard where the costs incurred are grossly disproportionate to the preventive effect of the measure or the severity of the damage. This task necessitates the weighing of the respective interests of the producer and the victim so that a just result will be achieved in each individual case, although the decision may be influenced by societal values that impact upon allocation of damages.

VI. CONCLUSION

There is no doubt that private regulation relating to public interest issues such as the protection of the environment, of health and safety, and of labour standards has legal effects in private law, even though these effects may rarely be intended. Legal effects of private regulation and common conduct are, however, limited to the establishment and furtherance of legal obligations on their authors or signatories, and on outsiders. First, private regulation establishes immediate obligations for those who adopt such rules. This is true for sales law and for advertising law, and also for tort law. Second, private regulatory instruments may have a generalising effect on a whole group of corporations, including outsiders, by determining what constitutes fair business conduct as well as due diligence in tort law, provided that the authors of the rules are sufficiently representative of the group in question. Thus, a truly transnational regulative effect may ensue from private regulation, which goes beyond the creation of individual obligations, but results in the setting of standards for all producers in the same category, thereby bridging the gap with private law mechanisms in instances where public law mechanisms are unavailable. Finally, standardising fairness requirements through private regulation appears possible if all groups concerned, including, for example, producers and consumers, have reached consensus. In contrast, private regulation cannot create a 'safe harbour' in tort law by limiting the legal obligations of those who adhere to the relevant rules, to the disadvantage of, for example, the victims of environmental degradation, because consensus on special burdens resting on individual victims is impossible to reach in a correct manner before the damage is done.

REFERENCES

Bachmann, G (2002) 'Privatrecht als Organisationsrecht', *Jahrbuch junger Zivilrechtswissenschaftler* 9.

Barron, A (2007) 'Reasonable Expectations, Good Faith and Self-Regulatory Codes' in G Howells *et al* (eds), *The Yearbook of Consumer Law 2007* (Aldershot, Ashgate).

Bodewig, T (2004) 'Das Recht des unlauteren Wettbewerbs in Großbritannien: Ein Dreiklang von Fallrecht, Gesetzesrecht und Selbstkontrolle' *Gewerblicher Rechtsschutz und Urheberrecht—Internationaler Teil* 543.

Böttger, K (2002) *Die Umweltpflichtigkeit von Auslandsdirektinvestitionen im Völkerrecht* (Baden-Baden, Nomos).

Brüggemeier, G (2004) *Common Principles of Tort Law* (London, British Institute of International and Comparative Law).

Denninger, E (1990) *Verfassungsrechtliche Anforderungen an die Normsetzung im Umwelt- und Technikrecht* (Baden-Baden, Nomos).

Deutsch, E and Ahrens, H-J (2001) *Deliktsrecht*, 4th edn (Cologne, Berlin, Bonn and Munich, Heymanns).

di Fabio, U (1997) 'Verwaltung und Verwaltungsrecht zwischen gesellschaftlicher Selbstregulierung und staatlicher Steuerung' 56 *Veröffentlichungen der Vereinigung der Deutschen Staatsrechtslehrer* 235.

Emmerich, V (2004) *Unlauterer Wettbewerb*, 7th edn (Munich, CH Beck).

Engisch, K (1987) *Einheit der Rechtsordnung* (reprint: Darmstadt, Wissenschaftliche Buchgesellschaft).

Falke, J (2000) *Rechtliche Aspekte der Normung in den EG-Mitgliedstaaten und der EFTA, vol 3, Deutschland* (Brussels, European Communities).

Falke, J and Schepel, H (2000) *Legal aspects of standardisation in the Member States of the EC and EFTA, vol 1, Comparative Report* (Brussels, European Communities).

Finke, K (2001) *Die Auswirkungen der europäischen technischen Normen und des Sicherheitsrechts auf das nationale Haftungsrecht* (Munich, CH Beck).

Fogt, M (2007) 'The protection of non-professional (private) sureties in Nordic law' in A Colombi Ciacchi (ed), *Protection of Non-professional Sureties in Europe: Formal and Substantive Disparity* (Baden-Baden, Nomos).

Gerlach, JW (1988) 'Grundstrukturen des privaten Umweltrechts' *Juristenzeitung* 161.

Glinski, C (2004) 'Haftung multinationaler Unternehmen beim Transfer von Produktionsrisiken in Entwicklungsländer', TranState Working Papers, No 4, available at http://www.sfb597.uni-bremen.de.

—— (2005a) 'Produktionsaussagen im Kauf- und Werberecht' in G Winter (ed), *Die Umweltverantwortung multinationaler Unternehmen* (Baden-Baden, Nomos).

—— (2005b) 'Haftung multinationaler Unternehmen für Umweltschäden bei Auslandsdirektinvestitionen' in G Winter (ed), *Die Umweltverantwortung multinationaler Unternehmen* (Baden-Baden, Nomos).

—— (2006) 'Self-regulation of Transnational Corporations: Neither Meaningless in Law Nor Voluntary' in S MacLeod (ed), *Global Governance and the Quest for Justice* (Oxford, Hart Publishing).

—— (2007) 'Corporate Self-Regulation: Moral or Legal Obligation?' in D McBarnet, A Voiculescu and T Campbell (eds), *The New Corporate Accountability: Corporate Social Responsibility and the Law* (Cambridge, Cambridge University Press).

Glinski, C and Rott, P (2003) 'Umweltfreundliches und ethisches Konsumverhalten im harmonisierten Kaufrecht' *Europäische Zeitschrift für Wirtschaftsrecht* 649.

Hart, D (1998) 'Ärztliche Leitlinien—Definitionen, Funktionen, rechtliche Bewertungen' *Medizinrecht* 8.

Henning-Bodewig, F (2005) 'Die Richtlinie 2005/29/EG über unlautere Geschäftspraktiken' *Gewerblicher Rechtsschutz und Urheberrecht—Internationaler Teil* 629.
Herberg, M (2001) 'Codes of Conduct und kommunikative Vernunft' 22 *Zeitschrift für Rechtssoziologie* 25.
—— (2005) 'Erzeugen multinationale Unternehmen ihr eigenes Umweltrecht?' in G Winter (ed), *Die Umweltverantwortung multinationaler Unternehmen* (Baden-Baden, Nomos).
—— (2007) *Globalisierung und private Selbstregulierung* (Frankfurt am Main, Campus)
Hoffmann-Riem, W (1996) 'Öffentliches Recht und Privatrecht als wechselseitige Auffangordnungen—Systematisierung und Entwicklungsperspektiven' in W Hoffmann-Riem and E Schmidt-Aßmann (eds), *Öffentliches Recht und Privatrecht als wechelseitige Auffangordnungen* (Baden-Baden, Nomos).
Howells, G and Weatherill, S (2005) *Consumer Protection Law* (Aldershot, Ashgate).
Howells, G, Micklitz, H-W, and Wilhelmsson, T (2006) *European Fair Trading Law* (Aldershot, Ashgate).
Huth, R (1992) *Die Bedeutung technischer Normen für die Haftung des Warenherstellers nach §823 BGB und dem Produkthaftungsgesetz* (Frankfurt, Lang).
Knieper, R and Fromm, H (1980) 'Anmerkung' *Neue Juristische Wochenschrift* 2020.
Kocher, E (2004) 'Unternehmerische Selbstverpflichtungen zur sozialen Verantwortung—Erfahrungen mit sozialen Verhaltenskodizes in der transnationalen Produktion' *Recht der Arbeit* 27.
—— (2005) 'Unternehmerische Selbstverpflichtungen im Wettbewerb—Die Transformation von "soft law" in "hard law" durch das Wettbewerbsrecht' *Gewerblicher Rechtsschutz und Urheberrecht* 647.
Köhler, H (2005) 'Zur Umsetzung der Richtlinie über unlautere Geschäftspraktiken' *Gewerblicher Rechtsschutz und Urheberrecht* 793.
Krut, R and Gleckman, H (1998) *ISO 14001—A Missed Opportunity for Sustainable Global Industrial Development* (London, Earthscan).
Ladeur, K-H (2000) 'Die rechtswissenschaftliche Methodendiskussion und die Bewältigung des gesellschaftlichen Wandels' 64 *Rabels Zeitschrift für ausländisches und internationales Privatrecht* 60.
Larenz, K and Canaris, C-W (1994) *Lehrbuch des Schuldrechts, II. Band, 2. Halbband*, 13th edn (Munich, CH Beck).
Lübbe-Wolf, G (2001) 'Europäisches und nationales Verfassungsrecht' 60 *Veröffentlichungen der Vereinigung der Deutschen Staatsrechtslehrer* 246.
Madalena, I (2003) 'Foreign direct investment and the protection of the environment: the border between national environmental regulation and expropriation' *European Environmental Law Review* 70.
Marburger, P (1979) *Die Regeln der Technk im Recht* (Cologne, Berlin, Bonn and Munich, Heymanns).
—— (1983) 'Die haftungs- und versicherungsrechtliche Bedeutung technischer Regeln' *Versicherungsrecht* 597.
—— (1992) 'Grundsatzfragen des Haftungsrechts unter dem Einfluß der gesetzlichen Regelungen zur Produzenten- und Umwelthaftung' 192 *Archiv für civilistische Praxis* 2.
Mavroidis, PC (2000) 'Trade and Environment after the *Shrimps-Turtles* Litigation' 34 *Journal of World Trade* 73.

Mertens, H-P (1994) Comment on §276 BGB in K Rebmann and FJ Säcker (eds) *Münchener Kommentar zum Bürgerlichen Recht*, vol 2, 3rd edn (Munich, CH Beck).
Micklitz, H-W and Keßler, J (2002) 'Europäisches Lauterkeitsrecht' *Gewerblicher Rechtsschutz und Urheberrecht—Internationaler Teil* 885.
Oppenhoff, W (1980) 'Anmerkung' *Gewerblicher Rechtsschutz und Urheberrecht* 861.
Parkinson, J (2006) 'Corporate Governance and the Regulation of Business Behaviour' in S MacLeod (ed), *Global Governance and the Quest for Justice* (Oxford, Hart Publishing).
Peifer, K-N (2001) 'Die Haftung des Verkäufers für Werbeangaben' *Juristische Rundschau* 265.
Sach, K (1994) *Genehmigung als Schutzschild?* (Berlin, Duncker and Humblot).
Sack, R (2005) 'Die lückenfüllende Funktion der Generalklausel des §3 UWG' *Wettbewerb in Recht und Praxis* 531.
Schepel, H (2005) *The Constitution of Private Governance* (Oxford and Portland, Hart Publishing).
Staudenmayer, D (2000) 'The Directive on the Sale of Consumer Goods and Associated Guarantees—a Milestone in the European Consumer and Private Law' *European Review of Private Law* 547.
Teubner, G (1971) *Standards und Direktiven in Generalklauseln* (Frankfurt, Athenäum).
—— (ed) (1997) *Global Law without a State* (Aldershot, Dartmouth).
—— (2004a) 'Global Private Regimes: Neo-spontaneous Law and Dual Constitution of Autonomous Sectors?' in K-H Ladeur (ed), *Public Governance in the Age of Globalization* (Aldershot, Ashgate).
—— (2004b) 'Societal Constitutionalism: Alternatives to State-centred Constitutional Theory?' in C Joerges, I-J Sand, and G Teubner (eds), *Constitutionalism and Transnational Governance* (Oxford, Hart Publishing).
von Bar, C (1999) *Gemeineuropäisches Deliktsrecht*, vol II (Munich, CH Beck).
Wilhelmsson, T (2002–2003) 'A Green Sales Law?' *Yearbook of New Zealand Jurisprudence* (Waikato, University of Waikato) 83.
Wurmnest, W (2003) *Grundzüge eines europäischen Haftungsrechts* (Tübingen, Mohr Siebeck).

3

Codes of Conduct and Framework Agreements on Social Minimum Standards—Private Regulation?

EVA KOCHER

I. INTRODUCTION

CORPORATE SOCIAL RESPONSIBILITY (CSR) is currently a widely discussed topic (Sheikh, 2002: 143–50; Riedel *et al*, 2003; Hauser-Ditz and Wilke, 2005; KPMG, 2005; Riess and Peters, 2005).[1] Many corporations and employer associations have tackled the subject and committed themselves to CSR policies. In addition, since the creation of the 'Global Compact' (Körting, 2006) there has been increased knowledge of what CSR comprises.

Many German companies (that is, those with German headquarters) claim to have always practised corporate social responsibility. However, doubts remain as to how CSR can be used in the specific context of German industrial relations that rely on collective bargaining between employee representation at the shop-floor level (Works Councils) as well as at the branch level (trade unions).

The European research project ESTER is an empirical study undertaken to determine whether the concepts included in CSR will serve to strengthen and export the 'European social model' or instead threaten it[2] (for the European social model see: Kaelble, 2000; Lavranu, 2000; Blanke and Hoffmann, 2006). In the summer of 2005, research teams in seven European countries each conducted about 40 interviews with representatives from different corporations, trade unions, employee representatives at the shop-floor level, advocatory NGOs, consumer organisations, business associations, etc. The study by no means intends to be representative, but rather hopes to glean deeper insights into the

[1] COM (2001: 366) Commission of the European Communities, Green Paper 'Promoting a European framework for Corporate Social Responsibility'.

[2] ESTER, Régulation Sociale des Entreprises Transnationales Européennes.

possible motives of and approaches taken by different actors from these anonymous interviews.

First results point towards possible conflicts between CSR concepts and traditional German labour relations (Hoffmann, 2004). Corporations are reluctant to use CSR concepts. On the one hand, there is a feeling that they have always practised corporate social responsibility by simply adhering to German labour laws or by complying with the ethics of their specific corporate identities or business (for example, family business or cooperative culture). On the other hand, there is the feeling among various actors that CSR may in fact mean something different from conventional German industrial practices. This is a main reason why many German trade union representatives are wary of CSR. As one interviewee puts it: 'So what made us a bit suspicious was that the employer associations demand the dismantling of codetermination, on the one hand; not complete dismantling, that is, but a reduction in the level of codetermination. And, on the other hand, they are promoting CSR at the same time.'[3]

In the cases studied, CSR policies have not been limited to internal organisational projects, sponsorship, or 'corporate citizenship' projects, but also relate to core business activities, by regulating the repercussions arising from production and distribution, such as employment conditions (cp Bassen *et al*, 2005; KPMG, 2005: 6). The voluntary and non-binding character of those CSR policies will be examined in this chapter, first by analysing the regulatory intentions and legal nature exhibited by corporate codes of conduct (section II). Section III explores hard law rules able to bind enterprises to their own rules once these have been adopted. Lastly, section IV asks whether corporate codes of conduct do not just affirm rules that enterprises would have to abide by in any event.

II. THE LEGAL NATURE OF CODES OF CONDUCTS: VOLUNTARY AND NON-BINDING?

A. Social Standards in Instruments of Self-Regulation

Unilateral corporate declarations of commitment are used as instruments of CSR policies. In 'codes of conduct', 'standards of engagement', and 'social charters', transnational enterprises publicly declare that they will adhere to certain minimum social standards in transnational production (that is, production in establishments operating outside Europe or in a transnational supply chain). In addition, and especially in Europe, there have been more and more contracts between transnational enterprises and social actors (namely international trade unions, but also sometimes European Works

[3] All quotes translated from the original German interviews.

Councils or World Works Councils)—so-called International Framework Agreements (IFAs). For example, Volkswagen's 'Declaration on social rights and industrial relations' was signed by the board of management, the World Works Council, and the International Metalworkers' Federation (Hammer, 2005; Hepple, 2005: 69–80; Greven, 2006: 10–15; Weinz, 2006).[4] The term 'code of conduct' will be used here as a general term, and will include within it International Framework Agreements.

In most of these instruments, companies commit themselves to apply the standards not only within the respective company, plants, and establishments inside and outside Europe, but also in the group of companies (that is, in dependent companies). Often, but not always, companies pledge to make sure that their business partners (contractors, subcontractors, suppliers) also meet certain standards (Wilhelm and Mauritz, 2005: 20–21). Sometimes, social standards are included as a supplier's obligation in corresponding commercial contracts with supplier companies in developing countries. In fact, many companies with complex supply chains, particularly in the textile and retail sectors, use this approach as a means to gain control over the supply chain and legally enhance supply chain management. Incorporating codes of conduct into these contracts is usually achieved by buyers imposing certain standard contract terms (van Liemt, 2000: 177; Fichter and Sydow, 2002: 357–80; Kocher, 2002: 265–80; Kocher, 2004a: 27–31). Furthermore, nowadays many European companies themselves must promise to observe certain social standards throughout the transnational supply chain in their contracts with commercial and other partners. This is true, for example, of suppliers in the automotive industry. In the retail and textile industries, certain actors such as political sports associations, in their capacity as sponsors and licensees, tend to demand that producers comply with social standards in the production of sportswear.[5]

B. Contents of Corporate Codes of Conduct and Framework Agreements

What is the common understanding of 'social standards' found in these codes? While transnational US or Dutch companies have been using codes of conduct since the beginning of the 1990s to institute transnational social standards, the current German understanding of CSR developed only in the late 1990s or early 2000 (KPMG, 2005: 4–6). The main reasons for this new

[4] Declaration of 6 June 2002, in *Arbeit und Recht* 2002 at 343; in addition, an 'Agreement on industrial health and safety policy' was signed by the same parties on 29 September 2004.

[5] See, eg Agreement of FIFA with the international trade union IC-FTU, September 1996.

corporate approach seem to be globalisation and the assumption of a global player's corporate identity. The revision of the OECD guidelines in 2000 may have also contributed to this development, but the ILO Declaration on core labour rights of 1998[6] (Alston, 2004; Langille, 2005: 409–37), and the establishment of the Global Compact in 1999/2000 seem to have been the decisive external turning points leading to these new approaches. This is due to the fact that normative orientations in Germany seem to have focused on the ILO core labour standards (to which the Global Compact and the new OECD guidelines also refer) (Tapiola, 2000: 9–16; Ölz, 2002: 330; Kocher, 2004a: 27–31).

As a consequence, German codes of conduct or social charters usually cover the abolition of child and forced labour,[7] non-discrimination,[8] and a guarantee of freedom of association and collective bargaining[9] (Dubin, 1999: 47–9; Engels, 2000: 219–31). Minimum standards on working time, wages, and other working conditions are also often included, although such guarantees are not always very specific. Framework agreements and some unilateral codes also mention standards on qualification of the workforce. Furthermore, there is always an assurance that standards set out under national law will be met (Herberg, 2002: 45).

Overall, the ILO core labour standards nowadays seem to constitute the lowest common denominator for German corporations when it comes to regulating social standards in private instruments (Kocher, 2004a: 27).[10] When asked about normative approaches, however, corporate representatives mention various sources for guidance. Most actors refer to the ILO core labour standards, the OECD guidelines, and the Global Compact. One actor mentioned 'the global eight', namely, the Global Compact, the ILO core labour standards, the OECD guidelines for multinational enterprises, ISO 14001, Accountability 1000, the Global Reporting Initiative (GRI), the Global Sullivan Principles, and Social Accountability 8000 (SA 8000). Other actors make reference to the Global Compact (which itself refers to the ILO core labour standards), the Charter for sustainable development of the International Chamber of Commerce, the OECD guidelines (revised, in 2000, in accordance with the ILO core labour standards), certification of production locations in accordance with the standards EMAS and ISO 14001, as well as the GRI guidelines.

[6] For the 1998 ILO Declaration on core labour standards, see also IV.B below.

[7] ILO Convention No 29 (on forced labour, 1930), No 105 (on the abolition of forced labour, 1957), No 138 (on minimum age, 1973), and No 182 (on the prohibition of the worst forms of child labour, 1999).

[8] ILO Convention No 100 (on equal pay, 1951), and No 111 (on non-discrimination at work, 1958).

[9] ILO Convention No 87 (on freedom of association, 1948) and No 98 (on collective bargaining, 1949).

[10] However, the ILO core labour standards are not always explicitly referred to.

C. Regulatory Character of Codes of Conduct and International Framework Agreements

1. *General Ideas*

Since codes of conduct are embedded in norms of both hard law (ILO Conventions, national law) and soft law (OECD Guidelines, ILO Declaration on core labour standards), one should be sceptical of the regulatory character attributed to them. Are these undertakings really meant to establish original 'regulation' of working conditions in subsidiaries or in the supply chain in Third World countries? Can they be considered as 'soft law'?

The term 'soft law' in its widest sense (Hailbronner, 1982: 113; Ballreich, 1989: 383; Ehricke, 1989: 1907) captures all kinds of standards, social rules, and business practices that create trust and, thus, give rise to the emergence of legitimate expectations, have relevance in formal/hard law, and can serve as catalysts in a process which may (in the future and via hard law bridges) lead to a binding legal norm (Teubner, 1971: 45; Scherrer *et al*, 1998: 12; Winter, 2005: 24–30).

'Private regulation' could be categorised as 'paralegal' or 'soft law', on the basis that corporate actors themselves seem to deliberately create legitimate expectations by referring to codes of conduct as setting out normative and regulative standards (Herberg, 2005: 110). However, on closer look at the undertakings we studied, we find, in fact, that they leave room for doubt as to their 'legal' or 'para-legal' character; it is not always clear if the corporate actors actually intend to create legitimate expectation through these specific instruments (see Simma and Zöckler, 1996: 80 whose work provides the basis for the approach taken in this section). First, it is doubtful that the adoption of codes of conduct results in the creation of new standards per se. This is because, as previously noted, corporate standards draw heavily on international regulation at ILO level or standards defined elsewhere. Second, it is clear that corporations mostly do not intend to create rights for their employees or those of their suppliers. As explicitly stated in the VW-Social Charter,[11] which is consistent with every other framework agreement signed by a trade union: 'No claims whatsoever by third parties may be asserted under this declaration.' Furthermore, corporations often imply, or sometimes even explicitly declare that the code of conduct is merely a restatement of what has always been corporate practice and policy, and that it only serves to 'document' the promotion of social rights and fundamental principles: this casts further doubt on the regulatory nature of such codes. Third, the lack of specifics in many unilateral declarations (Herberg, 2005: 83) and framework agreements points to an insufficiency of proper

[11] See n 3 above.

constitutive regulatory intent. For example, in the case of child labour, only a few of these codes set clear limits on the age of employees or their working hours. In fact, most codes provide only a general outline regarding the applicable labour standards, and ultimately refer to national law (for example, 'abolition of exploitative child labour ... and ... observance of the minimum age to be attained for the authorisation to take up employment in accordance with the respective national regulations'[12]). On the other hand, in three out of our four case studies, the wording of such codes usually goes beyond simply describing policy objectives. These private standards seem to constitute more than mere policy objectives which would have no legal or para-legal value and would not have the capacity to create legitimate expectations. Overall, it seems that corporate standards can most adequately be described as 'declaratory' and 'promotional', by setting out a normative framework or key corporate practices together with relevant implementation mechanisms.

2. *Relationship to Other Hard Law and Soft Law Standards*

It could be argued that there is no need for the codes to establish specific standards, since they implicitly refer to norms laid out in other instruments (especially in the ILO Conventions). However, although the codes often refer to various normative standards, these standards are by no means congruent with each other. For example, SA 8000 lays out a standard regarding workers' wages based on ensuring a livelihood ('living wage'); this differs from the Fair Labour Association's (FLA) code of conduct, which requires only that 'national minimum wages' be paid. All the companies studied used the standard requiring a 'legally prescribed minimum wage, or a wage customary in the trade if this exceeds the minimum wage' or some other formula. Moreover, none of the companies examined included the 'living wage' standard in their corporate codes, although two corporate representatives did mention that the SA 8000 approach was taken as a starting point: 'We have the SA 8000, of course, which we also took as a basis. But we found that it's too divorced from reality. It's very demanding, and that's a target to aim for, that you don't pay according to minimum wages.' A statement by a representative of a European Works Council (EWC) sheds further light on this issue:

> In the way we actually understand CSR, we ... always oriented ourselves, but never absolutely referred to, let's say, 100 per cent or 105 per cent RAI or SA 8000 or whatever, but actually always said, okay, we have to see for ourselves what our resources, what our requirements are, that are hardly comparable in South Africa or China or places like that ...—develop a lot in Germany, okay,

[12] Deutsche Telekom AG, Social Charter of 2003.

> but then, so to speak, implement it differently, according to the cultural situation as it is and the level of development, absolutely according to legal requirements in the respective countries.

Two corporate representatives explicitly stated that their codes of conduct were developed at their head office, and then adapted to meet local requirements placed on their regional offices. One of them said:

> Otherwise we're also very keen to apply aspects of our standards that are as specific as possible locally, and that's why we always resisted accepting standard clauses that, in our view, are totally unrealistic; we can put together any number of standards and codes, but what matters at the end of the day is how we can set up a process to work towards these standards and also gradually achieve comprehensive improvements. And a 110% standard is no help to us there; it's a question of reaching a standard in which the management of a supplying firm can find its views reflected.

3. *Relationship to National Law and Local Practice*

These citations confirm the suspicion that if one wishes to examine the regulatory character of these codes, the common references to 'national regulation', 'national law', or 'local practice' could give us more information on the regulatory intent and concept. The wording of the codes does not always give clear answers to the question whether the company standard will take precedence over local law or practice at the place of production, or if the interpretation of national law will rather determine the interpretation of the standards. The difficulty of reconciling possible contradictions between self-imposed obligations and national laws was mentioned in several interviews. One company representative cited Thailand as an example: here, the code of conduct called for a maximum 48-hour working week; where overtime was worked, the maximum increased to 60 hours. According to one interviewee, since the law in Thailand allowed for far more than 48 hours a week to be worked, suppliers there said 'quite rightly, of course' that employees could be found working more than 60 hours a week. Thus, the corporate representative in the German office was of the view that one could only gradually move towards the 60-hour limit. This decision seems to reflect an approach that favours applying the lowest standard required under national law.

Another problem regarding the application of social norms in transnational production might be termed the 'cultural objection'. As stated by one corporate representative on the question of the transfer of social standards: 'first, we don't want it, and, second, we can't do it anyway: to take abroad or transfer as an export hit, just like that, certain cultural things that have developed naturally in Germany.' It should be noted that this objection to a transfer of social standards arises in regard to standards that have been established in the company's 'voluntary' code of conduct and that are more or less congruent with standards set out by the ILO, that is global standards created for universal application. Another representative of a company that also publicly declared its adherence to universal ILO standards, including non-discrimination, stated:

> [O]n culture—we always go at it with our German way of thinking... . A Pakistani will either hire only men or only women. He'll never mix them because he's a Muslim. Like hell he will. So either he employs only men or only women ... and there we have classic discrimination. How are we going to deal with it? If he employs men and women together, he has a much bigger problem.

It is clear from this statement that the corporate representative does not intend to enforce or at least affirm the standard of non-discrimination against a cultural objection. Cultural relativism constitutes a fundamental problem for the implementation and enforcement of universal standards. However, none of the enterprises that uses a cultural excuse thinks of abandoning or adapting the standard of non-discrimination or some other standard.

It is also possible that the opposite situations can occur, such that a standard set out in national law is more protective than that set out in the code of conduct. In at least one of the cases we studied, the position taken on child labour in the corporate code of conduct was changed to reflect amendments to the national laws of the 'principal countries' of production, and the working age was raised from 14 to 15 years. As observed by one NGO representative:

> The NGOs in Central America, for example, say that the labour law that exists is much more important for them; that's national legislation, and a company is required to stick to it here. That means they actually have very little use for the code of conduct tool. And why should they? The labour law is good. They should simply stick to it.

In such cases, when NGOs campaign for the observance of national labour law, companies accordingly tend to concern themselves with national rules and thus seem to accept the prevalence of national law as a normative orientation to be respected. Issues of national law thus enter corporate CSR policies by way of 'agenda setting' by NGO campaigning; we were told, for example, of one case where the day of menstruation leave to be granted under Indonesian law was enforced this way.

Interesting in this respect is the handling of China, a country where implementation of social standards in production is generally viewed as problematic. In view of the general lack of industrial health and safety standards, but also certain deficiencies regarding freedom of association, representatives of companies with business activities or cooperations in China have made it clear that transnational enterprises do not regard themselves as firms that stand in opposition to the government. It was observed by some representatives that various organisations had failed in their attempts to gain greater influence in China, because they had confronted the government with expectations that the state could not ultimately meet. In view of the 'huge enforcement deficit' in China, one commentator was quoted as saying:

> [W]e assume that, of course, the Chinese government also has an interest in seeing that the laws there are in the country on this issue are gradually implemented ... And now the question arises as to how, by supporting the Chinese government, international companies can perform support, a supporting role.

Thus, where there are conflicts between 'local custom' and company standards such as codes of conduct (which contain 'guarantees' of freedom of association, collective bargaining, and non-discrimination), local practice, even where it is found to be insufficient, will be likely to have primacy. For example, when asked about the implementation of the guarantee of freedom of association in China, one company representative stated:

> We say there needn't be a union at the location, and if having a union is prohibited by law, then that does not meet our standard. It becomes difficult the moment the employees come and say, we want a union. Luckily, there isn't anything like that right now, thank goodness.

Obviously, this company is relieved not to have been forced to take a stand on the question of freedom of association, and, faced with an unsatisfactory local practice of non-compliance, has not acted. The same speaker said:

> [T]he important thing for us ... is that we also demand, by means of a standard, that employees in one way or another get the opportunity to represent their interests vis-à-vis company management. And, partly, these can be very simple things; it can be I have complaints management, I have a box and I can stick a letter in it, or I'm the responsible person from among my ranks who can then, let's say, can appear in front of management.

An internal complaints mechanism in corporate ownership is here identified with the promotion of freedom of association.

This example shows a relevant actor who does not expect the written document to actually function as constitutive standard-setting on its own. New standards will only be firmly established and specified as implementation policies are put in place, and subsequently monitored.

4. *Providing Enforcement Mechanisms for Existing Standards*

Corporate actors have cited the lack of adequate enforcement mechanisms as a key reason why, although ratified, the standards set out in the ILO and human rights agreements have not been observed in many states where suppliers or subsidiaries have business operations. In their view, codes of conduct function to give teeth to such existing standards by providing for enforcement mechanisms. Many declarations and contracts contain provisions that define how to monitor and implement compliance.

Control and monitoring procedures are diverse and varied, but they all have one common aspect: control and monitoring does not rely on legal and judicial mechanisms, but on mechanisms owned by the transnational standard-setters themselves. Only in rare cases, such as where the transnational corporation is facing political risks and/or market pressure, are independent or external actors and organisations chosen as auditors (Dubin, 1999: 62; Colucci, 2000: 277–89; van Liemt, 2000: 185).

As a consequence, what has been observed is more than just promotional standard-setting, which provides standards developed elsewhere with implementation and control mechanisms. Rather, specific standards emerge as a result of the implementation and monitoring processes. This could be referred to as the 'reflexivity' of standards (for the concept of reflexivity see: Teubner, 1984: 334; Teubner and Willke, 1984: 4; Habermas, 1997: 495; Calliess, 2000: 293). In the future, the involvement of legitimate actors in the implementation of standards as well as participative approaches to implementation and monitoring (especially trade union participation and, consequently, freedom of association/right to collective bargaining) will have to be discussed further.

III. CODES OF CONDUCT BETWEEN SOFT LAW AND HARD LAW

In view of these results, doubts arise as to the effective regulatory character of existing corporate codes of conduct. However, up to this point, only the performative value and normative quality of the texts, documents, and social practices of private standard-setting have been examined. Nevertheless, soft law standards such as unilateral declarations on minimum standards can be transformed into legal regulation and binding obligations through hard law norms. In the following section, the respective normative reference points and legal prerequisites for recognising a binding legal nature of standards will be examined (Kocher, 2002: 265–80; Dilling, 2005: 283–313; Glinski, 2005: 187–230; Kocher, 2005: 647–52).

A. Misleading Advertising

One key issue concerns cases where a company promotes its products on the basis that they were produced in compliance with certain minimum social standards, and specifically whether such a company could be found in violation of section 5(1)–(2) UWG (German Act against Unfair

Competition) prohibiting misleading or unfair advertising (Kocher, 2005: 647). It is clear that an advertisement will be found misleading if the company does not meet in practice what it claims to fulfil in the advertising. Moreover, the courts have demanded that the advertisement of an image, which is connected to certain socially desirable aims, be accompanied by a certain degree of information on what 'socially responsible' is actually supposed to mean (Ewert, 1997; Glinski, 2005: 210)[13]. This finding is more or less consistent with the provisions of the new Directive 2005/29/EC concerning unfair business-to-consumer commercial practices, which requires in Article 6(2):

> A commercial practice shall also be regarded as misleading if, in its factual context, taking account of all its features and circumstances, it causes or is likely to cause the average consumer to take a transactional decision that he would not have taken otherwise, and it involves any marketing of a product, including comparative advertising, which creates confusion with any products, trade marks, trade names or other distinguishing marks of a competitor.

The new regime now explicitly includes situations where a trader has failed to comply with certain commitments, which are not simply aspirational but are rather firm and capable of being verified, that he has undertaken as binding and where he has indicated through his commercial practice that he intends to be bound by the code (Glinski, 2005: 212). The commitments set out in many codes are likely not to meet the criteria of 'firm' and 'capable of being verified'; however, any determination depends on the specific wording of the code itself.

Where a commitment is found to be neither firm nor verifiable, one should consider whether it is a misleading practice for a company to suggest to consumers that it has made a firm commitment, despite the fact it has not. There are few cases where the social practices of transnational corporations have been questioned by means of the rules on unfair competition. The vast majority of these cases arose in the United States, where public interest actions are considered to have some legitimacy and where there is an institutionalised system and network for public interest legal advocacy (Pfarr and Kocher, 1998: 135; Kocher, 2004b: 216). For example, in the United States, NGOs have brought actions against the retail industry; the Saipan-case in particular garnered a huge amount of public attention. In this case, a whole group of retailers was accused of misleading advertising under the California Business and Professions Code, because they sold Saipan products in California as 'made in USA', suggesting that non-sweatshop production methods were used. In the consent decree that concluded the class action suit, 26 retailers and 23 production companies

[13] BGH, 5.12.1996 in *Der Betrieb* 1997 at 2119–20, BGH 20.10.1988 in *GRUR 1991* at 548–50.

paid a lump sum of USD 20 million (Kocher, 2004b: 209–23; Su-Ping, 1999/2000: 601–29; Glinski, 2005: 205). In this NGO attempt to control social practices in transnational production, the US rules on misleading advertising (functionally equivalent to the German regime) seem to have worked as an adequate instrument.

B. Consumer Contract Law

Regarding issues of consumer contract law, it is worth taking a closer look at the European Directive 1999/44 on certain aspects of the sale of consumer goods,[14] which states in Article 2(2d) that

> consumer goods are presumed to be in conformity with the contract if they show the quality and performance which are normal in goods of the same type and which the consumer can reasonably expect, given the nature of the goods and taking into account any public statements on the specific characteristics of the goods made about them by the seller, the producer or his representative, particularly in advertising or on labelling.

After transposition of the Directive, section 434 (1) BGB (German Civil Code) has been reworded accordingly (Rott and Glinski, 2003: 649–54; Glinski, 2005: 220). The German law on the sale of goods has already established that public declarations made for promotional purposes may have contractual value and, thus, create contractual obligations to consumers.[15] However, it is questionable whether a publicly advertised code of conduct which guarantees that certain minimum social standards were maintained during production will meet the requirement that such declarations be 'specific characteristics of the good' under the German provision. In the past, the German judiciary has been reluctant to recognise characteristics other than those physically attached to the purchase as 'characteristics of the good'. '[O]ther economical, social or legal attributes of the good ... that influence its usefulness or value may be considered. But such attributes must be based on the quality of the good and be attached to it for some time'.[16]

It is arguable that it is not simply a question of 'business ethics' where a company has advertised that it is in compliance with certain minimum social standards in the production of its goods. If the market recognises this aspect of the product, then the mode of production would have to be considered a feature of the good itself (Dilling, 2005: 288; Glinski, 2005: 223). On this basis, the code of conduct would then become a contractual obligation to be performed by companies for the benefit of consumers. Nevertheless, the strength of this obligation would still be dependent upon the specific wording

[14] OJ L 171, 07/07/1999 at 12–16.
[15] BGH, 21.6.1967, BGHZ 48 at 118.
[16] BGH, 28.3.1990, BGHZ 111 at 75 (trans).

and content of the code in question, and, as has been shown in this chapter, such commitments vary widely in respect of their regulatory character.

IV. CODES OF CONDUCT AS A CONTRIBUTION TO TRANSNATIONAL LAW

Another question is whether the corporate undertakings guaranteeing certain social minimum standards are really 'voluntary' in the sense that a company can freely decide to commit to these minimum standards. Are they not anyway bound to the same minimum standards that they 'voluntarily' commit themselves to? Since corporations publicly commit to consumers that they will meet certain social aims, both consumer law and the law on unfair competition will likely come to bear on this issue.

A. Social Dumping and the Law against Unfair Competition

Under German law, it is commonly (if questionably) assumed that an act which merely takes advantage of an international gradient in the level of protection without violating any legal norms cannot be considered unfair competition. 'Social dumping' as such will thus not be considered to be contrary to principles of fair competition.

Under sections 3 and 4, no 11 UWG (German Act against Unfair Competition) a commercial practice will be unfair if a competitor violates a legal provision that serves, inter alia, to regulate commercial behaviour in the interest of commercial actors. There have been few decisions on the question of whether the failure to meet certain minimum social standards aimed at protecting workers constitutes unfair trading for the purposes of this rule or under the new codification of these rules under section 4, no 11 UWG. However, the German Federal Civil Court (BGH) has found that an entrepreneurial action restricting itself to the production process will usually not be regarded as commercial trading activity. Thus, infringements of labour law standards constitute unfair competition only if the violation occurs where the commercial activity involves the sale of the product. Thus, violations of working time rules will not be considered unfair competition, but a violation of the rules on closing time for shops or a prohibition for bakeries to bake at night could be found to be unfair trading.[17] The Federal Civil Court held that a contravention of the minimum standards on wages

[17] BGH in *GRUR* 1989 at 116 (prohibition on baking bread at night); BGH, 7.6.1996 in *GRUR* 1996 at 786 (selling of flowers at petrol stations); BGH, 19.5.1982 in *BGHZ* 84 at 130 (marketing in airports after shop closing hours as unfair competition); BGH, 8.12.1983 in *NJW* 1984 at 872 ('information for housewives' after shop closing hours as unfair competition); BGH, 26.11.1987 in *NJW* 1988 at 2243*ff* (distribution of a advertising journal on Sundays as unfair competition).

or health and safety will be seen as a commercial activity if the violation is broad and systematic, and if the profits resulting from the violation are deliberately used to calculate a more favourable price for the goods.[18]

The principles on unfair competition set out by the German Federal Civil Court can be applied to cases where there has been a violation of certain minimum standards under international and foreign law, if the violated norms are found to be 'legal provisions' in the sense of section 4, no 11 UWG. For these purposes, the laws of the country of production are definitely to be considered 'legal provisions'. However, the ILO Conventions do not directly bind private enterprises. In the case of an infringement of ILO standards, the rules of section 4, no 11 UWG do not apply in the same way. In 1980, the German Federal Civil Court (BGH) had to decide a case where a producer of asbestos had purchased a considerable proportion of his products in South Korea, where the health and safety standards for workers were lower than in Germany. As a result, it was possible for this producer to undercut his competitors' prices. Since the asbestos production did not violate South-Korean law, the court did not see any unfair competition in the distribution of the goods. The fact that the conditions of production violated the ILO Convention on Asbestos (No 139 of 24 June 1974) was not seen as relevant (Knieper and Fromm, 1980: 2020; Oppenhoff, 1980: 862),[19] and the reform of the German law on unfair competition in 2004 has not changed anything in this respect. Nevertheless, it is important to note that, in the case of the asbestos products, the Convention on Asbestos had only been signed by 15 of the more than 100 Member States of the ILO. This factual detail was important in the case: the Federal Civil Court did consider that, under certain conditions, this might have been a case of unfair competition, for example, if there had been a common international understanding on what constituted ethical corporate conduct in this commercial area (Knieper and Fromm, 1980: 2020; Oppenhoff, 1980: 862; Hohloch, 1981: 691; Hollmann, 1981: 10; Katzenberger, 1981: 9; Sack, 1998: 510).[20] The common understanding could have been expressed in an international Convention signed by a considerable number of States.[21]

The new Act against Unfair Competition (UWG) no longer uses the standard of 'good commercial morals', instead referring to 'fairness in competition'. However, the new section 3 UWG still accepts the relevance of commercial customs and generally acknowledged rules (Köhler, 2004: 383).

[18] BGH, 27.6.1958 in *BGHZ* 28 at 54 (direct marketing by wholesalers to consumers constitutes unfair competition only in exceptional cases, ie, if the wholesaler takes advantages of his cost prices to undercut retail sellers). For infringements of rules laid down in collective bargaining in detail: BGH, 3.12.1992 in *NJW* 1993 at 1010–12.

[19] BGH, 9.5.1980 in *NJW* 1980 at 2018–20: *Asbestimporte*.

[20] Competition 'contra bonos mores', BGH, 9.5.1980 in *NJW* 1980 at 2018—*Asbestimporte*; the Convention had not even been ratified by the country of production, South Korea.

[21] BGH, 9.5.1980 in *NJW* 1980 at 2018–20—*Asbestimporte*.

As a result, the German Federal Civil Court's ruling in the *Asbestos* case still serves as a relevant reference point, since it focused on 'commercial' morals in trade. Consequently, internationally acknowledged norms and standards that mirror fundamental ideas of fair competition constitute important criteria for the assessment of the fairness of transnational commercial practices to the extent that these standards have achieved wide acceptance and are applicable to the distribution of goods, not exclusively to production (Däubler, 1995: 486).

B. Transnational Social Standards and the Relevance of Codes of Conduct

One of the reasons why the *Asbestos* case has rarely been applied in other rulings is due to the uncertainty of what internationally acknowledged minimum social standards are exactly (Leary, 1996: 202). What about the infringement of international minimum standards such as working hours, minimum working age, health and safety in the workplace, and the right to organise: In cases where they are violated in order to gain a competitive advantage, does such behaviour constitute unfair trading under German law?

Without legitimate or even democratic consent-finding procedures in the transnational sphere, it remains difficult to prove if, and if so, what kind of, universal consents on specific social values actually exist. With the 1998 Declaration on core labour standards, the ILO is continuously trying to focus its work on promoting the effective implementation of its Conventions through transnational corporations. Therefore, the ILO declared the standards set out under the ILO Conventions on the abolition of forced labour and child labour, on non-discrimination, on freedom of association, and on collective bargaining[22] to be core labour standards that are to be respected by every ILO Member State, regardless of ratification. Additionally, the ILO now also turns directly to enterprises and their associations for implementation.

In the wake of the 1998 ILO Declaration on core labour standards, considerable standardisation in standard-setting has taken place. Certification agencies and the labelling of products, processes, or firms have played important roles in this regard by professionalising the marketing of social standards. This includes, for example, the SA (Social Accountability) 8000-certificate (Köpke and Röhr, 2003: 78),[23] and in the textile and sports industry, the FLA label (Köhnen, 2002: 15; Köpke and Röhr, 2003: 76)[24]. Since their reform in 2000, the influential OECD-Guidelines for Multinational

[22] See nn 4–6 above.
[23] Cp 'Social Accountability International', (http://www.sa8000.org/SA8000/SA8000.htm).
[24] Cp Fair Labor Association, 'Workplace Code of Conduct' (http://www.fairlabor.org/all/code/index.html).

Enterprises also refer to the ILO core labour norms in the section on 'social standards'. The same is true for the Global Compact. One interviewee referred to these guidances as 'what is commonly accepted'.[25] Undertakings and agreements are, in part, also guided by model codes. Every global union federation has created a model code, which in turn draws on the model code of the International Federation of Free Unions. Some enterprise associations, such as the World Association of the Sports Goods Industry (WFSGI), also have model codes of conduct that are informed by the ILO core labour standards.

Another aspect of the legal relevance of codes of conduct is that they contribute to the emergence of transnational law. It is well accepted that international guidelines or private codes of conduct can express collective ideas of fairness and justice of the quality needed for their transformation into hard law. Their transformational value especially depends on the degree of consent on the part of relevant actors in the respective sector (Baade, 1979: 26; Meessen, 1981: 1131; Hailbronner, 1982: 116). Even when lacking a regulatory character, codes of conduct still serve to convert existing international law standards into standards 'commonly accepted' in transnational production and distribution.

V. CONCLUSIONS

Through the adoption of codes of conduct on transnational social standards, corporations aim to participate in the enforcement and adaptation of rules developed elsewhere. Even if the enforcement mechanisms included in such declarations exhibit weighty defects, the corporate undertakings still actively contribute to the emergence of transnational labour standards.

Private regulatory processes, which extend beyond the reach of nation states, have been described and analysed regarding their role in the emergence of 'transnational law' (Albert and Lehmkuhl, 2002: 159; Calliess, 2002: 188). Until now, the debate around the quality and importance of transnational law has focused on the *lex mercatoria* (Berger, 1996: 32; Berger *et al*, 2002: 12; Dasser, 2001: 189). However, the regulation of working conditions through corporate codes of conduct and framework agreements also exhibits the private character and the horizontal (as opposed to hierarchical) coordination of behaviour that are seen as characteristic for transnational law (Gessner, 2002: 280). These instruments of transnational law are important steps on the way from private standards to commercial rules and from commercial rules to law—that is, on the way from 'soft law' to 'hard law' (Berger, 1996: 192; Berger *et al*, 2002: 12).

[25] See also text at n 7 above for the 'global eight'.

In the case of social standards, through the ILO core labour norms, international law plays a leading role in the creation of transnational law. By entering into the field of social standards, private codes of conduct thus also contribute to making international labour standards legally binding in national 'reflective' hard law—which (like hard law rules on unfair competition) refers to transnational soft law.

REFERENCES

Albert, M and Lehmkuhl, D (2002) 'Transnationales Recht' 23 *Zeitschrift für Rechtssoziologie* 159.

Alston, P (2004) 'Core Labour Standards and the Transformation of the International Labour Rights Regime' *European Journal of International Law* 15.

Baade, HW (1979) 'The Legal Effects of Codes of Conduct for Multinational Enterprises' *German Yearbook of International Law* 26.

Ballreich, H (1989) 'Nachdenkliches über "Soft law"' *Gewerblicher Rechtsschutz und Urheberrecht Internationaler Teil* 383.

Bassen, A, Jastram, S, and Meyer, K (2005) 'Corporate Social Responsibility. Eine Begriffserläuterung' 6 *Zeitschrift für Wirtschafts- und Unternehmensethik* 231.

Berger, KP (1996) *Formalisierte oder 'schleichende' Kodifizierung des transnationalen Wirtschaftsrechts* (Berlin/New York, de Gruyter).

Berger, KP, Dubberstein, H, Lehmann, S, and Petzold, V (2002) 'Anwendung Transnationalen Rechts in der internationalen Vertrags- und Schiedspraxis' 101 *Zeitschrift für vergleichende Rechtswissenschaft* 12.

Blanke, T and Hoffmann, J (2006) 'Auf dem Weg zu einem Europäischen Sozialmodell. Voraussetzungen, Schwierigkeiten und Perspektiven einer europäischen Sozialpolitik' *Kritische Justiz* 134.

Calliess, G-P (2000) 'Das Tetralemma des Rechts' 21 *Zeitschrift für Rechtssoziologie* 293.

—— (2002) 'Reflexive Transnational Law' 23 *Zeitschrift für Rechtssoziologie* 188.

Colucci, M (2000) 'Implementation and monitoring of codes of conduct. How to make codes of conduct effective?' 37 *Bulletin of Comparative Labour Relations* 277.

Dasser, F (2001) 'Lex Mercatoria' in RP Appelbaum, WLF Festiner, and V Gessner (eds), *Rules and Networks: The legal culture of global business transactions* (Oxford; Portland, Oregon, Hart).

Däubler, W (1995) 'Sozialstandards im internationalen Wirtschaftsrecht' in F v Westphalen (ed) *Lebendiges Recht. Festschrift für Reinhold Trinkner zum 65. Geburtstag* (Heidelberg, Verlag Recht und Wirtschaft).

Dilling, O (2005) 'Die Produktionsbedingung als Produkteigenschaft' in G Winter (ed), *Die Umweltverantwortung multinationaler Unternehmen* (Baden-Baden, Nomos).

Dubin, L (1999) 'The Direct Application of Human Rights Standards to, and by, Transnational Corporations' 61 *Review of the International Commission of Jurists.*

Ehricke, U (1989) 'Soft law—Aspekte einer neuen Rechtsquelle' *Neue Juristische Wochenschrift* 1907.

Engels, C (2000) 'Codes of Conduct. Freedom of association and the right to bargain collectively' 37 *Bulletin of Comparative Labour Relations* 219.

Ewert, J (1997) *Wettbewerbsrechtliche Beurteilung von Umweltwerbung ohne Produktqualitätsbezug nach deutschem Recht und europäischem Gemeinschaftsrecht* (Berlin, Duncker & Humblot).

Fichter, M and Sydow, J (2002) 'Using Networks Towards Global Labor Standards? Organizing Social Responsibility in Global Production Chains' *Industrielle Beziehungen* 357.

Gessner, V (2002) 'Rechtspluralismus und globale soziale Bewegungen' 23 *Zeitschrift für Rechtssoziologie* 280.

Glinski, C (2005) 'Produktionsaussagen und Vertrauensschutz im Kauf- und Werberecht' in G Winter (ed), *Die Umweltverantwortung multinationaler Unternehmen* (Baden-Baden, Nomos).

Greven, T (2006) 'Auf dem Prüfstand: Gewerkschaftsstrategien zur Regulierung globaler Konkurrenz' *WSI-Mitteilungen* 10.

Habermas, J (1997) *Faktizität und Geltung*, 5th edn (Frankfurt am Main, Suhrkamp).

Hailbronner, K (1982) 'Rechtswirkungen des EG-Südafrikakodex' *Recht der Internationalen Wirtschaft* 113.

Hammer, N (2005) 'International Framework Agreements: global industrial relations between rights and bargaining' *Transfer*. European review of labour and research.

Hauser-Ditz, A and Wilke, P (2005) *Corporate Social Responsibility—Soziale und ökologische Verantwortung von Unternehmen. Eine Betriebsrätebefragung zu den Handlungsfeldern für Arbeitnehmervertretungen* (Düsseldorf, HBS-Arbeitspapier).

Hepple, B (2005) *Labour Laws and Global Trade* (Oxford/Portland, Oregon, Hart).

Herberg, M (2002) 'Codes of Conduct und kommunikative Vernunft' 22 *Zeitschrift für Rechtssoziologie* 45.

—— (2005) 'Erzeugen multinationale Unternehmen ihr eigenes Umweltrecht?' in G Winter (ed), *Die Umweltverantwortung multinationaler Unternehmen* (Baden-Baden, Nomos).

Hoffmann, J (2004) 'Co-ordinated Continental European Market Economies under Pressure from Globalisation: Germany's Rhineland capitalism' 5 *German Law Journal* No 8 (1 August 2004).

Hohloch, G (1981) 'Zum Urteil des BGH vom 9.5.1980 (Asbestimporte)' *Juristische Schulung* 691.

Hollmann, HH (1981) 'Anmerkung zur Entscheidung des BGH vom 9.5.1980 (Asbestimporte)' *Juristische Arbeitblätter* 120.

Kaelble, H (2000) 'Wie kam es zum Europäischen Sozialmodell?' in A Aust, S Leitner, and S Lessenich (eds), *Sozialmodell Europa* (Opladen, Leske+Budrich).

Katzenberger, P (1981) 'Inländischer Wettbewerb, ordre public und ausländisches Arbeitsschutzrecht' *Praxis des Internationalen Privat- und Verfahrensrecht* 9.

Knieper, R and Fromm, H (1980) 'Anmerkung zur Entscheidung des BGH vom 9.5.1980 (Asbestimporte)' *Neue Juristische Wochenschrift* 2020.

Kocher, E (2002) 'Private Standards between Soft Law and Hard Law—The German Case' *The International Journal of Comparative Labour Law and Industrial Relations* 265.

—— (2004a) 'Selbstverpflichtungen von Unternehmen zur sozialen Verantwortung' *Recht der Arbeit* 27.

—— (2004b) 'Mindeststandards vor Gericht' in T Brühl, H Feldt, B Hamm, H Hummel and J Martens (eds), *Unternehmen in der Weltpolitik* (Bonn, Verlag JHW Dietz).

—— (2005) 'Unternehmerische Selbstverpflichtungen im Wettbewerb' *Gewerblicher Rechtsschutz und Urheberrecht* 647.

Köhler, H (2004) 'Der Rechtsbruchtatbestand im neuen UWG' *Gewerblicher Rechtsschutz und Urheberrecht* 383.

Köhnen, H (2002) 'Haben Menschenrechtsverletzungen ein System?' *in Wal-Mart's Verhaltenskodex und die Realität bei Zulieferern in ausgewählten Ländern* (Düsseldorf, Hans-Böckler-Stiftung).

Köpke, R and Röhr, W (2003 *Codes of Conduct* (Köln, PapyRossa Verlag).

Körting, C (2006) 'Global Compact—Bilanz und Perspektiven' in J Martens, W Oesterheld, and P Eisenblätter (eds), *Verbindliche Regeln für Multis—Corporate Accountability—Zwischenbilanz und Zukunftsperspektiven* (http://www.globalpolicy.org/eu/de/publ/corporate-accountability-dokumentation.pdf).

KPMG (Kolk, van der Veen, Pinkse, Fortanier, Peters and Extercatte) (2005), *International Survey of Corporate Responsibility Reporting* (Amsterdam: KPMG) (http://ec.europa.eu/employment_social/soc-dial/csr/060403/kpmgsurvey2005_en.pdf).

Langille, BA (2005) 'Core Labour Rights—The True Story' 16 *European Journal of International Law* 409.

Lavranu, A (2000) 'Europa—Wertegemeinschaft oder Interessenkongruenz?' in A Aust, S Leitner, and S Lessenich (eds), *Sozialmodell Europa* (Opladen, Leske+Budrich).

Leary, VA (1996) 'Workers' Rights and International Trade: The Social Clause (GATT, ILO, NAFTA, US Laws)' in J Bhagwati and RE Hudec, *Fair Trade and Harmonization*, vol 2 (Cambridge, MA, MIT Press).

Meessen, KM (1981) 'Internationale Verhaltenskodizes und Sittenwidrigkeitsklauseln' *Neue Juristische Wochenschrift* 1131.

Ölz, M (2002) 'Die Kernarbeitsnormen der Internationalen Arbeitsorganisation im Licht der neuen handelspolitischen "Sozialklausel" der Europäischen Union' *Zeitschrift für internationales und ausländisches Arbeits- und Sozialrecht* 330.

Oppenhoff, W (1980) 'Anmerkung zur Entscheidung des BGH vom 9.5.1980' *Gewerblicher Rechtsschutz und Urheberrecht* 862.

Pfarr, H and Kocher, E (1993) *Kollektivverfahren im Arbeitsrecht* (Baden-Baden, Nomos).

Riedel, S, Deuerlein, I, and Pomper, F (2003) Die gesellschaftliche Verantwortung österreichischer Unternehmen. Ergebnisse einer empirischen Untersuchung (Wien, CSR Austria).

Riess, B and Peters, A (2005) *Die gesellschaftliche Verantwortung von Unternehmen* (Güterloh, Bertelsmann-Stiftung) (http://www.buergerstiftungen.de/cps/rde/xbcr/SID-0A000F0A-77FA41BB/buergerstiftungen/Unternehmensbefragung_CSR.pdf).

Rott, P and Glinski, C (2003) 'Umweltfreundliches und ethisches Konsumverhalten im harmonisierten Kaufrecht' *Europäische Zeitschrift für Wirtschaftsrecht* 649.

Sack, R (1998) 'Die wettbewerbsrechtliche Durchsetzung arbeitsrechtlicher Normen' in P Hanau (ed), *Festschrift für Günter Wiese zum 70. Geburtstag* (Neuwied, Luchterhand).

Scherrer, C, Greven, T, and Frank, V (1998) *Sozialklauseln, Arbeiterrechte im Welthandel* (Münster: Westfälisches Dampfboot).

Sheikh, S (2002) 'Promoting Corporate Social Responsibility Within the European Union' 13 *International Company and Commercial Law Review* 143.

Simma, B and Zöckler, M (1996) 'Law-making by Universal Organizations' in B Maydell and A Nußberger (ed), *Social Protection by Way of International Law* (Berlin, Duncker & Humblot).

Su-Ping, L (1999/2000) 'Corporate Codes of Conduct and the FTC: Advancing Human Rights through Deceptive Advertising Law' 38 *Columbia Journal of Transnational Law* 601.

Tapiola, K (2000) 'The ILO Declaration on Fundamental Principles and Rights at Work and its Follow-up' 37 *Bulletin of Comparative Labour Relations* 9.

Teubner, G (1971) *Standards und Direktiven in Generalklauseln* (Frankfurt am Main, Athenäum-Verlag).

—— (1984) 'Verrechtlichung' in F Kübler (ed), *Verrechtlichung von Wirtschaft, Arbeit und sozialer Solidarität* (Baden-Baden, Nomos).

Teubner, G and Willke, H (1984) 'Kontext und Autonomie: Gesellschaftliche Selbststeuerung durch reflexives Recht' 5 *Zeitschrift für Rechtssoziologie* 4.

van Liemt, G (2000) 'Codes of Conduct and International Subcontracting: A 'private' road towards ensuring minimum labour standards in export industries' 37 *Bulletin of Comparative Labour Relations* 177.

Weinz, W (2006) 'Globale Rahmenvereinbarungen zwischen Gewerkschaften und Konzernen' in J Martens (ed), *Corporate Accountability—Zwischenbilanz und Zukunftsperspektiven* (http://www.globalpolicy.org/eu/de/publ/corporate-accountability-dokumentation.pdf).

Wilhelm, A and Mauritz, C (2005) *Die Nachhaltigkeitsleistungen deutscher Großunternehmen* (http://www.scoris.de/download/scoris_dax30_studie_2005.pdf).

Winter, G (2005) 'Die Umweltverantwortung multinationaler Unternehmen' in G Winter (ed), *Die Umweltverantwortung multinationaler Unternehmen* (Baden-Baden, Nomos).

Part II

Standards of Transnational Business Networks and the Law

4

Proactive Compliance? Repercussions of National Product Regulation in Standards of Transnational Business Networks[1]

OLAF DILLING

I. INTRODUCTION

ACCORDING TO POPULAR opinion, economic globalisation and stringent environmental standards are at odds with one another. In the context of global trade and open markets, economic players are free to choose their location with regard to the most favourable—that is, least restrictive—legislation. The nation state, which used to be the sovereign author of mandatory regulation, has—according to this view—become driven by regulatory competition. In consequence, this is expected to lead to an erosion of often costly environmental requirements in OECD-countries (the so-called 'Delaware effect', or 'race to the bottom'). However, while the notion of regulatory competition makes some sense regarding the rules applicable to production processes in the context of foreign direct investments, product standards in the context of free trade follow a different logic (see Scharpf, 1994: 480*ff*).

In contrast to production facilities, which may circumvent environmental regulation by retreating to low standard jurisdictions, products have to be adapted to various regulatory contexts in order to be globally marketable. Instead of differentiating between production lines for various markets, transnational corporations must design uniform products complying with

[1] This chapter owes a lot to helpful comments on earlier drafts by Martin Herberg, Alexandra Lindenthal and Gerd Winter, and to the participants of our workshop in June 2005 at the International Institute for the Sociology of Law in Oñati, Spain. The relentless efforts of my mother, Karin Dilling (née Banfield), and Julian Hill helped to enhance English style and readability. Remaining flaws and idiosyncrasies are due to the author's stubbornness.

the strictest jurisdiction to reap the benefits of economies of scale and to avoid transaction costs (Douglas and Craig, 1995: 9; Vogel, 1995: 250). Thus, some political scientists and environmental lawyers stress that the 'race to the bottom' effect does not actually apply to environmental regulation in the context of free trade in general (Rehbinder and Stewart, 1985; Scharpf, 1994). The dynamics of environmental product regulation have even been described as a 'California effect' rather than a 'Delaware effect' (Vogel, 1995: 5*ff*).[2] Accordingly, rather than regulatory competition, another political mechanism called 'trading up' would better characterise the relation between globalisation and environmental standards: exporting corporations already complying with strict standards of importing countries are inclined to put pressure on their domestic jurisdiction to restore fair rules of competition by also raising environmental standards.

However, the idea that globally operating corporations invariably apply all national laws and therefore cogently contribute to a California effect seems to be based on an oversimplified model of regulatory compliance. Rather than fully determined by national laws, transnational corporate standards and practices are developing a life of their own (Teubner, 1997; Fischer-Lescano and Teubner, 2006: 41*ff*; see also earlier Luhmann, 1971). Regarding the issue of environmental protection, this autonomous development may have negative or positive effects: On the one hand, regulatory compliance is questioned by widely perceived implementation deficits, even in a national context; on the other hand, a proactive attitude of corporate actors practising self-regulation could also contribute to the emergence of new regulatory standards.[3] Accordingly, the question of how well environmental standards accompany economic globalisation should not be analysed only in the context of political mechanisms like regulatory competition or trading up. Rather, we should scrutinise the emergence of transnational corporate standards and their role in the evolution of global environmental governance (see also Perez, 2004). Many of these corporate standards affect not only environmental management practices within the organisation itself, but establish interorganisational duties that spread within transnational business networks. By analysing corporate product standards in business networks, this chapter will thus contribute to a more profound understanding of governance mechanisms in the context of economic globalisation.

In the following section, the proactive compliance hypothesis, on which the study is based, will be presented, before an account of the empirical

[2] The term 'Delaware effect' is derived from an example of regulatory competition in the US, as many corporations registered in Delaware because of lower costs of incorporation; the term 'California effect' was coined by Vogel with reference to Californian automobile emission standards spreading to other US States (Vogel, 1995: 259).

[3] See also the two different scenarios in Vogel, 1995: 248.

study on proactive compliance is given (in section III), and theoretical conclusions are drawn from it (in section IV).

II. PROACTIVE COMPLIANCE HYPOTHESIS

The criteria for analysing the corporate standards have been based on the following proactive compliance hypothesis, integrating the notion of more or less autonomous corporate standards into the 'California effect' theory. The hypothesis thus combines elements of regulatory compliance and of private self-regulation in a transnational context:

Concerning environmental product norms, corporate standards often apply national—or European—regulation to transnational product networks (global compliance) or even anticipate national regulation by means of self-regulation (anticipatory risk management), thereby partly assuming executive functions from the state and actively shaping environmental policy.

In the following two sections, the analytical framework of the hypothesis will be further developed, defining its scope with reference to the differences between product and production norms (II.A), considering the role of business networks (II.B), and developing the hypothesis's different elements (II.C).

A. Extra-territorial Impact of Product Norms

In general, the 'Delaware effect' and the 'California effect' theories characterise global environmental governance, although they are both based on specific phenomena that do not represent the whole policy sector.

David Vogel's analysis of the California effect focuses on the regulation of free trade, which only applies to product standards.[4] In contrast, proponents of the 'race to the bottom' theory base their arguments on the regulation of production processes, when debating pollution havens and industrial locations in general.

By its explicit restriction to statements on environmental product norms, the 'proactive compliance' hypothesis, developed in this chapter, tries to avoid such biased generalisations.

A differentiation between standards formally applying to products and those applying to processes shows how both views may be integrated into a more comprehensive theory: while regulatory competition works towards deregulation of production standards, it may foster trading-up mechanisms enhancing product standards.

[4] David Vogel did not systematically develop the difference between product and production-standards, but mainly based his explanation of the difference between 'Delaware effect' and 'California effect' phenomena on the argumentation that costs of environmental standards are negligible compared to the cost of labour: Vogel, 1995: 6, 256*ff*; for the distinction between product and production-related standards, see *ibid*, 6, 263.

This difference is due to a specific extra-territorial impact of norms that formally apply to products. Product standards, in that formal sense of applicability, either cause a disruption of trade or have de facto extra-territorial effects when foreign importers are forced to comply. While stringent standards for imported products can have the effect of a 'tax' on foreign production and are therefore a legal issue of free trade, production standards make domestic production more costly (Vogel, 1995: 21, 263). They are thus not discriminatory against foreign imports but, on the contrary, have the effect of a 'tax' on domestic production and are therefore primarily discussed in the political debate on industrial locations (Vogel, 1995: 20*ff*).[5]

It is, however, not always possible to draw a clear line between product and production standards (Howse and Regan, 2000). Between clear-cut product and production-related standards, there are certain hybrid forms, especially process and production measures (ppm). An example is the famous tuna–dolphin case of WTO law: the United States banned imports of tuna from Mexico, which are caught in fishing nets that do not prevent dolphins from being killed.[6] Another example is the labelling requirement for products manufactured with the use of ozone-depleting substances, such as CFCs. Even though the import regulations formally apply to the product, both aim at the production risk. Hence, legislators sometimes regulate production processes and their risks indirectly by developing rules which formally apply to products (Vogel, 1995: 18; OECD, 1997; see also Dilling, 2005: 283*ff*). Nevertheless, they are still substantially related to production methods. Such hybrid cases of regulation that formally apply to products, whilst substantially referring to the regulation of production processes, are also covered in this chapter. It could be expected that these—with respect to their contents—production-related standards show similar extra-territorial effects to product-related standards, if corporate standards comply globally.

On the other hand, there are standards applying to production processes with the purpose of enhancing environmental product quality, for example the ban on certain auxiliary substances, aiming at a reduction of product contamination. These standards, which formally refer to production but substantially aim at product risks, are sometimes mentioned in corporate standards.

While, of course, unambiguous cases of product standards, like the ban on lead in solders of electronic equipment, are also included in this study, this is not the case with standards unambiguously referring to production processes

[5] With respect to the regulation of inherent properties of tradeable manufacturing plants, a conflict between free trade and standards formally applying to production processes could arise. In this comparatively rare case, standards for products are at the same time standards for production facilities, as both categories coincide in one regulatory object; see also Rehbinder and Stewart, 1985.

[6] See GATT Dispute Panel Report on US Restrictions on the Imports of Tuna, 16 August 1991, 30 ILM 1594.

Table 1: References and Examples of the Product—Production Distinction

		Substantial Reference: Regulatory Issue or Purpose	
		Products	*Production*
Formal Reference: Scope of Application	*Products*	Ban on a substance in product, eg lead in solder	Labelling requirement for products manufactured using CFCs
	Production	Regulating auxiliary substance to prevent product contamination	*'End of pipe' emission thresholds*

such as emission thresholds for a production plant (see Table 1, in *italics*). Thus, standards on the one hand can be divided into those formally applying to products and those applying to production methods; and on the other hand, can be divided into those standards substantially aiming at product risks and those aiming at production risks.

B. Types of Proactive Compliance

According to the proactive compliance hypothesis, private standards for products are developed in the shadow of various jurisdictions relevant for the production of globally marketable products—and are sometimes even foreshadowing expected regulatory developments. On the other hand, the proactive compliance hypothesis acknowledges that corporate standards are not only determined by public regulation, but follow a logic of their own. Proactive compliance thus combines elements of regulatory compliance and self-regulation.

The orientation of corporate standards towards public regulation and public policy is manifested in (a) the transnationalisation and (b) anticipation of public regulation (see Table 2):

Table 2: Types of Proactive Compliance and Examples

	Compliance	**Self-regulation**
Transnationalisation of Norms and Policies	Global compliance of national norm: *de facto extra-territorial effects of EU lead ban*	Autonomous extra-territorial use of national norm: *ban on the use of CFCs as solvents*
Anticipation of Norms and Policies	Early compliance with legal norm: *early deadline for compliance with EU Directive*	Anticipatory self-regulation of political goal: *ban on substance not yet regulated*

(a) *Transnationalisation of norms and policies* can lead to the global application of territorially restricted public regulation. These transnationalisations could be either based on de facto extra-territorial effects, when economic efficiency forces corporate actors to apply a standard mandatory for some markets to all products (*compliance*), or on the voluntary adoption of national norms, for example norms without extra-territorial impact, such as production norms (*self-regulation*). An example of transnationalised global compliance is the adoption of the EU's ban on lead in the solder of electronic appliances, which has been implemented in various transnational corporate standards. An example of a self-regulatory transnationalisation is corporate standards banning the use of ozone-depleting chlorinated fluorocarbons (CFCs) as solvents in the production of semiconductors—irrespective of whether or not the producing countries are signatory states of the Montreal Protocol.

(b) *Anticipation of norms and policies* can lead to the application of legal norms earlier than formally required to enable a smooth transition period with effective compliance at the legal cut-off date (*compliance*), or even applying values and principles expressed in legal norms to other, not yet regulated cases with comparable toxic or ecotoxic risks (*self-regulation*). An example of anticipatory compliance with respect to the implementation of a legal norm can be found in corporate standards referring to the EU Directive on the restriction of hazardous substances in electronic and electrical equipment, setting a much earlier deadline for compliance than legally required. An example for the anticipatory implementation of a political goal was a corporate standard prohibiting TBBA, a flame retardant not yet regulated, after a political initiative for its prohibition had been launched.

III. EMPIRICAL STUDY

A. Sample

Throughout the following section, the proactive compliance hypothesis will be tested by empirical exploration of certain corporate environmental standards on the use of chemical substances in products and production processes. Textual analysis and descriptive statistics will be the major tool of study.

Internet research that I have undertaken[7] shows that environmental standards are employed by corporate actors with headquaters in Japan (18), the United States (11), the EU (9), South Korea (1) and Canada (1). These

[7] Examples were found between spring 2004 and autumn 2005 with the help of the search engine www.google.com, using typical catch-words (like 'supplier', 'controlled', or 'banned') and numbers of the Chemical Abstract Service (CAS) relevant for these lists. A complete list of standards can be found in the appendix to this chapter.

standards, predominantly concerning big multinational corporations, do not only apply to their own production, but are interorganisational corporate standards insofar as they are also applied to direct business partners, like suppliers or contract manufacturers—or even other agents in the supply chain with no direct contractual relation to the focal company at all. The study is based on 40 corporate standards that were publicly accessible via the internet. All standards belong to companies or corporate groups that are—at least to some extent—manufacturing electronic or electrical equipment. Most of them either specialise in electrical and electronic equipment (17), or in information technology hardware (17); five corporations combine electronics with mechanical engineering; one corporation specialises in telecommunication services.

More than half the corporations involved in the sample are included in a 2005 global ranking of the biggest 500 corporations.[8] In the fiscal year 2005, the combined revenues of all these corporations amounted to approximately one trillion US dollars. Compared to political economies, this figure comes close to the size of the German revenues in the budgetary year 2005. Many of the firms issuing the controlled substance lists are corporate leaders within their sector, with various business relationships inside and outside the electronics sector and often with paradigmatic influence on their competitors.

In this sector, complex products are manufactured, which are used by consumers. Compared to the automotive industry, the electronics industry is characterised by an even more dynamic technological development, a more fragmented organisational structure, and less integrating activities of industry associations.[9] The study analyses the management of toxic risk that is usually present from the early stages of the production chain and continues to be relevant until the end of the individual product's life cycle. As opposed to product risks generated at the last stage of the production chain, like electrical or mechanical risks for consumers' health, even more actors have to cooperate to manage effectively the overall toxic risk. Any toxic risk management coordinated by the private actors of those production networks should be even more difficult than in cases with less complex products, less unforeseeable uses, less dynamic technological development, less fragmented organisational production structures, and less involved production stages.

Because of these characteristics and the trendsetting, paradigmatic character of this sector, it seems plausible that the results of the empirical study have certain prospective value for product regulation in general.

However, it should also be considered that in contrast to the agricultural sector or, for example, the production of simple textiles, production

[8] See 'Fortune: The Global 500 2005' (www.cnn.com/fortune/, last visited 8 May 2006).
[9] For developments in the automotive sector, see Alexandra Lindenthal, ch 5, this volume.

of electronic equipment is highly globalised and export-oriented, and the various actors of the electronics production networks are highly interdependent. As the mechanisms analysed in this study are mostly based on both inter-firm and transnational interdependencies within the production chain, as well as export orientation of the final manufacturers, the results cannot be transferred to a sector still mainly dominated by domestic production or arm's length transactions of the free market. The fragmented network structures encompassing the many actors involved should not so much be seen as obstacles to coordination processes, since, in contrast to mere market relations, they rather help to spread standards and present possibilities of inter-firm governance.

B. Corporate Substance Lists

The analysed standards are the so-called 'Controlled Substance Lists' and 'Green Procurement Guidelines'. Basically, they are used to communicate the standards concerning the restrictions on use and disclosure requirements for chemicals used in products—and sometimes also production processes—to business partners and other actors in the supply chain. A typical example of a restriction would be a prohibition on the use of certain brominated flame retardants or compulsory disclosure of the use of PVC.

These standards have only recently emerged as formal company standards in the electronics sector. As many of the standards prominently refer to a 2003 EU Directive regulating the contents of electrical and electronic equipment (the RoHS-Directive),[10] their emergence could be directly related to this. In fact, the latest versions of the corporate standards referred to in the sample were issued mostly between 2003 and 2005, yet some are older—one list even dates from 2000.

However, according to the first release dates, given in overviews on the first page of the corporate standards, the earliest were established at the beginning of the 1990s by European companies.[11] At first, they seem to have served primarily as internal corporate norms for the design of new products (Hall, 2001: 30*ff*). In the 1990s Japanese Green Procurement Standards were developed and adopted by many Asian corporations. With the adoption of the above-mentioned RoHS-Directive in 2003, these standards have become increasingly common, not only among outstanding leading firms,

[10] Directive 2002/95/EC of the European Parliament and of the Council of 27 January 2003 on the restriction of the use of certain hazardous substances in electrical and electronic equipment. For international discussion of this European legislation and its effects on the US electrical industry see Boon, 2006; Courtney, 2006; and Sachs, 2006.

[11] 1992 is given as a first release date for BTExact Technologies, nd; 1994 for Siemens, 2003. The first developments seem to go back to the late 1980s/early 1990s, also Bosch, according to a German chemical risk management consultant (interview: Krefeld, 25 February 2005). In the automotive industry, the first standards seem to have been established by Ford in 1984 and Chrysler in 1987 (Ford, 2003; DaimlerChrysler, 1997).

but also among other actors in the supply chain, which do not receive as much public attention.

Still, the emergence of these corporate standards seems to have developed rather independently from legislative processes: 'global compliance' does not imply that compliance with EU Directives (or, rather, their corresponding national transposition acts) is the main or even the only motive for private standards. On the contrary, if our hypothesis is correct, it simply means that relevant national regulation and policy agendas can influence the details of already existing industrial standards.

The usual contents of a corporate standard on banned, restricted, and reportable substances are the following:

— Purpose
— Scope
— Definitions
— Disclaimer
— Reference documents
— Substance list

This structure (or at least the first part containing purpose, scope and definitions) resembles the usual contents of formal laws, as they are enacted by the political legislator. This is partly due to the common functional requirements of private standards and formal legal acts, both aimed at the protection of public interests. For example, an explicitly determined purpose can help a lot with the interpretation of the norm in a complicated case. To some extent, however, this quasi-legal formal structure may also be a rather stylistic means to stress the binding and authoritative character of that type of document. This is manifested in a sometimes superficially upheld formal structure. In many documents the purpose does not seem to be chosen carefully, but rather arbitrarily and thus varies considerably. Sometimes the paragraph on 'purpose' consists of an abstract of the whole document. Often either legal compliance, compliance with customer requirements, or the protection of the environment and workplace security, or a combination of these different objectives, are given as the main purpose.

The binding and authoritative character of the documents is a prevailing impression given in most standards. Many standards that actually only include formal legal requirements from different jurisdictions try to convince the reader that these are genuine requirements of the corporation. Of the complete sample of 40 standards, only two or three standards of German corporations include explicit exceptions from this authoritative and binding normative character. According to Siemens, its 'list of prohibited substances is for information only. It is not a legally binding document' (Siemens, 2003). The Bosch list explicitly sticks to the requirements given by European law and in a list of declarable materials by the German industry association of the automotive sector.[12] And furthermore, many of these 'requirements' are only to be applied if 'explicitly stipulated' in the individual contract (Bosch, 2004). Two other corporate lists were just not definite enough to allow a precise evaluation of their standards.

In the corporate standards there is a certain tension between an altruistic or ethical and a more opportunistic, strategic argumentation. Especially in the introductory parts of the Japanese Green Procurement Guidelines, deep concern for ecology and a healthy environment are declared to be an integral part of the corporate culture of the enterprise. Other standards seem to be much less ambitious: no clear commitment to corporate environmental and social responsibility is made; sometimes only compliance with the existent law and regulations is given as the purpose of the standard, as well as anticipation of future laws. The general appearance and formal layout of these substance lists resembles other corporate standards in the areas of quality management or workers' protection in that they have a more technical appearance.

The scope of the analysed standards explicitly covers products purchased from other manufacturers, which are either integrated into a company's own products or sold as its own products (in the case of production by contract manufacturers). These products could be substances, preparations, or articles, or—in the terminology of the electronics sector—materials and parts, as well as subassemblies and finished consumer products. The standards are all addressed to suppliers, but some are additionally addressed to internal organs of the corporation, such as the purchasing department. In some cases, the scope also covers substances which are used in the manufacturing process of the purchased parts and materials.

Many corporate standards give an overview of all included reference documents. These could be legal norms as well as customer requirements, and sometimes more general standards of the same corporation.

The fact that corporate standards of customers are displayed on an equal footing with formal legislation shows how important they are for their business partners, which in turn demonstrates the functional parallels between formal legal norms and private corporate standards. With reference to these lists, a disclaimer may be included giving notice that even though the relevant legal requirements should be integrated into the corporate standard, suppliers must still follow current legal developments.

C. Legal Frame

The regulation of substance risks through corporate standards in the transnational production of electrical and electronic equipment does not take place in a normative vacuum, but is framed by certain legal requirements.

[12] VDA Materials Declaration List; about the development in the automotive sector, see also Alexandra Lindenthal, ch 5, this volume.

Of particular importance for corporate standards is national or EU legislation. International law also plays a role in the regulatory field. For a concise analysis of the corporate standards and a distinction between the different forms of compliance and self-regulation, a survey of the legal context is necessary. According to the hypothesis, the legislation of jurisdictions with relevant economic potential for the global marketplace, like the EU, Japan, the United States, Germany—or, as an example from the sub-national level, the State of California—would be relevant.

To study the extra-territorial effects of national regulation, it is necessary to analyse cases of a clear regulatory divide between a high standard in one jurisdiction and low standards in other jurisdictions concerning one substance or substance group. If a ban or restriction on a specific substance group only exists in a single jurisdiction, this would help to isolate the impact of the jurisdiction on the global standards of corporations. To eliminate alternative independent variables, the highest standards should not always be found in the same jurisdiction, but for different substances in different jurisdictions. Otherwise it could, for example, be presumed that corporate standards are simply oriented towards one particular jurisdiction, for whatever reason.

1. *International Law*

In the last 15 years, some relevant conventions on international chemicals law have been signed, such as the prohibition of persistent organic pollutants by the Stockholm Convention and of ozone-depleting substances in the Montreal Protocol.

Under the Convention for the protection of the marine environment of the North-East Atlantic, the Paris Commission (Parcom) has issued several decisions with respect to the use and disposal of hazardous substances.

2. *EU and Member State Law*

With respect to bans on substances and their applications in the electronics, electrical equipment, and automotive sectors, the most demanding requirements are virtually always set by the EU or their Member States. The main legislative acts relevant are the previously mentioned Directive 2002/95/EC (the RoHS Directive), Directive 2000/53/EC on end-of-life vehicles, with specific substance bans for the production of electronics and automobiles, and, for chemicals in general, Directive 76/769/EEC on restrictions on marketing and use of certain substances and preparations.

The RoHS Directive belongs to the field of waste regulation. Yet, according to the preventive approach taken in EU waste regulation, both Directives aim at the reduction of certain hazardous substances, posing considerable problems for the recycling and disposal of these products. The RoHS Directive (and similarly the end-of-life vehicles Directive) therefore generally prohibits materials and components from containing heavy metals, such as lead, mercury, cadmium, and hexavalent chromium, and certain flame retardants.

Directive 76/769/EEC contains a regularly updated list of chemical substances, whose marketing and use is prohibited or restricted in the EU. Included substances relevant for the analysed sectors are asbestos, certain heavy metals, polychlorinated biphenyls (PCBs), and various others.

Directive 67/548/EEC on dangerous substances also includes relevant regulation on chemicals, especially labelling requirements. However, substances included in articles (that is, products having a permanent shape such as electronic or electrical equipment) are not subject to labelling, testing, and classification duties. Only in certain circumstances are they covered by the new REACH Regulation, which was passed after my empirical study had been completed.[13] According to Article 176 of the EC Treaty, EU Member State law can be stricter than those European legal acts based on Article 175 of the Treaty. As Directive 76/769/EEC is based on Article 95 of the EC Treaty, stricter national requirements have to be notified according to Article 95 (4) of the Treaty and must be approved by the European Commission. In one case, for example, the Netherlands has transposed a ban on short-chain chlorinated paraffins issued by the international Paris Commission. This transposition, which is stricter than Directive 76/769/EEC, has only been partly approved.[14]

Switzerland also has exceptionally strict requirements. Even though small countries, such as the Netherlands or Switzerland, may play a minor role as importing markets, explicit references to these jurisdictions can be found in some of the Japanese and US standards.

3. *US Federal and State Law*

US federal law is relevant, primarily the Toxic Substances Control Act and the Clean Air Act. The Toxic Substances Control Act includes prohibitions or restrictions for a few substances or substance groups like asbestos and PCBs. Under the Toxic Substances Control Act, the US Environmental Protection Agency (EPA) also prepares the regulation of highly persistent

[13] Regulation (EC) No 1907/2006 of the European Parliament and of the Council of 18 December 2006 concerning the Registration, Evaluation, Authorisation and Restriction of Chemicals (REACH), OJ L396, 30.12.2006, pp 1–849. The REACH Regulation uses the somewhat cumbersome definition of articles as objects 'composed of one or more substances or preparations which during production is given a specific shape, surface or design determining its end use function to a greater degree than its chemical composition does': Art 3. According to Art 7 REACH, registration requirements exist only in some cases for dangerous substances integrated into imported articles that are released during expected use.

[14] See Commission Decision 2004/1/EC of 16 December 2003 concerning national provisions on the use of short-chain chlorinated paraffins, notified by the Kingdom of the Netherlands under Art 95(4) of the EC Treaty.

and bio-accumulative substances still widely used in the semiconductor industry and many other sectors, as they are suspected to be carcinogenic.[15] The US Clean Air Act, Section 611, as amended in 1990, not only requires the labelling of products containing ozone-depleting substances, but also the labelling of products imported to the United States manufactured with certain ozone-depleting substances. These requirements of the US Clean Air Act could thus indirectly affect offshore production. In 1993, additional rules of the US EPA clarified that only if the manufacturer itself uses ozone-depleting substances under certain conditions can these labelling requirements apply.

US State law concerning toxic properties of products includes the State of California Safe Drinking Water and Toxic Enforcement Act of 1986 (Proposition 65), which requires a warning to be given for chemicals known to cause cancer or reproductive defects.

4. *Japanese Law*

Japanese chemical laws are partly based on international obligations, but also have genuine requirements, especially concerning the authorisation of certain substances dangerous to the marine environment. Many relevant substances are regulated by the Japanese Chemical Substance Control Law.[16] Regulated substances, as well as products in which such substances are used, either require authorisation (see Articles 2(2), 6, and 14 of the Chemical Substance Control Law), or notification and labelling. Polychlorinated naphthalenes are regulated in Japan, but not in the EU (nor the United States), which may be due to the fact that they have a low production volume and only one supplier in the EU. However, in Switzerland a ban on polychlorinated naphthalenes exists, albeit rarely cited in corporate standards.[17] Other relevant substances are also regulated in the EU—at least labelling requirements exist.

5. *Conclusions for the Research Design*

There are several cases of relevant substances with a clear regulatory divide, with the EU operating as a high standard jurisdiction, whereas low standards exist in the United States and Japan. Examples of substances in recent use in the electronics and automotive sector which have been—with exemptions—prohibited only in the EU by the RoHS Directive are lead,

15 See eg the initiative of the US EPA on perfluoroalkyl sulfonates (PFAS), and especially perfluorooctanic acid (PFOA), see http://www.epa.gov/oppt/pfoa/, last visited 21 February 2007.

16 Law Concerning the Evaluation of Chemical Substances and Regulation of their Manufacture, etc, Law No 117, 16 October 1973 as last amended by Law No 49, 28 May 2003 (available in provisional translation by the Ministry of Economy, Trade and Industry).

17 Previously StoV, Annex 3 1; in May 2005 replaced by the Chemical Risk Reduction Ordinance (ChemRRV): see Annex 1.1 to Art 3 ChemRRV.

cadmium, mercury, and hexavalent chromium. Lead is still common in the electronics industry, especially for use in solders. Under the RoHS Directive, additional prohibitions of PBBs (polybrominated biphenyls) and PBDEs (polybrominated diphenyl ethers) exist. PBDEs are a group of flame retardants, still used in the sector and often referenced in corporate standards, but nowadays are of minor importance, as they can be substituted. However, many of the substitutes (often other brominated flame retardants) are also suspected to have adverse effects on human health and the environment.

Both Directive 76/769/EEC and the Netherlands' transposition of the Paris Commission decision, mentioned above, contain restrictions on short-chain chlorinated paraffins, although the restrictions of the EU Directive do not, or only marginally, concern specific applications in the electronics sector. They could therefore serve as an example for the effectiveness of product regulation by the jurisdiction of a relatively small political economy, although in this example, it should be considered that corporate standards are also directly influenced by the international Paris Commission decision. Chlorinated paraffins are used as plasticisers in paints, coatings and sealants, and flame retardants in rubber and plastic. It seems to be not quite clear, if or to what extent, they are still used in the electronic sector, but they are classified as a chemical substance group with a high production volume still with several producers or importers in the EU.[18]

An outstanding regulatory initiative from the United States is the labelling requirement for the use of CFCs and other ozone-depleting substances in offshore production. It is interesting to see how the United States can help to spread standards for the environmentally friendly manufacture of semiconductors worldwide—by introducing regulatory measures for products manufactured with the help of ozone-depleting substances.

Regarding Japanese law, the authorisation requirement for polychlorinated naphthalenes is considered the strictest regulation within one of the main jurisdictions. However, the Swiss ban on polychlorinated naphthalenes is an example of an even stricter regulation in a small jurisdiction. In the electronics sector, polychlorinated naphthalenes were formerly used for similar purposes as PCBs (for capacitors etc) and may have been recently used for flame retardants. Since the 1970s, they have been phased out. Today, even in the industrialised world, the facts about their use seem to be unclear (van der Plassche and Schwegler, 2002).

The Table 3 below gives an overview of the divide between regulations and regulatory loopholes in the EU, the United States, and Japan, regarding the use of substances of concern in the electronics sector; five exemplary substances and substance groups are selected. In this table, 'BAN' either

[18] See HPV–LPV Information on 'Alkanes, C10-13, chloro' in the European chemical Substances Information System (ESIS) supplied by the European Chemicals Bureau (http://ecb.jrc.it/ESIS/, last visited 21 February 2007).

Table 3: Examples of the Regulatory Divide between the EU, the United States, and Japan

Substance (Group)	EU*	Japan	US**	Commonness of application in OECD
PBDEs	BAN			May be still be used as flame retardants in polymers
Lead and compounds	BAN		DIS	Commonly used for solders, cables, wires, etc
Short-chain chlorinated paraffins	RES			Before phase-out used in metalwork fluids, as flame retardant, plasticiser and lubricant
Polychlorinated naphthalenes		DIS		Before phase out used as additive to lubricants, rubber, paints, etc
ODS I used in off-shore production***			DIS	Before phase-out used as solvent in semiconductor production

Notes:
* Relevant restrictions on short-chain chlorinated paraffins (also known as alkanes, C10-C13, chloro) apply in the Netherlands only.
** The indicated disclosure requirement for lead applies in the US State of California only.
*** Ozone-depleting substances; the ODS I group covers all substances listed in Annexes A and B of the Montreal Protocol; ODS II covers all HCFCs listed in Annex C, Group I.

signifies the prohibition of the use of a substance in electrical and electronic equipment or its phasing out within a definite deadline over the next five years, although certain minor applications may be exempted.[19] 'RES' refers to material restrictions other than prohibitions of substances. This could be a threshold limit, as in the case of short-chain chlorinated paraffins, restricted by Directive 76/769/EEC, or a restriction on certain applications as in the Chlorinated Paraffins Decision of the Netherlands. 'DIS' indicates a requirement of labelling or disclosure (including the duty to supply safety data sheets), or requirements of notification or authorisation. A cell left blank signifies that in the indicated jurisdictions no regulations for the substance exist which are applicable to products in the electronics sector.

With respect to the use of lead in electronic equipment, apart from the EU ban, a disclosure requirement exists in the US State of California. It has been assumed that the ban is a stricter regulation than the disclosure requirement—even though, in certain cases, public disclosure requirements can have a prohibitive effect comparable to a ban.

[19] For such prohibitions a typical threshold limit would be 1,000 ppm (the equivalent to 0.1% by mass) for unintentional contamination: that is, eg, solder containing less than 1,000 ppm is considered to be lead-free.

D. Empirical Analysis of the Different Types of Proactive Compliance

To study compliance of corporate standards more closely, five substance groups were selected, including PBDEs, lead and its compounds, short-chain chlorinated paraffins, polychlorinated naphthalenes, and certain ozone-depleting substances used in the offshore manufacturing of semiconductors (see Table 3). For these substances a systematic evaluation of the 40 corporate standards has been carried out.

Our question always has been as to how far the highest standard of one of the three main jurisdictions of the global market (the EU, the United States, and Japan) could also be found in the corporate substance list as a universally applicable transnational standard. Theoretically, a globally compliant standard would consist of a combination of the highest standards of different jurisdictions. In practice, a comprehensive substance list, which has considered all applicable public regulations of all jurisdictions, can hardly ever be found. Whenever a universally applicable standard incorporating the strictest public regulation regarding a certain substance could be found in a corporate substance list, it was considered as 'globally compliant'. To exclude the alternative reading that the compliance of corporate standards is still based on traditional mechanisms of national law enforcement, the compliance rate of 'domestic' corporations with their headquarters in the strictest jurisdiction is compared to 'foreign' corporations with headquarters outside the relevant jurisdiction (see Table 4).

During the evaluation of the lists, it was found that four of the 40 standards could not be considered globally compliant with respect to any or most of the six substances, even though they did not directly violate national legislation. These standards either explicitly restrict themselves to being merely 'informative' with respect to prohibited substances or claim the territorially restricted applicability of national regulations.

In many other cases, standards were globally compliant with regard to some substances, but did not explicitly refer to other regulated substances. There are many possible reasons for this; a substance may not be included into the standard, because the corporation wants it to be used by its suppliers and contract manufacturers without restrictions, or because the use of the substance in materials, parts, and products is regarded as improbable—or is just ignored.

It also had to be considered in the evaluation that both the public and private regulation of substance risks is a dynamic process. In terms of time, global compliance is not a fixed category, but constantly changes alongside the publication of new laws and regulations and the issuing of new and amendment of existing corporate standards. As the requirements of the RoHS Directive for hazardous substances in electrical and electronic equipment have only been applicable from 1 July 2006, at the time of the evaluation of the standards, no corporation was formally obliged to adhere to these requirements. Still, it has been considered in the empirical analysis whether or not the standards have already been adapted to the obligations of the Directive.

There is no common standard for corporate substance lists as to which substances should be included. Hence the substances covered by the individual standards vary to a great extent. Some substances irrelevant for the sector may be included, or other relevant substances may be left out. Substance bans are thus only useful as indicators of legal compliance if the use of the substances is relevant for the sector and has not been abandoned for other reasons.

But even if an evaluation is restricted to those relevant substances, considerable differences can be found. These variations do not necessarily imply that the corporation positively decided not to regulate a certain substance. They could in some cases be explained by the differences in the range of substances considered relevant for the individual corporate profile with respect to manufactured products and contracted suppliers.

1. *Transnationalisation of Regulatory Standards*

Compliance with environmental law presupposes knowledge of the regulatory basis. Environmental management systems, like ISO 14001 and other environmental management schemes, therefore require documentation and regular updates on all relevant regulations. In almost half the standards, such regulatory information is given, either in the form of reference lists, or in a special column of the restricted substance list, often referring to legal norms as reasons for the inclusion of a substance. Such references also enable the supplier to independently keep track of regulatory developments. A review of all the standards shows considerable differences concerning detail and precision. Often, no accurate first-hand knowledge seems to be available for the main jurisdictions of the global market—and sometimes even for the domestic jurisdiction of the corporation.

Hence, reasons for substance bans given in standards can also be misleading. In many cases, companies declare bans or other measures to control substance risk as their own demands, even if they are legally required to do so. Typical examples are the labelling requirement for nonylphenol, which is given in Directive 67/548/EEC, and for polychlorinated naphthalenes, which even require authorisation according to the Japanese Chemical Substance Control Law. Restrictions on formaldehyde and dioxin, given in the German Ordinance on the Prohibition of Chemicals, as well as in Swedish and Austrian regulations, are also passed as own self-regulatory standards in many corporate lists. Some standards base restrictions on other self-regulatory standards or customer requirements. The ban of short-chain chlorinated paraffins, for example, is based on the German Blue Angel Mark and a Swedish eco-label for office equipment emissions, because, as it is explained, 'no laws and regulations regulate this category of hazardous substances', whereas the existing Dutch regulation is ignored (Maxim Integrated Products and Dallas Semiconductors, nd).

On the other hand, in some corporate standards for certain substances, regulations are given that do not exist, are outdated, or do not apply to the substance or its application. The standard of a US manufacturer of mobile phones bans PBDEs, based on 'Canadian Regulation' (Motorola, 2005). However, no Canadian regulation for PBDEs as yet exists, although voluntary strategies are currently developed in cooperation with the industry.[20] A Californian manufacturer of computer processors and chipsets bans all uses of mercury except for lamps and relays, switches, contacts, and guards, basing this on Directive 89/677/EEC, even though this Directive only restricts uses of mercury not relevant for the electronics sector, like anti-fouling paints, wood preservation, textile impregnation, or water treatment.

In one case, a Japanese electronics corporation refers to a non-existent EU Directive to explain the ban of polychlorinated naphthalenes, without considering that there exists the Japanese authorisation requirement and the Swiss prohibition.

Possible reasons for this lack of knowledge are the fragmentation of the regulatory framework for economic transactions in production and marketing networks, poor transparency of regulatory requirements—even though the recent development of online resources facilitates research of national legislation—and insufficient doctrinal reflection of the global legal regime for chemical products by environmental lawyers. Compared with these deficiencies, the resulting material contents of the corporate standards are, at least at first sight, nevertheless relatively homogenous and comprehensive.

a) Global Compliance with Product Quality Standards Most requirements of corporate standards concern problematic substances in the finished product. Typical product standards, which can be found in the lists of almost every corporation, are restrictions or bans on asbestos, PCBs, ozone-depleting substances, some heavy metals, and certain brominated flame retardants.[21]

A corporate standard is considered as globally compliant if it adopts the most ambitious product-related public regulations relevant for a substance which is used in the production chain. Not globally compliant, in this sense, are corporate substance lists adopting a standard only for products destined for the territory where the regulation formally applies. As demonstrated in Table 4, global compliance with public product regulation can only partly be found in corporate standards.

[20] See the official website of the Canadian Ministry of Environment (http://www.ec.gc.ca/CEPARegistry/documents/subs_list/PBDE_draft/PBDEfaq.cfm, last visited 21 February 2007).

[21] Other potential candidates for corporate bans and restrictions include polychlorinated terphenyls, pesticides like DDT or mirex, azo dyes, phthalates, polychlorinated naphthalenes, short-chain chlorinated paraffins, organotin compounds, ethylene glycol ethers, perfluoroorganic compounds and radioactive substances.

Table 4: Corporate Standards Compliant with Selected Jurisdictions

Highest Regulatory Standard			**Global Compliance of Corporate Standards*:**	
Jurisdiction	**Substance (group)**	**Regulation type and date****	**Domestic**	**Foreign**
EU			Standards of EU firms (9)	Standards of non-EU firms (31)
	PBDEs	BAN 01/03	6	28
	Lead and compounds	BAN 01/03	5	18
NL	SCCPs***	RES 11/99	3	14
Japan			Standards of Japanese firms (18)	Standards of non-Japanese firms (22)
	Polychlorinated naphthalenes	DIS 1988	16	7
United States	Offshore production using CFCs		Standards of US firms (11)	Standards of non-US firms (29)
		DIS 11/90	6	8

Notes:

* Figures relate to those of the 40 analysed standards positively considered as globally compliant, regarding the current regulation of a specific substance—other standards do not necessarily violate the law! For example, some of the standards found on the internet could not be considered globally compliant, as they were issued before the publication of the RoHS Directive and did not therefore include its obligations; other standards do not list the substance in question for whatever reason, or have only informatory status.

** 'BAN' = prohibition of substance for electrical and electronic equipment; 'RES' = threshold limit level for product applications requirement; 'DIS' = authorisation, notification, or labelling duties. The dates give the month/year of formal publication of the regulation.

*** Short-chain chlorinated paraffins.

This raises doubt regarding a linear perception of the trading-up process: the horizontal transfer of norms should be seen as a selective and interactive process rather than as inevitable determination. Even in the domestic context, sociologists of law have stressed the difference between law in the books and law in action, and questioned the effectiveness of legal regulation, as they usually found low compliance rates in empirical studies. Hence, it should come as no surprise that the rates of global compliance are even slightly lower than those of domestic compliance. While full global compliance of corporate standards seems to be an ideal rather than a reality, a more qualitative evaluation of the standards shows that there is still a significant influence of national public regulation on global corporate standards.

Polybrominated Diphenyl Ethers (PBDEs) With respect to the ban on PBDEs, only six of the 40 corporate standards were not globally compliant. Standards of corporations outside the EU were no less compliant than standards of EU corporations. Apart from three standards of EU firms that are not globally compliant in any single case for lack of a definite normative binding character, only one Japanese, one British, and one Canadian corporation standards were not considered as 'globally compliant' with the RoHS prohibitions, as they only required substitution without a definite deadline. As these standards had been researched about a year before the prohibitions of the Directive were to be applied, this can be considered a good rate of global compliance. Nevertheless, it should be noted that regarding a PBDE ban, not as much seems to be at stake for the electrical and electronic equipment industry. Most of its applications have already been phased out, and for the remaining applications alternatives exist, albeit not necessarily less problematic ones than PBDEs. Often other brominated flame retardants are used as flame retardants, for example in printed circuit boards, which are also substances of concern (Lohse and Lißner *et al*, 2003: 100*ff*). Moreover, certain voluntary industrial initiatives for PBDEs have existed in Europe since the 1980s (Leisewitz and Schwarz, 2001: 37*ff*). In the United States in 2003, the only domestic manufacturer of two chemicals of the PBDE group declared that production would be stopped by the end of 2004 after the US EPA had recommended a phasing-out.[22] In the meantime several US States, as well as the federal US EPA, initiated regulation procedures concerning PBDEs.

Apart from lead, the other substances prohibited by the RoHS Directive—mercury, cadmium, hexavalent chromium, and PBBs—show similar results. At least regarding their application in mobile phones, they either are not functionally required or are easily substituted.[23]

Lead Compared with the other substances prohibited by the Directive, listed above, many fewer corporations have adopted the requirements of the RoHS Directive for the use of lead in electronic and electrical equipment in standards governing their worldwide transactions with business partners. However, two thirds of the EU, and more than half the non-EU, corporate standards have already integrated the ban on lead. Many of the foreign standards are directly influenced by the EU Directive. This can be concluded from at least five Japanese standards which more or less literally repeat the exemptions of the Directive's Annex.

It is even more rewarding to look closely at those cases where no global compliance could be assumed. The prohibition on lead in solder in the EU

[22] See http://www.epa.gov/oppt/pbde/pubs/qanda.htm, last visited 21 February 2007.

[23] Guidance Document—Environmentally Sound Management of Used and End-Of-Life Mobile Phones, Basel Convention 'Mobile Phone Partnership Initiative', Draft, March 2006, http://www.basel.int/industry/mppiwp/guid-comment/guidoc200406.pdf, last visited 21 February 2007.

RoHS-Directive is sometimes ignored by competent and well-informed corporate leaders, such as Intel or Samsung. Instead of adopting the prohibition, these firms first require disclosure of the presence of lead in electronic parts and materials, probably to get an overview of actual uses and substitution possibilities. This may also be regarded as a more realistic approach to preparation for full compliance, as a text passage in the IBM standard shows. According to IBM, the maximum concentration level requirements of the RoHS Directive are still not established. Therefore, IBM requires of its suppliers only disclosure of the presence of lead in all materials, parts, and products supplied for IBM applications. However, IBM already reserves the right to introduce 'other more stringent IBM specifications' that may supersede the disclosure requirement (IBM, 2003).

Other companies are even more explicit on the problems they face with the strict requirement of lead substitution in most electronic and electrical equipment applications:

> Maxim will continue to supply leaded parts to customers that prefer leaded parts, therefore lead will not be totally eliminated from solder and surface finish operations. Customers demanding lead-containing parts are typically those that are not impacted by European legislation … . In addition, the technology to eliminate lead from certain products has not been developed and proven acceptable for commercial applications. Flip chip and BGA products currently have no lead free alternatives' (Maxim Integrated Products and Dallas Semiconductors, nd).

At the same time, this citation implies that some customers of the electronics industry still supply regionally restricted markets.

Short-chain Chlorinated Paraffins (SCCPs) Short-chain chlorinated paraffins are persistent, bio-accumulative pollutants with adverse effects on marine organisms. Therefore, the Parcom Decision 95/1 demanded a two-step phasing-out process lasting until 2004, of short-chain chlorinated paraffins, used for example as flame retardants and plasticisers. However, this decision remained ineffective, as it was apparently only transposed into national law by the Netherlands. Even this Netherlands transposition has been only partly approved by the European Commission as it was considered to be not in compliance with Directive 76/769/EEC.[24]

Short-chain chlorinated paraffins are listed in only 29 of the 40 corporation standards. Even according to the standards of Royal Philips Electronics, the only corporation in the sample with its corporate headquarters in the Netherlands, short-chain chlorinated paraffins are only banned by the specifications of certain product divisions. It is striking to see that the standards

[24] See Commission Decision 2004/1/EC of 16 December 2003 concerning national provisions on the use of short-chain chlorinated paraffins, notified by the Kingdom of the Netherlands under Article 95(4) of the EC Treaty.

of EU corporations show even less compliance (3 out of 9) than those of non-EU corporations (14 out of 31). This could be due to the fact that the Dutch law on SCCPs is disputed in Europe and that corporate standards are directly influenced or even explicitly refer to the Decision 95/1 of the Paris Commission, although this is an act of public international law formally addressed at states only.

Polychlorinated Naphthalenes Regarding polychlorinated naphthalenes there is a high compliance rate in Japan: of 18 corporate standards, 16 prohibit the substance group, and the remaining two require disclosure of information so that authorisation requirements can be fulfilled. In contrast, less than half of the non-Japanese corporate standards are globally compliant in that they explicitly ban the substance or require disclosure. However, the substance group, which had been historically in use in the electronic industry for transformer and capacitor fluids (even before PCBs were introduced) and in electroplating, was phased out in the late 1970s in the United States and in the 1980s in most of Europe (van de Plassche and Schwegler, 2002; Santillo and Johnston, 2004). In Europe it is today classified as a low production volume substance, with only one French supplier.[25] Additionally, even though the information on national regulatory requirements worldwide has improved enormously since the emergence of the internet, Japanese laws are still difficult to track down and exist only in provisional translations into English.[26] It may well be that the substance group (and its Japanese regulation) was not considered relevant enough to be included in non-Japanese corporate standards.

b) Extra-territorial Use of Production-Standards Standards aimed at the regulation of production risks could also be disseminated horizontally to other jurisdictions, if they were included into corporate product standards. This could mitigate the stark contrast often drawn between the ambitious harmonisation of product regulation and the 'race to the bottom' effects of production regulation.

However, the evaluated standards showed rather diverse results regarding such production requirements. Some corporate standards explicitly exclude substances used in the manufacturing processes of suppliers.[27] Other corporations are often not only concerned with the contents of their products,

[25] See the ESIS-database (http://ecb.jrc.it/esis/, last visited 21 February 2007).

[26] See the Japanese Law Concerning the Evaluation of Chemical Substances and Regulation of Their Manufacture, etc (http://www.meti.go.jp/english/information/downloadfiles/cChemicalControl.pdf) and its enforcing ordinance (http://www.meti.go.jp/english/information/downloadfiles/kashin1.pdf), last visited 21 February 2007.

[27] For example, 'Chemical substances used for the production of the Purchased Goods are not subject to chemical substance control, on condition that the chemical substances are used only for processing at the suppliers or the contractors of the suppliers and the chemical substances do not remain in the Purchased Goods.' (Nippon Chemi-Con Corporation, 2003).

but also with the regulation of production processes, especially with respect to auxiliary substances. A number of corporate standards therefore extend all bans and restrictions to all substances used in manufacturing processes of suppliers and contract manufacturers.

Nevertheless, both extreme positions—that corporations either explicitly take no responsibility at all or they take full responsibility for all substances used by business partners—seem to be the exception. The general rule is rather an intermediate level of responsibility for substances used in the production processes of other economic agents in the supply chain. Ten corporate standards therefore include restrictions for certain auxiliary substances, especially ozone-depleting substances and ethylene glycol ethers.

Intel even distinguishes between suppliers and contract manufacturers ('OEMs') and has stricter standards for auxiliary chemicals used in the production processes of contract manufacturers. This shows even more differentiated levels of responsibility: basic responsibility for suppliers manufacturing only parts and materials; increased responsibility for business partners manufacturing products which bear the lead firm's label; and full responsibility for substances included in their own products or for auxiliary substances used by the lead firm itself.

Other standards avoid the issue of auxiliary substances used in the manufacturing processes of business partners or leave the question open.

CFCs and Other Ozone-depleting Substances The most important group of auxiliary substances which are regulated in corporate standards are ozone-depleting substances, commonly used as solvents in the production of semiconductors. In some standards, these are the only substances prohibited in manufacturing processes of 'upstream' business partners. An evaluation of such a ban on CFCs and other ozone-depleting substances should take into account that a phasing-out of CFCs as halogenated solvents has been on the political and industrial agenda at least since the 1980s. The Montreal Protocol required some ozone-depleting substances to be phased out by the late 1990s. The US Clean Air Act required in Section 604(b) a complete phasing out of the production of CFCs for the domestic market before the year 2000. The European Union and Japan both implemented the Montreal Protocol in the 1990s. The production and use of ozone-depleting substances had thus been heavily regulated before the analysed standards were issued.

However, it does make sense for corporations to regulate the use of ozone-depleting substances as auxiliary substances in manufacturing processes of suppliers and contract manufactures: as conceded in Article 5 of the Montreal Protocol, CFCs can still be produced for export to developing countries for their basic domestic purposes.[28] The obligations of the

[28] See also s 604(e) of the US Clean Air Act.

Protocol or national regulation may thus be circumvented by the offshore outsourcing of manufacturing processes to developing countries or even countries not signatories to the Protocol. Corporations banning these substances from the manufacturing processes of their products and components therefore commit themselves to resisting such circumvention. Further, other ozone-depleting substances like HCFCs are still in common use as CFC substitutes and a complete phasing-out according to the Montreal Protocol will only be required by 2030. Yet several US, European, and Japanese standards already now ban the use of HCFCs as auxiliary substances.

Bans may concern all or some of the substances listed in the annexes to the Montreal Protocol. Corporate standards sometimes use a distinction between two classes of ozone-depleting substances (basically CFCs and HCFCs), which does not follow the classification in the annexes to the Montreal Protocol, but corresponds to Sections 601*ff* of the US Clean Air Act.[29] Section 611(d) of the Clean Air Act requires under certain conditions the labelling of products manufactured with CFCs and some other substances. The use of HCFCs can also lead to labelling requirements, if a petition based on adequate data is accepted by the public administration. As mentioned above, the Intel standard distinguishes between the manufacturing processes of suppliers and those of contract manufacturers: while for contract manufacturers the use of all ozone-depleting substances in manufacturing processes is prohibited, suppliers just have to avoid the use of CFCs and some other especially problematic substances.

In the IBM standard, a clear reason is given for the inclusion of standards for the manufacturing processes of the suppliers: 'the use of certain materials in manufacturing materials, parts, and products for IBM applications may restrict IBM's ability to market products in certain countries or jurisdictions' (IBM, 2003). In particular, the prohibition of such substances in manufacturing processes helps to avoid potential labelling duties contained in Section 611 of the US Clean Air Act. However, only one of the corporate standards requires disclosure of ozone-depleting substances. It seems that the requirement to label products manufactured by means of ozone-depleting substances is so unattractive to many manufacturers that they would rather completely prohibit those substances.

Still, only 14 out of the 40 standards explicitly ban CFCs from the manufacturing processes of suppliers or contract manufacturers. This relatively low rate of explicit compliance could be explained by the fact that the obligations of the Clean Air Act are rather restrictively applied (only to the manufacturing processes of the manufacturer, not to those of suppliers). Therefore, most of the standards concerning the use of ozone-depleting substances in

[29] According to the US Clean Air Act, Class I substances include CFCs and halons, as well as carbon tetrachloride and methyl chloroform listed in annexes A and B to the Montreal Protocol; Class II covers the HCFCs in annex C, group I of the Protocol.

manufacturing processes may be characterised by self-regulation rather than compliance.

2. *Anticipatory Effect of Regulatory Standards*

The horizontal transfer of standards can partly be understood as a factual result of compliance with formal product legislation of various markets. An example of more autonomous forms of private self-regulation are standards anticipating either existing legal acts, regulations not yet in force (early compliance), or public debates and political initiatives on substances of concern which have not even yet led to regulatory outcome (voluntary standards).

a) Early Compliance In some cases, corporations are demanding their suppliers to substitute certain substances earlier than legally required. While for the RoHS Directive of the EU the original compliance deadline was 1 July 2006, almost half the Japanese and US corporations, and one European corporation, set earlier target dates for substitution. These periods of early compliance range from a few months to more than three years. Only six (mostly German) corporations explicitly stick to the legal date. The fact that many German corporations take a formalistic attitude corresponds to their conception of the standards having a merely informatory character. Other corporations do not give any specific date of compliance, or state that they already comply. It is argued that a reason for fulfilling requirements in advance is that this alone will 'ensure a successful transition' to compliance with the RoHS Directive (HP, 2005). This reason is of special relevance if both manufacturers and suppliers are situated outside the EU: in this case the implementation process has to be organised without the administrative infrastructure provided by public authorities and industry associations in the EU. Effective compliance is then only possible if production networks do not stick to a passive attitude of formalistic compliance. Often, complex transition processes provoked by public regulation are difficult to control and predict. Therefore, margins of safety have to be introduced in order to check out and control the implementation process and thereby guarantee effective compliance. Within the transition period an active implementation process must be organised by the lead firms of the production networks.

b) Voluntary Standards for Substances of Concern Some requirements found in corporate standards are not based on existing public regulation at all. For example, the use of certain glycol ethers is forbidden in several cases in production processes and products. In many other cases they are categorised as restricted, reportable, or controlled substances.

Only under the German workplace standard TRGS 609 is the substitution (as far as possible) of methylene and ethylene glycol ethers and their acetates required. They are not to be used by young or pregnant workers, and special measures must be taken to reduce workplace exposure. They are also classified as dangerous according to Directive 67/548/EEC, with the result that disclosure is legally required within the EU.

However, the corporate standards go beyond these restrictions. The far-reaching commitment to prohibit their use not only within the corporation itself, but also to ban them in the production processes of business partners may have resulted from the considerable scandalising potential of these substances: they are highly teratogenic and therefore pose a serious threat, especially to pregnant workers and their unborn babies. According to a reference in one standard, the semiconductor industry has voluntarily committed itself to the phasing out of ethylene glycol ethers in manufacturing processes. Considering the extensive offshore outsourcing to South-East Asia in semiconductor production, it is not surprising that public authorities of OECD countries tend to avoid direct regulation and prefer alternatives without territorial restrictions such as voluntary commitments by industry associations or single companies.

Another example concerns perfluoralkyl sulfonates, which are sometimes prohibited in corporate standards. This is a case of self-regulation anticipating already initiated regulatory projects, as the US EPA prepares a significant new use rule under the Toxic Substances Control Act.[30]

In various other corporate standards, substances like PVCs, phthalates, formaldehyde, and so on are banned, but only in singular cases, so that no clear patterns have emerged.

Most corporate requirements that exceed legal obligations do not concern bans, but are rather soft instruments such as disclosure requirements or recommendations to search for substitutes.

In the context of the Basel Convention, there is a voluntary initiative on waste mobile phones, including the reduction of hazardous substances.[31] In 2006, this initiative led to detailed guidelines on product development and design, collection of waste mobile phones, transboundary movement of collected mobile phones, refurbishment and recycling.[32] However, compared to corporate standards these guidelines are less binding, as they only consist of recommendations for the sound management of waste mobile phones.

c) Procedural Requirements Beyond Legal Compliance The substantial demand that certain substances, for example those listed in the Montreal Protocol, shall not be used in the manufacturing process, even if they are not

[30] See http://www.epa.gov/EPA-TOX/2006/April/Day-10/t3400.htm, last visited 21 February 2007.

[31] Basel Convention on the Control of Transboundary Movements of Hazardous Wastes and their Disposal (http://www.basel.int, last visited 9 February 2008).

[32] See the 'Mobile Phone Partnership Initiative' under the Basel Convention (http://www.basel.int/industry/mppi/documents.html, last visited 9 February 2008).

found in the final products, is often combined with the procedural requirements for environmental management systems. These procedural requirements are not required by law.

More than half of the standards, especially those of Japanese and US corporations, require the certification of an environmental management system for all their suppliers. In many cases, these certifications could either be made according to introduced systems like ISO 14001, or according to individual specifications or minimum requirements given in questionnaires attached to the corporate standards.

3. *Interorganisational Aspects of Corporate Standards*

Compliance with product-related standards directly relevant for the physical qualities of the product itself requires cooperation throughout the supply chain from the raw materials to the finished consumer product. Manufacturers and their suppliers thus try to integrate environmental and health standards into supply chain management.

Production network structures and interorganisational standards can therefore help to spread standards globally and across different industry sectors. This is made possible by complex interdependencies between the actors within the corporate production networks. It is precisely this open organisational structure of the networks that helps to spread standards to all linked firms (see also Teubner, 2005: 116).

The analysed corporate standards are used by different actors in the supply chain. They are not necessarily restricted to distinct industry sectors. For example, companies of the electronics industry also refer to standards of the automotive sector, and manufacturers of polymers must adhere to the standards of the relevant sectors producing consumer goods depending on their customers. Thus, corporate standards are not restricted to one business sector but may spread across the whole global market.

Reference to other corporate standards, which can often be found in corporate substance lists, shows how suppliers 'cascade the requirements' (Motorola, 2005) to sub-tier suppliers without direct contractual relationship with the producer of the final consumer product, so that the entire supply chain is confronted with the standard of lead firms. Also, some standards directly address the responsibility of the suppliers. This means that suppliers are not only obliged to comply with the material standards, for example where they have to substitute lead in certain applications, but they also have to assure that their own suppliers stick to the standards of the customer. This can be even more ambitious where not only product standards but production standards also come into play, as in the case of IBM.

The full impact of this cascading effect is only understood when business relations are not visualised as linear value chains, but rather as complex production networks: customers multiply the circulation of a standard if they have multiple inputs from many suppliers. In addition, due to economies of scale, a supplier with many customers will also proliferate his customers' standards effectively by selling complying products to all other customers. In the electronics and the automotive sector, recent structural changes have led to the emergence of influential 'first tier suppliers'. Often these suppliers are supplying system components to more than one final assembler and therefore have comparable economic power. They often develop product design as well as production standards in close cooperation with their customers (Womack *et al*, 1990: 146*ff*). These characteristics are not only typical for the electronics and automotive sector, as corporate networks in various other sectors are marked by close business relationships with intense cooperation and control.[33]

Still, in most cases the final product manufacturer will take the initiative for developing standards. This is also demonstrated by the fact that the standards found were mostly those of leading final product manufacturers. One possible explanation for this fact may be that these lead firms engage in brand-building and are more exposed to a critical public that holds multinational corporations globally responsible for their business partners' actions. This has led to the widespread use of corporate codes of conduct and environmental and social reporting for big multinational corporations.[34]

But, even if standards are unilaterally set by the manufacturer, suppliers do not necessarily accept them. An interview partner from a corporation supplying system components for the automotive industry reported that they did not accept one customer's threshold level for a certain substance and wanted to renegotiate the contract. According to the supplier, which had not been consulted beforehand in this case, the threshold value for the substance was later changed by the customer, a well-known US automobile manufacturer.[35]

Rather than establishing pre-modern informal social bonds between business partners, the organisation of customer–supplier relations in modern industrial production seems to be characterised by formalised routines. Systems of monitoring, benchmarking, and certification encourage the participation of suppliers in product and production design and set a common framework for collective learning processes (Sabel, 1994). These routines generate, and continuously enhance, interorganisational standards that are essential to ensure an integrated quality management throughout the supply chain.

Thus, the hierarchically structured corporation of mass production, as famously conceived and implemented by Henry Ford, has neither been

[33] For a comprehensive overview see the contributions in Gereffi and Korzeniewicz, 1994.

[34] See, with further references, the contributions by Eva Kocher and Oren Perez; for corporate codes of conduct see also Martin Herberg, all in this volume (chs 3, 6, and 1, respectively).

[35] Interview with a supplier of electronic system components for the automotive industry, Frankfurt am Main, 25 February 2005.

replaced by anonymous arm's-length markets nor by hierarchically structured supply chains with standards exclusively determined by lead firms.

E. Summary

The empirical study shows that most corporate leaders of transnational business networks are not passive subjects of the law, but are actively selecting legal norms, taking the law into their own hands, or adapting standards according to their particular needs. At the same time, corporate actors often use legal regulation at the national level as a reference point which provides them with normative orientation. The results therefore confirm the assumption that private product standards in the transnational field are neither characterised by a formal application of national regulation nor by forms of autonomous self-regulation which are completely out of touch with state-based law.

The term 'proactive compliance' may sound too optimistic regarding the quantitative rates of explicit compliance. Regarding the selective application of laws and the wide self-regulatory scope, corporate standards seem to have an appropriative rather than a proactive character. However, a more thoroughgoing qualitative analysis showed that in cases of lower (or less anticipatory) compliance, the concerned substances were either no longer used in the sector, so that they were not considered relevant and therefore not included into corporate substances lists (for example polychlorinated naphthalenes) or, in the case of lead, for some applications, no technical substitute had been developed until the standards were issued. Therefore leading firms first aimed at getting an overview over the actual use of the substance and thus required disclosure—possibly as a first step of the implementation process. In the case of ozone-depleting substances, the labelling requirements of the US Clean Air Act have been applied very restrictively by the US EPA. It is therefore no wonder that the impact on non-US corporations has been relatively low.

The empirical study supports our theory of anticipatory effect more obviously than that of global compliance, which might result from the fact that the analysis (regarding the early implementation of the RoHS Directive) is methodically less difficult. The phenomenon of anticipatory compliance also shows how the distinction between compliance and self-regulation can become blurred: on the one hand, it seems impossible to change the contents of a complex product from one day to the next; on the other hand, it can hardly be determined exactly how far in advance the conversion process should start. Some standards even banned the use of substances immediately after the EU Directive was published. This also shows that multinational corporations often do not stick to legal norms in a formalistic manner, but rather take requirements as a rough orientation for their own autonomous standards.

The cases of 'true' self-regulation, that is private standards for substances of concern not yet regulated, share this anticipatory characteristic, as they often appear in the context of regulatory initiatives, whether these be at the national or international level. Corporate self-regulatory standards often explicitly put forward this reason as a purpose for self-regulation, for example: 'These lists ... have been compiled to meet existing and anticipated legal requirements and market demands' (Ericsson, 2003).

However, just as compliance and self-regulation are often seen in combination, the most important motives for developing the standards, namely 'observing the law' and 'protecting the environment', are more or less interchangeable: it could not be found that different argumentations in the section of the standards on 'purpose' correlate with more or less stringent standards, neither regarding compliance nor self-regulation.

IV. THEORETICAL CONCLUSIONS

The above analysis focuses on the influence of national and European public regulation on corporate standards. Scholars of political science and legal theory often explain private standards in the transnational sphere with reference to factors other than (expected) regulatory requirements. They usually refer to public pressure, generated by civil society agents or by socially and environmentally conscious consumers, fear of litigation, and sometimes also to factors within the corporate sphere, such as the professional ethos of employees (see, for example, Haufler, 2001). It would not make much sense to argue that regulation has priority over these factors. Still, it is interesting to consider what role public regulation can play regarding the other factors.

Litigation has not played an important role so far with regard to chemical risk management in the electronics sector. The same applies for environmentally conscious consumption schemes, such as eco-labels.[36] Regarding public pressure, changing social perceptions of the responsibility of transnational corporations and business networks can play an important role in the development of interorganisational standards dealing with social and ecological issues. This has been witnessed in the clothing industry and sports equipment industry, where big global players like Nike began developing social and environmental codes after massive protests about the working conditions in Asian 'sweatshops'. Even if manufacturing has been outsourced, and is therefore in the hands of legally independent suppliers or contract manufacturers, responsibility for working conditions can still be attributed to transnational corporations. By developing interorganisational ethical

[36] Although the TCO-Label exists for electronic office equipment and has some testing and emission requirements for chemical substances, especially brominated flame retardants, it is rarely referenced in corporate standards: see http://www.tcodevelopment.com/, last visited 21 February 2007.

standards they often accept this responsibility. This was also seen as the only means to protect the image of the brand from attacks by NGOs. Similarly, questions of ecological and social responsibility for offshore production have been raised in the electronics sector. This was shown when substandard practices of recycling and waste disposal in China were publicly documented (Puckett and Smith, 2002).

The risks of product liability, of NGO pressure, and of image-deficits may thus be important driving forces for corporate risk-management in the electronics sector. However, neither a judge nor the average consumer is usually competent and capable enough to decide hard cases and complex mechanisms of toxic risk management. Even if judges or consumer organisations were always able to ask for scientific expertise, it rarely helps to achieve definite certainty. But whenever one of the major jurisdictions imposes a ban on a certain substance or one of its applications, this signals the transformation of arbitrary suspicions within the realm of scientific debate into the solid facts of regulatory policy. In the transnational sphere the probability of classical law enforcement mechanisms may be drastically reduced. That does not make public regulation 'merely symbolic', and thus ineffective. On the contrary, it is exactly the 'symbolic' quality of national regulation that seems to make it so effective in influencing the behaviour of globally operating corporations (Führ, 2003; Berman, 2006: 945*ff*, 951*ff*). These symbolic qualities may have less appeal to public inspectors, who already have restricted means of controlling multinational corporations, but be more appealing to consumers and environmental organisations, the media, or perhaps even juries in US product liability trials. And similarly, on the side of the addressees of legal duties, these symbolic qualities may appeal less to small and medium-sized businesses, which have no public image to lose, but rather to global players with well-recognised brands. Nevertheless, for the credibility of performance within a specific business sector, it seems increasingly important for smaller firms to fulfil certain social and environmental standards (Sabel *et al*, 2000).

The orientation of transnational private standards towards public regulation and the anticipation of public policies are characteristic of a changed relationship between state and private sector, especially concerning multinational corporations. In contrast to the classic hierarchical relationship, the phenomenon of proactive compliance implies that interdependencies between public regulation and corporate standardisation arise from the mutual reliance of globally operating corporations and national legislators. In the field of product risk management, both actors are constrained by the demand to adapt products or product standards to various possible contexts: big corporations tend to design uniform products for the global market, principally complying with all regulatory environments. Similarly, national public authorities have to anticipate the variety of functional contexts of the products to make comprehensive risk assessments and draw regulatory consequences. Agents of the private and public sector are both overburdened by unforeseen—regulatory and technological—developments in the respective other area. To reduce this mutual unpredictability, public and private standards have to be developed in coordination. This presupposes a mutual reflection of the other sector's rationality, that is, each sector has an interest that its objectives are reflected in the other sector's planning. The phenomenon of proactive compliance can accordingly be described as the reflection of national regulation and public interests in corporate standards with global reach, combining elements of regulatory compliance and industrial self-regulation.

REFERENCES

Berman, PS (2006) 'Dialectical Regulation, Territoriality, and Pluralism' 38 *Connecticut Law Review* 929.

Boon, J (2006) 'Stemming the Tide of Patchwork Policies: The Case of E-Waste' 15 *Transnational. Law & Contemporary Problems* 731.

Courtney, R (2006) 'Evolving Hazardous Waste Policy for the Digital Era' 25 *Stanford Environmental Law Journal* 199.

Dilling, O (2005) 'Die Produktionsbedingung als Produkteigenschaft—Ein Fallbeispiel für die Haftung bei Werbung mit ethischen Produktionsstandards nach der Schuldrechtsreform', in Gerd Winter (ed) *Die Umweltverantwortung multinationaler Unternehmen*, (Baden-Baden, Nomos-Verlagsgesellschaft).

Douglas, S and Craig, S (1995) *Global Marketing Strategy* (New York, McGraw-Hill, Inc).

Fischer-Lescano, A and Teubner, G (2006) *Regime-Kollisionen. Zur Fragmentierung des globalen Rechts* (Frankfurt am Main, Suhrkamp Verlag).

Führ, M (2003) *Eigen-Verantwortung im Rechtsstaat* (Berlin, Duncker und Humblot).

Gereffi, G and Korzeniewicz, M (1994) *Commodity Chains and Global Capitalism* (Westport, CN/London, Praeger).

Hall, JC (2001) *Product Design to Reduce Restricted Substances—The experience of brominated flame retardants in vehicle design* (Lund, IIIEE Reports, 2001: 2).

Haufler, V (2001) *A Public Role for the Private Sector* (Washington, DC, Carnegie Endowment for International Peace).

Howse, R and Regan, D 2000: The Product/Process Distinction—An Illusory Basis for Disciplining 'Unilateralism' in Trade Policy *EJIL* 249.

Leisewitz, A and Schwarz, W (2001) *Formulation of proposals for measures to be taken to substitute environmentally relevant flame retardants in printed circuit boards, outer casings for IT and TV appliances and polyurethane insulation and one-component foams* (Frankfurt am Main, UBA).

Lohse, J, Lißner, L, Ahrens, A, Heitmann, K, Lundie, S, Wagner, A, and Wirts, M (2003) *Substitution of Hazardous Chemicals in Products and Processes*, Report for the DG Environment of the EU Commission (Hamburg, Ökopol).

Luhmann, N (1971) 'Die Weltgesellschaft' 57 *Archiv für Rechts- und Sozialphilosophie* 1.

OECD (1997) *Processes and Production Methods (PPMs): Conceptual Framework and Considerations on the Use of PPM-based Trade Measures* (Paris, OECD).

Perez, O (2004) *Ecological Sensitivity and Global Legal Pluralism—Rethinking the Trade and Environment Conflict* (Oxford, Hart Publishing).

Puckett, J and Smith, T (eds) (2002) *Exporting Harm—The High-Tech Trashing of Asia* (San Jose, CA, Silicon Valley Toxics Coalition).
Rehbinder, E and Stewart, R (1985) *Environmental Protection Policy—Integration through Law*, vol 2 (Berlin, de Gruyter).
Sabel, CF (1994) 'Learning by Monitoring. The Institutions of Economic Development', in Neil J Smelser and Richard Swedberg (eds), *The Handbook of Economic Sociology* (Princeton, NJ, Princeton University Press) 137.
Sabel, CF, O'Rourke, D, and Fung, A (2000) *Ratcheting Labor Standards: Regulation for Continuous Improvement in the Global Workplace*, KGS Working Paper No. 00-010 (Harvard, MA, Harvard University).
Sachs, N (2006) 'Planning the Funeral at Birth: Extended Producer Responsibility in the European Union and the United States' 30 *Harvard Environmental Law Review* 51.
Santillio, D and Johnston, P (2004), *An overview of potential ongoing sources of polychlorinated naphtalenes (PCNs) to the marine environment of the North East Atlantic (OSPAR) area*, Greenpeace Research Laboratories—Technical Note 04/2004 (http://www.greenpeace.to/publications/GRL_TN_04_2004.pdf).
Scharpf, FW (1994) 'Mehrebenenpolitik im vollendeten Binnenmarkt' 5 *Staatswissenschaften und Staatspraxis* 457.
Teubner, G (ed) (1997) *Global Law without the State* (Dartmouth, Aldershot).
—— (2005) 'Codes of Conduct multinationaler Unternehmen: Unternehmensverfassung jenseits von Corporate Governance und Mitbestimmung', in C Hohmann-Dennhardt, M Schmidt, and A Seifert (eds), *Arbeitnehmermitwirkung in einer sich globalisierenden Arbeitswelt: Liber Amicorum Manfred Weiss* (Berlin, Berliner Wissenschafts-Verlag) 109.
van de Plassche, E and Schwegler, A (2002) *Polychlorinated Naphthalenes* (Royal Haskoning, The Netherlands (http://www.unece.org/env/popsxg/docs/2000-2003/pcn.pdf).
Vogel, D (1995) *Trading Up—Consumer and Environmental Regulation in a Global Economy* (Cambridge, MA/London, Harvard University Press).
Womack, JP, Jones, DT, and Roos, D (1990) *The Machine that Changed the World: The Story of Lean Production* (New York, Rawson Associates).

APPENDIX—EVALUATED CORPORATE STANDARDS

Agere Systems (2002) 'List of Banned, Restricted and Materials Requiring Disclosure', Issue 2.
Agilent Technologies (2004) 'General Specification for the Environment'.
Bosch Rexroth AG (2004) 'Central Standard—Prohibition and Declaration of Substance—Products components, materials and preparations', ZN 07950-11.
Brother (2002) 'Green Procurement Standard'.
BTExact Technologies (nd) 'GS-12 Standard for Materials Used by Contractors', Issue 8.0.
Canon (2003) 'Green Procurement Standards—Parts and Materials'.
D&M Group (2004) 'Green Procurement Guideline'.
Daikin Industries Ltd (2003) 'Green Procurement Guidelines'.
Electrolux (2005) 'Restricted Materials List'.
Ericsson (2003) 'The Ericsson lists of banned and restricted substances'.
Fujitsu Limited (2003) 'Fujitsu Group Green Procurement Direction'.

Heidenhain (2003) 'Environmentally Compatible Products', Heidenhain Standard HN 373132-1.
Hewlett-Packard (2005) 'General Specification for the Environment', HP Standard 011-0 (GSE), A-5951-1745-1.
IBM (2003) 'Environmental Requirements for Materials, Parts and Products', ES 46G3772.
Intel (2003) 'Environmental Product Content Specification for Suppliers and Outsourced Manufacturers'.
Matsushita (2003) 'Electronic Components Group Chemical Substances Management Guidelines'.
Maxim Integrated Products and Dallas Semiconductors (nd) 'Control of Banned and Restricted Substance Policy', Document ID 10-0300, Revision A.
MEN Mikro Elektronik GmbH (2003) 'Liste verbotener und deklarationspflichtiger Inhaltsstoffe—List of Prohibited and Declarable Substances'.
Minebea Group (2004) 'Green Procurement Standard'.
Motorola (2005) 'Material and Methods Specification', No 12G02897W18 Global Common Specification.
National Semiconductor (2004) 'Corporate Standard Procedure—National Semiconductor's List of Banned and Reportable Substances', (SC) CSP-9-111S2.
NEC Corporation (2005) 'Standards Pertaining to Procurement Restrictions for the Inclusion of Chemical Substances in Products (for Suppliers)', Kankatu-04-006.
Nippon Chemi-Con Corporation (2003) 'Manual for Controlled Chemical Substances', CEM-3558-03A/E.
Nokia (nd) 'Substance List', Version 6.0.
Nortel Networks (2000) 'Environmental Specification'.
Omron Corporation (2004) 'Green Procurement Standards'.
ON Semiconductors (2003) 'Product Chemical Content Brochure', BRD8022/D.
Pioneer Group (2003) 'Environmental Hazardous Substances List'.
Royal Philips Electronics (2004) 'List of Banned Substances', CSO-BP01-2004-1.
Ricoh Company Ltd (2002) 'Ricoh Group's green procurement policy'.
Samsung Electronics (2004) 'Position Paper of Samsung Electronics with regard to the use and phase out of certain substances when appropriate'.
Seiko Epson Group (2003) 'SEG Green Purchasing Standard for Production Material'.
SGI (2001) 'Environmental Assessment and Declaration for Suppliers'.
Sharp Corporation (2001) 'Green Purchasing Guidelines'.
Siemens (2003) 'Umweltverträgliche Produkte—Teil 2: Gefährliche Stoffe, Verbotsliste', Vermeidungsliste, SN 36350-2.
Sony (2004) 'Management Regulations for the Environment-related Substances to be Controlled which are included in Parts and Materials', SS-00259.
Tamura Corporation (2003) 'Green Procurement Standard', ST-S2-1602.
TDK Corporation (2004) 'TDK Green Procurement Standard', TSG-14-01-03.
ULVAC Group (2004) 'IV. List of Surveyed Chemical Substances under Voluntary Control for Green Procurement'.
Yamatake (2004) 'List of target chemical substance groups for Yamatake Group management'.

5

Transnational Management of Hazardous Chemicals by Interfirm Cooperation and Associations[1]

ALEXANDRA LINDENTHAL

I. INTRODUCTION

IN THE CONTEXT of the debate on global governance, political scientists are concerned with the question if, and to what extent, the role of the state has changed and what the driving forces, as well as the consequences, of this development are. Recently, the role of transnational private actors has attracted the interest of students of political science and the discipline recognises that private actors may play a significant role in global governance (Börzel, 2000: 1). This Chapter adheres to this observation. While the major strand of research focuses on public private relationships in global governance (Ronit and Schneider, 2000), this chapter concentrates on questions of self-regulation among private actors. Its field of study is the efforts of corporations in different industries to produce common practices with regard to the management or phasing out of chemicals beyond the borders of nation states. Although business goals are generally different to those of the public sector, this does not mean that certain activities of corporations cannot contribute to the provision of public good (Ronit and Schneider, 2000: 87). Hence, it is argued that the transnational management of chemicals, considered as self-regulation, contributes to a healthy environment (cf Knill and Lehmkuhl, 2002: 86). The firms' self-regulatory practices may contribute to solve global environmental problems and thus may take over functions that were previously assigned to single nation states or international institutions. To handle chemicals in a careful way

[1] The author thanks Olaf Dilling, Martin Herberg, Martin Koch, and Gerd Winter, as well as the members of the law dimension colloquium of the Collaborative Research Center 'Transformations of the State' (cf next footnote) for helpful comments on earlier drafts of this article, and Dörthe Hauschild and Julian Hill for making the text more readable. The author bears responsibility for any shortcomings.

is necessary because of their possibly negative effects on health and the environment. Harmful substances may cause environmental problems if they reach the ecosystem, for example via their usage in consumer goods. Consequently, a safe handling of chemicals is an important condition for a global protection of the environment.

This chapter comprises two main parts. First, the emergence of the transnational management of chemical substances in a particular section of a production chain will be described, with a few examples that constitute different forms of self-regulation.[2] Second, it will be exposed which factors facilitated, and which hindered, the development of the transnational management of chemical substances. Even though common practices have emerged referring to the handling of chemicals, it is sometimes questionable as to what extent these benefit the public interest in environment and health protection.

II. EMPIRICAL EXAMPLES OF THE TRANSNATIONAL MANAGEMENT OF CHEMICALS

Against the background of an increasing disparity between the transnationalisation of trade and the regulatory jurisdiction of nation states, multinational corporations may join forces to solve environmental problems by designing and establishing rules and procedures among themselves that have consequences for the rest of society. Here, their specialised knowledge, and financial and management potential, as well as their transnational organisational structures, may be extremely valuable (cf Messner and Nuscheler, 2003: 16; Cutler *et al*, 1999: 4). It will be shown in the following sections that in specific realms, such as the trade in hazardous products, self-regulation does create suitable arrangements of transnational management.

Focusing on transnational self-arrangements of corporations bearing upon environmental protection is not to say that there is no state-based regulation of chemicals. For example, the European Economic Community adopted the first Directive on classification, packaging, and labelling of dangerous substances as early as 1967 (Directive 67/548/EEC). Since then, chemicals have been a field of intense activity within the EU's environmental policy. With respect to our research, some legal acts are of major importance, such as Directive 2000/53/EC on the management of end-of-life vehicles (the ELV Directive). The Directive stipulates that vehicle manufacturers and material and equipment manufacturers must, among other

[2] The empirical study is based on an analysis of documents as well as on interviews that were conducted with representatives of the automotive and chemical industry. The interviews were carried out together with Olaf Dilling in the context of the research project 'Transnational Governance and International Law' at the Collaborative Research Centre 'Transformations of the State' (University of Bremen).

things, reduce the use of hazardous substances when designing vehicles and make sure that components of vehicles placed on the market after July 2003 do not contain mercury, hexavalent chromium, cadmium, or lead. Further, Directive 2002/95/EC on the restriction of the use of certain hazardous substances in electrical and electronic equipment requires that from July 2006, new electrical and electronic equipment that is placed on the market may not contain lead, mercury, cadmium, hexavalent chromium, or the brominated flame retardants PBBs[3] and PBDEs.[4]

As the state attempts to influence firms' behaviour by setting environmental policy targets and/or by creating a framework designed to promote particular behaviour in private actors, strictly autonomous self-regulation is rare (Rehbinder, 1997: 2). Yet there are a number of possibilities for self-regulation in a broader sense, even when surrounded by state regulation.[5] In the context of the empirical study in this chapter, a variety of modes of self-regulation appeared, including: firms developing systems to notify each other of (new) laws and private standards; firms ensuring that their trading partners complied with legal and private requirements; firms coordinating their behaviour to make compliance with legal requirements possible; firms rectifying their practices prior to any new regulation[6] and even regulating their behaviour in the absence of laws or going beyond existing legal requirements where they were believed to be insufficient. As these coordination processes reach beyond the command of individual states, they can be referred to as a transnational form of self-regulation (cf Ronit, 2001: 568). In terms of modes of governance, self-regulation manifests itself through guidelines in the form of restricted substances lists or assessment requirements and through concrete practices like the handling of safety data sheets or substitution processes (cf Ronit, 2000: 91; Haufler, 2001: 12), as will be shown in the following sections.

The section of the production chain that is central for the empirical study is composed of producers, suppliers, and finishing companies belonging to the chemical and automotive industries. To get a full overview of the management of chemical substances, not only the chemical industry which produces and distributes chemical substances, but also industries using chemicals must be analysed. As will be demonstrated in the following, the automotive industry highlights its commitment to the protection of health and the environment. Whether this industry is able to produce goods which

[3] Polybrominated biphenyls.

[4] Polybrominated diphenyl ethers.

[5] This notion of self-regulation comes close to the concept of 'regulated self-regulation' where both public and private actors own a 'high level of governance capacity'. In contrast, the idea of 'private self-regulation' assumes that the state's capacity to intervene is restricted and private self-regulation is dominant (Knill and Lehmkuhl, 2002: 93).

[6] Differentiating between self-regulation and compliance, Dilling (ch 4, this volume) calls this 'proactive compliance'.

can adequately address these demands depends to a certain degree on the input of its respective suppliers. The automotive industry is of special interest to this study because parts suppliers and global car producers are located in different regions of the world and thus operate under different legal requirements. It remains to be seen how the automotive industry handles this situation in its exchange relationships.

The organisations of the chemical and the automotive industry are formally autonomous but interdependent; they are connected to one another by material as well as by immaterial exchange processes. The firms participating in the production chains share a common goal: the successful production and purchasing of goods. To pursue this goal it is necessary not only to provide materials and parts, but also to exchange information in these matters as well as on applications of chemicals.[7] To obtain information on the management of chemicals, the interactions of some firms of the chemical and automotive industry were analysed. Interviews were conducted with representatives of the chemical industry (producers, distributors, and consultants) and the automotive industry (car manufacturers and parts suppliers) and an analysis of documents was carried out (cf addendum).

In this chapter, I will make some short, exemplary comments on the public's perceptions of the chemical and the automotive industry concerning environmental and health aspects as well as on the industry's reaction to such perceptions. This is to show that the societal embeddedness of industrial sectors is an impetus for self-regulation. Thereafter, some examples of the transnational management of hazardous chemicals will be discussed.

A. Societal Embeddedness of the Chemical and the Automotive Industries

For several decades, chemical corporations have had a 'very bad public image', because 'They are seen as causing environmental hazards' (Ronit, 2000: 84). Especially following some momentous chemical accidents in the past, the public image of the chemical industry has deteriorated. Globally, the most well-known accident was the one in Bhopal (1984) where some thousands of people died and thousands of others were injured when toxic chemicals were released into the atmosphere (Greenpeace, 2004; Nathan and Kovoor-Misra, 2002: 253).[8] The disaster caused widespread consumer protest against the liable chemical manufacturer, and the chemical industry

[7] Cf Gereffi to whom a value chain comprises 'the whole range of activities involved in the design, production, and marketing of a product' (Gereffi, 1999: 38).

[8] The gas explosion in the Indian city of Bhopal is regarded as the worst accident in industry's history. According to Greenpeace, in the first days after the incident 8,000 people died. Since then, more than 20,000 people have died from the direct or indirect consequences of the catastrophe (Greenpeace, 2004).

reacted by establishing Responsible Care, a global programme to ensure the responsible treatment of chemicals (Kollman and Prakash, 2001: 401). This worldwide, voluntary initiative of the chemical industry challenges chemical companies 'to improve all aspects of performance which relate to protection of health, safety and environment' (Druckrey, 1998: 981).[9] Worldwide, chemical corporations at different stages of the value chain are committed to this programme.[10] Chemical corporations allude to their environmental efforts in their company profiles, for example, they emphasise their commitment to the Responsible Care initiative and the idea of sustainable development in general. These environmental and health statements are often linked with declarations on the chemical corporations' web pages that they are in need of societal acceptance and trust.

These efforts by the chemical industry were not enough to bring critical discussions to an end. The risk of some of the substances produced and distributed by the chemical industry to human health and the environment have been further discussed in public. As 'critical observers' of the chemical industry (Ronit and Schneider, 2000: 19), environmental organisations play an important role in spreading information on the risk of substances. An example is polyvinyl chloride (PVC). The mass plastic PVC is a product of chlorine chemistry; it is used in the automotive industry, for example in cables, car undercoatings, and interior components. Not only the production of PVC but also its disposal is ecologically critical. With the entering into force of the ELV Directive in October 2000 this has also become a problem for automotive producers (cf Greenpeace, 1999: 1; 2003: 22). PVC contains flame retardants[11] and phthalates[12]—substances which are a risk to human health. To 'ensure a high level of protection for the environment and human health', Greenpeace demanded that hazardous chemicals like the phthalate DEHP, brominated flame retardants and chlorinated paraffins be 'substituted with less hazardous, or preferably non-hazardous,

[9] One aspect of Responsible Care is product stewardship, where, eg, chemical distributors pledge themselves to offer only products that may be transported, used, and disposed of in a safe way, according to current knowledge (Verband Chemiehandel eV, 2004).

[10] Among them are some of the most well-known producers of chemicals.

[11] According to Greenpeace, brominated flame retardants—eg chlorinated paraffins—are harmful to human health and the environment (Greenpeace, 1999: 4; Greenpeace *et al*, 2004: 2). Chlorinated paraffins 'are used mainly in plastic articles made of PVC, in which they act as a flame retardant and/or plasticiser' (Greenpeace, 2003: 26). The German Bundesumweltamt calls for the substitution of flame retardants that are harmful to health and the environment and especially mentions decabromdiphenylether, which is a component of plastic (http://www.umweltbundesamt.de/uba-info-presse/presse-informationen/p-0155d.htm). The agency also calls for a substitution of chlorinated paraffins (http://www.umweltbundesamt.de/umweltvertraegliche-stoffe/weichmacher.htm).

[12] A widely dispersed phthalate is DEHP (Di-2-ethylhexylphthalat), which is regarded as harmful to health. DEHP is predominantly used in plastic articles made of PVC (Greenpeace, 1999: 3; 2003: 22; BUND, 2005: 1). At the EU level, DEHP was classified as harmful to reproduction. The German Umweltbundesamt calls for a substitution of DEHP in plastics (http://www.umweltbundesamt.de/umweltvertraegliche-stoffe/weichmacher.htm).

alternatives' (Greenpeace, 2003: 3).[13] The PVC industry reacted with a voluntary commitment—to embrace the principles of the Responsible Care initiative—to meet the challenge of sustainable development. Among others, the commitment contains a strategy to improve the product management in all phases of the life cycle of PVC (Vinyl 2010, 2001; 2003).

The self-portrayals of corporations belonging to the automotive industry, concerning their attitudes towards the protection of the environment are similar to those of the chemical industry. On their websites, the automotive producers and their suppliers declare their intention to protect human health and the global environment and their commitment to the concept of sustainable development. One reason for the commitment to sustainable development, as pointed out by one of the global car producers, is that the corporation wants to maintain and expand its societal acceptance. While, in particular, the car producers emphasise their social responsibility, the argumentation of the automotive suppliers is more pragmatic. They argue that 'green' products offer higher performance and that they comply with the highest environmental legal requirements for logistic reasons.[14] As one of our interviewees stated:

> We are of course obligated to observe the law. Because we go global, it's always a global perspective. Anything that could be valid somewhere is immediately a worldwide benchmark for us. For logistic reasons, it wouldn't be practicable to supply different material compositions in different parts of the world… . So, the maximum requirement is valid for us in reality. While one has to say 95% of the laws that get passed are similar or identical. (Interview, February 2006)

Even though there are no environmental or health scandals in the automotive industry (cf Bolli, 2000: 55), the public awareness of the risks associated with substances such as PVC, brominated flame retardants (BFRs), and phthalates also concern the automotive industry as these substances are contained in their products. A recent study of an Austrian environmental protection organisation analysed the contaminant loads in new cars. According to the study, 98 chemicals pollute the air of passenger compartments. Among others, the phthalate DEHP, a potentially carcinogenic plasticiser, was detected (Global 2000, 2005).[15] A study, commissioned by the US environmental protection agency (EPA), on product stewardship

[13] Because PVC is hazardous to health and to the environment, Greenpeace demands an end to the use of cables containing PVC and points to the fact that there are alternatives which are more environmentally friendly (Greenpeace, 1999).

[14] Bolli points out that for automotive suppliers, 'the environment has become an important competitive issue. It is vital for them to declare the ecological properties of their products, otherwise they are out of business' (Bolli, 2000: 63).

[15] All of the detected substances were put on the market before 1981—hence they belong to the group of 'existing chemicals'. The difference between new and existing chemicals is that 'While new chemicals have to be tested before they are placed on the market, there are no such provisions for existing chemicals' (European Commission, 2004).

opportunities within the automotive industry, showed that car manufacturers and suppliers recognised BFRs[16] and PVC as important issues. The use of these materials is reduced in several applications. In cases where they are still used, alternative design and materials exist or are under development (Five Winds International, 2003: 11, 83–7). A study on the experience of BFRs in vehicle design showed that at least one of the companies interviewed regarded the use of these substances in vehicles as a high risk for the company image (Hall, 2001: 36).[17] On the other hand, as one of our interviewees explained, the reason to stop the use of PVC was because the corporation wanted to reduce fire hazards in its production plants (interview, November 2004).

B. International Material Data System/Global Automotive Declarable Substance List

The development of the automotive industry's international material data system (IMDS) and the development of the global automotive declarable substance list (GADSL) are illustrative examples of the industry-spanning management of chemical substances. IMDS was developed by European and US car producers and came into operation in June 2000. Meanwhile, Asian car manufacturers committed themselves to this system.[18] IMDS, a voluntary industry-led initiative, files and administers information on all materials used in the automotive manufacturing chain and stores chemical information (Fisher, 2005). It is the aim of this initiative to collect data on chemical substances that are part of the automobiles produced. Suppliers have to generate these data, because they are requested by law and/or by their customers' delivery conditions.[19] This system is designed to make compliance with the national and international standards and laws concerning hazardous substances for automobile producers and their suppliers easier. For instance, the IMDS makes it easier to comply with the ELV Directive. This Directive requests that vehicle manufacturers provide authorised treatment facilities with comprehensive information, in particular about hazardous materials, in order to facilitate the dismantling and recovery of end-of-life vehicles.[20] Further, this system is helpful

16 Eg the study shows that the automotive industry is moving away from using the flame retardants PBDE and PBB.

17 Hall deduces that this indicates that automotive companies 'must be responding to some consumer pressure on the use of BFR [brominated flame retardants]' (Hall, 2001: 36).

18 International Material Data System (www.mdsystem.com).

19 Recently, most automakers in the U.S., the European Union and Japan require their suppliers to disclose all materials used in vehicles by entering this data into an international materials database system (IMDS) (Five Winds International, 2003: 10).

20 German car manufacturers, especially, opposed the European Commission's proposal because they feared additional costs of this 'EU car take back legislation' (Bolli, 2000: 53). A study on product stewardship within the US automotive industry says: 'The ELV Directive

for automobile producers because if a substance of concern is prohibited by law, a producer knows which of its suppliers uses this substance and can call on them to remove the substance from their products (Johnson Controls, 2001). The suppliers using the database are able to monitor the substances contained in their products. If a customer has questions regarding the composition of product parts, the supplier should be able to answer them. In reality, this can sometimes be complicated as the following statement shows:

> We can look into the data for any product by means of a complete pedigree—provided that the data are available, which is more difficult for old parts than for new ones. (Interview, February 2005)

To simplify the communication and exchange of information concerning the usage of substances in car parts at different stages of the production chain, the international Global Automotive Stakeholders Group (GASG) has been formed. It consists of automobile producers, and suppliers of the automotive and chemical industries. To meet its objective, the GASG developed the Global Automotive Declarable Substance List (GADSL).[21] The GADSL, implemented in 2005, is a globally harmonised list of declarable substances.

The accomplishment of this list was not easy, because some of the suppliers were not willing to pass information on to the car producers. For example, manufacturers of plastics used in the production of automobiles argued that raw materials for polyurethane could not be revealed because the protection of the know-how of a product should be ensured (Fachverband Schaumstoffkunststoffe eV, 2003). To tackle the issue of confidentiality between car producers and suppliers, individual agreements can be used, as another case revealed in our interviews shows: one global automotive producer practises bilateral non-disclosure agreements in order to assure that suppliers reveal the chemical substances contained in their products (interview, March 2005).

In spite of the difficulties in coming to an agreement, those firms which were really interested in the issue came together and did reach a consensus. One interviewee emphasised that his corporation appreciated the list because it was able to contribute to it and because it is a 'synopsis of all global material requests' concerning both legal demands and requirements

in the European Union is, to some extent, driving activities of manufacturers, suppliers and end-of-life managers in the US' (Five Winds International, 2003: 34). Currently, automotive suppliers domiciled in the US tend to comply with the ELV Directive and adapt their lists of substances of concern to it. Hence, 'Requirements within the ELV Directive are an important driver for the automotive industry on a global scale' (*ibid*). Of course, this can be explained by the fact that all manufacturers selling automobiles into the EU have to comply with the ELV Directive.

[21] GADSL (http://www.mdsystem.com/).

from the car producers (interviews, February/March 2005). Complying with this list means complying with both legal and private standards; hence, this list is an important aid for the suppliers. Before the GADSL and its forerunner, the less successful International List of Reportable Substances,[22] each automobile producer developed individual lists of restricted substances. As a consequence, suppliers had to report in relation to multiple lists (interview, February 2005).

The decision to list a substance on the GADSL is based on clear criteria. A substance is listed if it is already regulated, is expected to be regulated by a governmental agency,[23] or if it is demonstrated—by testing under OECD guidelines—'that the substance may be associated with a significant hazard to human health and/or the environment, and its presence in a material or part in a vehicle may create a significant risk to human health and/or the environment'.[24] Accordingly, three 'reason codes' have been developed to explain to the participating firms why a substance has been included in the GADSL. The first code means that a substance is 'legally regulated'. The code 'for assessment' indicates that a substance is expected to be regulated by government agencies. The code 'for information' denotes a substance:

> tracked for information purposes only, upon decision by the GASG Steering Committee. After discussion at the GASG Steering Committee and on an exceptional basis, a car producer may include an individual substance or family of substances on the list under this reason code.[25]

According to official statements, the purpose of the GADSL is to 'help the automotive industry to monitor the usage of these substances and to facilitate compliance with current and future regulations'[26] as well as to 'help take into account customer requirements to ensure sustainable products'.[27] In practice, the parts suppliers to the automotive industry often do

[22] The GADSL replaced the International List of Reportable Substances (ILRS) in April 2005. Like the GADSL, it was the aim of the ILRS to summarise the different requirements of car producers concerning the declaration of substances. Different from the GADSL, the ILRS was planned without the support of the automotive suppliers and the chemical industry (http://www.mdsystem.com/).

[23] Hence, the automotive industry is able to rectify its practices prior to regulation, eg the automotive industry agrees on limit values before a substance will be regulated (interview, March 2005).

[24] GADSL (http://gadsl.org/files/2005_Ver_1.0.pdf).

[25] *Ibid*. Apparently, adding substances is an exception, because some of those firms that participated in the development of the GADSL feared that the legislator might accept this and regulate these substances formally. The list itself was not without controversy: Some of the suppliers were not willing to lay their information open to the car producers. Thereupon, the producers threatened to go back to individual negotiations between suppliers and producers. As a result, the suppliers accepted the list (interview, March 2005).

[26] IMDS model office (http://www.model.mds.eds.de/html/data/imds_standard101_ilrs.pdf).

[27] GADSL (http://gadsl.org/files/2005_Ver_1.0.pdf).

not know which substances are contained in their products. Consequently, they forward these requests up the production chain, which in some cases reach the chemical industry (interview, February 2005). Whether chemical distributors get the information from the chemical producers depends on the size of the producer; big producers are normally willing and able to provide the information. However, as the chemical distributors have reduced their staff in recent years, the handling of these inquiries has been delayed (interview, February 2005).

It is the official intent of the GADSL:

> to become the company specific list for declaration of parts composition within the automotive industry. It provides a definitive list of substances requiring declaration with the target to minimise individual requirements and ensure cost-effective management of declaration practice along the complex supply chain.[28]

Again, empirical evidence shows a different picture. For instance, one global automobile producer which is represented on the GASG steering committee has its own restricted substance management standard (RSMS). This standard is, so the firm's portrayal suggests, global and addresses all legislation on the restriction of substances as well as its own strategy that 'may go beyond substance restrictions and bans in local markets'.[29] Compliance with this standard is part of the terms of doing business with this car producer. It is the responsibility of its suppliers to forward this standard and all its requirements upstream through the value chain.[30] The car producer checks if its suppliers comply with this standard. Non-compliance has consequences for the awarding of new contracts. The RSMS exceeds the GADSL in protection level. Even after the coming into existence of the GADSL, the RSMS standard has remained valid and will be further updated. The car manufacturer in question regards it as necessary to exceed existing standards of chemical regulation regarding, for example, the passenger compartment (interview, March 2005). In contrast, a common standard was in the best interest of the suppliers because it would have simplified the reporting processes:

> The suppliers' industry is, of course, interested in having one single standard, because this simplifies the processes. In this case you can say: 'We do it according to the list, hence we are legally clean and we fulfil the common standard to which we contributed.' (Interview, February 2005)

> 'This is something that especially the suppliers wish, that we [the car producers] harmonise [the requirements we ask them for] so they do not have to produce differently for different producers. (Interview, March 2005)

[28] GADSL (http://gadsl.org/files/2005_Ver_1.0.pdf).

[29] Before the implementation of the ELV Directive, the manufacturer put the regulated substances on its own declaration list (interview, March 2005).

[30] Document available to the author.

Hence, compliance with this global list would have meant that all laws and the automotive standard were observed. The fact that car producers insist upon their own standards once again makes individual negotiations between supplier and car producer necessary (interview, February 2005).

The example illustrates, on the one hand, that global car producers are able to dictate to their suppliers what kind of chemical substances they do not want to have in the delivered products and, on the other hand, that the car producers depend, to a certain degree, on their suppliers' willingness to cooperate. Sometimes suppliers of parts do not want to exchange information with the producers because they are afraid of revealing sensitive information on the composition of substances. The suppliers fear that the car producers could use this knowledge and change to another supplier, passing the confidential information on to them (interviews, November 2004, February/March 2005).

C. European Single Assessment Document

The European Single Assessment Document (ESAD) is a document developed for the assessment of chemical distributors. It was developed jointly by chemical manufacturers and chemical distributors in order to prevent the situation where each chemical manufacturer uses its own assessment procedure and that consequently distributors get assessed by all of their suppliers. According to official statements, the ESDA offers 'a measurement of the commitment of distributors to their Responsible Care Programme'[31] as well as 'a common tool for suppliers to evaluate, against their individual requirements, the safety, health and environmental performance of their distributors'.[32] The ESAD was launched in 1999. It has been developed by a joint task force from the European Chemical Industry Council (CEFIC)—the European association of national chemical associations—and the European Association for Chemical Distributors (FECC). It should demonstrate the determination of chemical suppliers and distributors to address common issues in the context of safety, health, and environmental aspects. It is intended that the ESAD should lead to a reduction in the number of assessments of the chemical distributors conducted by the chemical suppliers.[33]

Any chemical distributor may decide—on its own initiative or at the request of a chemical company—to have an assessment performed. The assessor, selected by the distributor from a list of accredited assessors, enters

[31] As stated above, Responsible Care is a global initiative. This voluntary code of conduct was first launched in 1985 in Canada. The programme is administered by national chemical associations and varies 'according to national cultures and circumstances' (Druckrey, 1998: 983). Cf Prakash, 2000 for the programme's achievements in the United States.

[32] ESAD II: General Guidelines, 2004 (http://www.fecc.org/page.php?id=72).

[33] FECC (1999) Press Release (http://www.fecc.org/en/). In 2005, ESAD was replaced by ESAD II. Under ESAD I only 80 distributors' sites were assessed. A key change of ESAD II was to create a centrally trained group of independent auditors to assess more distributors than in the past (http://www.envirocentre.ie).

the draft assessment report in an electronic database. For one month, only the distributor is entitled to view the report, which means it is his responsibility to review the report and he may also add comments on the complete assessment. Thereafter, a final assessment report is launched on the database and becomes accessible to those authorised chemical companies that are members of the ESAD service group.[34] The chemical companies can provide feedback on the results of the assessment. Based on this feedback, the distributor develops an improvement programme in respect of any unsatisfactory issues concerning his safety, health and environmental performance.[35]

The third party assessments of the chemical distributors are carried out via structured questionnaires. The questionnaires contain 'mandatory questions' as well as 'industry standard questions'. Mandatory questions 'cover items that are statutory in most countries in Europe, but not necessarily in all. *They represent basic requirements that should be met by all distributors*' (emphasis added). Even if a question does not concern a statutory requirement in the country where the assessment is carried out, it needs to be answered. In contrast, industry standard questions 'cover items that the chemical industry normally requires from its distributors in order to have an acceptable level of control'. The total number of questions for all sections of the assessment questionnaire is 650.[36]

Relating to legal requirements, the distributors have to answer, among others, the following questions[37]:

— Are you aware of current legislation relevant to your business?
  - Is there a library of relevant safety, health and environmental regulations?
— Does the company have a means of ensuring that it keeps abreast of legislative requirements and how to comply with them?
  - Is a person designated or a source defined to keep the company abreast of legislative developments in the area of safety, health and the environment?
— Is there a means of confirming that the company and personnel comply with legal requirements?
  - Is a regular review made of the system for compliance with licences?

Concerning the provision of information, the distributors are asked, among other things[38]:

[34] All companies supplying chemicals through distributors in Europe can join the ESAD Service Group (http://chemie.de/news/e/40263).
[35] ESAD II: General Guidelines, 2004 (http://www.fecc.org/page.php?id=72).
[36] See for this paragraph: ESAD II: General Guidelines, 2004 (http://www.fecc.org/page.php?id=72).
[37] ESAD II: Questionnaire, 2004 (http://www.fecc.org/page.php?id=72).
[38] *Ibid.*

— Are customers supplied with adequate health, safety and environmental information and other technical data on the products supplied to them?
- Does the company have a written procedure covering the issue of safety data sheets for all products and to all organisations?

As regards ongoing improvements, the manufacturers want to know, among other things[39]:

— Are customer complaints (all types) monitored and reviewed and corrective action taken?
- Do management reviews consider trends in customer complaints?

Other main topics in the ESAD questionnaire are risk management, policies and documentation, training, emergency response, and community interaction.[40] An additional questionnaire assesses the management of chlorinated solvents. One of the main topics is 'legal requirements and important guidelines'. It is asked if the distributors are aware of current legislation and important guidelines relevant to chlorinated solvents. Further, the distributors have to answer if they have a means of ensuring that they are up to date with new or changed guidelines regarding chlorinated solvents in addition to the legislative developments.[41]

Even though one interviewee asserted that some of the questions were redundant, he regarded the questionnaires as helpful as they released instructive processes of reflection and resulted in a meaningful changing of practices:

> Actually, the questionnaire was extremely helpful for us. There are a lot of aspects we thought about and realised them. (Interview, April 2005)

Likewise, another interviewee considered the ESAD as 'a very strong' code of conduct. He regarded the ESAD elements like product safety and environmental protection as reasonable, but emphasised also the expense factor:

> This is also a cost factor. Environmental protection ... that's all well and good, but I have to be able to pay for it. If I ruin my company with it, I won't have achieved anything. (Interview, February 2005)

D. Material Safety Data Sheets

In short, material safety data sheets contain safety information on the handling of hazardous substances. They provide essential information on chemicals in order to minimise health or environmental dangers (cf Ronit, 2000: 91).

In the 1970s, firms from different industries began to provide their own safety data sheets. For example, car producers and chemical distributors developed their own data sheets as they wanted to be informed by their

39 *Ibid.*
40 *Ibid.*
41 ESAD II Questionnaire: Chlorinated Solvents (http://www.fecc.org/page.php?id=72).

suppliers on the chemical composition of products as well as on the adequate handling of hazardous chemicals (interview, February 2005).[42] In the 1980s, the German chemical industry association (VCI) and the German Association of the Automotive Industry (VDA) issued their own association-specific data sheets.[43] According to a voluntary initiative of the industry, the safety data sheets were harmonised in Germany (interview, February 2005). At first, these harmonised safety data sheets were not coordinated with data sheets used by industry in other countries. The situation changed with Directive 91/155/EEC on safety data sheets. In the forefront of the Directive, the Federation of German Industries (BDI) arranged a committee of representatives of the VDA and the VCI to participate in the development of a harmonised European safety data sheet. The VDA data sheet can be said to be the precursor of the European data sheet. This can be explained by the fact that as the European Commission, preparing the Directive on safety data sheets, was asking for adequate instruments, the VDA safety data sheet was already widely used and therefore qualified as a model:

> As the European Commission asked 'are there any instruments in the individual countries?', everyone pulled out his own translated VDA data sheet and hence it went rather consistently in this direction. So we had the European data sheet. (Interview, March 2005)

Directive 91/155/EC determines that any person established within the Community who is responsible for placing a dangerous substance or preparation on the market, whether they be the manufacturer, importer, or distributor, shall supply the recipient who is an industrial user of the substance or preparation with a safety data sheet.

The major difficulty with the data sheets is that the information contained in them is often deficient, or even lacking, or the wrong data sheet has been used (interviews, February/March 2005).[44] This can be explained by the fact that the design of safety data sheets is different in different regions. For example, an Asian corporation that wants to export a dangerous substance has to deal with different data sheets in the United States and in the EU. If information on chemical substances is lacking, a European corporation uses its personal contacts with its supplier outside of the EU to get the missing information in an informal way. In spite of these problems, safety data sheets are more accepted currently than at the beginning; corporations' staff pay more attention to them. If they do not want to compile safety data sheets on

[42] Cf http://www.storck-verlag.de/pdf/edaskonzept.pdf.

[43] A publisher of expert information on hazardous materials summarised the development of EDAS, an electronic data processing format for structured electronic exchange of safety data sheets. Against this background, the publisher gives a short survey of the development of safety data sheets (http://www.storck-verlag.de/pdf/edaskonzept.pdf).

[44] Cf, for deficiencies in safety data sheets, the Eclips Report (Eclips Working Group, 2004).

their own, corporations may contact chemical consulting firms—these firms emerged in the 1980s—that compile data sheets, for example under the provisions of the aforementioned Directive (interview, February 2005).

Since the implementation of the Directive on safety data sheets the chemical and automotive industries have not been inactive. For example, some representatives of automotive manufacturers and suppliers of automotive parts, as well as a representative of a global chemical producer, are active members of a working group that was established to develop an efficient electronic system to exchange European data sheets. Finally EDAS,[45] a harmonised data format, was designed. According to VDA, this data format allows an 'electronic interchange of structured data between suppliers and recipients', it is 'essential on cost grounds' as structuring the data 'allows the information to be readily evaluated and incorporated into hazardous substance logs, area analyses and instructions for the employees'.[46]

In the 1990s, a globally harmonised system for hazard communication (GHS) was developed that includes a common approach on substance data sheets. Key participants in developing the system include various governments and some international organisations.[47] Work on the GHS has been ongoing since the United Nations Conference on the Environment and Development in Rio de Janeiro in 1992.[48] In the case of safety data sheets, the harmonisation process was able to build on the previous efforts of the industry to standardise the approaches of the data sheets requirements (Silk, 2003: 447, 451).[49]

E. Substitution Processes

A final example of emerging industry-spanning management of chemical substances is the substitution of hazardous chemicals. In recent years, the automotive industry began to substitute methylene chloride. The EU classifies this substance as 'category 3', the category containing substances 'that need attention due to their possible carcinogenic properties for humans' (Tukker and Simons, 1999: 38). A global car producer, together with a leading global producer of chemicals, started to substitute this substance[50]

[45] See n 43 above.

[46] Cf the information of VDA on safety data sheets and their electronic exchange via the ESAD format (http://www.vda.de/en/service/jahresbericht/auto2000/Auto+umwelt/u_30.html). Cf also the EDAS homepage (http://www.edas.org).

[47] Canadian centre for occupational health and safety (http://www.ccohs.ca/oshanswers/chemicals/ ghs.html).

[48] According to an international agreement, 'it is desirable to have as many countries as possible adopt the GHS by 2008' (Silk, 2003: 451).

[49] Finally, there was agreement on a 16-section data sheet including, among others, information on ingredients, and toxicological, ecological, and transport information (Silk, 2003: 451).

[50] Among other uses, methylene chloride is used as a paint remover and a solvent.

in automotive repair lacquers. In contrast to the substitution of methylene chloride, its substitution in repair lacquers proved to be difficult at first. As the cancer-causing effect of methylene chloride had already been discussed,[51] the car manufacturer quickly searched for an adequate solution:

> Substituting methylene chloride in paint removers was quite easy. However, it didn't work with repair lacquers. Hence it was said, this little soupcon of it in repair lacquers doesn't matter. But the cancer-causing effect of methylene chloride was discussed and some cases of death did occur, among the people who did the paint-removing. And so we said, we have to see immediately if we can do something else. (Interview, March 2005)

Therefore, the car manufacturer contacted a global chemical producer which developed a less harmful repairing lacquer. As this solution proved to be effective, the chemical producer promoted it and offered the new lacquer to other producers of automobiles. Meanwhile, the substitution of methylene chloride in repairing lacquers proceeded in the automotive industry (interview, March 2005). In another case, a producer of lacquer developed a solvent-free lacquer and ceased the production of lacquers with solvents, so its customer, a global car producer, had to purchase the substitute (interview, November 2004).

Nonetheless, some of the interviewees expressed their scepticism about the substitution of substances. They were of the opinion that it might be more reasonable to handle a hazardous, but well-known substance in a careful way, rather than apply a substitute without knowing how to handle it properly:

> Sometimes it's more favourable to stick to something one knows the hazard of, where one knows the functional chain and is able to introduce the appropriate management procedure to prevent that a high risk potential leads to a high risk. Today it's a matter of common knowledge how to deal with asbestos reasonably. (Interview, March 2005)

Other interviewees challenged the idea that substitutes are as effective as the substances used initially.

In the chemical industry, it is unusual that substitution processes are initiated by chemical distributors. Rather, their customers demand substitutes or their suppliers advertise new substances and offer training programmes for their distributors (interviews, April 2005). Of course, the substitution processes may fail. This was the case when a car producer demanded a product free of nitrosamines, a cancer-producing substance, from his supplier. The supplier regarded this demand as unfair and announced a price increase for the demanded product. This resulted in the car manufacturer withdrawing his demand. Other suppliers would not have been able to fulfil this customer requirement either (interview, February 2005).

[51] Eg in 1995 Greenpeace published a study on the effects of chlorine on human health and alluded to the health hazards of this chemical substance (Greenpeace, 1995: 61).

Further, a substitution of hazardous substances or at least their restrictive use can be triggered by internal developments within a corporation. On the one side, the corporation's staff may become alerted to the risk of the substances they have to handle:

> An enhanced awareness of hazards of the firms' own staff can be seen. It has been said: 'Come on, we would like to know more about it!' (Interview, February 2005)

On the other side, the employers may want to protect their staff, sometimes because they fear a law suit:

> Even before the Directive on end-of-life vehicles we restricted the substances regulated in it. The reason was employment and environment protection. Our staff have to deal with these substances as well. (Interview, March 2005)
>
> It becomes a problem for us if our name is written on it [a product], and if someone initiates legal action, like in the case of asbestos at present. People whose skin mutated somehow and who worked for a long time in a garage partially initiated legal action. (Interview, February 2005)

The example of BFRs shows that the substitution of hazardous chemicals is not uncomplicated, hence restricted BFRs 'are not yet out of vehicles' (Hall, 2001: vii). In her study on BFRs in vehicle design, Hall gives two reasons for this: First, 'industry is not able to apply suitable alternative solutions for all applications in vehicles and components'. Second, 'vehicle producers and suppliers ... do not know all cases where brominated flame retardants are used' (*ibid*).

F. Evaluation of Empirical Findings

Above, some examples of the transnational management of chemical substances in a selected section of a production chain have been described. It has been shown that firms and associations have established their own practices to handle chemicals.

The example of the IMDS/GADSL demonstrates that initially corporations involved at the same stage of a production chain tried to design and enforce their own rules individually. As this proved to be ineffective, the addressees of the regulation were consulted to design and enforce the rules more effectively in cooperation. For this purpose, the GASG was created. As it was created intentionally with a specific purpose, the GASG can be seen as a strategic network.[52] It remains to be seen if the GASG network will

[52] Strategic networks are rather small groups of 'legally autonomous organizations with high levels of interdependence and cooperative working', principally for-profit organisations engaging in collective action (Knight, 2002: 430). These kinds of networks are created intentionally, they are coherent and purposive in character (Whetten, 1981: 8).

commonly solve the problems that have resulted from the non-compliance of some automobile producers; it would be advisable if the network reacted to this by revising the list of declarable substances in such a way that all important actors—even the 'pioneers'—will consider it as useful. Further, the network should assure that all firms fill in the list correctly, so single corporations do not have to ask their suppliers individually for missing information. This example reveals that a common design of rules and standards in a network is easier to achieve than its common enforcement against non-complying corporations.

While it is a vital interest of each single automotive manufacturer to assess their suppliers on the basis of their own standards,[53] chemical manufacturers and chemical distributors launched a single assessment which is common for all distributors. Contrary to those of the automotive industry, the results of the assessment are accessible to a group of authorised chemical manufacturers, which have the opportunity to give a feedback. Like car manufacturers, chemical manufactures are in a powerful position in that they can request that their customers prepare an assessment as well as, if necessary, develop an improvement programme. While the global car producers tend to dictate their product requirements to their suppliers, the described single assessment document of the chemical industry is based on commonly established and accepted procedural rules. Even though this is approved by the industry, it seems to be arguable whether the questions listed above really do provide a basis to detect grievances. The fact that someone has been designated to keep the company abreast of legislative developments does not necessarily mean that this person is able to cope with such a task: for example it might be the case that the company is not willing to provide the necessary working hours or other essential resources. Further, the fact that the distributor chooses an assessor may result in a conflict of interests if the assessor is dependent on his customer.

In the case of the safety data sheets, a cooperation of different national industry associations resulted in a common European safety-data sheet, which was later incorporated in EU Directive 91/155/EEC. A few years later, firms at different stages of the value chain managed to develop an electronic system for the structured exchange of European data sheets.

The last case demonstrates that substitution processes have taken place between direct partners of the production chain. Those processes were launched either by suppliers who invented a new product or by customers who were not content with a certain substance for a variety of reasons. The substitution of a chemical substance may fail if a car producer is not able to enforce it against his supplier or if he does not accept the new product.

[53] Car producers conduct their own rankings whose results decide who might be considered as a supplier; a producer will not conclude any further agreements with a supplier which does poorly in a ranking (interviews, November 2004/February 2005).

As the example of the car producer who acted as a pioneer by substituting a hazardous chemical substance shows, other firms are also willing to take it on if the substitute proves to be effective. Hence, the original substance which had been substituted was found to be no longer acceptable in the whole industry—even without governmental regulation.

In addition to emerging practices, some common views, interpretations, and goals as to the transnational management of chemicals have been established. One example is the recognition of the automotive and the chemical industry that it is necessary to cooperate and to produce a common standard, the GADSL. Further, it is the common goal of the chemical manufacturers and distributors to reach a commonly accepted quality level with the ESAD initiative; the ESAD questionnaires were regarded as helpful as they resulted in a meaningful change of practices. The example of the increasing acceptance of safety data sheets shows that firms consider it as important to be informed on the composition of products and their safety handling. Requests from different industries for a harmonised European safety data sheet, as well as the desire for an electronic exchange system, demonstrate that new common goals are emerging. The substitution case also shows that the chemical, and primarily the automotive, industry turned out to be responsive to public concerns relating to environmental and health dangers while being aware of the risk of introducing a new, but unknown substance instead of a hazardous but well-known substance. Nonetheless, the fact that neither the car producer nor its supplier were willing to voluntarily bear additional costs for a phasing-out of nitrosamines show that, sometimes, common views and interpretations are established that run counter to the responsible management of hazardous chemicals.

III. CONDUCIVE AND HINDERING CONDITIONS FOR THE TRANSNATIONAL MANAGEMENT OF CHEMICALS

Against the background of the examples discussed above, the following section exposes those conditions which facilitated or impaired the development of transnational management of chemical substances.

First of all, the existence of so called 'lead firms', that argued for a more safety-conscious handling of chemicals, was conducive to the development of transnational management of chemicals. Controlling access to major resources, lead firms are able to influence and guide other corporations in their sphere of activity towards their own interest (compare Gereffi, 1999: 38; 2001: 1622). The examples given reveal that lead firms are placed on both sides of the production chain: Upstream, chemical manufacturers acted as lead firms; downstream, car producers could also be referred to as lead firms. The examples show that these firms made use of their powerful positions as multinational corporations by using different strategies. On the one hand, car manufacturers individually exerted pressure on their suppliers, which in most cases accepted the demands and, if so requested, forwarded their requirements upstream through the value chain because they depended on their customers' orders. Hence, the car manufacturers are, by and large, able to dictate to their suppliers what kind of chemical substances they do not want to have in the delivered products. On the other hand, car manufacturers, as well as chemical manufacturers, built up networks that incorporated firms at different stages of the production chain to look jointly for more effective ways of problem-solving. As especially the launch and development of the IMDS/GADSL, the ESAD, and the electronic system to exchange safety data sheets show, chemical manufacturers and car producers assumed a 'strategic management function' (Rycroft, 2003: 312) in initiating and coordinating the described processes which was conducive to a more responsible handling of chemicals. This is not to say that they did not try to exert pressure on their customers and their respective suppliers. The substitution processes, as well as the example of the car manufacturer who decided to go beyond the GADSL, demonstrate that lead firms may act as pioneers by setting an example for other corporations—even if this is not primarily for environmental but for economic reasons.

As lead firms, both chemical manufacturers and automobile producers were able to influence other corporations in the production chain. Nonetheless, both depended on other (societal) actors. First, both automobile and chemical producers were vulnerable as they depended to a certain degree on their public image. The examples of the substitution of chemical substances and the initiation and diffusion of the Responsible Care programme demonstrate that firms are motivated by self-interest not to damage their own reputation; they perceive themselves as socially embedded actors. The examples indicate an enhanced awareness of the hazardousness of chemical substances in the chemical and the automotive industry, on occasion created by environmental organisations. That the chemical industry in general has become more active on environmental issues, especially through the 1990s (Ronit, 2000: 86), can be explained by the intention to enhance their reputation after chemical accidents in the past. The chemical industry has tried to improve its image by 'demonstrating a responsible behavior' (Ronit and Schneider, 2000: 19). Global car producers are important actors insofar as they—as finishing companies—are very 'visible' in public and hence accordingly vulnerable. The fact that car producers are the ones who finally have to sell the manufactured products and, linked to this, their interest in a good reputation, explains why they have taken the initiative on the responsible management of chemicals.[54] For automobile manufacturers as finishing companies it is particularly important that they

[54] On the other hand, there might be less public pressure on car manufacturers to substitute flame retardants if, eg, customers assess fire safety as more important than a low exposure to hazardous substances in passenger compartments (cf Hall, 2001: 36).

can offer marketable products. To achieve this goal, car producers have exerted their influence on their suppliers on whose materials' and parts' quality they depend.

That lead firms and other less powerful firms in the value chain, like automotive suppliers, addressed the issue can be further illustrated by the increased scepticism of the firms' staff members who have to handle chemical substances and who cared for their health. These concerns were taken seriously by the corporations, as demonstrated by their efforts to establish better working conditions.

Another reason is the intention of firms to reduce hazards that could also endanger smooth production. The example of the corporation that began to stop using PVC not primarily because it does harm to health and to the environment, but because the firm wanted to reduce fire hazards in its production plants substantiates this.

Further, the launch of ESAD and the Responsible Care programme, as well as the development of a harmonised safety data sheet, gives an indication of the contribution of associations with regard to the establishment of transnational chemical management. In contrast to the GADSL initiative, it was important that associations supported and diffused environmental ideas or at least established instruments that made an exchange of information on chemical substances possible.

Last but not least, the case of ESAD exemplifies that the laws that existed in some nation states were conducive to the extension of the private transnational management of chemicals as these regulations were integrated into the ESAD assessment questionnaires and compliance was demanded even from chemical distributors in countries that did not have such a legal foundation. A similar trend could be observed in the automotive industry. As automotive suppliers deliver their products to car producers in different regions of the world, they are often confronted with divergent standards. Many of them therefore decide to produce according to the highest standards in order to meet them all.

Some factors impaired the development of the transnational management of chemical substances. One such factor was economic concerns. So, the example of the failed substitution shows that the automotive supplier refrained from environmentally sound behaviour because the substitution would have been too costly. Likewise, another interviewee emphasised that environmental protection is important, but in the end it must not endanger the existence of the corporation.

A significant element of the management of chemicals is the exchange of information on hazardous substances. In some cases, this exchange was problematic at the interface between the chemical industry and the automotive industry. For instance, employees of parts suppliers to the automotive industry that asked their own suppliers for information on chemical substances did not use the same terminology as the chemical experts they contacted. This hindered an information exchange on an equal footing (interview, February 2005). Further, the cutbacks in financial and personnel resources, even in large corporations within the chemical industry, rendered the exchange of information on chemicals more difficult and time-consuming. Generally, the transmission of information was hampered if corporations like chemical distributors or automotive suppliers were afraid of revealing sensitive information on the composition of substances or parts. The suppliers wanted to keep their business secrets confidential; they feared that their customers could change to other suppliers and pass the confidential information on to them.[55]

As the example of the failed substitution process exemplifies, car producers sometimes depend on their suppliers' willingness to cooperate. Knowing that other suppliers would also have been unable to produce the desired parts without price increases, the supplier was able to refuse the demands of the car producer.

The case of the GADSL indicates some further problems with the transnational handling of chemical substances. On the basis of the example of the ILRS, the precursor of the GADSL, one may suppose that the initiative did not work at first because not all of the important stakeholders and their special interests were taken into consideration. To incorporate the relevant stakeholders was, in this special case, probably more difficult since the stakeholders were located in different regions of the world. Further, some corporations first tried to prevent a private regulation fearing that this could attract the attention of law-making institutions, which could take up these initiatives and formulate binding laws.

Finally, it is significant that car producers did not advertise, for example, chemical-free passenger compartments. This is because it would have had negative consequences for the automotive industry as a whole, as it would have focused public attention on the fact that there are serious problems with chemicals in automobiles. In contrast to the chemical industry, automotive producers do not have to restore their reputation but they do have to uphold it. Consequently, an advertising campaign featuring cars that contain fewer chemicals was not possible from the perspective of the automotive industry. Since the negative environmental and health effects of chemical substances in cars are not widely discussed in public, a sufficient demand for chemical-free automobiles is lacking. Hence, an important trigger for the responsible private handling or phasing out of chemicals seems to be missing.

[55] Likewise, Hall declares in her study on BFRs in vehicle design that: 'Secrecy and lack of trust often characterise relationships between companies, their suppliers and other actors in the product chain. These have been identified as major obstacles for realising environmental initiatives' (Hall, 2001: 28).

IV. CONCLUSION

The examples presented illustrate that corporations, partially supported by associations, identified realms where self-regulation was possible and thus created adequate arrangements that could be referred to as corporation- and industry-spanning transnational management of chemicals. The examples of the IMDS/GADSL and the ESAD demonstrate that these self-regulating arrangements are partially based on existing laws. In the former case, corporations used these databases to diffuse information on existing and new laws. In the latter case, the ESAD questionnaires were used to control distributors' knowledge of existing laws and their actual compliance. Yet the IMDS and GADSL systems provided a basis for an exchange of information on private standards regarding the regulation of chemicals as well as on new scientific evidence concerning the consequences of chemicals for health and the environment. Further, the ESAD questionnaires were used to review whether the distributors had complied with the chemical manufacturers' standards concerning the handling of chemical substances.

The development of harmonised material safety data sheets illustrates that firms from different industries managed to design a unified data sheet. Later on, they succeeded in influencing the form of the European safety data sheet. Likewise, the example of the new Regulation on the registration, evaluation, authorisation and restrictions of chemicals (REACH), which entered into force on 1 June 2007, shows that the EU Regulation takes up the practices of private actors. It can be read in the recitals of the REACH Regulation that not only manufacturers and importers but also downstream users are responsible for ensuring a high level of protection for human health and the environment. According to Article 37(4) of the REACH Regulation, downstream users of a substance shall prepare a chemical safety report for any use falling outside the conditions described in an exposure scenario or, if appropriate, a use and exposure category communicated to them in a safety data sheet or for any use their supplier advises against. This reflects the interest of the lead firms of the supply chain in also making the downstream user responsible.

Finally, the substitution of hazardous chemicals in lacquers demonstrates that corporations have phased out substances without a legal foundation. It seems remarkable that firms not only tried to inform each other on existing and new laws but that they attempted to impose laws on corporations in countries where such laws were non-existent. Further, the demands of global car producers and chemical manufacturers reach, via the production chain, even firms in the automotive and chemical industries in countries with lower regulatory standards. Hence, the diffusion of standards and laws could lead to a 'trading up' (Vogel, 1997).[56] An example of this is the

[56] Cf for the discussion of the mechanisms of trading up in Dilling, ch 4, this volume.

ELV Directive. It has been shown above that car producers in the United States also try to comply with this EU Directive; this may result in the observance of its requirements even for markets outside the EU—assuming that companies design and produce their vehicles 'according to the highest world wide governmental health and safety regulations' (Five Winds International, 2003: 33).[57]

Private rule-making and monitoring of compliance, as well as sanctioning mechanisms, are important elements of successful self-regulation (Ronit and Schneider, 2000: 23). Against the background of the launch of the GADSL and the ESAD, corporations of the automotive and the chemical industry have learnt that a collaborative setting of private standards with corporations involved at different stages of the value chain is beneficial for effectively solving problems with handling chemicals. It remains to be seen if the common lists will be suited to the interests of the participating firms. In relation to the IMDS/GADSL, it seems that common monitoring and enforcement mechanisms are lacking, as some of the corporations individually detected compliance problems with their trading partners and reacted to these difficulties on their own. Further, the automotive producers conducted assessments of their suppliers to establish whether their suppliers complied with their demands. The case of the safety data sheets also reveals that corporations tried to solve problems with the data sheets individually with their direct trading partners. In contrast, the ESAD provides a common monitoring mechanism as independent auditors were appointed to assess chemical distributors. Further, it guides improvement processes whereas the automotive industry handles cases of non-compliance individually via the awarding of contracts. While the former case approximates to the model of peer pressure from members, the latter is a model of hierarchical sanctioning (cf Ronit and Schneider, 2004: 24).

The industry's practices concerning the management of hazardous substances show that self-regulation by private actors has some positive effects for the environment and/or for human health. A careful handling, reduction or avoidance of hazardous substances will not only benefit the staff of corporations involved in the manufacture of cars but also consumers and the environment. Finally, the disposal or recycling of automobiles will be less complicated and more environment-friendly. Other cases reveal that self-regulation was primarily useful for the efficient coordination of production processes, but that the environmental benefits are questionable. Hence, it may be beneficial for automotive suppliers that it is difficult for their customers, the car producers, to exceed the GADSL; however, it may prove to

[57] According to a study on product stewardship within the automotive industry, this 'enables companies to shift products among markets with minimal changes to each model for different markets, which would be more costly than building a single vehicle that meets the majority of standards and regulations around the world' (Five Winds International, 2003: 33).

be unfavourable for environmental reasons. The examples given demonstrate that the responsible handling of chemicals, having positive effects on human health and the environment, was motivated by the firms' pragmatic interest in smooth production rather than by deep-rooted ecological principles. Hence, in situations where firms refrain from environmentally sound behaviour, public regulation remains important.

V. ADDENDUM

The empirical insights are based on interviews and an analysis of documents. The interviews were conducted to expose similarities concerning a management of chemicals that spanned across corporations. The interviews were arranged with representatives of corporations primarily belonging to the automotive and the chemical industry. All in all, ten interviews took place. Five interviews were conducted in the automotive industry. Here, two interviews were conducted with employees of global car manufacturers. Two further interviews were conducted with employees of global automobile suppliers and another one with a local supplier of parts. In the chemical industry, four interviews were conducted: one with a global producer of chemicals and one with a chemical consulting firm, and two further interviews with distributors of chemicals. In addition, one interview was conducted with a chemical trade association. The interview quotations were translated into English by the author. The interviews were interpreted according to qualitative-interpretive methods (Wernet, 2000; Froschauer and Lueger, 2003). For this analysis, environmental reports of corporations, corporation guidelines, management standards, and similar documents were examined.

REFERENCES

Börzel, TA (2000) *Private Actors on the Rise? The Role of Non-State Actors in Compliance with International Institutions* (Bonn, Max-Planck-Projektgruppe Recht der Gemeinschaftsgüter).

Bolli, A (2000) *Environmental Communication and Competitiveness. A Case Study of the Car Industry* (Lund, International Institute for Industrial Environmental Economics (IIIEE), Lund University) (http://www.iiiee.lu.se/Publication.nsf/$webAll/7DB36EB102603D37C1256C37002CC457).

BUND (2005) Bundschau, (http://www.bund.net/lab/reddot2/pdf/bundschau_1_2005.pdf).

Cutler, AC, Haufler, V and Porter T (1999) 'Private Authority and International Affairs' in AC Cutler, V Haufler and Porter, T (eds), *Private Authority and International Affairs* (New York, State University of New York Press).

Druckrey, F (1998) 'How to Make Business Ethics Operational: Responsible Care—An Example of Successful Self-Regulation?' 17 *Journal of Business Ethics* 979.

Eclips Working Group (2004) *European Classification and Labelling Inspections of Preparations, including Safety Data sheets*, Final Report (http://www.cleen-eu.net/projects/ECLIPS_Final_report.pdf).

European Commission (2004) 'Why do we need REACH?' (http://europa.eu.int/comm/enterprise/reach/docs/reach/reach_in_brief-2004_09_15.pdf).

Fachverband Schaumstoffkunststoffe eV (2003) *Presseinformation: Abstimmungs-Meeting zur Automobilteile-Datenbank IMDS bringt wichtige Kunststoff-Zulieferer zusammen* (http://www.fsk-vsv.de/de/index.html).

Fisher, MM (2005) Standards Development for Reporting of Declarable Substances. American Society for Testing and Materials (http://www.astm.org/SNEWS/JUNE_2005/fisher_jun05.html).

Five Winds International (2003) *Product Stewardship Opportunities within the Automotive Industry* (http://www.moea.state.mn.us/publications/autoPSreport.pdf).

Froschauer, U and Lueger, M (2003) *Das qualitative Interview. Zur Praxis interpretativer Analyse sozialer Systeme* (Wien, WUV-Universitätsverlag).

Gereffi, G (1999) 'International Trade and Industrial Upgrading in the Apparel Commodity Chain' 48 *Journal of International Economics* 37.

—— (2001) 'Shifting Governance Structures in Global Commodity Chains, With Special Reference to the Internet' 44 *American Behavioral Scientist* 1616.

Global 2000 (2005) *Schadstoffbelastung in Neuwagen* (http://help.orf.at/dateien/1903_Autotest_Luft.pdf).

Greenpeace (1999) *Es geht auch ohne PVC* (Wien) (http://marktcheck.greenpeace.at/uploads/media/halogenfreie-kabel-3.pdf).

—— (2003) *Chemicals out of control. The systematic failure of EU chemicals policy in the last 20 years* (http://www.greenpeace.fr/vigitox/dossiers/Studie_10x10_BW.pdf).

—— (2004) *Bhopal 1984–2004: Zwanzig Jahre Verantwortungslosigkeit.* (http://www.greenpeace.de/fileadmin/gpd/user_upload/themen/umweltgifte/greenpeace_bhopal.pdf).

Greenpeace, Epha Environment Network, Chemical Reaction, European Environmental Bureau, and BUND (2004) *Chemikalien außer Kontrolle. Für eine EU-Chemikalienpolitik zum Schutz von Gesundheit und Umwelt.* (http://www.bund.net/bundgegengift/pdfs/gp_reach_report_ge_jan05.pdf).

Hall, JC (2001) *Product Design to Reduce Restricted Substances. The Experience of brominated flame retardants in vehicle design* (Lund, International Institute for Industrial Environmental Economics (IIIEE), Lund University) (http://www.iiiee.lu.se/Publication.nsf/$webAll/C455D7F4D27FA27CC1256BE9003E9BB0).

Haufler, V (2001) A Public Role for the Private Sector. Industry Self-regulation in a Global Economy (Washington, DC, Carnegie).

Johnson Controls (2001) *IMDS User Guideline* (http://ag.johnsoncontrols.com/SupplierHandbook/pdf/imdsuserd.pdf).

Knight, L (2002) 'Network Learning: Exploring Learning by Interorganizational Networks' 55 *Human Relations* 427.

Knill, C and Lehmkuhl, D (2002) 'Governance and Globalization: Conceptualizing the Role of Public and Private Actors' in A Héritier (ed), *Common Goods: Reinventing European and International Governance* (Oxford, Rowman & Littlefield).

Kollman, K and Prakash A (2001) 'Green by Choice? Cross-national Variations in Firms' Responses to EMS-Based Environmental Regimes' 53 *World Politics* 399.
Messner, D and Nuscheler A (2003) *Das Konzept Global Governance. Stand und Perspektiven* (Universität Duisburg-Essen/Standort Duisburg, Institut für Entwicklung und Frieden).
Nathan, ML and Kovoor-Misra, S (2002) 'Vicarious Organizational Learning. From Crises in an Inter-Organizational Field' 38 *The Journal of Applied Behavioral Science* 245.
Prakash, A (2000) 'Responsible Care: An Assessment' 39 *Business & Society* 183.
Rehbinder, E (1997) *Environmental Agreements. A New Instrument of Environmental Policy* (Florence, European University Institute).
Ronit, K (2000) 'The Good, the Bad or the Ugly?' in K Ronit and Schneider, V (eds), *Private Organizations and their Contribution to Problem-solving in the Global Arena* (London, Routledge).
—— (2001) 'Institutions of Private Authority in Global Governance. Linking Territorial Forms of Self-Regulation' 33 *Administration & Society* 555.
Ronit, K and Schneider V (2000) 'Private Organizations and their Contribution to Problem-Solving in the Global Arena' in K Ronit and Schneider, V (eds), *Private Organizations and their Contribution to Problem-solving in the Global Arena* (London, Routledge).
Rycroft, RW (2003) 'Technology-based Globalization Indicators: The Centrality of Innovation Network Data' 25 *Technology in Society* 299.
Silk, JC (2003) 'Development of a globally harmonized system for hazard communication' 206 *International Journal of Hygiene and Environmental Health* 447.
Tukker, A and Simons, LPH (1999) *Methylene Chloride: Advantages and Drawbacks of Possible Market Restrictions in the EU*, Final report for DG III of the European Commission (http://europa.eu.int/comm/enterprise/chemicals/docs/studies/tno-methylene_chloride.pdf).
Verband Chemiehandel eV (2004) *Verantwortliches Handeln im Chemiehandel* (Köln) (http://www.vch.de).
Vinyl 2010 (2001) *The Voluntary Commitment of the PVC Industry* (http://www.vinyl2010.org/DOWNLOAD/PR/2001upd/VC2001_en.pdf).
—— (2003) *Die Freiwillige Selbstverpflichtung der PVC-Industrie zur nachhaltigen Entwicklung*, Fortschrittsbericht 2003 (http://www.hydropolymers.com/library/attachments/de/progress2003_de.pdf).
Vogel, D (1997) 'Trading up and Governing across: Transnational Governance and Environmental Protection' 4 *Journal of European Public Policy* 556.
Wernet, A (2000) Einführung in die Interpretationstechnik der objektiven Hermeneutik (Opladen, Leske + Budrich).
Whetten, DA (1981) 'Interorganizational Relations: A Review of the Field' 52 *Journal of Higher Education* 1.

6

The New Universe of Green Finance: From Self-Regulation to Multi-Polar Governance

OREN PEREZ*

THE EMERGENCE OF green finance challenges the traditional constructs of financial law.[1] New 'green' instruments are poised to transform conventional investment practices ('ethical investment'), lending standards associated with project finance ('environmental/social impact assessment'), and accounting conventions ('green/social reporting'). To a large extent this process was inspired and motivated by civic forces: environmentally and socially conscious citizens, environmental groups, and private financial institutions. International organisations such as the World Bank and the United Nations Environment Programme ('UNEP') added further impetus to this process. From a legal perspective the phenomenon of 'green finance' reflected a highly inconsistent social process, comprised of segregated contractual instruments and uncoordinated organisational routines, none of which were subject to meaningful global discipline.

This chaotic picture of detached legal structures evolving in an uncoordinated fashion has started to change over the last few years with the emergence of new global centres of governance. While these new normative centres are highly diverse in terms of their institutional structure and mode of operation, they are all dominated by non-state actors. My main goal in this chapter is to expose the contours of these emerging regulatory orders,

* I would like to thank Olaf Dilling and Gerd Winter for helpful comments on an earlier version of this chapter. An earlier version was also delivered at the University of Victoria Law School (BC, Canada) on 28 September 2006, where I was a guest of the Sustainability Project and the Environmental Law Clinic. I want to thank the students of the law school for their comments.

[1] Green finance is part of a broader phenomenon—the incorporation of various non-financial or ethical concerns into the financial universe. I will limit my observations, however, to the environmental aspects of this phenomenon.

highlighting the move from self-governance to multi-polar governance. In particular, I want to explore the question of the coordination of regulatory powers: what were the processes that shaped the allocation and redistribution of normative power at the global level? In that respect, the chapter explores two theoretical issues. The first concerns the historical forces that shaped the contemporary governance structure, specifically relating to the dominant role of non-state forces and the relatively minor role of state regulation. This division of normative powers seems to be changing, however, with signs of increasing governmental intervention. To a large extent, one can view the emergence and transformation of the field of green finance as the product of two conflicting narratives: first, neo-liberal capitalism with its emphasis on free trade, deregulation, and small government; and second, the emergence of globally oriented civic networks that highlighted the adverse social and environmental repercussions of the neo-liberal order. The second issue involves the question of whether the current normative structure, with its idiosyncratic distribution of normative powers, is the most efficient model in terms of achieving a more sustainable society. I will argue, in this context, that the contemporary governance structure, with its multiple layers, and private and public components, constitutes a *regulatory ensemble* whose synergistic capacities compensate for some of its evident shortcomings.

In answering these questions, I will take the following approach. First, I will describe the various instruments that constitute the new field of 'green finance', distinguishing between three fields of financial regulation: project finance, ethical-green investment, and environmental reporting. Project finance represents the supply side of the market, while green investment represents the demand side. Environmental reporting is part of the institutional framework that facilitates the work of the financial market.[2] In each of these domains, I will explore the evolution of new global centres of governance. In the following section, I will discuss the causal question of the extent to which the new centres have been successful in effectuating social change. The final section will explore the historical forces that shaped the contemporary normative structure of the field of green finance and examine its ecological impact, drawing on the idea of 'ensemble regulation'.

[2] The Basel Accord is another example of framework regulation. It sets minimum capital requirements for the banking industry. The new Basel Capital Framework ('Basel II'), which was published on June 2004, replaced the current 1988 Capital Accord ('Basel I'). The new Framework is based on the following three mutually reinforcing pillars: (1) minimum capital requirements, which refine the measurement framework set out in the 1988 Accord; (2) supervisory review of an institution's capital adequacy and internal assessment process; (3) market discipline through effective disclosure to encourage safe and sound banking practices. For further details see the Basel II website: http://www.bis.org/publ/bcbsca.htm, last visited 22 June 2006.

I. WALKING THE NORMATIVE MAZE: MAPPING THE CONTEMPORARY GOVERNANCE STRUCTURE OF THE FIELD OF GREEN FINANCE

A. Environmental Assessment and Project Finance

Since the beginning of the 1990s environmental considerations have started to play a bigger role in the field of project finance, influencing and shaping the organisational practices governing lending decisions. The incorporation of environmental risk assessment into the banking sector was led by development banks—prominently the World Bank—with the private sector following suit. This process had two motivations. First, the recognition that environmental concerns could also reflect financial risks, so that examining environmental risks alongside conventional (for example, economic or political) risks was seen as a reasonable business practice. The second reason arose from an ideological commitment not to support ecologically problematic projects. Whereas the first motivation was instrumental, aligned to the banks' profit-maximisation ethos, the second was normative.

Underlying the instrumental approach to environmental risks was a threefold distinction, dividing environmental risks into three categories. The first group, *direct risk*, relates to the possibility that a bank could incur direct legal liability for cleaning up contaminated land that was owned by one of its borrowers (for example, if the borrower becomes insolvent). The second category is *indirect risk,* which concerns the risk that a borrower's environmental liability might affect his ability to repay loans. Finally, *reputational risk* involves the potential damage to the bank's image from being associated with environmentally problematic investments (Thompson, 1998).[3] The US Superfund Act,[4] which increased the direct risk to lenders, has contributed to the incorporation of environmental considerations into the financial decision-making process (UNEP FI Secretariat, 2002: 54). The US approach has also influenced other financial institutions with worldwide operations.[5]

[3] Financial institutions additionally face environmental risks in their role as advisors in mergers and acquisitions. In this context, financial advisors (eg investment banks) are also expected to perform environmental risk due diligence, focusing on potential risks such as contaminated land, sick buildings, and outdated technology. Insurance companies, which play a key role in the global financial market, evaluate environmental risks in terms of their potential influence on the insurer's liability under a certain policy, most often regarding general liability or professional indemnity policies (EPA Victoria, 2003: 6).

[4] The Comprehensive Environmental Response, Compensation, and Liability Act (the 'Superfund Act') 42 USC paras 9601–75 (1988). The Superfund Act established a comprehensive liability scheme and a federal fund for the clean-up of disposal sites for 'hazardous substances'. The Act was amended in 1986 by the Superfund Amendment and Reauthorisation Act, Public Law No 9-499 (1986).

[5] See Strasser and Rodosevich (1993) and Thompson (1998). In 2000, the European Commission published a White Paper on Environmental Liability, which outlines the structure of a future framework of community liability for environmental damages (2000). The

In response to this new understanding, banks and other financial institutions, such as insurance companies, have begun to develop risk management and environmental assessment schemes in order to manage 'environmental risks' and identify their financial implications.[6]

Within the public sector—and the World Bank in particular—the instrumental considerations were also accompanied by a newly embraced commitment to environmental values. In response to severe criticism from environmental groups in the late 1980s and early 1990s with respect to its lending practices, the World Bank has made an effort to *integrate ecological considerations* into the mainstream of its lending activities (Bridgeman, 2001: 1037; Nielson and Tierney, 2003: 253–71).[7] The introduction of an environmental impact assessment requirement for all of the Bank's loans was a central tenet of this policy.[8] Article 1 of the Bank's Policy on Environmental Assessment[9] requires an 'environmental assessment (EA) of projects proposed for Bank financing to help ensure that they are environmentally sound and sustainable, and thus, to improve decision-making'.[10] Similar requirements were adopted by other development banks, such as

White Paper, which was consequently consolidated into a formal directive, explicitly rejects the expansive US approach to the liability of financial institutions, by clarifying that lenders who do not exercise operational control should not be considered liable. See Pozzo (2001) and Directive 2004/35/EC of the European Parliament and of the Council of 21 April 2004 on environmental liability with regard to the prevention and remedying of environmental damage.

[6] For a general survey of these schemes, see Jeucken (2001) and UNEP FI Secretariat (2002).

[7] As Nielson and Tierney note, the historical narrative of this policy change is complex and reflects the intricate relationships between the Bank and its member governments, and the internal dynamics of the Bank. I am more interested, however, in the ultimate consequences of this complex process.

[8] This requirement was consolidated as Operational Directive 4.01 in 1989 and was converted in 1999 into a new format: Operational Policy (OP) 4.01 and Bank Procedures (BP) 4.01. Both documents are available at: lnweb18.worldbank.org/ESSD/envext.nsf/47ByDocName/Policy (last visited 12 June 2006). A commitment to environmental assessment is also included in the *World Bank Pollution Prevention and Abatement Handbook* ('*PPAH*') (1998), pp 22–26 ('The Environmental Assessment Process'). The *PPAH* is also used by the International Finance Corporation, see: http://www.ifc.org/ifcext/enviro.nsf/Content/PPAH (last visited 22 February 2008). For further discussion of the environmental reform at the World Bank, see Nielson and Tierney (2003: 262–6).

[9] Part of the OP 4.01, revised August 2004. A complementary text exists for BP 4.01.

[10] The exact details of the environmental assessment procedures are set out in the Bank's Environmental Assessment policy, *ibid*. These procedures cover a wide range of lending operations, including investment lending, sector lending, rehabilitation lending through financial intermediaries, and Prototype Carbon Fund and Global Environmental Facility co-financed projects. The International Finance Corporation of the World Bank group adopted similar practices, codified in the new Environmental and Social Review Procedures (version 1.0, 30 April 2006), which are available at: http://www.ifc.org/ifcext/enviro.nsf/AttachmentsByTitle/pol_ESRP2006/$FILE/ESRP2006.pdf (last visited 22 June 2006).

the Asian Development Bank, the European Bank for Reconstruction and Development, and the Inter-American Development Bank.[11]

Following the lead of development banks, private banks—especially big banks with international operations—have introduced risk assessment procedures into their internal 'rule-book' (UNEP FI Secretariat, 2002: 54–5). This codification process has mainly been driven by instrumental considerations that recognise the business logic of taking environmental risks seriously. Its evolution has been highly fragmented, reflecting the accumulated experience of each institution.[12] Nonetheless, it marked an important change in the operational practice of international banks, by subjecting lending decisions to some form of environmental regulation—even though this remained a completely internal process. The approach of private banks to ecological risks was highly important given the increasing role of private capital in the financing of big infrastructure and industrial projects across the globe since the mid 1990s.[13]

The foregoing processes reflected uncoordinated normative phenomena, which took place simultaneously at separate locations. This fragmented picture seems to be changing, however. Several important initiatives representing public–private cooperation seek to provide a global normative framework for the incorporation of environmental considerations into the business practices of financial institutions. The first initiative is the United Nations Environmental Programme Finance Initiative (UNEP FI). UNEP FI was established in the early 1990s as a global partnership between UNEP and the private financial sector. UNEP's initiative seeks to strengthen the commitment of private financial institutions to environmental values.[14]

[11] See the Asian Development Bank Environment Policy, 2002 (www.adb.org/Environment/envpol/default.asp) (last visited 13 February 2006), the Environmental Policy of the European Bank for Reconstruction and Development (http://www.adb.org/Environment/envpol/default.asp) (last visited 13 February 2006), and the 2006 Environment and Safeguards Compliance Policy of the Inter-American Development Bank (http://www.iadb.org/sds/env/site_5512_e.htm) (last visited 13 February 2006).

[12] Some banks have relied on the World Bank guidelines in designing their internal risk assessment procedures (UNEP FI Secretariat, 2002: 55).

[13] There was a substantial increase in the 1990s in the amount of private capital flows going to developing countries, with a similar increase in the level of private financing of infrastructure projects (although since the late 1990s there was a steady decline in annual investment flows to private infrastructure projects in developing countries): see Botchwey (2000: 3) and Dailami and Leipziger (1998: 1284–5). It is important to note, however, that these capital flows were not equally dispersed. Low income countries in Africa and South Asia had relatively very low levels of private capital inflows (Botchwey, 2000: 5–8).

[14] UNEP FI focuses on three topics. First, it explores questions of carbon finance, and renewable energy investment through its Climate Change Working Group. Second, it explores how social, environmental, and governance considerations can be incorporated into investment practice. Finally, it emphasises the issue of sustainability reporting, and has developed with the Global Reporting Initiative Unique Reporting Guidelines for financial institutions (Financial Services Sector Supplement (Environmental Performance)). See UNEP FI core activities at http://www.unepfi.org/work_programme/index.html (last visited 16 February 2006). This supplement is part of the GRI disclosure protocol; I will therefore review it more closely at II.C below.

As part of its work programme, UNEP initiated the formulation of two statements, translating its general vision into pragmatic principles. The first statement, entitled 'Statement by Financial Institutions on the Environment and Sustainable Development', covers the banking sector;[15] the second, 'Statement of Environmental Commitment by the Insurance Industry', targets the insurance market.[16]

Both statements emphasise the need to incorporate environmental considerations into standard risk assessment processes by banking and insurance firms. Thus, Article 2.3 of the Banking Statement provides:

> We recognise that identifying and quantifying environmental risks should be part of the normal process of risk assessment and management, both in domestic and international operations. With regard to our customers, we regard compliance with applicable environmental regulations and the use of sound environmental practices as important factors in demonstrating effective corporate management.

Article 2.1 of the Insurance Statement similarly provides:

> We will reinforce the attention given to environmental risks in our core activities. These activities include risk management, loss prevention, product design, claims handling and asset management.

Another important initiative, led by the International Finance Corporation (IFC) of the World Bank Group, is the Equator Principles.[17] The Principles provide a framework for addressing environmental and social risks in project financing. Similar to the UNEP Financial Initiative, the Equator Principles are a public–private initiative; indeed, many financial institutions which have adopted these Principles are also signatories to the UNEP Banking Statement. Unlike the UNEP Statements the Equator Principles provide a detailed environmental and social impact assessment manual, adopting the practices of the IFC and the World Bank.[18] The Principles include risk categories for different types of projects, lists of issues which

[15] The banking statement was originally launched in 1992 under a slightly different name. The current, revised statement was launched in May 1997. See www.unepfi.org/signatories/statements/index.html (last visited 16 February 2006).

[16] See www.unepfi.org/signatories/statements/index.html (last visited 16 February 2006).

[17] The first version of the Equator Principles (EP) was released in 2003; a second version was released in July 2006. See http://www.equator-principles.com. The new text has expanded the class of projects to which the Principles apply by lowering the 'project threshold' to projects which cost $10 million or more (instead of the $50 million threshold in the 2003 version). As of January 2006 the EP have been adopted by 45 banks representing about 80% of project finance funds worldwide; Paul Watchman and Charles July, 'A new environment' *Legal Week*, 2 February 2006, 24 (http://www.legalweek.com). The list of institutions that have adopted the EP is available on the EP website.

[18] The EP are based on the IFC 'Safeguard Policies'. The introduction of the 2006 version was triggered by a change in the IFC Safeguard Policies (February 2006) (BankTrack, 2006: 3).

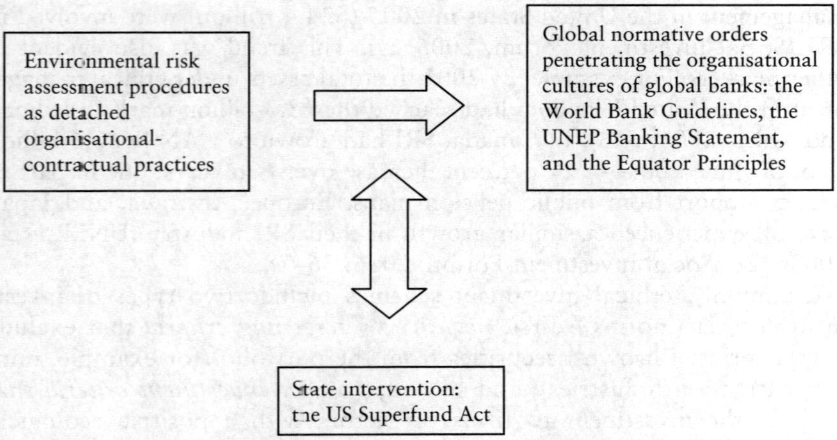

Figure 1 ***The Normative Evolution of 'Green' Project Finance.***

should be addressed by the environmental assessment process, and monitoring and follow-up guidelines.

Figure 1 depicts the normative evolution which took place in this domain.

B. The Maze of 'Green' Investment

An increasing number of institutional investors across the globe, but especially in the US, Europe (particularly the UK), and Canada, are now managing their investment portfolios according to 'socially responsible' principles.[19] This trend reflects a widening demand for investment vehicles that will be guided, not just by the criterion of financial performance, but also by moral and social concerns. Thus, ethical investment has been defined by one of the leading 'ethical' research groups as 'an investment process that considers the social and environmental consequences of investments, both positive and negative, within the context of rigorous financial analysis. It is a process of identifying and investing in companies that meet certain baseline standards or criteria of Corporate Social Responsibility' (Social Investment Forum, 2006: iv).[20]

The market for socially responsible investment (SRI) has been growing steadily over the last few years. In the United States, assets in socially screened mutual funds increased from $12 billion in 1995 to $179 billion in 2005. Nearly 10 per cent of total assets that were under professional

[19] For a detailed analysis of this trend see, eg, UNEP *et al* (2003, 126–7), the report of the US Social Investment Forum (2006), and Heal (2004).

[20] Other forms of responsible investment, such as shareholder advocacy and community investing, will not be considered in this chapter; see, eg, Social Investment Forum (2006: 16–36).

management in the United States in 2005 ($24.4 trillion) were involved in SRI (Social Investment Forum, 2006: iv). This trend was also evident in other markets. For example, by 2001 the total assets under ethical management in the United Kingdom had reached the £3.3 billion mark (Friedman and Miles, 2001: 543). In Canada, SRI had grown to CAN $65.46 billion as of 30 June 2004—a 27 per cent increase over two years, due in part to strong support from public pension plans. Europe, Australia, and Japan have all experienced a similar growth in their SRI industry (UNEP *et al*, 2003: 126; Social Investment Forum, 2006: 36–7).

Commonly, ethical investment schemes include two types of investment criteria ('norms'): first, *negative* or *screening criteria* that exclude inappropriate ('brown') securities from the portfolio (for example, mineral extraction industries); and second, *positive investment criteria* that channel the investment to firms or sectors with a positive ecological 'signature'. Positive investment criteria can either be based on considerations associated with the ecological qualities of the firm's core activity (for example, renewable energy) or on best practice benchmarking (that is, choosing the best environmental performers from a certain sector) (Brink and Woerd, 2004: 187–203). From a legal perspective, ethical investment represents a form of private rule-making, in which investors contract with financial institutions to invest on their behalf, subject to certain investment rules that are designed by the financial institution and (passively) accepted by the investors. It is thus a process of both *self-regulation* and *standard contracting*. This process has evolved in a highly fragmented environment, with each financial institution devising its own set of investment criteria, sometimes relying on external consultancies.[21] Its development has resembled the incorporation of environmental considerations into project finance. Initially, governmental intervention was limited to providing a very general regulatory framework governing the fiduciary duties of institutional investors (for example, managers of

[21] While the field of ethical investment evolved in a deeply fragmented fashion, as noted above, there are similarities between the criteria used by different investment institutions. This convergence evolved spontaneously, however, without central coordination. Thus, most ethical funds use the following negative/positive screening criteria: tobacco, alcohol and gambling, defence/weapons, community relations, environment, labour relations, and employment-equality (Social Investment Forum, 2006: 7–8). The Social Investment Forum report does not provide comprehensive data about the sub-fields, but I believe there is much more divergence at this sub-level. A comprehensive mapping of the standards used by 'green' funds is beyond the scope of this chapter. To get a sense of the criteria used by environmental funds, see the investment statements of two leading British mutual funds, Jupiter Ecology Fund and Morley Sustainable Future Funds: see, Jupiter Ecology Fund, 'Interim Report for the six months ended 30 September 2005' 2–3 (http://www.jupiteronline.co.uk/) (last visited 22 June 2006), and Friends Provident, 'Ethical and Value-Based Fund Options' (http://www.friendsprovident.com/doclib/xinv27e.pdf) (last visited 28 May 2007) (further information can be found at http://www.friendsprovident.com/sri).

pension funds, mutual funds, and other types of collectively managed funds).[22] This passive approach has changed somewhat since 2000, with governments seeking a more active role in the regulation of the ethical investment market. I will further elaborate on this regulatory shift in the following sections.

The evolution of new centres of governance seems to change this disordered picture.[23] The four key sources of governance are: transnational networks involving different stakeholders, the new Principles for Responsible Investment, sustainable indexes, and governmental initiatives. Transnational networks reflect an attempt to pool together the expertise of different organisations, and to create an international forum for exchanging ideas and coordinating action. There are many examples of such networks, such that it is impossible to cite all of them here. Let me give just a few examples. The European Social Investment Forum is a pan-European network which seeks to provide an international forum allowing various stakeholder groups to work together on questions related to socially responsible investment and corporate governance, and to collect input from members and communicate their ideas to European policy makers. Current members of the European Social Investment Forum include pension funds, financial service providers, academic institutes, research associations, and NGOs.[24] The Enhanced Analytics Initiative is an international collaboration between asset owners and asset managers aimed at encouraging better investment research, in particular research that takes account of the impact of extra-financial issues on long-term investment.[25] The SiRi Network represents another phenomenon—the global alignment of consulting agencies. The SiRi Group was formed in 2000 by 11 research organisations based in Europe, North America, and Australia.[26] Global cooperation, which brings together knowledge and expertise from different social domains, allows the network to provide superior consulting and research services in a field that is inherently global in nature.[27]

22 For a comparative discussion of these fiduciary duties, see Freshfields Bruckhaus Deringer and UNEP Finance Initiative (Asset Management Working Group) (2005).

23 Other observers have also noted the lack of standardisation in screening strategies, as well as the lack of transparency. See, in particular, the EU Commission Green Paper on promoting a European framework for Corporate Social Responsibility, COM (2001) 366 final (18/07/2001), at 22 (http://europa.eu.int/comm/employment_social/soc-dial/csr/index.htm) (last visited 22 June 2006).

24 See http://www.eurosif.org/ Leading members are Triodos Bank, Eiris, SAM, FTSE, HSBC, DNV, WWF, BNP Paribas, UBS, Fidelity, KLD, and SiRi Group. See Eurosif website, 'Members' (last visited 2 March 2006).

25 See http://www.enhancedanalytics.com (last visited 2 March 2006). Leading members are ABP Investments, AGF Asset Management, and BNP Paribas Asset Management.

26 For the full partners list see http://www.siricompany.com/partners.shtml (last visited 6 March 2006).

27 For further details about SiRi, see http://www.siricompany.com.

The Principles for Responsible Investment ('the Principles') were introduced in 2006,[28] and were co-sponsored by the UNEP Finance Initiative, the UN Global Compact, and a group of private financial institutions. The Principles provide a menu of possible options for the incorporation of environmental, social, and corporate governance (ESG) issues into mainstream investment decision-making and ownership practices. The Principles are voluntary, and not prescriptive. They require the signatories, among other things, to address ESG issues in investment policy statements and to support development of ESG-related tools, metrics, and analyses.

Sustainable indexes constitute another, and increasingly influential, source of governance. The primary players in this field are the Dow Jones Indexes and the FTSE Group, the world leaders in the stock index market.[29] Dow Jones Indexes launched the Dow Jones Sustainability Indexes in 1999 as an instrument for tracking the financial performance of the leading sustainability-driven companies worldwide. The first index in this 'family'—the Dow Jones Sustainability World Index ('DJSI World')—covers the top 10 per cent of the biggest 2,500 companies in the Dow Jones World Index in terms of economic, environmental, and social criteria; it was first published on 8 September 1999. Since 1999, other indexes have been added to the group.[30] The FTSE4Good Index Series was launched in July 2001. It was designed to measure the performance of companies that meet globally recognised corporate responsibility standards, and to facilitate investment in those companies.[31] Due to space constraints, I will focus on the Dow Jones indexes' environmental criteria. A brief discussion of the FTSE environmental criteria is included in Annex A. The Dow Jones Sustainability Indexes and the FTSE4Good Indexes Series provide order to the ethical investment market in two ways. First, the methodologies used by the two index families to select and rank companies constitute a normative benchmark for the whole ethical investment market. Second, the ultimate selections of the Dow Jones and FTSE4Good schemes themselves constitute an ordering mechanism.

[28] The full text of the Principles and further details about the development process and signatories is available at http://www.unpri.org/ (last visited 23 May 2006).

[29] Two other noteworthy social–environmental indexes are the KLD Select Social[SM] Index and the Canadian the Jantzi Social Index, see http://www.kld.com/indexes/ssindex/index.html and http://www.jantzisocialindex.com/ (last visited 6 February 2007).

[30] These include the Dow Jones STOXX Sustainability Index, the Dow Jones EURO STOXX Sustainability Index, the Dow Jones Sustainability North America Index, and the Dow Jones Sustainability United States Index, and subset indexes using further screens such as alcohol, gambling or tobacco. See http://www.sustainability-indexes.com/htmle/indexes/overview.html (last visited 28 February 2006). In February 2005 the SAM Group launched a sustainable index in Australia—the Australian SAM Sustainability Index (AuSSI)—using the same methodology as used by the Dow Jones World Index: see http://www.aussi.net.au/.

[31] Currently the series include five benchmark indices: FTSE4Good Global, FTSE4Good UK, FTSE4Good Europe, FTSE4Good US, and FTSE4Good Japan: see http://www.ftse.com/Indices/FTSE4Good_Index_Series/Constituents.jsp (last visited 1 March 2006).

The Dow Jones Index is constructed according to a highly structured selection process. The core of this process is the Corporate Sustainability Assessment Criteria, which provide a scheme for measuring and comparing corporations. The criteria are divided into three dimensions: economic, environmental, and social. Each dimension includes a list of criteria and weighting. Thus, for example, the environmental dimension includes the following areas:[32]

Table 1: Dow Jones Index—Corporate Sustainability Assessment Criteria—Environmental Dimension

Dimension	Criteria	Weighting (%)	Sub-criteria
Environment	Environmental performance (eco-efficiency)	7.0	Key Performance Indicators (KPI)—Energy KPI—GHG KPI—Waste KPI—Water coverage
	Environmental reporting	3.0	Content—Environmental Reporting Coverage
	Industry-specific criteria	Depends on industry	Environmental management systems Climate strategy, biodiversity impacts, product stewardship, etc. Media and stakeholder analysis (MSA): selected industry-specific criteria

In order to select and rank companies in accordance with the Corporate Sustainability Assessment Criteria, the Dow Jones uses the services of a consulting agency.[33] The agency analysts use the criteria as a framework for evaluating the sustainability performance of a company, assigning to each company, at the end of the evaluation process, a *sustainability score*. The sustainability score is used to identify the leading sustainability companies in each sector.[34] The data that is collected by SAM analysts in order to determine the composition of the Index is not disclosed to the public,

[32] See Dow Jones Sustainability World Indexes Guide, Version 8.0, August 2006 (http://www.sustainability-indexes.com (last visited 6 February 2007) at 10–11.

[33] Sustainable Asset Management Group Holding AG.

[34] For each company, the informational input sources for the Corporate Sustainability Assessment consist of responses to an online questionnaire, submitted documentation, policies and reports, publicly available information, and direct engagement between SAM Research analysts and the companies. The information provided in the questionnaire is then verified, which includes cross-checking the answers with documentation provided by the company, verifying a company's track record and incident and crisis management with media and stakeholder reports and, if necessary, direct interaction and clarification with the company.

although the criteria, methodology, and, of course, the names of the selected firms are made public.[35]

Finally, governments have started to take an increasing interest in the ethical investment market, recognising the growing popularity of this new investment trend. While government intervention has been quite limited up to now, I believe that the prospects are good for an increase in the scale of intervention as the ethical investment market expands. Governments have, so far, primarily intervened in the pension market, focusing on issues such as freedom of choice and transparency. As a result, several countries have introduced rules that ensure that individuals can freely choose their personal retirement plans, as well as rules that require pension funds to disclose their investment policies.[36]

The approach taken in the United Kingdom illustrates the potential impact of such governmental intervention. According to the new rules, which came into force on 1 July 2000, pension fund trustees are required to declare their policy on social, environmental, and ethical issues in their Statement of Investment Principles.[37] The new disclosure rules have already induced several pension funds to adopt ethical investment criteria. Thus, for example, Friends Provident decided to manage all of its £15 billion assets in equity investment portfolios according to a new strategy of 'responsible engagement overlay', which will encourage good practice with regard to human rights, child labour, and environmental pollution.[38] The BT Pension Scheme (£25 billion) and the Universities Superannuation Scheme (£20 billion) have already published their SRI policies, which include special provisions on environmental 'good practice'.[39]

Figure 2 describes the evolution of the ethical investment governing apparatus.

C. The Emergence of 'Green' Accounting: The Story of the Global Reporting Initiative

The field of green—or, more generally, non-financial—accounting has undergone a similar transformation from self-regulation to external, globally

[35] See Dow Jones Sustainability World Indexes Guide, n 32 above, 8–9.

[36] Rules pertaining to freedom of choice were adopted by Australia, Japan, the UK, and the US (UNEP FI Secretariat, (2002: 18). Disclosure rules were adopted by Australia, Austria, Belgium, France, Germany, Hungary, Spain, Sweden, the Netherlands, and the UK (Freshfields Bruckhaus Deringer and Group 2005: 11) and the Compendium on national public policies on CSR in the European Union (http://ec.europa.eu/employment_social/emplweb/csr-matrix/csr_matrix_en.cfm) (last visited 1 June 2006).

[37] See the Occupational Pension Schemes (Investment, Assignment, Forfeiture, Bankruptcy etc) (Amendment) Regulations 1999, SI 1999/1849, reg 2(4). These Regulation were made under the Pensions Act 1995.

[38] See 'Friends Plans to Give Ethical Lead', (2000) *Financial Times*, 8 May, 25.

[39] 'Ethics Under the Microscope' (2000) *Financial Times Survey—Pension Fund Investment*, 12 May, 8. On the reaction of the UK pension market to this regulatory change see further Friedman and Miles (2001: 526).

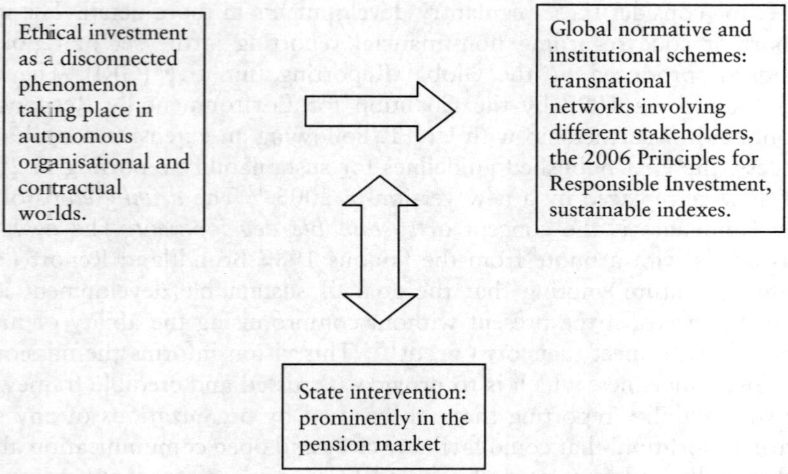

Figure 2 ***The Normative Structuration of Ethical Investment.***

oriented governance. The three vertices of the governance game in this field have been transnational corporations ('TNCs'), global institutions, and governments. Firms, especially TNCs, have been publishing non-financial information since the 1980s. However, these social–environmental reports varied greatly in both style and form, disclosing relatively little quantitative data.[40] While there was a process of convergence and reciprocal learning between firms (Tile, 2001), the lack of central coordination was highly apparent.

The disordered landscape of the 1990s is currently being transformed into a much more ordered domain. This process is inspired by three sources of governance: first, *private codes* that set out clear rules for non-financial reporting and external assurance; second, increasing and wide-scale *government intervention*; and finally, *indirect pressure* towards more extensive disclosure reflecting the normative changes in the fields of environmental risk assessment and ethical investment, as well as parallel transformations in the field of corporate law. Particularly important in this regard is the influence of global environmental management standards (such as ISO 14001) and corporate codes (such as the Ceres Principles).[41]

[40] See *Disclosure of the impact of corporations on society: Current trends and issues*, Report by the UNCTAD Secretariat, TD/B/COM.2/ISAR/20, 15 August 2003 (http://www.unctad.org/en/docs/c2isar20_en.pdf), paras 34 and 38, and Maltby (1997).

[41] See Potoski and Prakash (2005) for a discussion of ISO 14001, and see http://www.ceres.org/coalitionandcompanies/principles.php for the CERES Principles. Also noteworthy is Principle 10 of the 2006 Equator Principles, which requires each subscribing institution to publish an annual report elaborating on the way it has implemented the Principles.

Let me consider these regulatory developments in more detail. The most important code regarding non-financial reporting is the set of reporting standards produced by the Global Reporting Initiative (GRI). The GRI was founded in 1997 by the Coalition for Environmentally Responsible Economies in partnership with UNEP. Following an extensive consultation process, the GRI published guidelines for sustainability reporting in 2002, which were replaced by a new version in 2006.[42] The *driving ethos* of the new Guidelines is the concept of *sustainable development*. The new text thus opens with a quote from the famous 1987 Brundtland Report ('Our Common Future') noting that the goal of sustainable development is to 'meet the needs of the present without compromising the ability of future generations to meet their own needs'.[43] This vision informs the mission of the GRI Guidelines, which is to provide a 'trusted and credible framework for sustainability reporting that can be used by organizations of any size, sector, or location' that could facilitate clear and open communication about sustainability using a 'globally shared framework of concepts, consistent language, and metrics'.[44]

The 2006 Guidelines, as the 2002 scheme they replaced, distinguish between three aspects of organisations' activities: economic, environmental, and social.[45] This choice is supported by the idea that '*achieving sustainability* requires balancing the complex relationships between current economic, environmental, and social needs in a manner that does not compromise future needs' (emphasis added).[46] A sustainability report issued in accordance with the GRI Guidelines should include information on each of these three aspects of corporate behaviour (although I will focus only on the environmental segment of the Guidelines here). It is assumed that the sustainability report will be issued in *conjunction* with the corporate conventional financial statement.[47]

In contrast to the traditional rules of financial reporting, which are *bounded* by the ethos of profit maximisation, the GRI Guidelines are *driven* by a *distinctive* environmental concern. This fundamental difference influences the nature of environmental disclosure that is required by each scheme. Whereas the traditional accounting conventions require the disclosure of environmental data only when it is presumed to have some impact on the firm's profit, the GRI Guidelines seek to measure the organisation's 'impact on living and non-living natural systems, including eco-systems, land, air

[42] GRI, *Sustainability Reporting Guidelines* (Amsterdam: Global Reporting Initiative, 2002); GRI, *RG—Sustainability Reporting Guidelines*, (Amsterdam: Global Reporting Initiative, 2006). Both versions can be obtained from the GRI website (http://www.globalreporting.org). In the following discussion I will refer to the 2006 text.

[43] 2006 Guidelines, at 2.

[44] *Ibid.*

[45] 2006 Guidelines, at 8, 25–34; 2002 Guidelines, at 9, 34.

[46] 2002 Guidelines, at 9; see also, 2006 Guidelines, at 8.

[47] 2006 Guidelines at 37. The two reports might, in some instances, overlap; in general, however, they should be complementary, 2002 Guidelines, at 45.

and water'.[48] This is achieved by requiring the reporting organisation to provide comprehensive data about the ecological aspects of its behaviour. Thus, the Guidelines' Environmental Indicators cover 'performance related to inputs (eg, material, energy, water) and outputs (eg, emissions, effluents, waste). In addition, the indicators cover performance related to 'biodiversity, environmental compliance, and other relevant information such as environmental expenditure and the impacts of products and services.'[49]

The 2006 Guidelines provide a detailed description of each indicator in a separated annex.[50] The indicators include data about total material use, direct and indirect energy consumption, energy conservation measures, total water withdrawal by source, location, and size of land owned, leased, or managed in, or adjacent to protected areas and areas of high biodiversity value, significant impacts on biodiversity, greenhouse gas emissions, emissions of ozone-depleting substances, NOx, SOx and other significant air emissions by type, total amount of waste by type and destination, initiatives to mitigate environmental impacts of products and services, and extent of impact mitigation, and monetary values of significant fines and total number of non-monetary sanctions for non-compliance with environmental laws and regulations.

Although the GRI Guidelines are somewhat ambiguous regarding the meaning of sustainability, they take a highly exacting approach with respect to the design of 'green' behavioural (or performance) indicators. The Guidelines introduce a variety of rigorously defined economic, environmental, and social indicators. The choice of indicators reflects, of course, an embryonic vision of sustainability, delineating the general boundaries of sustainable development as a concept. What is probably the most important aspect of the Guidelines is that they facilitate interpretative dialogue on 'sustainability' within the corporate realm.

The GRI, together with UNEP FI, developed special rules setting out distinctive disclosure requirements for financial institutions. This resulted in the GRI Financial Services Sector Supplement (Environmental Performance) that provides a method for measuring the ecological impacts of financial institutions, which are different from conventional industrial impacts. The performance indicators in the GRI Supplement relate primarily to the systems used by institutions to incorporate environmental considerations into their business processes.[51] The indicators distinguish between three elements—policy, procedures, and practice. Each of these elements is measured by a detailed

[48] 2002 Guidelines, at 48; see also 2006 Guidelines, at 27.
[49] 2006 Guidelines, at 27.
[50] Indicator Protocols Set: Environment, available at www.globalreporting.org/Services/ResearchLibrary/GRIPublications.
[51] The GRI Financial Services Sector Supplement (Environmental Performance), Pilot Version 1.0, March 2005: 6.

set of questions that seek to make explicit the content, organisation, and implementation of the organisation risk assessment system. The GRI Supplement provides a normative benchmark for financial institutions.[52]

In parallel to the development of the GRI Guidelines, and in response to concerns regarding the reliability of the reported information, several bodies produced global standards on external assurance. The prominent examples are the International Standard on Assurance Engagements (ISAE 3000),[53] the AA1000 Assurance Standard produced by AccountAbility,[54] and several guidance documents on the assurance of sustainability reports produced by the European Federation of Accountants.[55] The International Standard on Assurance Engagements is likely to be widely adopted, since the International Federation of Accountants, which has produced the standard, is the global organisation for the accountancy profession, working with 163 member organisations.[56]

Alongside these civic-oriented initiatives there are two other important developments at the governmental level. First, there was increasing recognition from national regulators that securities regulations—although not based on ecological rationale—require more extensive disclosure of environmental data. It seems that stock markets do not provide all the necessary environmental information that should be disclosed under the traditional materiality principle—which requires environmental disclosure when *the data has an influence on the firm's future revenues*.[57] This recognition led, for example, the US Environmental Protection Agency (EPA), in cooperation with the US Securities and Exchange Commission (SEC), to take several steps aimed at improving the level of compliance with SEC disclosure requirements.[58] Another important development is the establishment of mandatory reporting schemes, imposing independent reporting obligations. Mandatory disclosure programmes, such as the US Toxics Release

[52] Its potential audience is broad, covering a wide range of financial institutions: retail banking, commercial and corporate banking, asset management and insurance, *ibid*, at 5. It is thus also relevant to the field of ethical investment, which will be discussed below, as well as to the operations of insurance companies, which will not be discussed in detail in this chapter.

[53] See http://www.ifac.org/Guidance.

[54] See www.accountability.org.uk.

[55] See www.fee.be. Also important are several standards produced by ISO on the auditing of environmental management systems and environmental performance (eg, ISO/AWI 14064, ISO 19011).

[56] See, generally, AccountAbility, 'The Future of Sustainability Assurance' (2004), ACCA Research Report No 86, http://www.accountability.org.uk/uploadstore/cms/docs/rr-086-001.pdf.

[57] For a more detailed discussion of this issue see Perez (2006).

[58] In October 2001 the EPA's Office of Enforcement and Compliance Assurance issued an Enforcement Alert urging companies to abide by the requirements of Regulation S-K, which sets out the disclosure requirements under US Securities Regulations; it has also improved its information-sharing with the SEC in order to expand the SEC's enforcement capacities: see EPA Enforcement Alert, vol 4, No 3 (October 2001) (www.epa.gov/compliance/resources/newsletters/civil/enfalert) (last visited on 1 April 2005).

Inventory (TRI) programme, the European Pollution Emissions Register (EPER), and the Canadian National Pollutant Release Inventory (NPRI) Scheme require manufacturers, which meet certain conditions (usually in terms of size and type of business), to provide estimates of their chemical emissions for a designated set of toxic substances.[59] The GRI scheme goes beyond the requirements of these two state-sponsored projects, both by extending the scope and scale of the ecological data that must be disclosed (moving beyond chemical emissions) and by not basing the disclosure requirement on an economically defined notion of materiality. Nonetheless, the expansion of the disclosure obligations under state law clearly provided support for the adoption of the more stringent disclosure requirements prescribed by the GRI Guidelines.

Figure 3 describes the normative evolution of this field.

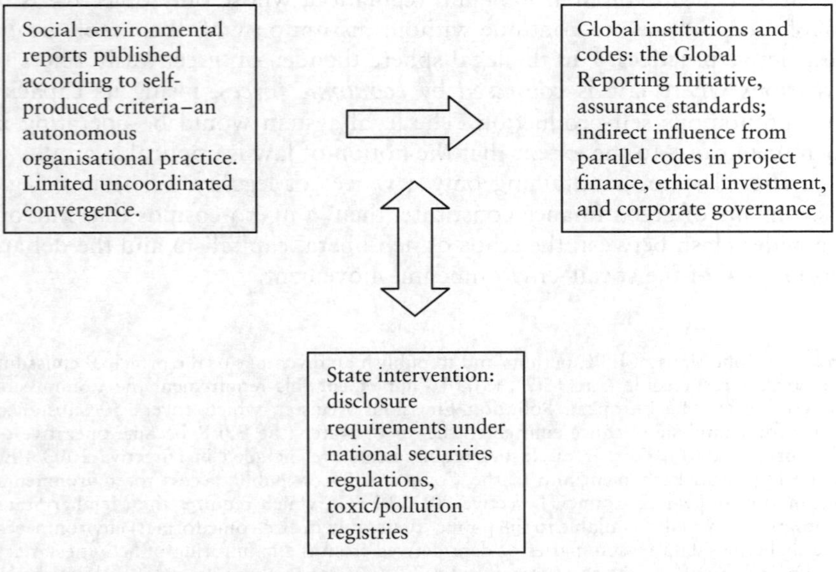

Figure 3 *Green Accounting—Normative Trends.*

[59] See Brehm and Hamilton (1996: 445). More details about these three programmes can be found at http://www.epa.gov/tri/, http://eper.eea.eu.int/eper/ and www.ec.gc.ca/pdb/npri, respectively. Other prominent examples include the Swiss Pollutant Emission Register, the Mexican pollution inventory (http://www.ine.gob.mx/?lang=_e), the Australia National Pollutant Inventory (http://www.npi.gov.au/index.html), the Swedish Pollutant Release and Transfer Register (http://www.naturvardsverket.se/prtr/), and the British Pollution Inventory (www.environment-agency.gov.uk/pi). Let me expand upon the relatively new European scheme. The European Pollution Emissions Register implements the data dissemination requirements included in Directive 96/61/EC concerning integrated pollution prevention and control ('the IPPC Directive'). The IPPC Directive requires the Member States and the Commission (respectively) to publish the results of monitoring of releases as required

II. THE CAUSAL QUESTION: LEGAL TALK, GREENWASH, AND ECOLOGICAL CHANGE

As outlined in the previous section, the field of 'green finance' was transformed from a field governed by multiple, self-standing organisational contractual instruments, to one governed by a relatively small number of transnational codes. This transformation has taken place, almost simultaneously, in all of the fields discussed above, including project finance, ethical investment, and environmental reporting. In all of these areas, state intervention remained both patchy and hesitant. While these processes seem to reflect a notable legal phenomenon, the impact of these processes on other worlds of meaning (social systems and individuals) and the natural environment remains unclear. Indeed, one has to deal here with the recurring accusation that these so-called 'soft' legal instruments are nothing but 'greenwash': a façade of environmental regulation, whose only objective is to enable corporations to continue without disruption with their ecologically destructive practices.[60] In the legal sphere the idea of 'greenwash' refers to situations where law is *colonised* by *economic forces*, losing its capacity for autonomous self-production. The legal system would be operating in such scenarios—to the extent that the notion of law is applicable at all—in a corrupted state, maintaining only a veneer of legality.[61] The new legal instruments of green finance constitute, then, a micro-cosmos that mirrors the wider clash between the ethos of neo-liberal capitalism and the defiant world-view of the social–environmental movement.

under the conditions of IPPC permits and to publish an inventory of the principal emissions and sources responsible (Art 15(2), (3)). To implement this requirement the Commission has established the European Pollution Emissions Register, which covers 50 substances of environmental significance emitted to the air or water (the EPER became operative on 23 February 2004). Further disclosure requirements are included in Directive 2003/4/EC of the European Parliament and of the Council 2003 on public access to environmental information (repealing Council Directive 90/313/EEC), which requires the Member States to progressively make available to the public (preferably in electronic format) environmental data including 'data or summaries of data derived from the monitoring of activities affecting, or likely to affect, the environment' (Art 7(2)(e)). For further information about the US scheme and a list of pollution registers in other countries, see UNEP *et al* (2003: 110–12). A significant advance in the adoption of pollution registers came in May 2003, when a broad coalition of countries signed the Protocol on Pollutant Release and Transfer Registers (PRTR) under the Aarhus Convention. The PRTR Protocol reflects an ambitious effort to expand mandatory disclosure requirements for toxic pollutants. For further discussion of the PRTR Protocol, see UNEP *et al*, *ibid*, at 114–15.

[60] See, for example, Kenny Bruno, 'Earth Day 2000 Greenwash Sweepstakes: The World Bank', CorpWatch, April 22nd, 2000 (http://www.corpwatch.org/article.php?id=240, last visited 4 June 2006). For a more nuanced critique of ethical investment, see Friends of the Earth, 'Ethical Investment', March 2005 (http://www.foe.co.uk/campaigns/corporates/resource/investors.html, last visited 4 June 2006). For a definition of greenwash see CorpWatch, 'Greenwash Fact Sheet', 22 March 2001 (http://www.corpwatch.org/print_article.php?id=242) and Lyon and Maxwell (2007).

[61] Using Luhmann's distinctions, see (2004: 109).

In exploring the integrity of these new legal regimes, I would like to focus on two causal issues. First, what is the impact of the normative clustering depicted above on the structure and behaviour of financial institutions? Examples of *structural changes* include the creation of new organisational units, routines, and hierarchies. Examples of *behavioural changes* include shifts in the composition of loans or stocks portfolios (in banks and investment institutions, respectively). Second, what is the ecological impact of the new normative framework? In considering this question, one can either try to observe nature directly, or, alternatively, focus on close proxies, such as the behaviour of (polluting) industries. These two issues do not exhaust the causal puzzle. Other questions such as the general influence on the economic system (in terms of fluctuations in stock market), the influence on individuals in their dual role as investors and citizens, and the reciprocal relationship between these new global regimes and national normative processes are also important; however, although I will return to the last issue in the next section, it will not be possible to fully consider such questions in this chapter. Nonetheless, the two issues highlighted above provide a rich enough picture of the external impact of the new regimes.

Before commenting on these two questions it is important to set out the limitations of this kind of causal analysis. The causal forces underlying the problem of pollution control are highly complex. The normative processes depicted above take place alongside multiple legal and non-legal processes, each having their own causal influences. It is not possible to create a laboratory experiment, in which the variables discussed in this chapter—environmental risk-assessment, investment criteria, and disclosure rules—are manipulated, while everything else is held constant.[62] As a result, the following observations will be necessarily contingent and tentative, especially given the fact that the normative phenomena explored here are very recent.[63]

Consider first, the field of project finance. In this context, a distinction needs to be made between private banks and development banks. There are some indications that private banks have been influenced by the new regimes. First, UNEP Banking and Insurance statements and the Equator Principles have already attracted a significant number of signatories, many of which are global leaders. The UNEP statements had 168 signatories as of 1 February 2007, among them key players such as Barclays Group plc, Citigroup, Credit Suisse Group, and Deutsche Bank AG.[64] The Equator Principles had 45 signatories.[65] Many leading institutions such as ABN

[62] Experimental economics explores economic dilemmas with such laboratory experiments, but it usually deals with much more structured and simpler causal situations: see eg Kahneman *et al* (1990).

[63] For a discussion of these limitations, following Luhmann, see also King (2006).

[64] See http://www.unepfi.org/signatories.

[65] See http://www.equator-principles.com.

AMRO Holding NV, Citigroup, HSBC Holdings plc, JPMorgan Chase, and the Royal Bank of Scotland Group take part in both initiatives. The lack of transparency which characterises the operations of private financial institutions, however, makes it difficult to assess to what extent these institutions have actually implemented their commitments under these regimes. Whereas public financial institutions, such as the World Bank, operate in a relatively transparent manner, the practices of private financial institutions remain, in general, highly secretive.[66] Nonetheless at least one recent report argues that the Equator Principles had a substantial impact on the financial market, describing them as a 'shining beacon for responsible banking' (Freshfields Bruckhaus Deringer and Group, 2005: 1).[67] There are also some indications that the practice of environmental risk assessment spread beyond the circle of UNEP/Equator signatories (McKenzie and Wolfe, 2004).[68]

With respect to development banks, the data is somewhat richer, allowing for more detailed empirical research. Particularly noteworthy is an ambitious research project funded by the US National Science Foundation—Project-Level Aid (PLAID)—which has compiled data on development finance for the years 1970–2001, covering 430,000 development projects. The project evaluates each of the projects for its projected impact on the environment (using a novel coding system).[69] Up to now, studies using

[66] Whereas the World Bank, for example, provides extensive information about its decision-making rules (eg lending criteria) and its loans portfolio, this information is usually not available with respect to private banks. See Paul Watchman and Charles July, 'A new environment' (2006) *Legal Week*, 2 February, 24 (http://www.legalweek.com), WWF (2005: 3) and BankTrack (2006: 9–10). The lack of transparency is reflected also by the fact that as of 8 June 2006 only 25 financial institutions (out of 163 organisations) have committed to publishing annual reports *in accordance* with the GRI Guidelines see http://www.globalreporting.org/ guidelines/reporters_IA.asp. It is interesting to note in that regard that only five of the 25 financial institutions that have published *in accordance* reports have also subscribed to the Equator Principles (ABN AMRO Bank, Caja Navarra, Rabobank Groep, WestLB AG, and Westpac Banking Corporation). Principle 10 of the 2006 Equator Principles (EP) requires each of the subscribing institutions to publish an annual report about the way it has implemented the EP. It may thus reduce some of the information asymmetry that currently characterises the financial realm.

[67] The Freshfields study was based on detailed questionnaires, which were sent to EP and non-EP banks, project sponsors, consulting agencies, and NGOs: *ibid* at 45.

[68] A UNEP study found that 56% of the banks that participated in the survey (including banks from the EU, North America, and Oceania) conduct environmental risk assessments in their financing decisions (UNEP FI Secretariat, 2002: 54–5). Other studies report similar findings. See, for example: McKenzie and Wolfe (2004), McDermott *et al* (2005: 8–9), Hoijtink (2005: 50), Gee-Janssens (2004: 42–66). While the foregoing studies seem to indicate that the world of private banking has undergone significant institutional change, their results are somewhat limited, because they rely either on questionnaire-based surveys, in-depth interviews, or examination of data in financial and social–environmental reports. None of these studies examined closely the banks' loan portfolio or the financed projects themselves. While this methodological deficiency may be understandable given the secretive nature of the banking business, it nonetheless casts doubts on the conclusions of these studies.

[69] See http://www.wm.edu/irtheoryandpractice/plaid/ (last visited 6 February 2007).

the PLAID database have mainly focused on the World Bank. The studies show that the World Bank has significantly changed its lending practices, and that these changes triggered statistically significant changes to its loan portfolio, reflecting a shift toward categories whose environmental impact is negligible, non-existent, or even positive.[70]

Looking next at the area of ethical investment, the normative transformation of the field of ethical investment has triggered significant institutional changes, reflecting the fact that the new 'ethical' investment vehicles have attracted increasing amounts of money, causing substantial changes in the investment portfolios of pension funds and investment houses.[71] What is less clear is whether this normative-institutional phenomenon, and the associated shift of investment money from 'regular' to 'green' funds, has had any effect on the behaviour of firms themselves.[72]

The research into the possible and actual effects of ethical funds is still in its early stages. Several studies offer theoretical models showing that the existence of green or ethical investors may induce firms to change their behaviour (for example, adopt green technologies) by changing the cost of capital of 'green' firms. However, the force of this 'green' stimulus depends on the proportion of green/ethical money in the total universe of investment capital (Heinkel *et al*, 2001; Aslaksen and Synnestvedt, 2003). Economic theory also predicts that ethical/green investment funds are likely to underperform neutral investment vehicles because 'by restricting the universe from which stocks can be picked, a fund manager cannot improve his performance and may worsen it' (Heal, 2004: 22). Empirical studies of these two predictions are still quite limited and leave many open issues. There has not been much work exploring the efficacy of ethical/green funds in changing corporate behaviour. A recent study exploring the FTSE4Good index examined this question indirectly, by conducting a questionnaire survey of companies listed on the FTSE4Good UK and Europe indices (as of September 2003). The questionnaires were sent to public/investor relations departments. The results suggest that the FTSE4Good initiative had some impact on the internal dynamics of listed companies, especially with respect to reporting, policy decisions, and management systems (Cobb *et al*, 2004: 26). This study suffers, however, from various methodological shortcomings, and thus, its results require further corroboration (Cobb *et al*, 2004: 25–6). There are also

[70] See Nielson and Tierney (2005: 788–9).

[71] See the Social Investment Forum (2006).

[72] It is possible to distinguish in this context between two motivations driving individuals to invest in green funds. Ethical investment can be seen, first, as a reflection of personal integrity. People want to ensure that their deeds conform to their moral principles and beliefs. From this perspective profitability and financial cost are simply irrelevant. But ethical investment can also be seen as an instrument for inducing firms to behave more responsibly—in terms of the environmental and social side effects of their behaviour. From this perspective ethical investment is seen as an instrument for changing the world.

conflicting findings with respect to the performance of ethical funds (Heal, 2004: 22).

In the field of environmental reporting, the emergence of the GRI as a dominant normative source has had substantial impact on global disclosure practices. A report published by KPMG in 2005 outlines the scale of this impact (KPMG, 2005). The KPMG survey analyses trends in corporate responsibility reporting of the world's largest corporations, including the top 250 companies of the Fortune 500 (G250) and top 100 companies in 16 countries (N100). With its vast coverage of more than 1,600 companies, the survey provides a truly global picture of reporting trends over the last 10 years. The report documents a dramatic change in both the style and scale of environmental reporting. First, the focus of corporate responsibility reporting has changed from purely environmental reporting up until 1999 to sustainability (social, environmental, and economic) reporting, reflecting the structure of the 2002 GRI Guidelines. Second, in terms of scale, the report notes that sustainability reporting has now become mainstream among G250 companies (68 per cent) and is fast becoming so among N100 companies (48 per cent).[73] The influence of the GRI Guidelines was also reflected by the fact that 40 per cent of the reporters mentioned that the Guidelines were the tool used by the corporation to decide about the content of the sustainability report.[74] The increasing influence of the GRI Guidelines on global reporting trends was also noted by the SustainAbility 2004 survey of corporate sustainability reporting.[75]

But did the institutional move from conventional to sustainable reporting make a difference in terms of the environmental performance of the reporting organisations? This is a much more difficult question, mainly because one cannot design a proper experiment to test this hypothesis, while other measurement techniques, such as econometric methods and elite interviews raise various methodological questions.[76] The literature has yet to tackle this question, so I can only refer to a few preliminary indicators. For instance, a KPMG report explored the question of what drives companies to take on sustainability reporting. Almost half of the companies reported risk management or risk reduction as one of their key reasons, which seems to suggest that sustainable reporting had an impact on they way these firms are managed.[77]

[73] KPMG (2005: 4).
[74] *Ibid* at 20.
[75] See Standard&Poor *et al* (2004: 38–42, 47).
[76] For example, to mention just two: the problem of building a reliable control set, and the self-selection bias.
[77] KPMG Report (2005: 18 (table 1)). Other key reasons were economic considerations (74% of the sample), ethical considerations (53%), innovation and learning (53%), and employee motivation (47%). These data are based on a textual analysis of the reports: *ibid* at 8.

To conclude this section two general observations may be made. First, the new global legal apparatus has triggered discernible changes in the practices and organisational routines of financial institutions and transnational corporations. However, it is too early to predict the extent to which these changes will lead to meaningful ecological improvement. Answering this question involves difficult methodological and empirical problems, reflecting the lack of reliable and coherent data about the behavioural profile of industrial corporations and the state of the environment. The evidence seems, then, to weigh against the 'greenwash' hypothesis, although there is insufficient data to dismiss it completely.

III. COORDINATING THE COORDINATORS: REFLECTIONS ON THE PAST AND FUTURE OF GOVERNANCE IN THE FIELD OF GREEN FINANCE

In considering the normative apparatus which governs the field of green finance, one is confronted with two questions. The first concerns the historical forces that led to the contemporary governance configuration, and specifically, the dominant role played by non-state forces in this regard. The second involves a different question: is the current normative structure, with its idiosyncratic distribution of normative powers, the most efficient one in terms of achieving a more sustainable society? While the former question adopts a position of detached sociological observation, the latter takes the bolder and more problematic perspective of social engineering.

Let me comment, first, on the historical question. The emergence and transformation of the field of green finance should be considered, as noted above, in light of the cultural struggle between neo-liberal capitalism and the new social movements. The origins of the green finance wave can be traced back to the environmental campaign against the World Bank and the GATT in the 1980s and beginning of 1990s.[78] This campaign received some political support from the US Government and other governments (particularly Japan, West Germany, the Netherlands, and Denmark) leading to a significant reform at the World Bank, and, to a lesser extent, influencing the structure of the newly established WTO.[79] This environmental critique brought to light the linkage between the trade–financial world and the environment, triggering the emergence of green-financial instruments. This environmental sentiment was supported by certain regulatory changes, in particular, the enactment of the Superfund Act in the United States.[80]

[78] For a review and discussion see Esty (1994), Wade (1997), and Nielson and Tierney (2003).

[79] Nielson and Tierney (2003: 261) and Perez (2004: chs 1 and 3).

[80] The Act imposed liability for land contamination on banks lending to environmentally sensitive industries; see Hooley (2001) and Boyer and Porrini (2003).

On another front, financial institutions and industrial corporations began to recognise that ecological risks also represent financial and operational risks.

The parallel processes of broadening environmental sentiments, stricter environmental regulation, and increased business interest in ecological risks led together to the evolution of the first generation of green financial instruments. The ensuing legal map was highly fragmented, reflecting the absence of global coordinating forces. State intervention remained limited, reflecting the strong influence of the neo-liberal perspective. The leap to the second generation of regulatory instruments was facilitated by several processes.[81] *First*, the recognition—by various 'green entrepreneurs'—that the increased interest in green financial instruments on the one hand, and the lack of global centres of governance, on the other, constitutes a business opportunity. For private entities such as the FTSE and Dow Jones groups, environmental consulting agencies, and global standardisation bodies such as the ISO, the relative chaos that characterised the field of green finance and corporate social responsibility, marked a new business terrain. The evolution of sustainable indexes represents a particularly fascinating example in this context. In providing governance to the ethical investment market, groups like the FTSE and the Dow Jones Indexes were building on their reputation and experience in the parallel business of tracking companies' financial performance. They were using their experience as leverage for gaining normative supremacy in this newly created 'market'.

A *second factor* was the increasing involvement of international organisations such as the World Bank and UNEP. In most cases, these organisations have joined forces with transnational corporations. UNEP Finance Initiative, the Equator Principles project, the 2006 Principles for Responsible Investment, and the Global Reporting Initiative are all examples of such joint projects. Increasing consumer interest—particularly in instruments of ethical investment—provided further impetus to this process, boosting the interest of financial institutions and providing public legitimacy for these initiatives. Finally, new governmental initiatives, such as the imposition of transparency rules in the pension market, and the introduction of mandatory disclosure schemes such as the US Toxics Release Inventory and the European Pollutant Emission Register, also contributed—even if indirectly—to the codification process which was led by private institutions and global organisations. These latter processes seem to reflect a certain retreat from the basic prescriptions of neo-liberal capitalism, and a willingness to accept some of the civic critique against it.

What is likely to be the next phase in this evolving process? While I think that the normative leadership will remain in the hands of non-state

[81] For a discussion of this historical process, see also Utting (2000: 2–5).

organs, such as NGOs, TNCs and international organisations, and various hybrid combinations of these entities, I believe that governments are likely to extend their intervention, creating a normative ensemble of multi-layered regulation. Government intervention is likely to take place in several areas. The *first* regulatory dimension in which governments are likely to expand their intervention is *transparenacy*.[82] There will be continued pressure to develop (and extend) environmental reporting registers, which would operate independently of the emerging practice of sustainability reporting.[83] In the field of pension law there will be increasing pressure to ensure that citizens have the freedom to choose among different investment philosophies, and that fund managers provide full information with respect to their ethical, social, and environmental policies.[84]

Second, while I do not foresee governments intervening directly in the content of the new regimes (for example in the investment criteria of 'green' mutual funds), there will be more attempts to invoke domestic norms governing *framework issues* such as misrepresentation in securities laws, and laws regarding the fiduciary duties of fund managers.[85] One of the more puzzling question concerns the response of traditional legal doctrines to the challenges created by the new field of green finance. For example, how can damages be measured in the case of a misrepresentation or omission regarding ecological information, if such misrepresentation or omission did not cause financial damage to the investor? Furthermore, is it possible to bring a claim of a breach of fiduciary duty against a pension fund manager for failing to implement the fund's social-environmental policy, if it can be shown that this breach has financially benefited the fund's beneficiaries?[86] A possible legal response, which was developed by the Israeli Supreme Court, is the creation of a new tort remedy that does not focus on the question of financial damage, but instead on the *grievance to the individual's integrity or autonomy*, manifested in the deliberate disregard of his moral beliefs and preferences.[87] Finally, there will also be increasing pressure to incorporate social–environmental criteria into public procurement rules.

[82] See, in general, eg the data provided on the EC website Compendium on national public policies on CSR in the European Union (http://ec.europa.eu/employment_social/emplweb/csr-matrix/csr_matrix_en.cfm) (last visited 11 June 2006).

[83] See above n 63.

[84] For a survey of recent developments in this field see Freshfields Bruckhaus Deringer and UNEP Finance Initiative (Asset Management Working Group) (2005).

[85] For a discussion of these doctrinal issues, see, for example Vashista *et al* (2005) and Freshfields Bruckhaus Deringer and UNEP Finance Initiative (Asset Management Working Group) (2005). These norms can be invoked both through criminal or administrative actions initiated by state regulators and through private litigation.

[86] See, Freshfields Bruckhaus Deringer and UNEP Finance Initiative (Asset Management Working Group) (2005: 7–12).

[87] *Daaka v Carmel Hospital—Haifa*, Supreme Court Case 2781/93, and *Tnuva v Ravi Tufic*, Supreme Court Case 1338/97.

Such clauses can already be found in the public procurement regimes of the Czech Republic, France, Lithuania, and Sweden.[88]

Regarding the question of regulatory efficiency, two conflicting arguments have been raised. First, the thesis of reflexive law, which highlights the systemic barriers facing the project of social engineering, points to the advantages of bringing together under a single institutional umbrella both financial expertise and norm-creation capacities. Allowing financial institutions to take an active role in shaping the norms that will regulate the financial market—from risk assessment procedures to investment criteria and disclosure protocols—sets the ground for a more responsive legal structure. A second important advantage has to do with the shortcomings of global politics, namely, the grave difficulties of reaching transnational agreements. Private entities such as the FTSE and Dow Jones, and hybrid structures such as the GRI can circumvent these difficulties.

On the other hand, these hybrid associations—which are very different from the organisational structures that dominate the national realm, in which the legal and economic worlds are embedded in highly separated institutions—are much more prone to the risk of corruption or colonisation. The question, then, is who will guard the regulators (Utting, 2000)? In other words, can this new multi-layered regulatory network withstand the inevitable pressures of the global economic system? This is a legitimate concern. I think that the unique structure of the new regulatory apparatus, with its 'ensemble' architecture, makes the prospects of absolute economic domination unlikely. The different regulatory layers that constitute this field create a *mutually supportive* structure, whose synergistic capacities compensate for some of its shortcomings (like the lack of developed compliance mechanisms).[89] Three points are particularly noteworthy in this context. First, the multi-polar structure of the current regulatory framework ensures that an orchestrated attempt to link the various green-finance initiatives, creating a global greenwash cartel, will face formidable transaction costs. Second, there is a developed network of transnational environmental NGOs, which observes and monitors the developments in this field, thus limiting the capacity of financial actors to totally undermine the integrity of the new global instruments.[90] Finally, the broadening governmental intervention is also likely to suppress such corrupting pressures.

[88] See the public procurement section at http://ec.europa.eu/employment_social/emplweb/csr-matrix/csr_matrix_en.cfm (last visited 11 June 2006). Another potential avenue for state intervention is tax law. Thus, eg, the Dutch authorities have introduced a tax cut on dividends from green funds (Aslaksen and Synnestvedt, 2003: 221).

[89] Thus, for example, environmental groups have criticised the Equator Principles for their lack of compliance and grievance mechanisms: see BankTrack (2006) and Freshfields Bruckhaus Deringer and UNEP Finance Initiative (Asset Management Working Group) (2005: 36–44, reviewing and responding to the NGOs' critique).

[90] For recent NGO actions in this field see the Collevecchio Declaration on Financial Institutions and Sustainability, April 2003, (http://www.foe.org/camps/intl/declaration.html, last visited 22 June 2006), and the activities of BankTrack, a network of civil society organisations

ANNEX A

FTSE4Good Environmental Criteria

To be included in any of the FTSE4Good indexes, companies must meet requirements in five areas: environmental sustainability, relationships with stakeholders, universal human rights, supply chain labour standards, and countering bribery.[91] In addition, companies having business interests in the following industries are excluded from the FTSE4Good Index Series: tobacco producers, companies associated with the nuclear industry or nuclear weapons systems, companies manufacturing whole weapons systems. The FTSE4Good team developed detailed criteria covering each of the foregoing areas.[92] The environmental criteria, which are reproduced below, assign companies with a high, medium, or low impact weighting according to their industry sector.[93] The inclusion criteria are more stringent, the higher the environmental impact of the company's operations. Similarly to the Dow Jones Index, FTSE4Good uses a consultancy group—Eiris—in order to assess companies against the FTSE4Good criteria. The final

	High Impact Companies	Medium Impact Companies	Low Impact Companies
Policy	Policy must cover the whole group and either: • meet all five core indicators plus one desirable indicator • or meet four core plus two desirable indicators	Policy must cover the whole group and meet four indicators, three of which must be core.	Companies must have published a policy statement including one commitment indicator.
	Core Indicators • Policy refers to all key issues • Responsibility for policy at board or department level • Commitment to use of targets • Commitment to monitoring and audit • Commitment to public reporting		**Desirable Indicators** • Globally applicable corporate standards • Commitment to stakeholder involvement • Policy addresses product or service impact • Strategic moves towards sustainability
Management	If environmental management systems (EMS) are applied to between one and two-thirds of company activities, all six indicators must be met, and targets must be quantified. If EMS are applied to more than two-thirds of company activities, the company must meet five of the indicators. One of these indicators must be documented objectives and targets in all key areas. Companies with ISO certification and EMAS registrations are considered to meet all six indicators.	EMS must cover one third of the company and meet four indicators. If the EMS covers less than one third of the companyís operations, the company must meet six indicators, including quantitative objectives and targets. ISO14001 certified or EMAS registered systems are considered to meet all six indicators.	No requirement.
	Indicators • Presence of environmental policy • Identification of significant impacts • Documented objectives and targets in key areas • Outline of processes and responsibilities, manuals, action plans, procedures • Internal audits against the requirements of the system not limited to legal compliance) • Internal reporting and management review		
Reporting	The Report must have been published within the last three years, cover the whole group, and meet three core indicators. Reports which do not cover the whole group must meet all four indicators. or three core indicators together with two desirable indicators.	No requirement.	No requirement.
	Core Indicators • Text of environmental policy • Description of main impacts • Quantitative data • Performance measured against targets		**Desirable Indicators** • Outline of an EMS • Non-compliance, prosecution, fines, accidents • Financial dimensions • Independent verification • Stakeholder dialogue • Coverage of sustainability issues

Figure 4 ***The FTSE4 Good Environmental Criteria (from: FTSE4Good Index Series Inclusion Criteria (FTSE International Limited, 2006, 3).***

tracking the operations of the private financial sector (http://www.banktrack.org, last visited 22 June 2006).

[91] See *FTSE4Good Index Series Inclusion Criteria* (FTSE International Limited, 2006), at 1 (http://www.ftse.com/Indices/FTSE4Good_Index_Series/Downloads/FTSE4Good_Inclusion_Criteria_Brochure_Feb_06.pdf).

[92] *Ibid*.

[93] *Ibid*, at 3.

decision whether to include or delete a company from the index is made by FTSE4Good Policy Committee.[94]

REFERENCES

Aslaksen, I and Synnestvedt, T (2003) 'Ethical investment and the incentives for corporate environmental protection and social responsibility' 10(4) *Corporate Social Responsibility and Environmental Management* 212–23.

BankTrack (2006) *Equator Principles II: NGO Comments on the Proposed Revision of the Equator Principles*, 26 April 2006 (http://www.banktrack.org/, Publications/BankTrack on Equator Principles).

Botchwey, K (2000) *Financing for Development: Current Trends and Issues for the Future* (Geneva: United Nations Conference on Trade and Development).

Boyer, M and Porrini, D (2003) 'The Choice of Instruments for Environmental Policy: Liability or Regulation?', in T Swanson (ed) *An Introduction to the Law and Economics of Environmental Policy: Issues in Institutional Design* (London, Elsevier Science Ltd).

Brehm, J and Hamilton, JT (1996) 'Noncompliance in environmental reporting: Are violators ignorant, or evasive, of the law?' 40(2) *American Journal of Political Science* 444–77.

Bridgeman, NL (2001) 'World Bank Reform in the "Post-policy" Era',13 *Georgetown International Environmental Law Review* 1013–46.

Brink, TWM van den, and Woerd, F van der (2004) 'Industry Specific Sustainability Benchmarks: An ECSF Pilot Bridging Corporate Sustainability with Social Responsible Investments' 55(2) *Journal of Business Ethics* 187–203.

Cobb, G, Collison, D, Power, D, and Stevenson L (2004) 'FTSE4Good: Perceptions and Performance' Paper presented at the Seventh Alternative Perspectives on Finance Conference, Stockholm University, 8–10 August.

Dailami, M and Leipziger, D (1998) 'Infrastructure Project Finance and Capital Flows: A New Perspective' 26(7) *World Development* 1283–98.

EPA Victoria (2003) *Risk, the Environment and the Role of the Insurance Industry* (Victoria, Australasian Advisory Committee on Insurance and UNEP Finance Initiatives).

Esty, DC (1994) *Greening the GATT: Trade, Environment, and the Future* (Washington, DC, Institute for International Economics).

EU Commission (2000) *White Paper on Environmental Liability* (Brussels, European Commission).

Freshfields Bruckhaus Deringer and UNEP Finance Initiative (Asset Management Working Group) (2005) *A Legal Framework for the Integration of Environmental, Social and Governance Issues into Institutional Investment* (Geneva, UNEP Finance Initiative).

Friedman, AL and Miles, S (2001) 'Socially Responsible Investment and Corporate Social and Environmental Reporting in the UK: An Exploratory Study' 33 *British Accounting Review* 523–48.

[94] See: Ground Rules for the Management of the FTSE4Good Index Series, Version 1.3 August 2005 (www.ftse.com/Indices/FTSE4Good_Index_Series/Downloads /indexrules.pdf).

Gee-Janssens, P (2004) 'The Socially Responsible Investment Fund Market in Belgium and The Netherlands: ABN AMRO and KBC Case Studies: SRI and Sustainable Banking' Master of Arts in European Studies, Katholieke Universiteit Leuven, Leuven.

Heal, GM (2004) *Corporate Social Responsibility—An Economic and Financial Framework* (http://ssrn.com/abstract=642762).

Heinkel, R, Kraus, A and Zechner J (2001) 'The effect of green investment on corporate behavior' 36(4) *Journal of Financial and Quantitative Analysis* 431.

Hoijtink, A (2005) *The Sustainability Attitude of Commercial Banks* (Tilburg, University of Tilburg).

Hooley, R (2001) 'Lender Liability for Environmental Damage' 60(2) *The Cambridge Law Journal* 60(2) 405–18.

Jeucken, M (2001) Sustainable Finance and Banking: the Financial Sector and the Future of the Planet (London, Earthscan).

Kahneman, DJ, Knetsch, L, and Thaler RH (1990) 'Experimental Tests of the Endowment Effect and the Coase Theorem' 98 *The Journal of Political Economy* 1325.

King, M (2006) 'What's the use of Luhmann's Theory', in M King and C Thornhill (eds) *Luhmann on Law and Politics: Critical Appraisals and Applications* (Oxford, Hart).

KPMG (2005) *KPMG International Survey of Corporate Responsibility Reporting 2005* (Amsterdam, University of Amsterdam and KPMG Global Sustainability Services TM).

Luhmann, N (2004) *Law As a Social System.* trs KA Ziegert (Oxford, Oxford University Press).

Lyon, TP and Maxwell, JW (2007) *Greenwash: Corporate Environmental Disclosure under Threat of Audit*, Indiana University, Kelley School of Business, Working Paper (May 23, 2007).

Maltby, J (1997) 'Setting its own Standards and Meeting those Standards: Voluntarism Versus Regulation in Environmental Reporting' 6 *Business Strategy and the Environment* 83–92.

McDermott, T, Stainer, A, and Stainer, L (2005) 'Contaminated land: bank credit risk for small and medium size UK enterprises' 5(1) *International Journal of Environmental Technology and Management* 1–13.

McKenzie, G and Wolfe, S (2004) 'The Impact of Environmental Risk on the UK Banking Sector' 14(14) *Applied Financial Economics*) 1005–16.

Nielson, DL, and Tierney, MJ (2003) 'Delegation to International Organizations: Agency Theory and World Bank Environmental Reform' 57 *International Organization* 241–76.

—— (2005) 'Theory, Data and Hypothesis Testing: World Bank Enviromental Reform Redux' 59 *International Organization* 785–800.

Perez, O (2004) *Ecological Sensitivity and Global Legal Pluralism: Rethinking the Trade and Environment Conflict* (Oxford, Hart Publishing).

—— (2006) 'Facing the Global Hydra: Ecological Transformation at the Global Financial Frontier: The Ambitious Case of the Global Reporting Initiative', in C Joerges and E-U Petersmann (eds) *Constitutionalalism, Multilevel Trade Governance and Social Regulation* (Oxford, Hart Publishing).

Potoski, M and Prakash, A (2005) 'Green Clubs and Voluntary Governance: ISO 14001 and Firms' Regulatory Compliance' 49(2) *American Journal of Political Science* 235–48.

Pozzo, B (2001) 'Towards Civil Liability for Environmental Damage in Europe: the "White Paper" of the Commission of the European Communities' 1(2) *Global Jurist Topics*.

Social Investment Forum (2006) '*2005 Report on Socially Responsible Investing Trends in the United States: 10-year Review*' (Washington, DC, Social Investment Forum).

Standard&Poor, SustainAbility, and UNEP (2004) *Risk & Opportunity: Best Practice in Non-Financial Reporting* (http://www.sustainability.com/).

Strasser, KA and Rodosevich, D (1993) 'Seeing the Forest for the Trees in CERCLA Liability' 10(2) *The Yale Journal on Regulation* 493–560.

Thompson, P (1998) 'Assessing the Environmental Risk Exposure of UK Banks' 16(3) *International Journal of Bank Marketing* 129–39.

Tile, CA (2001) 'The content and disclosure of Australian corporate environmental policies' 14(2) *Accounting, Auditing & Accountability Journal* 190–212.

UNEP FI Secretariat (2002) *Finance and Insurance* (Geneva, United Nations Environment Programme/Finance Initiatives).

UNEP, World Bank, and World Resources Institute (2003) *World Resources 2002–2004: Decisions for the Earth: Balance, Voice, and Power* (Washington, DC, World Resources Institute).

Utting, P (2000) 'UN—Business Partnerships: Whose Agenda Counts?', Paper presented at seminar on Partnerships for Development or Privatization of the Multilateral System, organised by the North–South Coalition, Oslo, Norway, 8 December.

Vashista, A, Johnson, DR, and Choudhury MS (2005) 'Securities Fraud' 42 *American Criminal Law Review* 877–941.

Wade, R (1997) 'Greening the Bank: The Struggle over the Environment, 1970–1995', in D Kapur, JP Lewis and R Webb (eds) *The World Bank: Its First Half Century*, vol 2 (Washington, DC, Brookings Institution Press).

WWF (2005) 'Shaping the Future of Sustainable Finance: Moving from Paper Promises to Performance' http://www.wwf.org.uk/filelibrary/pdf/sustainablefinancereport.pdf (Surrey, WWF-UK).

Part III

Consumer based Self-Regulation and the Law

7

The Social and Technical Self-Governance of Privacy

RALF BENDRATH

I. PRIVACY AND REGULATION IN A GLOBAL CYBERSPACE[1]

A. The Internet as a Case of Global Governance

PRIVACY PROTECTION IS a policy field with growing importance in the information society. Although its foundations date back to early liberal philosophy, which drew a clear border between the public and private spheres of a citizen's life,[2] it has only been the subject of intentional political regulation since the second half of the 20th century. This development was closely connected to the rise in computer use. The first generations of privacy and data protection laws, enacted in Western Europe and the United States in the 1970s and 1980s, envisaged few centralised databases that could be easily controlled. The rise of personal computers and widespread internet use changed this situation drastically. Since then, self-regulatory approaches, like codes of conduct, contracts, standards, and technical means, have become more widespread. More and more personal data can be collected, processed, and transferred online. Therefore, the internet empirically is a good case to explore recent developments in the field of privacy or data protection.

The internet should also theoretically be a most likely case to observe changes in the type of governance structures. As a global space for all kinds of human interaction, it should show the typical signs of globalised governance beyond the nation-state (spatial dimension). As it is mainly run

[1] Research for this chapter was conducted in the project 'Regulation and Legitimacy on the Internet' at the Collaborative Research Centre 'Transformations of the State', Bremen University. I thank my colleagues Jeanette Hofmann, Volker Leib, Peter Mayer, Johannes Moes, Gregor Walter, and Michael Zürn for ideas and comments on the privacy case study and on earlier papers. Thanks also go to Olaf Dilling, Martin Herberg, and to two anonymous reviewers at the centre for their helpful comments. Clemens Haug, Nino Jordan, Dulani Perera, and Monika Tocha provided valuable research assistance.

[2] See Warren and Brandeis (1890) as a prominent example. Rössler (2001) provides a good systematisation of the liberal arguments for privacy.

by private and transnational companies, with its technical standards being developed by transnational bodies, it should also be a most likely case for self-regulatory forms of private governance (organisational dimension). Unlike telephone networks, which were designed by hierarchical forms of coordination in and between nation states, the internet seemed to be immune to any form of central control. Certainly, the core resources of the internet, like the root server for the domain name system or the allocation of IP address ranges, are organised centrally. However, normal usage is not affected by this, as routing and packet switching take place in a decentralised way.

Because the internet crosses and, to some extent, ignores national borders, it undermines territorial forms of control (Drake, 1993). In the view of many observers, this could only mean that cyberspace had to develop its own form of post-nation state control (Johnson/Post, 1997). Consequently, the as yet young internet community discussed various scenarios of 'non-governmental governance' for the net (Baer, 1997) that ranged from Barlow's famous 'Declaration of the Independence of Cyberspace' (Barlow, 1996) to articles on the 'virtual state' (Rosecrance, 1996) that only plays a networking role and is no longer based primarily on territorial space. This debate did not end with the bursting of the dot.com bubble. Some years into the new millennium, we still find academic visions and findings of the 'peer-production of internet governance' (Johnson *et al*, 2004), or the emergence of 'global civil constitutions' in cyberspace (Teubner, 2003).

No academic discussion, let alone any political vision, comes without sceptics. Already, in the initial stages of this debate, they raised their voices against the 'cyber-separatists' (for an overview of the debate, see Mayer-Schönberger, 2003). They viewed 'reports of the imminent death of the state as greatly exaggerated' (Post, 1998: 521), and deconstructed the libertarian cyber-optimism as a new 'Californian ideology' (Barbrook and Cameron, 1995). There are two groups of scholars that still believe in a role for the state (Mayer-Schönberger, 2003). The 'traditionalists' insist that people and corporations acting online are still present in the physical space, and that the internet also depends and runs on a physical infrastructure comprised of cables, servers, and routers. As these are located in national territories, they can become objects of the state monopoly of force. Implementation of regulation and enforcement of law on the internet may be more difficult, but not impossible (for a recent empirical account in this perspective see Goldsmith and Wu, 2006). The 'internationalists' are more concerned with the non-Cartesian characteristics of cyberspace, where physical distance is compressed to the question of how many hyperlinks apart two websites are, and where 'safe havens'—the proverbial server on the Antilles—can be used for escaping regulation while still providing worldwide services. Because of the global extension of cyberspace, the internationalists see multilateral cooperation between states as a necessity for functioning regulation. The proper medium for global governance of cyberspace therefore would be international law—still state-based, but with global reach (Berg, 2000).

This surely sounds familiar to scholars who study the legal forms of global governance. In the offline-world, the equivalent of 'cyber-separatism' is transnational self-regulation or 'lex mercatoria', the realm of independent rule-making and norm-setting by private transnational actors, mostly specialised for different industry sectors. The equivalent of 'internet traditionalism' is legal traditionalism, which still sees real law as only possible within nation-states, as this is where the last resort for law enforcement—physical force applied through the police—is located. And 'internationalism' resembles the traditional forms of multilateral governance, where international law is seen as the only adequate form of reacting to interdependence and globalisation.

B. Social and Technical Governance Structures

There is a different dimension to the internet in terms of rule-setting and rule enforcement. In the offline world (the 'meat-space', as many 'netizens' say), norms are *social* rules. They are generated, communicated, adapted, and enforced by social interactions. They may have strong compliance mechanisms, and the most successful rules are surely the ones we have internalised and do not even recognise as such any more. But in principle, they can be followed *or not*. Let me give an example from an offline infrastructure that has many common characteristics with the internet—the road traffic system. If the speed limit is set to 30 kilometres per hour in residential areas, many drivers will accept this because they think it is reasonable, and they may themselves have kids who play football on their own street. But a car driver in a hurry can still decide to not obey the law and drive faster. Rule enforcement then sometimes works locally and socially, for example if pedestrians directly show their dissatisfaction with this behaviour through, more or less, rude gestures. But mostly it works through a legal sanctioning mechanism: the speeding ticket. If the risk—calculated from the cost of the penalty and the chances of being caught—is high enough, many drivers will refrain from speeding in anticipation of the consequences. But the underlying mechanism here is the risk of ex post sanctions. In principle, drivers are free in their individual decisions to speed or not to speed, even under legal rules.

It is different when physical or architectural constraints are involved. Imagine a street in a residential neighbourhood where the speed limit has been set to 30 kilometres per hour, but where many drivers still rush through it. This is often the case where the street is straight, paved, and has few crossroads or traffic lights. In many instances, communities that do not wish to bother with the high transactional costs of speed cameras rely on a different mechanism. They set up speed humps. These make the drivers slow down automatically, because they do not want to damage their cars' suspension, or they are afraid of losing control of the car in speeding over the humps. To most drivers, it is plainly impossible to speed over speed humps. The physical characteristics of a street—its architecture—have a huge impact on the drivers' behaviour. This does not operate through social norms and the risk of ex post sanctions, but through the architecture and ex ante enforcement. Still, in the offline world, speed humps can be ignored to some extent by acquiring very good suspension, huge tyres, or—as an extreme example—a tank. Street traffic is based on physics, and the limitations built into the infrastructure can be overcome by using the laws of physics.

The political nature of technologies, and the fact that their design can influence and control social behaviour, has been widely discussed in the science, technology and society community (Bijker, 1992; Winner, 1986a). Structures like road bumps, bridges, and even the design of locks for backyard doors (Latour, 1994) can determine how people move and behave. In cyberspace, architecture has an even more constraining role than in the offline-world. If you are connected to the internet through a dial-up modem, you can have a very fast computer, but you will still not be able to have the data packets flow any faster than 56 kilobits per second. And even if you have a high-speed connection, say at a university research laboratory, some websites will not respond very fast, because the servers they are running on are slow and/or busy, or their uplinks are congested. While this still very much resembles the street analogy, with fast or slow cars and highways or bumpy tracks, many more constraints are possible through programming the servers, switches, and routers through which the data packets flow. A street that automatically slows down every car headed towards a particular location is unthinkable, but in cyberspace, this is reality. In Germany, the internet service provider Tiscali for example, automatically slows down all traffic from its broadband customers that comes from specific ports of their computers, namely the ports used for peer-to-peer file-sharing. There are many more examples of this, from Chinese automated content filtering to the technical blocking of specific forms of internet usage at the workplace through companies' firewalls. The Chinese government can enact a law prohibiting visits to critical websites (and has done so in the past), and companies can establish social rules that discourage their employees from using instant messaging services in the office (as many have also done). But they can also build these rules into the architecture of the routers, switches, and firewalls—and many have done so.

The internet is a technical infrastructure, but it also is a social space that enables, facilitates, and shapes online interactions between individuals and groups. Because all of these interactions are taking place in a technically mediated environment, the range of freedom and individual options for behaviour are also being determined by the way the network architecture is built. This differs from large industrial socio-technical systems, which by technical design impose a strong discipline on the workers,[3] but where the latter can still go on strike and leave the factory. In cyberspace, you can not leave the data 'machines' constituted by the operating systems and network protocols. It was these regulatory characteristics of cyberspace that made Joel Reidenberg (1998) speak of a 'lex informatica' that is different from state-based law, in resemblance to the 'lex mercatoria' of international private trade regulation. Lawrence Lessig (1999) in a similar way has called the software code—which makes the internet and our computers run—the 'law of cyberspace'. Very much to the point, he distinguishes 'West coast code' (Silicon Valley-based software) from 'East coast code' (Capitol Hill-based laws). We can distinguish different levels of rigidity for lex informatica. The operating systems our computers run on (and even more so the underlying hard-wired code in the hardware) and the networking protocols can be compared to the constitution. They provide the foundation on which other applications run, and they determine what options for user control (for example different user account settings in multi-user operating systems like Windows XP or Unix) and identification (eg dynamically or statically assigned Internet Protocol numbers) are possible. The equivalent of common 'laws' then, are applications like office software, mail clients, and web browsers and servers. While the users have some choice in this level (and can change some settings, such as cookie policies), the design of web servers, websites, and the underlying databases is dependent on the choice of the corporation running it.

Software code does not of course work in a vacuum. Naturally, social and community norms also exist on the internet with regard to how to and how not to behave in different contexts (so-called 'netiquette'). But even some codes can still be influenced by the user, depending on the degree of access he has to the computer controlling his online behaviour. If a website filter for indecent content is running on my own computer which I have root access to, I can deactivate it or change its settings. If it is running on my company's web proxy server, I would have to convince the network administrator to let me visit specific websites that would normally be blocked. If it is run by my internet service provider (ISP), I would have to change ISP. If it is run by a national exchange point or international gateway, there is normally not much I can do personally. What is even more interesting for political scientists as well as legal scholars are the complicated and still emerging links between state-based law, self-regulatory norms, and the lex informatica. How are lawmakers and private norm-setting bodies reacting to technological change, and how are the technical codes influenced by law and social norms?

Applied to privacy issues, the design of websites can force users to give away more personal data than they would like to do—and more than they

[3] 'The automatic machinery of a big factory is much more despotic than the small capitalists who employ workers ever have been' (Engels, 1978: 731, quoted in Winner, 1986b).

would do in the real world. If you want to read the *New York Times* (NYT) online, for example, you can only do so after registering with their customer database and giving away information about your address, age, job, and more. The NYT web server then can follow your 'click-stream', that is, the way you move around on the site, which articles you read, which advertisements you click on, and more. With 'cookies' or other means, this information can even be linked to the databases of large marketing companies like DoubleClick that earn their revenues by profiling customers for other corporations. Online privacy, as now should be clear, is heavily dependent on the technical design of the internet. This chapter sets out to contribute to this debate with empirical findings on the role of self-regulatory norms for the protection of privacy on the internet, and especially how social and technical codes interrelate here. 'Data protection' (the European term) or 'informational privacy' (the American term) as a subject of regulation emerged with the broader use of computers in the 1960s. As technology continues to change, so have the forms of data protection regulation. Data protection norms also have made an impact on the design of the technological architectures.

Self-governance structures in the privacy field have not emerged in isolation. They often have often come as a reaction to consumer demands, pressure from public interest groups, and from the usual widely reported data-leak scandals. But the general norms of privacy protection have developed mostly in the state-based national and international governance structures of Western Europe and North America. In order to understand the emergence and growing importance of privacy self-governance, it is therefore necessary to first take a brief look at the history of public and law-based privacy and data protection regulation. Against this backdrop, we can then better understand the different self-regulatory instruments for privacy protection that have been developing since the 1990s. There are now a number of different social and technical codes in the private sector, with varying degrees of scope, reach, enforcement, and control over the data by customers and companies. Self-governance is surely growing in importance within the privacy field, and some of its forms can be seen as private equivalents of legal regulation. But the story does not end here. Self-governance mechanisms of privacy protection have again recently become the subject of closer inspection by governments and other public bodies. As we will see, the state is coming back—but in a different shape. The new privacy governance pattern no longer has the state as its hierarchical enforcer, but rather a *primus inter pares* that still holds some carrot-and-stick-capacity. Indirect regulation through intermediaries and the use of network effects seem to be a more successful way of establishing the wider use and application of privacy standards in the private sector. In addition, the use of technical codes is becoming more popular, but their success is still dependent on the social codes and underlying norms which they are supposed to reflect.

II. SETTING THE STAGE: STATE-BASED PRIVACY GOVERNANCE

A. National Laws and International Harmonisation

'Privacy' has been internationally regarded as a fundamental civil liberty since the 1940s. The Universal Declaration of Human Rights (1948) contains a paragraph on privacy. The 1950 European Convention on the Protection of Human Rights and Fundamental Freedoms includes a similar clause. The United States has had a judicial tradition of privacy protection since the 1890 seminal article by Samuel Warren and later Supreme Court judge Louis Brandeis, who coined the phrase, the 'right to be let alone' (Warren and Brandeis, 1890).

These early privacy rules were originally intended as a protection against unreasonable police searches of private property and an overly intrusive press. As a result of World War II and experiences with the Nazi regime,[4] people became more afraid of leaving too much personal information in the hands of powerful government bureaucracies. The use of computers in accounting and personnel management that emerged in the 1960s transformed the policy problem of limiting the compilation, access, and use of personal files from a purely bureaucratic task into a political-technological endeavour. Now, it became 'informational privacy' or 'fair information practices' (the US version) and 'data protection' (in Europe) (Schwarz and Reidenberg, 1996). The discussion on the 'Big Brother state' was also growing.[5] Thus began parliaments' first efforts in drafting laws to protect personal information against unlimited computer use.

The world's first data protection law was enacted in the German state of Hessen in 1970. Shortly afterwards, Sweden (1973) and the United States (1974) followed suit. A bit later, West Germany at the federal level (1977), Denmark, Austria, France, Norway and Luxembourg (all 1978) also introduced privacy protection laws. Up to the beginning of the 1980s, seven countries—all in Western Europe—had enacted data protection laws, and in the 1980s, ten more followed, among them Israel, Japan, Canada, and Australia (for a systematic four-country comparison between the United States, Germany, Sweden and the United Kingdom from 1960 to 1980, see

[4] The Netherlands had maintained comprehensive population registers since the 1930s, which were seized by the German government in the first three days of the occupation. The Dutch Jews as a result had the highest death rates of all occupied countries in Western Europe. See Seltzer and Anderson (2001).

[5] Lyon (2001) has elaborated the thesis that 'privacy' only became a social value when the technologically enabled surveillance society was already a fact.

Bennett, 1992). By the 1990s, 22 more states from all continents had joined the throng, followed by a smaller number into the new millennium. The reasons for this general spread of privacy legislation are not the topic of this chapter.[6] We can keep in mind that there were several 'waves' or 'generations' of data protection legislation (Mayer-Schönberger, 1998).

Technical systems at the time were envisioned as centralised large computer facilities that would be easy to control and supervise, and where the data, once entered, would remain.

> In other words, there were huge cabinets full of digitised data where before there had been huge cabinets full of files, but still, they were huge cabinets. (Fink, 2002: 85, my translation)

By the 1980s, the picture had already begun to significantly change. The globalisation of the economy had led to an increase in transborder data flows. On the other hand, one of the official goals of international economic policy was (and is) free trade. Personal data, as soon as it became more widely available than before, also became a valuable commodity (Weichert, 2000). As early as 1970, an expert group in the Council of Europe identified the transnational character of the computer and the according need for international regulatory harmonisation (Bennett, 1992: 134). Due to the fact that various national data protection laws often contain differing procedural regulations with regard to transnational data transfers, difficult legal conflicts still arose, even though they rested on the same basic set of principles (EU JRC, 2003: 90). In the late 1970s, the Council of Europe and the European Parliament began discussions on how to remove these trade barriers whilst preserving data protection. The objective soon became clear: International harmonisation of data protection was needed. The European Parliament even called for the 'creation of a genuine common market in data-processing' (European Parliament, 1979).

During the following years, several international treaties and documents were developed in an attempt to harmonise international data protection. The most binding international agreement for 15 years was the Council of Europe's 1981 Convention for the Protection of Individuals with Regard to Automatic Processing of Personal Data. This 'influential treaty' (Bennett and Raab, 2003: 3) mandated the signatories to translate (or incorporate) its rules into national law. Citizens of one country party to the treaty now had the right to legally fight any misuse of their personal data in another country that had ratified the treaty. The Convention included regulations on transborder data flows and also allowed restrictions in cases where the data was to be transferred to a country with lower protection levels. This

[6] Bennett and Raab (2003) mention a change in public opinion, policy-learning, diffusion through epistemic communities, and the influence of external actors (EU, Council of Europe, OECD).

rule had a harmonising impact within Europe, especially on the second generation of data protection laws that were enacted in the 1980s. The Convention was not relevant for data flows to third party countries which had not signed the treaty. This remained a matter of national legislation. The Council of Europe subsequently adopted a number of recommendations for implementing the Convention in specific areas that ranged from medical databases (1981) to privacy protection on the internet (1999) (EU JRC, 2003: 120).

In order to avoid further complications, the OECD developed its 1980 Guidelines on the Protection of Privacy and Transborder Flows of Personal Data (OECD, 1980) in close coordination with the Council of Europe. Unlike the Council of Europe's 1981 Convention, the guidelines are not binding, and they had been preceded by fierce conflicts between the United States and some European governments. The Europeans perceived the very low or (for the private sector) non-existing level of data protection in the United States as unacceptable and suspected that behind it was an attempt to globalise the dominance of the US computer industry with the buzz phrase 'free flow of information'. The United States in turn accused the Europeans of protectionism by means of data protection (Bennett, 1992: 136*f*). The guidelines themselves are only a short document listing basic fair information practices. The OECD followed up in 1985 with another declaration on transborder data flows that dealt with data flows within transnational corporations, trade barriers, and related aspects of data protection, and envisioned better cooperation and harmonisation (OECD, 1985).

The OECD for a decade was the only supra-regional international organisation that dealt with privacy and data protection. It was only in 1990 that the UN General Assembly adopted the, also voluntary, Guidelines concerning computerised data files, which had no follow-up mechanism and therefore no real impact.

The European Parliament, as mentioned above, had adopted several resolutions on data protection since 1976 and urged the EC Commission to draft an EC Directive for the harmonisation of national legislation. The Commission was rather hesitant and until 1982 requested only that Member States join the Council of Europe Convention (Bainbridge, 1996: 22). Not until 1990, with the European common market fast approaching, did the Commission react by presenting a draft European data protection Directive. This step was a surprise to many, as the EC was still seen as an economic community that did not deal with human rights issues. But the Commission used the same argument as the EC parliamentarians, the OECD, and the Council of Europe. It referred to Article 100a of the EC Treaty and presented its move as necessary for the functioning of the European common market. It took five more years of negotiations in Brussels and the Bangemann report, *Europe and the global information society* (EU, 1994) that made the common European information space its utmost priority, before the Directive was enacted as Directive 95/46/EC (EU, 1995; see Bainbridge, 1996: 23–32).

The EU data protection Directive is unanimously described as 'the most influential international policy instrument to date' (Bennett and Raab, 2003: 5). It contains regulations on the private and public sectors' use of personal data, applies to manual and automated data processing, has detailed rules on implementation and mandatory data protection commissioners, and creates a coordination body at the European level (the 'Article 29 Working Party') as well as a Commission-chaired committee that can make binding decisions. It was supplemented in 1997 by a special Directive for privacy in the electronic communications sector, which was further amended in 2002 to include latest technological developments (EU, 1997; EU, 2002). Here, the EU tried to take into account caller identification for telephone calls, location data for mobile phones, cookies, spam, and other new technological possibilities. Since the 1999 Treaty of Amsterdam, the Directive also applies to data processing within the EU bureaucracy, which has since had its own internal data protection commissioner.

The brief overview of international state-based privacy regulation shows a familiar pattern: The more binding the regulatory instruments, the shorter their reach is. National data protection laws, even if harmonised through the EU Directive, are still the most precise legal regulations, and they can also be enforced by supervisory authorities (the public data protection commissioners) and, as a last resort, by the courts. The EU Directive is wider in scope and still fairly detailed. It has the Commission committee and the Article 29 Data Protection Working Party as executive bodies, and it stipulates some fundamental—substantial and institutional—provisions for the national laws. But as it is an EU Directive, specific implementation and direct compliance control over the private sector is still delegated to the national level, according to the subsidiarity principle. The Council of Europe's Privacy Convention is wider in reach than the EU Directive, as the organisation includes European States that are not EU Members. But although it is a binding international treaty, it provides only a basic set of fundamental data protection principles. It is less precise in giving institutional directions to its parties, having created no day-to-day supervisory body, instead relying on the European Court of Human Rights. The OECD guidelines not only apply to Europe, but also to North America and the Asian developed countries. However, they are completely voluntary and do not constitute international law. Instead, they rely on the OECD Committee for Information, Computer and Communications Policy's attempts to achieve adoption of the guidelines by the private sector. The UN Guidelines are, in principle, global in reach, but they are neither precise nor binding, and they do not have any follow-up or implementation mechanism. Precision and enforcement of state-based privacy regulations are therefore the strongest at the national level within the EU, weakening in concentric circles that are constituted by the EU, the OECD, and the United Nations.

B. The Internet, Safe Harbour, and the Rise of Self-governance

Thirty years after the first generation of data protection laws were enacted, the technological developments turned out less like 'Big Brother' and more as 'Little Sisters'. Centralised control by hierarchically structured, but territorially bound bureaucracies no longer seemed to be the main problem. The European model of registering and overseeing a few large databases hosted in large computer facilities was already reaching its limits in the late 1970s, spurred on by the emergence of mini-computers. In the mid 1980s, when the personal computer hit the market, the use and processing of all kinds of data—including personal data—was finally put beyond reach of effective government supervision. After the advent of the internet as a mass medium in the 1990s, this problem became even worse, as the trade and flow of personal data across borders now took only a matter of seconds. The big corporations were still easy to control, but they also had the resources to fight encroaching government controls and prohibitions. Swire and Litan (1998: 200–204) use the instructive metaphor of elephants and mice: Elephants are large and easy to spot, but they also have the ability to inflict considerable damage on their environment. The problem, however, is that the mice—the small companies that can easily relocate—are hard to control and 'breed annoyingly quickly' (Swire and Litan, 1998: 201). Data protection, therefore, could only work if government supervision was combined with functioning self-regulation in the private sector. This has been the US approach since the enactment of their first Privacy Act controlling government use of data in 1974. The EU Directive also reflected this approach, because it discontinued the mandatory registration of databases with the data protection supervisory authorities. Companies can instead now appoint internal data protection commissioners (or even outsource this job to specialised service providers) and thereby comply with the directive and the relevant national laws.

The driving force behind the move towards a more self-regulatory approach in data protection therefore was a change in the structure of the regulated problem. If everybody becomes a potential user and collector of personal data, then top-down enforcement and central supervisory mechanisms do not work any more—at least this was the perception. The answer was an attempt to infuse data protection ideas and their social agents into the private sector itself.

The other influence beyond these technological developments was political, and here, 'transatlantisation' was more important than globalisation. The negotiations over the OECD guidelines from 1980 had already led to heavy conflicts between European governments and the US government.

The conflict between American 'free flow of information' and European 'privacy' was barely covered in the guidelines. On one hand, the guidelines are completely voluntary by nature, which was desired by the United States, but on the other hand, at least they have set some lowest common denominator for fair information principles and therefore met the interests of the Europeans.

In 1995, the problem became more apparent following the enactment of the EU directive. For the first time, the directive as an international instrument harmonised and regulated data transfers to third party countries. This feature made its impact felt far beyond the European Union, and that is why we can speak of 'globalisation' here, not just 'Europeanisation'. EU Member States are only allowed to approve data exports of personal data if there is an 'adequate level of protection' present in the recipient country. If there is no comparable legislation in place, the companies wanting to export the data can only do so if it is based on a contract with the company that receives the data. The contract also has to ensure adequate protection for further re-export. This clause has created a significant adaptational pressure on third countries (Charlesworth, 2000). In addition, the EU later developed standard contract clauses for data exports (EU Commission, 2002). The EU's adequacy provisions are 'the *de facto* rules of the road' for global data processing (Bennett and Raab, 2003: 6).

As there was no comprehensive data protection legislation for the private sector in the United States, but binding third party data export rules in the EU, there existed a dilemma: Either the EU Commission could have treated the US data protection regulation as 'not adequate' and risked another transatlantic trade war, or it could have turned a blind eye on the United States and heavily damaged the credibility of the whole directive. Even before the transatlantic conflict was resolved, the EU Directive helped create pressure on the United States to raise its level of data protection for the private sector. The Clinton administration was afraid that the EU Commission could lock US companies out of the large European market for e-commerce, because the lack of comprehensive data protection legislation in the United States could mean an 'inadequacy' rating. Before the Directive had to be implemented at national level in 1998, the US government therefore tried to convince the EU that self-regulation worked (for example with a comprehensive compendium: US DoC, 1997). At the same time, it also started pushing the private sector into seriously self-regulating data protection. Some parts of the administration, especially in the Federal Trade Commission, even threatened to adopt legal measures if self-regulation would not work quickly. As a result, the self-regulatory instruments have been referred to as 'the Directive's bastard offshoots' (Shaffer, 1999: 433). The international trade regulation provided some unexpected assistance with regard to this matter. The World Trade Organization's 1994 General Agreement on Trade in Services (GATS) makes reference to privacy, not so much as an obstacle to trade, but as an exception from otherwise liberalised trade in services, including data services (WTO, 1994).[7] By doing this, trade liberalisation not only curbed the need for the United States to raise its level of privacy protection, but limited its ability to retaliate (Shaffer, 2000: 86).

After long negotiations, the EU Commission and the US Department of Commerce sealed a 'Safe Harbour' agreement in July 2000 (Fink, 2002; Farrell, 2003; Heisenberg, 2005). It has been described as a 'hybrid' or 'interface solution' (Farrell, 2002), as it links two different regulatory approaches: the European, law-based and comprehensive privacy regulation; and the American, private sector-based and sectoral privacy regulation. Under the Safe Harbour agreement, the object of the Commission's important adequacy rating is no longer a country, but a single company. Therefore, the United States could keep its data processing industry partly unregulated, and the EU could allow data transfers to US companies under the condition they subjected themselves to the Safe Harbour principles. The mechanism is quite simple:

> The decision by U.S. organizations to enter the safe harbor is entirely voluntary. Organizations that decide to participate in the safe harbor must comply with the safe harbor's requirements and publicly declare that they do so. (US DoC, 2005)

As of January 2008, 1,353 companies had entered the Safe Harbour (US DoC, 2008). The agreement is—as is natural for a compromise—weaker than the EU regulation. There is no possibility for EU citizens to legally insist on being given information about what is happening to their data in the United States, or for European data protection commissioners to inspect the processing companies on the other side of the Atlantic. The European Parliament strongly resisted the agreement, but as judgment on 'adequacy', in accordance with the 1995 Directive, is delegated to the Commission, could do little against it. But the agreement still involves some public supervision and enforcement as it utilises a general clause in US trade regulation. Companies that have joined Safe Harbour and are caught red-handed can be fined by the Federal Trade Commission for 'unfair and deceptive trade practices'. There is also an arbitration procedure for cases of complaint, where the arbitrator can be chosen from either private providers like TRUSTe or public authorities like the EU data protection commissioners (US DoC, 2005).

The regulatory regime of Safe Harbour therefore consists of several layers. The EU sets the substantive data protection standards, the companies

[7] 'Nothing in this Agreement shall be construed to prevent the adoption or enforcement by any Member of measures … necessary to secure compliance with laws or regulations … including those relating to … the protection of the privacy of individuals in relation to the processing and dissemination of personal data and the protection of confidentiality of individual records and accounts.' (WTO, 1994, Art XIV).

voluntarily commit to them, private or public bodies provide arbitration services, public enforcement is carried out by a US agency, and the EU Commission still has the last word and can terminate the whole agreement if compliance or public supervision in the US is not working. It can therefore be described as a hybrid arrangement that combines transnational self-regulation on the one hand, and nation-state-based intergovernmental public regulation on the other hand, to produce a complex, multi-layered regime.

III. SELF-GOVERNANCE INSTRUMENTS OF PRIVACY PROTECTION

In the Safe Harbour regime, the private sector has a much more important role than in the traditional European regulation model, which is predominantly based on public supervision and inspection bodies. Under Safe Harbour, most of the regulatory functions, as well as the day-to-day supervision, are carried out by the private sector itself. States only set the minimum data protection level, but may employ means of last resort in cases of serious non-compliance. In this regard, the process leading up to the agreement was a learning experience for European data protection commissioners and regulators, and it has greatly enhanced the acceptance for private-sector self-regulation instruments. In this section, I will give an overview of the different instruments available today. As we will discover, they still differ greatly in terms of precision, reach, scope, and enforcement mechanisms.

A. Social Codes

1. *Internal Corporate Rules*

The simplest form of self-regulation is where a company publicly declares its adherence to a minimum set of privacy principles. This has become quite popular on the internet. A 'privacy policy' is nowadays found on most corporate websites, but the idea dates back to the early days of transborder data flows. The OECD has repeatedly urged the private sector to adopt the 1980 privacy guidelines. It has even developed an online privacy-statement generator to help website providers be more transparent about what data they collect, how they use it, what dispute resolution mechanisms are available, and so on.[8] According to OECD staff, this is not meant as a legal instrument, but rather as a means of making corporate data handlers think more closely about the mechanisms and organisational requirements for a sound data protection policy. Often, corporate privacy commitments

[8] See http://www.oecd.org/sti/privacygenerator.

are more a reaction to bad publicity or a public relations operation than a serious attempt to change the company's internal and external data usage. They more resemble indications of what the management or the customer relations department believe should happen than an internal policy for employees or a guide for binding organisational practices (Bennett and Raab, 2006: 154).

More recently, companies have started to translate their privacy statements into clear guidelines for their employees—so-called 'organisational codes'. Early examples of these were developed by multinational companies such as American Express and Readers' Digest, some of which followed as a result of customer surveys. Some global corporations have also started to adopt 'binding corporate rules' for privacy protection that apply to all worldwide subsidiaries, regardless of whether their country of residence has privacy legislation in place or not. Prominent examples are DaimlerChrysler, General Electric, and Siemens. They have come closest to inventing a new form of internal corporate private laws for data protection.

Many companies have also now established internal supervision mechanisms for ensuring compliance with organisational privacy codes. This model goes back to early German data protection legislation, which from the beginning had a unique model of institutionalising self-regulation in the private sector. Here, companies can avoid the burden of registering their data banks with the public supervisory bodies if they appoint an independent corporate data protection commissioner. This model has been incorporated into Directive 95/46/EC (recital 49) and since then has been widely adopted all over the corporate world. These 'chief privacy officers', as they are mostly called now, are organised in transnational professional bodies like the International Association of Privacy Professionals (IAPP), and they regularly meet with the public privacy commissioners.

2. *Codes of Conduct for Business Associations*

More widely encompassing are the codes that have been developed for whole industry sectors ('sectoral codes': Bennett and Raab, 2006: 155–57). Found mainly in the United States, a number of codes of conduct are now available from different industry and trade associations, ranging from the Direct Marketing Association to the Associated Credit Bureaus. These sectoral codes have become quite popular in the last few years. If they do not apply to a specific sector but to generic business functions like customer relations management or human resources management, they are also called 'functional codes' (*ibid*: 157).

Different from organisational codes, application of and adherence to these sectoral or functional codes is often mandatory for members of the respective trade or business association. They are also offered by specialised third party entities like auditing services or consultancy firms. Many of these self-regulating mechanisms are giving 'privacy seals' to websites that publicly declare their adherence to the specific data protection standard. The most popular are TRUSTe and Better Business Bureau (BBB) OnLine. Enforcement in general is not very strict, but industry associations play an increasing role in educating their members about privacy best practices. The inherent problem is that the certification providers are dependent on funding from their members or customers, so it is extremely unlikely that tough measures will be taken against those who break the rules. TRUSTe, for example, was placed under public pressure after it failed to adequately address accusations made against one of its members, Microsoft (Richardson, 2000; Boutin, 2002). A 1999 study, carried out by Forrester Research, concluded that privacy seal providers had become more of an advocate for the industry than for the consumer (EPIC and Privacy International, 2004: 110). On the other hand, industry associations are playing an increasing role in educating their members about privacy best practices, through specialised seminars, training services, and newsletters. This form of self-regulation more closely resembles the 'managed compliance' approach than the enforcement approach.

The purely technical environment of the internet and the World Wide Web allows for new forms of oversight. TRUSTe has started to automate its compliance checks through a mechanism called 'seeding', whereby unique data is entered into websites, allowing the detection of privacy-invasive data handling by the respective web-service at a later stage. Even more stringent is a programme called WebTrust, developed jointly by the US and Canadian associations of certified public accountants. Based on the high professional standards of the accounting profession, it is now being offered throughout North America as well as in Hong Kong, Australia, and a growing number of European countries (Bennett and Raab, 2006: 166). It can be expected that these professional efforts, combined with public pressure from consumer groups and privacy advocates, will serve as a strong incentive for self-regulatory bodies to strengthen their privacy compliance and control mechanisms.

The main problems with these self-regulatory mechanisms lie elsewhere. First, they only certify adherence to a minimal set of fair information practice principles. These are often less supportive of privacy than comparable EU legislation, for example with opt-out instead of opt-in mechanisms for commercial marketing as the norm. That is, unless the customer objects, his data will be used for marketing purposes. Second, these voluntary agreements have a relatively low level of participation and naturally can only regulate the behaviour of companies that subscribe to them. In January 2008, only 724 websites participated in the BBBOnLine privacy programme (BBBOnLine, 2008), and 2,490 sites had been certified by a TRUSTe seal (TRUSTe, 2008).

Mandatory membership of professional associations can therefore be a strong support for self-regulatory privacy protection instruments. A very strong version of privacy codes of conduct are 'professional codes' (Bennett and Raab, 2006: 14). They apply to professional associations, which have a direct influence on their individual members, but not on companies. Well-known examples are the age-old codes for physicians and lawyers, who are bound to professional discretion in their relationships with their patients or clients. As membership of professional organisations such as medical associations or the Bar is made mandatory in order to practise in that respective profession, misconduct can potentially lead to exclusion and loss of professional licence.

Today, codes of conduct are a standard instrument of privacy governance and their mechanisms for compliance and certification have become stronger. Most of them have emerged in the United States, as their prime users are US companies, but due to the transnational nature of many businesses, they have been constantly growing in their spatial reach. Some of these efforts are now being developed on a global scale, the most prominent being the Global Business Dialogue on electronic commerce's guidelines for 'consumer confidence' (GBDe, 2001) and the International Commerce Exchange's 'Global Code of Conduct'. Other global efforts in this direction have begun in the International Air Traffic Association (IATA) and the Federations of Direct Marketers (Bennett and Raab, 2006: 156). Typically, these transnational codes of conduct have been developed in close connection with the international community of data protection commissioners, some even involving the active participation of privacy advocacy groups. TRUSTe was actually founded by a joint effort of the Boston Consulting Group and the Californian NGO Electronic Frontier Foundation (EFF). But this is not a typical example, as cooperation between corporate entities, NGOs, and public commissioners is normally much less institutionalised and less formalised. Instead of the highly formalised forms of business–NGO cooperation found in other industry sectors, the field of privacy policy is still dominated by a loose diffusion of ideas through constant and decentralised discussions within an epistemic community comprising public commissioners, privacy advocates, and corporate chief privacy or chief technology officers.

3. *Contractual Solutions in Business Networks*

Contracts are often used as a case-by-case substitute for missing privacy legislation. They are common in big corporations that hold large amounts of personal data about customers and employees and contract out (or outsource) some of the related work. The business agreement then has sections that regulate how the contractor may use the data, who holds property rights to it, if and how it can be transferred to third parties, and so on. Specific privacy contracts have been used since the late 1970s to allow transborder data flows under national data protection laws. In France, the use of private contracts has been quite popular since the early days of data protection regulation, but other European states have also relied on contracts to ensure that personal data exported to other countries is handled according to the legislation in force in the country of origin. The national data protection authorities have played a crucial role in pushing for the use of this private-law instrument (Ellger, 1996).

By as early as 1992, the Council of Europe had developed a template contract for transborder data flows with the cooperation of the EU Commission and the International Chamber of Commerce. Other groups, such as the 'Düsseldorfer Kreis' of German data protection commissioners, have also been active in this area (Ellger, 1996). The EU followed after the adoption of its data protection Directive in 1995, which accepts standard contractual clauses to ensure an adequate level of protection for transborder data flows to third countries. These standard clauses must be verified or developed by the EU Commission, which has updated them several times since.

There are several limitations to this approach. First of all, what consequences arise from the fact that the affected party—the citizen, customer, or user—is not subject (or privy) to the contract? This may not be a problem in the continental European tradition, but the Anglo-Saxon *common law* countries traditionally do not recognise the concept of third parties' rights derived from a contract between two other parties. However, the United States has given up the strict use of the privity of contract doctrine and now allows third party beneficiaries from private contracts (Ellger, 1996: 765). The legal enforcement of these contract clauses is still difficult. Enforcement of contract clauses depends not only on the jurisdiction chosen as the basis, but also on the national laws in the import country and on the interests of the receiving party. Specific laws (for example for intelligence agencies) may override strong protections in private contracts.

On the other hand, these contracts are also used to raise the data protection level within a country. If organisations, either voluntarily or due to public pressure, want to mandate high data protection standards for their contractors, they can insist on incorporating standard data protection clauses into their business agreement. Government agencies, with their huge purchasing power, have used this as leverage where mandatory data protection laws are lacking.

This private data protection law of contracts has proven to be a useful instrument, especially in extending the EU's data protection standards to countries where national legislation is lacking or not deemed adequate. Thus, the use of EU data protection standards is slowly being incorporated into private sector data usage all over the world. This demonstrates how private law can help to spread a regional legal standard through the use of mandatory data export control clauses (Reidenberg, 1999).

4. *Harmonisation by Standardisation Organisations*

Privacy standards go further than commitments to voluntary codes of conduct, because they simultaneously provide a set of objective criteria and a defined process by which compliance can be tested. Standards here do not mean technical standards or networking protocols, but a standardised way of measuring the performance of how technology and social practice are integrated within an organisation. There has been some discussion going on about general privacy standards, based on the generic quality management standards of the ISO 9000 series. Standards normally also have strict supervision and compliance mechanisms that go further than voluntary codes and are more comparable to professional codes.

The first real privacy standard was the Canadian Model Code for the Protection of Personal Information. It was developed in 1992 by trade associations and consumer organisations together with the Canadian government and the Canadian Standards Association (CSA). The objective was to harmonise the different self-regulatory codes, but it also reflected the failed attempts of the OECD in this field. The model code was officially recognised as a 'National Standard of Canada' in 1996. Organisations that voluntarily adopted the standard were then bound to mandatory quality controls by the CSA. Similar standards to the Canadian Model Code have been developed elsewhere. In 1999, the Japanese Standards Association published the standard JIS Q 15001 ('Requirements for Compliance Program on Personal Information Protection'), which is modelled in detail on the structure of the environmental management standard ISO 14001 (Bennett, 2004a: 234). JIS Q 15001 was developed from a government-issued norm, the 1997 Data Protection Guidelines from the Ministry of International Trade and Industry (MITI) (Privacymark.org, 2006). In 1998, the Australian Privacy Commissioner published National Privacy Principles that also resemble the Canadian model (Bennett, 2004a: 234).

At the international level, the Council of the International Standards Organisation (ISO) initiated a process for the development of an international privacy standard in 1996, as a result of pressure from ISO's Consumer Policy Committee (Bennett, 2004a: 236). Because of heavy lobbying from US corporations and critique from European data protection commissioners, ISO has not been able to agree on a standard as yet. A more modest approach to '"set a common privacy terminology, define privacy principles when processing PI information, categorize privacy features and relate all described privacy aspects to existing security guidelines"' was started within ISO in 2006 under the leadership of the German standards institute, DIN (ISO/IEC, 2006). The European standards body Comité

Européen de Normalisation (CEN) has also been studying the feasibility of an international privacy standard. CEN works together with the EU's data protection commissioners. (CEN, 2002)

5. *Comparison*

Compared against each other, the mechanisms analysed above reflect different characteristics with respect to their level of protection and reach. While privacy requirements of national standardisation organisations have been successful in a number of cases, an agreement on a global privacy standard has proven to be extremely difficult. At the other extreme, privacy codes of conduct within single corporations are very binding and detailed. Sectoral codes and global industry guidelines still tend to be more lists of general principles rather than specific routines. Other codes of conduct with institutionalised compliance mechanisms are somewhere in the middle. Theoretically, they apply to a large number of corporations across the globe, but, in practice, these corporations still must subscribe to them (and pay for them) individually. Contractual solutions only apply to those trading partners that include them in their business agreements, and they are mostly used by EU-based corporations that want to transfer data to third countries. As there are no highly integrated 'supply chains' for personal data, the network of contractual privacy protections is still pretty loose, and it does not have the broad trickle-down effect that can be seen in the product standards of the car manufacturing sector. The most binding forms of privacy self-regulation are still the very old professional codes for lawyers, physicians, and priests. Here, compliance is to a large extent self-enforcing, as customer confidence in the secrecy of their information is at the core of the business model. On top of this, non-compliance may also lead to losing the licence required to further practise in that profession.

This resembles what we have discovered above in regards to state-based privacy regulation efforts. There is a trade-off between reach on the one hand, and obligation, precision, and enforcement on the other. At first glance, the same pattern seems to apply to privacy self-regulation. The more detailed the privacy codes are in terms of regulating data use, the less likely they are to have a wide applicability. But whereas state-based regulation differs along territorial or regional borders (nation, Europe, OECD), private self-regulatory instruments apply to organisations or sectors and, to a growing extent, ignore geography. While DaimlerChrysler's internal binding rules for privacy only apply to the corporations' employees and data subcontractors, they are valid and enforceable all over the world, from Stuttgart to Detroit, Johannesburg to Mumbai. The IATA privacy code of conduct applies to all air carriers that are members of this organisation, just like the confessional secret is binding on priests of the Catholic Church. The 'death of distance' brought on by the internet and the increasing trend of integration within the global economy have also made privacy self-governance instruments outgrow their territorial origins and realise worldwide adoption. The privacy seals for websites that are provided by companies like TRUSTe or BBBOnLine, while they were a purely US-based reaction to the EU Directive and the transatlantic Safe Harbour agreement, are now also available for and used by companies in the Far East. In 2000, the Japanese Information Processing Development Centre (JIPDEC) entered into a mutual privacy seal recognition programme with BBBOnLine (Bennett and Raab, 2006: 167). Standard contract clauses for business-to-business data transfers first emerged in the EU as a means of making data exports possible to countries that lacked adequate legislation. But they have developed in close cooperation with the International Chamber of Commerce, which now recommends their use to corporations all over the globe.

As the futile efforts to develop a global privacy standard show, a homogenous regime for the self-governance of privacy is not yet within sight. While there is a global consensus on basic principles (more or less based on the 1980 OECD guidelines), the instruments differ in scope, reach, precision, and enforcement mechanisms. Albeit, they are gradually making their way through the global network of private business governance structures, becoming more and more interlinked with each other. More recently, they have also found their implementation in the form of technical codes.

B. Technical Codes

The regulatory efforts for privacy protection in the 1970s were early attempts by the states concerned to more or less directly regulate the technology. The first data protection laws were a response to electronic data banks run by governments and large corporations (Mayer-Schönberger, 1998). The computer was the problem, and the privacy laws of the first generation therefore aimed at the technical systems that stored and processed the data. They set up registration and even licensing mechanisms for databases. They regulated access controls and were filled with terms like 'data', 'data file' and 'data record'. In some countries such as Sweden, the public supervisory agency possessed the power to direct specific design changes for data banks, access controls, data transfers, and the like. When international harmonisation started in the Council of Europe, the OECD, and later the EU and transatlantic agreements, privacy governance instruments lost their technological focus and concentrated on the normative principles and institutional mechanisms. Only with the emergence of the internet did the privacy implications of technological design gain wide attention again, although in this case, the development towards privacy-friendly technologies came neither from governments nor from corporations, but as a result of user concerns and demands.

1. *User Self-help Tools*

The growing ubiquity of data processing converged with another development that had also begun in the 1980s—the new legal and political concept of 'informational self-determination' that the German constitutional court had developed in a landmark census ruling in 1983 (Bundesverfassungsgericht, 1983). Contrary to the first generation of data protection laws that attempted to regulate the corporations, the new laws and amendments, and the developing case-law in the 1980s, gave citizens a say in the process. Their consent, at least in Europe, became a precondition for the use and processing of personal data. 'Informational self-determination' also reached beyond just the collection of the data and included control of the individual over all later stages of the processing and use of the data (Mayer-Schönberger, 1998).

This development received a new boost from the internet. Cyberspace was initially seen as a great place for user empowerment. Until the mid 1990s, most of the 'netizens' did not want the government to have a role in the new final frontier land. John Perry Barlow's 'declaration of the independence of cyberspace' (Barlow, 1996) is a famous example of the high expectations people had for the power of cyber self-regulation without government involvement. This 'Californian Ideology' (Barbrook and Cameron, 1995) was mirrored in the Clinton administration's policy towards the new medium. A majority in Washington, and elsewhere, were strictly against disturbing the growth dynamic of the 'new economy' by government interventions or regulations. 'Government has largely taken a hands-off approach to the new economy', as the report *State of the Internet* concluded even as late as 2000 (United States Internet Council, 2000: 29).

The reaction in Europe was more sceptical, but also relied heavily on the users. The Council of Europe issued a set of recommendations for privacy on the internet in 1999, following up on its 1980 Convention. The wording is telling, as it reads like a capitulation of state regulation:

> For Users: Remember that the Internet is not secure. However, different means exist and are being developed enabling you to improve the protection of your data. Therefore, use all available means to protect your data and communications. (Council of Europe, 1999)

Technology was—and for many still is—the best and only chance for users to ensure their privacy online. A number of privacy-enhancing end-user tools have been developed in the last 10 years. As personal computers became easier to use with graphical user interfaces like Windows, MacOS, and the several Linux desktop managers, privacy-enhancing technologies were also developed from cryptic command-line tools into user-friendly packages. Because of the internet, they are now readily accessible to all. Many of them are available for free distribution, and some of them work directly online. The first widespread tool for encrypting data on personal computers was Phil Zimmerman's 'Pretty Good Privacy' (PGP). It triggered a landslide of attention and after a six-year long legal and political struggle in the United States, resulted in a liberalisation of export control restrictions on cryptography technology in 1999 (Bendrath, 2001).

The tools available today include: strong encryption software for data, emails, and web access; web anonymising proxies; tools that automatically delete cookies; anonymous re-mailers; blocking software for advertisement banners and pop-up windows; disposable email addresses and even databases with fictional individual data sets for anonymously using websites that require registration; traffic scrambling networks; and much more.[9] They generally offer two kinds of privacy protection. Most of the encryption and traffic scrambling tools help their users to hide data, internet traffic patterns, and the traffic's content from prying eyes, whether law enforcement agencies or network providers. They therefore allow online interactions between trusted parties, be they friends, business partners, or political activists. The main threat from the perspective of their users is still more or less based on the 'Big Brother' scenario, one also made popular by movies such as 'Enemy of the State' and widely reported snooping activities carried out by intelligence agencies like the National Security Agency. The other group of privacy-enhancing tools are directed against corporate data collectors who track visitors to their websites and online services. They include tools that allow the deleting of corporate tracing instruments like cookies and 'web bugs' on the hard drives of the users' computers, as well as online services that provide disposable identities for anonymously accessing registration-based online services.

These privacy-enhancing tools give users considerable protection. Many of them are still not widely used, but some functions, like automatic cookie deletion, have been included in newer versions of most web browsers and, as such, have become mainstreamed into most computer desktops.

2. *Negotiation-based Codes*

There is one problem that all of the above mentioned privacy-enhancing tools fail to address. If the user is doing an online purchase, he or she must enter their real name, credit card number, and other information into a corporate website. If the item bought is not a digital item like a music file, the company also needs the address and further information for delivery. How can users be certain this information will not be misused at a later date? This is where negotiation-based technical codes come into play, which act like an agent between the user and the companies. The user can apply tools that automatically negotiate his privacy preferences with the website

[9] For an overview, see http://www.epic.org/privacy/tools.html.

he visits. A well-known example of this is the P3P standard ('Platform for Privacy Preferences Project') for websites. It was developed by the World Wide Web Consortium (W3C) with the involvement of corporations, technology experts, and data protection commissioners (Cranor, 2002). P3P presumes no set level of privacy protection, but enables the user to define his privacy 'choices' for different types of websites. The concrete data transactions are then automatically negotiated between the user's web browser and the company's web server. The standard has been applauded by public data protection commissioners as a model for technological enforcement of privacy protection mandated by law. The European Commission is also following this approach. In 2003, it stated that technological measures 'should be an integral part in any efforts to achieve a sufficient level of privacy protection' (EU Commission, 2003: 16).

On the other hand, privacy advocates have criticised P3P as being merely an automation of the data collection that many websites do anyway. The standard development process for P3P even started under the name 'Open Profiling Standard' (Article 29 Working Party, 1998). An assessment by the Electronic Privacy Information Center mentioned the lack of enforcement options, because 'P3P provides no means to ensure enforcement of the stated privacy policies' (EPIC and Junkbusters, 2000). Nowadays, about 10 per cent of all major websites have some P3P functionality (Byers *et al*, 2003), but most web browsers except Internet Explorer have ceased to support P3P, while still keeping privacy settings as part of their functionality. The EU's Data Protection Commission had already requested that the default settings in browsers should reflect the highest level of protection, even before the P3P standard was adopted (Article 29 Working Party, 1998). This was not the case, and with the internet becoming a mass medium, the average user now is even less familiar with these technological solutions or with how to set up personal privacy preferences in browsers.

3. *Privacy and Identity Infrastructures*

These technological approaches are currently being developed into more comprehensive infrastructures under the label 'Privacy and Identity Management' (PIM). They are expected to provide two features at the same time: (1) a simple and user-friendly administration of a person's online identity; and, (2) a technological implementation of data protection standards. Most PIM concepts include some kind of single sign-on service that makes the handling of different logins and passwords for several websites and online services easier for users.

It is not yet clear if whether this will actually lead to better data protection or even to the end of anonymity on the net. Microsoft's heavily criticised 'Passport'/'.Net' programs with centralised databases are regarded as PIMs, as are decentralised online infrastructures that ensure role-based pseudonymity (so-called 'federated' PIMs). Sophisticated designs include public key encryption schemes that allow the individual to not only control the delivery of his or her personal data to corporations and other users, but also the use of this data after it has been submitted (for an overview, see ICPP Schleswig-Holstein and Studio Notarile Genghini IMS, 2003). Complementary to the P3P front-end standard that allows the user to control which data he gives to websites, meta-data protocols are currently being developed to ensure that once personal data has entered the corporate data warehouses (back-end), its processing can only be done in accordance with the preferences of the person it belongs to. The Enterprise Privacy Authorisation Language (EPAL), such a privacy meta-data standard, is already being used by companies like eBay. As with P3P, the EPAL standard was submitted to the World Wide Web Consortium for adoption, and again like P3P, has been developed by the industry (IBM Laboratories Zürich) in cooperation with data protection commissioners (Borchers, 2004).

Recently, a lively debate has kicked off online and at various meetings and conferences concerning 'user-centric identity management'. It has been actively driven by Microsoft's privacy and identity staff, who—after the market failure of 'Passport'—seem to now understand that a single customer database controlled by a monopoly-like corporation is neither what users are looking for, nor what companies want as an intermediary for their customer relations. The basic idea for the design of this new identity management architecture is the use of credentials. This would only allow the transfer of the minimum amount of personal data required. To return to our earlier road traffic analogy, if stopped by a police officer on a highway, drivers would only have to provide proof that they in fact possess a driving licence (legal driver credential), but not further details such as their name, address or other personal information that is not relevant in that specific context. Most of the participants in the development towards identity management come from large, US-based information technology corporations, with a few academics and freelance consultants also taking part. Privacy advocates, as well as public data protection commissioners, are largely missing.[10]

The development of these infrastructural concepts is still in its early phase, and a broad user-base is still lacking. But, if successful, the technical design of the systems will have a broader impact on how anonymously people can 'move' on the internet in the future. In reference to the famous cartoon 'on the Internet, nobody knows you're a dog' (Steiner, 1993), companies now might not always have to know that there is a dog, but

[10] A central hub for this development is a loose network called the 'Identity Gang' (http://www.identitygang.org) and the 'Identity Commons' group (http://www.idcommons.net). I regularly discuss developments around these issues in my blog (http://bendrath.blogspot.com).

would ask for the dog's age, gender, credit card number, or other pieces of information, depending on the service provided. The technical differences between the various emerging identity management standards can be overcome through interfaces and gateways, but the different levels of data protection incorporated within them are more difficult to harmonise (Farber, 2003). Therefore, EPAL allows for the creation of templates through which the different legal data protection provisions in different countries can be implemented (Borchers, 2004).

4. *Comparison*

As in the realm of social codes for privacy self-governance, there is no single technical standard for privacy protection on a global scale. This is partly due to the fact that different threats to privacy require different tools for protection. On the other hand, it also reflects the different interests and needs of corporate data processing and the respective policies and technical architectures. In the technical field, we can once more observe a trade-off between the reach of the technical codes and the privacy protection they provide. But, differing from the social codes, individuals do not necessarily depend on private corporations and their privacy codes of conduct. Instead, their level of control over their own data, as well as the variety of tools available for protecting it, is varying with the architectural scope of the technical codes. For users who individually want to hide their data while surfing the web or sending emails, there is a whole range of tools available that allows for more or less perfect protection. Nevertheless, whether people use these tools, how intensively they use them, and in what combination still depends on their computer literacy and personal privacy preferences.

For exchanging private information with other parties, there are still a number of different privacy tools available, but because of interoperability needs, there are only a few standards that are widely adopted. The user base for these tools is growing due to the network effects—that is, the more users a communications standard has, the more it will attract new users. This is especially true for tools that aim at protecting communications privacy or at exchanging encrypted data between trusted parties. Pretty Good Privacy (PGP) has become the de facto standard for private data security for this mechanism, with the OpenPGP standard having been submitted to the Internet Engineering Task Force (IETF, 1998) providing the basis for many other implementations (Bendrath, 2001). Here, if the parties to a communication use the same standard, they can be confident that their personal information and communication is protected.

Internet users who must provide personal data to website providers because of a business relationship can use the Platform for Privacy Preferences web standard P3P to automatically negotiate their privacy preferences with the respective corporation. But user control has its limits here, as only a minority of websites and browsers support P3P, and even if they do, there are no technical measures available yet that allow the individual control over what happens to their information once it has entered the corporate data warehouses. Comprehensive and strong user-centric privacy and identity management architectures are still under development, and technical back-office privacy standards like EPAL that limit data use within the corporate data warehouse only provide a generic framework. The level of privacy protection they implement depends on the social codes that apply in the respective company, be they self-governance codes of conduct or legal obligations. This lack of technically supported control for users over their personal data once they have given it to private corporations, combined with ongoing compliance problems in the private sector and constant consumer mistrust in e-commerce, has fuelled new state-based regulation efforts in recent years.

IV. COMPLIANCE PROBLEMS AND THE NEW ROLE OF THE STATE

A. Ongoing Low Compliance Rates

In 1997, the OECD Committee for Information, Computer and Communications Policy conducted a survey of websites that openly questioned the effectiveness of the official mechanisms like the OECD privacy guidelines, and national privacy legislation. The researchers found:

> a marked discrepancy between the world of the various institutions and organisations that develop ideas and instruments for data protection on the one hand, and the world of Web sites on the other. (OECD, 1998a: 23)

Around the same time, several well-published cases of misuse of personal information from companies such as online marketing giant DoubleClick, the steady rise of spam and junk mail, security holes in customer databases, and a growing fear of credit card data being stolen on the net (for an overview, see Junkbusters, 2005) led to a public demand for more effective online privacy protection. Users, according to a number of other surveys, were not satisfied with the state of online data protection (for an overview, see Bennett, 2004b). A March 2004 EuroBarometer survey found that of the 84% of EU citizens who did not shop online, 25% said it was because they did not trust the medium (EuroBarometer, 2004).

This was noted by many. A number of governments and international organisations tried to work on online privacy under a general 'trust' framework. Consumers' lack of trust in privacy and other rights on the web was and is still perceived as a major problem standing in the way of a large-scale breakthrough for e-commerce. This was repeatedly stated between 1997 and 2003 in a number of national and international forums, from the White

House to the EU, the OECD, and the World Summit on the Information Society.[11]

Therefore, states have been trying, either directly or indirectly, to influence the development of technical codes for privacy protection, and have also started public auditing and certification programmes for social codes of privacy self-governance. In addition, the most recent development is the return of the good-old state-centrist model of regulation. A public demand for legislation in the absence of meaningful private sector regulation can now loudly be heard.

B. The State's Seal on Social Codes

The 'adequacy' rating for the privacy protection levels in third countries by the EU Commission in a way equates to the job done by rating agencies in the financial sector. Elsewhere in the data protection universe, states have started to certify private instruments like privacy standards, organisational procedures, or private contractual arrangements. The Canadian Model Code for the Protection of Personal Information, for example, is a model in a twofold sense: a model for good privacy practices, and a model for the creeping-in of a more prominent role of the state. The code has been developed since 1992 by trade associations and consumer organisations together with the Canadian government and the Canadian Standards Association (CSA). It was officially recognised ('rated') as a 'National Standard of Canada' in 1996. Organisations that voluntarily adopt the standard are then bound to mandatory quality controls by the CSA, comparable to the web privacy seals in the United States. The model code even served as the basis for comprehensive privacy legislation for the private sector—the 2001 Personal Information Protection and Electronic Documents Act (PIPEDA) (Bennett and Raab, 2006: 162). Under PIPEDA, audits of corporate data handling can in turn be delegated from privacy commissioners to accounting firms or standards certification bodies (*ibid*: 138).

The 1995 EU Directive also contains options for the certification of private self-governance instruments by public authorities. They were conceived as exceptions that should rarely be used, but since the Safe Harbour breakthrough even the European data protection commissioners have actively supported and promoted them. The basic idea is to let business associations develop privacy codes of conduct, but to embed them in a legal framework and have them certified by public authorities. The data protection

[11] See, eg, the the EU Commission's 1997 'European Initiative in Electronic Commerce' (EU Commission, 1997), the White House's 1997 'Framework For Global Electronic Commerce' (White House, 1997), the OECD 1997 Turku conference, 'Dismantling the Barriers to Global Electronic Commerce' (OECD, 1998b), the OECD 1998 Ottawa ministerial conference, 'Realising the Potential of Global Electronic Commerce' (OECD, 1998c), the 2003 World Summit on the Information Society's 'Declaration of Principles' (WSIS, 2003).

commissioners have a strong role here. Several adoptions of this certified self-regulation have been developed at the national level. Under the reformed German Federal Data Protection Law of 2001, trade associations can submit their codes of conduct to the data protection authorities, which check these against compliance with data protection laws. These decisions are not binding, however; and therefore the individual data processors (corporations, website owners, or other entities) can submit their individual products or privacy policies to an audit mechanism and thereby get an official certificate and a seal of approval. This is also regulated in the Data Protection Law and in the new Media-Services Treaty between the Federal States of Germany (Berlin Data Protection Commissioner, 2001; Rossnagel, 2000). The German Federal State of Schleswig-Holstein has been offering such an audit mechanism since 2001, with the Data Protection Commissioner's independent centre as the official public certification authority. Interest among corporations in this official auditing is high, which shows a greater trust in the state's legitimising function even in the private sector. Ironically, what is still missing is a federal law that regulates the exact auditing process, including certification and selection of the official experts who are supposed to do the auditing (Sietmann, 2004). The privacy seal nevertheless is currently being taken to the European level by the EU-funded project "European Privacy Seal" (ICCP, 2008). A similar movement can be observed in Australia, where the standard principles were incorporated into national law in 2001. Here, the Privacy Act allows organisations and industries to have and to enforce their own privacy codes in order to allow for some flexibility in the application of the privacy law. The codes developed by the different industry associations then have to be certified by the national privacy commissioner (Australian Privacy Commissioner, 2005).

Some public certification schemes even work with additional incentives. One method is minimising the risk of lawsuits. In the United States, the 1998 Children's Online Privacy Protection Act also introduced the possibility of an official certification of private privacy programmes by the Federal Trade Commission (FTC). Companies that receive this certificate significantly reduce the risk of liability lawsuits in case problems do arise. As it fits into the US model of privacy protection through the courts, it could possibly be used as a model in other areas of privacy protection as well (Cranor and Reidenberg, 2002: 19). It also follows the trend in the United States by focusing on formalised compliance methods, with legal obligations, in order to minimise risks, prompting calls of an emerging 'audit society' (Power, 2002). Another model is reducing the bureaucratic task of having to get a new privacy certificate for each jurisdiction that a company wishes to do business in. The EU Directive envisions consultations between privacy commissioners and business associations at the national level for countrywide codes of conduct, and an examination by the group of national commissioners (the 'Article 29 Working Party') for EU-wide regulation. The European Union has recently started using this model of regulated self-regulation in order to certify the global adherence of its data protection standards within multinational corporations. The procedure for this has already been harmonised among the EU data protection commissioners (Article 29 Working Party, 2005), thereby providing a one-stop certification mechanism for the whole EU. In May 2005, DaimlerChryser became the first corporation to receive a certificate that was valid throughout the entire EU for its global Privacy Code of Conduct from the French supervisory agency CNIL. Others, such as General Electric, have been following in their footsteps. In its first report on the implementation of the 1995 Data Directive in 2003, the EU Commission noted its importance, stating that 'certification schemes play a crucial role' (EU Commission, 2003: 16).

C. The State's Impact on Technical Codes

Some states have begun to mandate so-called 'privacy impact assessments' (PIAs) for government databases. The first country to make PIAs mandatory for federal agencies and departments in the early stages of system development was Canada (EU Commission, 2003: 16). In the United States, under the E-Government Act of 2002, every federal agency must conduct a PIA before it can develop or introduce new information systems that use personally identifiable data. These PIAs must be published and supervision is provided by the Office of Management and Budget. The P3P standard for websites is also mandated by the above-mentioned E-Government Act, as are privacy notices on all government websites. The privacy notices must include which information is collected, why it is collected, with whom the information is shared, what form of 'notice' is available to the individual, and how the information is secured (*Privacy Times*, 2 December 2002). Government *use* of these technological systems, standards, and protocols of data protection, such as P3P, is of course not a regulation of the private sector, but it can help spread their adoption beyond the public sector. The large number of its own computers, which the government can use as a leverage, can create the critical mass for widespread adoption through network externalities, and the official use also functions like a certificate.

Another approach is for government agencies to actively participate in and support the development of privacy-enhancing technologies. As mentioned above, public data protection authorities and commissioners regularly participate in industry expert groups that design technical codes for privacy protection like P3P and EPAL. The European Union has funded a large section of P3P development and supports several privacy and identity management projects within its framework research programmes.[12]

[12] PRIME (Privacy and Identity Management for Europe), FIDIS (Future of Identity in the Information Society), and RAPID (Roadmap for Advanced Research in Privacy and Identity Management).

The German Federal Ministry of Economics has financed the GNU Privacy Guard—a free software implementation of the OpenPGP standard for encryption. Other governments have carried out extensive studies on privacy-enhancing technologies to further the debate and the exchange of knowledge (as a prominent example, see Borking and Hes, 2000).

In a few cases, state-based governance structures have intervened directly in the technological design of computer systems sold by private corporations. Microsoft's 'Passport' program is such an example of how the European Union is now making an impact on global technical developments and thus on global data protection compliance. In its original architecture, Microsoft planned for the centralisation of all data collected from visitors to its affiliates' websites in order to provide authentication services for the latter. Microsoft abandoned this plan following privacy complaints from consumer groups and pressure from EU data protection commissioners (EPIC and Privacy International, 2004: 131). Another example is search engine giant Google's free email service 'Gmail', which automatically scans all its users' mail and places context-sensitive advertisements within them. After strong protests from a number of privacy NGOs and an official complaint to several European data protection authorities by Privacy International, the EU group of data protection commissioners stated that Google's service may be in violation of the European data protection Directive (Links & Law, 2004). Google had to ensure that mail scanning was only done by machines and only with the explicit consent of the users. Whilst the EU data protection bodies merely threatened to initiate legal action against Microsoft and Google in these cases, later entering into discussions with both companies, the California State Senate adopted a Bill restricting Google's search and transfer abilities of GMail users' data (Hansen, 2004).

The state, it seems, is again starting to focus on the technological design of the computer and the networks and is less reliant purely on users' self-help or industry self-regulation. But instead of regulating individual data banks and data centres, as was the norm in the 1970s, it is concentrating on technical infrastructures and standards that will potentially have a widespread impact on the use of personal data.

D. The Return of Legal Enforcement

The call for government regulation over private sector privacy policies and behaviour has been continually growing over the past few years. Beth Givens, director of the privacy rights clearinghouse, concluded her comments on the 1999 Georgetown privacy survey with a recommendation that the FTC should 'exert a stronger leadership role in evaluating the adequacy of privacy protection policies and practices in e-commerce' (Givens, 1999). Even the FTC itself in its 2000 report on online profiling made a significant change. To the surprise of many, it said that legislation was needed to complement industry initiatives like the standard proposed by the Network Advertising Alliance and others. The most important reason given was the defection problem, still prevalent within most self-governance mechanisms.

> Self-regulation cannot address recalcitrant and bad actors, new entrants to the market, and drop-outs from the self-regulatory program ... Only legislation can guarantee that notice and choice are always provided in the place and at the time consumers need them. (FTC, 2000)

The FTC's call was a clear sign that the official 'do self-regulation, or else we regulate you' approach, which had been a constant pattern in the United States, is reaching its limits. The Bush administration has hesitated to adopt a comprehensive data protection law for the private sector and since the attacks of 2001 is not known as a strong supporter of privacy protection in general; however, Congress has seen a rising number of initiatives for data protection legislation since then (Smith, 2006). Several US States have already moved further and passed laws that protect data more comprehensively than current federal legislation.[13] In 2003, California passed the 'Shine the Light' law, enabling customers to find out how businesses sell their personal information. Since then, companies that do business with Californian residents must either allow customers to opt out of information-sharing, or disclose to them in detail how their personal information is shared with others. The Bill was a landmark because it was one of the first legislative attempts in the United States to address 'list brokerage', the compilation and sale of individuals' personal information for marketing campaigns, including spamming, telemarketing, and junk mail. Prior to this, businesses were under no obligations to inform customers and visitors of their information business activities even though many companies, both online and offline, sell their customer lists to list brokers (EPIC, 2005a).

The persistence of consumer distrust in corporate privacy self-governance, as well as the growing burden of having to comply with a number of different national and state-level privacy laws, has recently led to a number of large corporations in the information sector rethinking the need for state-based governance of privacy. In November 2005, in a widely perceived move, Microsoft called for a comprehensive privacy law in the United States (Smith, 2005)[14]. The call was repeated in June 2006 by an industry consortium including Microsoft, Oracle, Intel, Hewlett-Packard, Google, and other big players in the information technology field (Consumer Privacy Legislative Forum, 2006).

[13] See http://www.epic.org/privacy/consumer/states.html for an older, but very comprehensive overview.

[14] The author is Senior Vice President, General Counsel, and Corporate Secretary of Microsoft.

V. CONCLUSION: THE COMPLEX NETWORK OF PRIVACY GOVERNANCE

A. The Role of the State in a Different Shape

Even in private sector self-regulation, there is a growing interest by corporations in getting the state 'back in' ('pull'), while at the same time the failures of pure private sector regulation have created a rising public demand for more state control and enforcement ('push'). Be it public funding and promotion of privacy-enhancing technologies, government supervision over private seal mechanisms, officially certified auditing of privacy policies, or the recent US developments in favour of private sector regulation mandated by law, the state is gaining a more prominent role than it used to have, especially when we consider the 'hands-off' approach towards the internet that was prevalent 10 years ago.

However, what is different from the state-centric approach to privacy and data protection regulation of the first generations is the more prominent role of intermediaries. The state does not regulate big databases and computer centres directly, as it did in the 1970s and 1980s. This would be unfeasible, especially since the rise of the internet. Instead, the state is now trying to control or steer what the important agents set as standards and procedures. The public governance of privacy is no longer pursued directly, but through private intermediaries (Perritt, 1997). These are:

- — trade associations that receive their privacy codes of conduct sealed;
- — technology companies, like Microsoft, who develop identity-management infrastructures;
- — standards organisations like the World Wide Web Consortium (for the P3P web privacy standard);
- — consortiums that develop new infrastructural designs under an explicit mandate from the state, like the EU's funding for the 'Privacy and Identity' projects or the P3P development;
- — organisations that develop model contracts for transborder data flows between private parties like the ICC.

This is all happening within the 'shadow of the law' (in the United States) or even within a legal framework (in other OECD countries), and with an important role still being played by private sector self-governance. The agents and tools of data protection regulation therefore are diverse, with a growing role for the state again. The distributed nature of this new regulatory pattern shows the changing role of the state, which is more an 'enabler' than an 'enforcer' and must work with all types of other agents, sometimes cooperating, sometimes enforcing, and sometimes enabling. This convergence of the EU and US patterns of privacy regulation (and with other regions following) is one striking result of the globalisation of personal data flows through the internet. States in general are no longer willing to tolerate every possible use of personal data in the online environment. Issues with increasing 'spam' are adding to the problem. This has been the subject of several UN discussions, and under the lax CAN-SPAM Act of 2003,[15] we have already witnessed the first big court cases against spammers in the United States.[16]

The Safe Harbour agreement of 2000 embodies the paradigmatic convergence between the self-governance and law-based approaches. It is still based on public law and an intergovernmental agreement, but leaves the certification and operation of privacy governance to the private sector. It also limits the scope of privacy adequacy ratings from whole countries to individual companies. By doing this, it allows for a transnational trading up of protection levels with potentially global reach. At first sight, this resembles the trading-up effect of Californian rules for car emissions (Vogel, 1995). If you are able to change the privacy policy of a big corporation in one jurisdiction, you will help spread this standard worldwide. There is certainly some truth in this, as the example of Microsoft's Passport project has shown. But car manufacturing is based on economies of scale. Things are different in the computer world. It certainly makes sense to have *one* version of a new Microsoft system operating on global scale, but if you maintain only a few localised websites and your business model basically rests on one huge customer database, then it is much easier to reprogramme it so you can distinguish between the use of personal data of EU and US citizens. The external effects of specific privacy regulations are therefore much more effective when they explicitly focus on extraterritorial and third party effects, as the 1995 EU Directive did, and where they are based on law, rather than voluntary compliance.

The trading-up effect through transnational business networks is also still in place. It works more through the interoperability of standards and the reduction in transaction costs they provide. These standards can be technical codes like P3P or social codes like standard contract clauses or a privacy management standard. They will produce a learning effect (if I use this standard here, I know how to use it there), and they also produce a network effect (if everybody else uses this standard, it is much easier for me if I use it too). The critical mass to generate these network effects can be generated by a critical mass of state and corporate users, or by a critical mass of states that mandate the use of privacy codes for corporate users.

[15] The full title is 'Controlling the Assault of Non-Solicited Pornography and Marketing Act of 2003', Public Law 108-187. Critics say the 'CAN' refers not to canning the spam but allowing it, as only fraudulent emails and a lack of opt-out information is considered a breach of the law. See EPIC (2005b) for an overview.

[16] In April 2005, the first spammer was sentenced to nine years in prison; see 'Sie haben Post!', (2005) *Der Spiegel*, 18 April, at 73.

B. The Role of Social and Technical Codes

The distinct technical nature of the internet allows for means of regulating behaviour other than social or legal norms and rules. *Lex informatica*, the ex ante enforcement of specific behaviour in online environments, can certainly be a strong regulator of citizens' and corporate use of personal data. The way websites and servers are programmed either: (a) forces users to either reveal their personal data or be locked out of a service; or (b) can free them from these obligations. Political discussions of the technical design of new infrastructures have certainly become more popular in recent years, with data protection agencies and parliaments trying to enforce more user- and customer-friendly systems design.

A growing nuisance for companies as well as privacy advocates is that there is now a wide variety of national, sectoral, and international privacy laws, codes, standards, and commitments. Although they are more or less based on the same privacy principles, they have different levels of protection and different compliance and public supervision mechanisms, as well as different degrees of control by users and customers over their data. Because they work under conditions of global transnational communications, they cannot be neatly separated by territorial borders or industry sectors any more. In a global cyberspace where proximity and distance in the classical territorial sense have vanished, rezoning the internet into separate national or organisational sub-nets has not been possible as yet, and it is certainly something most users, companies, and developers would oppose anyway.[17] In many respects, it is a return to the 'conflict of law' problem, this time for transnational self-governance. Reidenberg's (2000: 1358) hope that 'multiple technical standards can coexist for information flows in cyberspace'—which would reflect the multiple regulatory approaches—has failed to materialise so far. Applying and translating the several national, international, and private sector privacy governance instruments into technical protocols that automatically manage compliance across different jurisdictions and organisations—and then even offering users some choice in the matter—has yet proven too complex a task to find workable applications and convenient widespread use. We will therefore witness for some time to come, a global privacy regime that is diverse, overlapping, and contradictory. Until truly global privacy norms and standards are established, the next best thing we must settle on is the 'adequacy' rating method, which is increasingly being applied to social and technical codes alike.

[17] This will only be possible if the underlying internet addresses (IP numbers and domain names) are rezoned according to national boundaries. Even for countries that have established border gateways for internet traffic like the proverbial 'Great Firewall of China', circumvention has been a constant nuisance. For a different view, see Goldsmith and Wu, 2006.

The attempts of governments and the European Union to encourage technological regulation schemes may have a harmonising effect, and possibly create a wider use of privacy-enhancing technologies. As most of the developments described in this chapter are very recent, it is too early to judge their effectiveness. Especially approaches like privacy impact assessments in the early stages of systems development or the EU's research funding for privacy-enhancing technologies will only play out in the mid-term. But their widespread adoption will only take place if there is a global agreement on the *content* of the technical rules, on the level of privacy protection that is desired. The seed crystals for such a global privacy standard are slowly emerging as the result of regional mandatory laws such as the EU data protection Directive, their third party effects which have a globalising impact, the development of privacy standards schemes and global sectoral codes of conduct, the political influence on the design of large technical infrastructures, and the private transnational contracts that reference standards and codes of conduct. Technical codes can help enforcement and are a new kind of binding regulation for computer-mediated social interaction spaces. But their widespread adoption still depends on a political consensus that defines the material content of the *lex informatica*. In the end, social codes still reflect social values and norms, and as long as there are different opinions on them, we will not see globally harmonised privacy protection.

REFERENCES

Article 29 Working Party (1998) *Platform for Privacy Preferences (P3P) and the Open Profiling Standard (OPS)*, Opinion 1/98, Document WP 11 (Brussels, EU Commission).

—— (2005) 'Setting Forth a Co-operation Procedure for Issuing Common Opinions on Adequate Safeguards Resulting From "Binding Corporate Rules"', Working Document, Document WP 107 (Brussels, EU Commission).

Australian Privacy Commissioner (2005) Privacy Codes (http://www.privacy.gov.au/business/codes/index.html).

Baer, WS (1997) 'Will the Global Information Infrastructure Need Transnational (or Any) Governance?' in B Kahin and E Wilson (eds), *National Information Infrastructure Initiatives: Visions and Policy Design* (Cambridge, MA, MIT Press) at 532–52.

Bainbridge, D (1996) *The EC Data Protection Directive* (London, Butterworths).

Barbrook, R and Cameron, A (1995) *The Californian ideology* (different versions available at http://www.hrc.wmin.ac.uk/theory-californianideology.html).

Barlow, JP (1996) *A Declaration of the Independence of Cyberspace*, Davos, Switzerland, 8 February 1996 (http://homes.eff.org/~barlow/Declaration-Final.html).

BBBOnLine (2008) Consumer Privacy Website, (http://www.bbbonline.org/consumer/Privindex.aspx).

Bendrath, R (2001) 'PGP—die ersten zehn Jahre' in *Telepolis*, 19 March (http://www.heise.de/tp/deutsch/inhalt/te/7175/1.html).

Bennett, CJ (1992) *Regulating Privacy. Data Protection and Public Policy in Europe and the United States* (Ithaca: Cornell University Press).
—— (2004a) 'Privacy Self-Regulation in a Global Economy: A Race to the Top, the Bottom or Somewhere Else?' in K Webb (2004) *Voluntary Codes: Private Governance, the Public Interest and Innovation* (Ottawa: Carleton Research Unit for Innovation, Science and Environment), 227–48 (http://www.carleton.ca/spa/VolCode/Ch8.pdf).
—— (2004b) 'Privacy in the Political System: Perspectives from Political Science and Economics' (http://web.uvic.ca/~polisci/bennett/pdf/westinbook.pdf).
Bennett, CJ and Raab, CD (2003) 'The Governance of Global Issues: Protecting Privacy in Personal Information', Paper presented at the ECPR Joint Sessions of Workshops, Edinburgh, 28 March–2 April.
—— (2006) *The Governance of Privacy. Policy Instruments in Global Perspective*, 2nd (updated) edition (Cambridge, MA, MIT Press).
Berg, T (2000) 'www.wildwest.gov: The Impact of the Internet on State Power to Enforce the Law', 25 *Brigham Young University Law Review* 1305–62.
Berlin Data Protection Commissioner (2001) Berliner Beauftragter für Datenschutz und Informationsfreiheit Unabhängiges Landeszentrum für Datenschutz Schleswig-Holstein Neuregelungen im Bundesdatenschutzgesetz, Berlin.
Bijker, WE (ed) (1992) Shaping Technology, Building Society: Studies in Sociotechnical Change (Cambridge, MA: MIT Press).
Borchers, D (2004) 'Eine Sprache für den Datenschutz' in *Heise News* 14 May (http://www.heise.de/newsticker/meldung/47361).
Borking, J and Hes, R (eds) (2000) *Privacy-Enhancing Technologies. The path to anonymity*, revised edition (Den Haag, Registratiekamer).
Boutin, P (2002) 'Just How Trusty is Truste?' *Wired News*, 9 April (http://www.wired.com/news/exec/0,1370,51624,00.html).
Bundesverfassungsgericht (1983) BVerfGE 65, 1—Volkszählung. Urteil des Ersten Senats vom 15. Dezember 1983 auf die mündliche Verhandlung vom 18. und 19. Oktober 1983—1 BvR 209, 269, 362, 420, 440, 484/83 in den Verfahren über die Verfassungsbeschwerden, (http://www.datenschutz-berlin.de/gesetze/sonstige/volksz.htm).
CEN (2002) 'Initiative on Privacy Standardization in Europe', Final Report (Brussels: CEN/ISSS).
Charlesworth, A (2000) 'Clash of the Data Titans? US and EU Data Privacy Rules', 6 *European Public Law* 253–74.
Consumer Privacy Legislative Forum (2006) 'Statement of Support in Principle for Comprehensive Consumer Privacy Legislation', 20 June 2006 (http://www.cdt.org/privacy/20060620cplstatement.pdf).
Council of Europe (1999) Recommendation No R(99)5 of the Committee of Ministers to Member States for the Protection of Privacy on the Internet. Guidelines for the Protection of Individuals with Regard to the Collection and Processing of Personal Data on Information Highways, adopted by the Committee of Ministers on 23 February 1999 at the 660th meeting of the Ministers' Deputies.
Cranor, LF (2002) 'The role of privacy advocates and data protection authorities in the design and deployment of the platform for privacy preferences' in Association of Computing Machinery (ed), *Proceedings of the 12th Computers, Freedom and Privacy Conference* (New York City, Association of Computing Machinery) (http://portal.acm.org/citation.cfm?id=543506).

Cranor, LF and Reidenberg, JR (2002) 'Can user agents accurately represent privacy notices?', Paper for the Telecommunications Policy Regulation Conference (http://tprc.org/papers/2002/65/tprc2002-useragents.PDF).

Drake, WJ (1993) 'Territoriality and Intangibility' in K Nordenstreng and H Schiller (eds) *Beyond National Souvereignty: International Communications in the 1990s* (Norwood/NJ: Ablex) at 259–313.

Ellger, R (1996) 'Vertragslösungen als Ersatz für ein angemessenes Schutzniveau bei Datenübermittlungen in Drittstaaten nach dem neuen Europäischen Datenschutzrecht' 60 *Rabels Zeitschrift für ausländisches und internationales Privatrecht* 738–70.

Engels, F (1978) 'On Authority' in Robert Tucker (ed), *The Marx–Engels Reader* 2nd edtion (New York: W.W. Norton).

EPIC (Electronic Privacy Information Center) (2005a) 'California SB 27 "Shine the Light" Law' (http://www.epic.org/privacy/profiling/sb27.html).

—— (2005b) 'SPAM—Unsolicited Commercial E-Mail' (http://www.epic.org/privacy/junk_mail/spam/).

EPIC and Junkbusters (2000) : *Pretty Poor Privacy: An Assessment of P3P and Internet Privacy* (http://www.epic.org/reports/prettypoorprivacy.html).

EPIC and Privacy International (2004) *Privacy & Human Rights 2004 An International Survey of Privacy Laws and Developments* (Washington, DC: EPIC).

EU (1994) 'Europe and the global information society. Recommendations to the European Council', Report of the High-level Group on the Information Society, 26 May (http://europa.eu.int/ISPO/infosoc/backg/bangeman.html).

—— (1995) Directive 95/46/EC of the European Parliament and of the Council, on the protection of individuals with regard to the processing of personal data and on the free movement of such data, 24 October.

—— (1997) Directive 97/66/EC of the European Parliament and of the Council, concerning the processing of personal data and the protection of privacy in the telecommunications sector, 15 December.

—— (2002) Directive 2002/58/EC of the European Parliament and of the Council, concerning the processing of personal data and the protection of privacy in the electronic communications sector, 12 July.

EU Commission (1997) 'A European Initiative in Electronic Commerce. Communication to the European Parliament, the Council, the Economic and Social Committee and the Committee of the Regions', COM(97) 157, 15 April.

—— (2002), Commission Decision 2002/16/EC on standard contractual clauses for the transfer of personal data to processors established in third countries, under Directive 95/46/EC, notified under document number C(2001) 4540, 27 December, with annex 'Standard Contractual Clauses'.

—— (2003) First report on the implementation of the Data Protection Directive (95/46/EC), COM (2003) 265 final, 15 May.

EU JRC (European Union Joint Research Centre) (2003): *Security and Privacy for the Citizen in the Post-September 11 Digital Age: A Prospective Overview*, Report to the European Parliament Committee on Citizens' Freedoms and Rights, Justice and Home Affairs.

EuroBarometer (2004) *E-Commerce Survey March 2004* (http://europa.eu.int/comm/consumers/topics/btoc_ecomm.pdf).

European Parliament (1979): 'Resolution on the protection of the rights of the individual in the face of technical developments in data processing' in Official Journal of the European Communities, No. C 140/35, 5 June 1979.

Farber, D (2003) 'Federated identity, PingID and standards cartels', *ZDNet Tech Update* 19 October (http://techupdate.zdnet.com/Federated_identity_PingID_standards_cartels.html).

Farrell, H (2002) 'Hybrid Institutions and the Law: Outlaw Arrangements or Interface Solutions?' 1 *Zeitschrift für Rechtssoziologie* 25–40.

—— (2003) 'Constructing the International Foundations of E-Commerce: The EU–U.S. Safe Harbor Arrangement', 2 *International Organization* 277–306.

Fink, S (2002) 'Datenschutz zwischen Staat und Markt. Die "Safe Harbor"-Lösung als Ergebnis einer strategischen Interaktion zwischen der EU, den USA und der IT-Industrie', Masters Thesis, Department of Political and Adminstrative Science, University of Konstanz, November 2002 (http://www.ub.uni-konstanz.de/v13/volltexte/2003/1012//pdf/magarbsfink.pdf).

FTC (Federal Trade Commission) (2000) *Online Profiling. A Report to Congress, Part 2: Recommendations*, July 2000 (Washington, DC., Federal Trade Commission) (http://www.ftc.gov/os/2000/07/onlineprofiling.htm).

GBDe (Global Business Dialogue on electronic commerce) (2001) 'Consumer Confidence: Trustmarks' (http://www.gbd.org/pdf/recommendations/trustmark00.pdf).

Givens, B (1999) 'The Emperor's New Clothes: Privacy on the Internet in 1999' (http://www.privacyrights.org/ar/emperor.htm).

Goldsmith, J and Wu, T (2006) *Who Controls the Internet? Illusions of a borderless world* (New York, NY, Oxford University Press).

Hansen, E (2004) 'California Senate approves anti-Gmail bill', CNET News.com, 27 May (http://news.com.com/2100-1028_3-5222062.html).

Heisenberg, D (2005) *Negotiating Privacy. The European Union, the United States and Personal Data Protection* (Boulder, CO, Lynne Rienner).

ICPP (Independent Centre for Privacy Protection) Schleswig-Holstein and Studio Notarile Genghini (2003) *IMS (Identity Management Systems) Identification and Comparison Study for the EU Joint Research Centre Kiel* (http://www.datenschutzzentrum.de/idmanage/study/ICPP_SNG_IMS-Study.pdf).

ICPP (Independent Centre for Privacy Protection) Schleswig-Holstein (2008) *EuroPriSe—Europäische Datenschutz-Pilotzertifzierungen beginnen*, Press Release, 30 January (https://www.datenschutzzentrum.de/presse/20080130-europrise-pilotzertifizierung.htm)

IETF (Internet Engineering Task Force) (1998) RFC 2440, OpenPGP Message Format (http://www.ietf.org/rfc/rfc2440.txt).

ISO/IEC (2006), 'New Work Item Proposal on A privacy framework', ISO Joint Technical Committee 1, Document ISO JTC N8172, 22 June.

Junkbusters (2005) 'News and Opinion on Marketing and Privacy', constantly updated (http://www.junkbusters.com/new.html).

Johnson DR, Crawford, SP, and Palfrey, JG Jr (2004) *The Accountable Net: Peer Production of Internet Governance* (Cambridge, MA, The Berkman Center for Internet & Society Research) (http://ssrn.com/abstract=529022).

Johnson, DR and Post, DG (1997) 'The Rise of Law on the Global Network' in B Kahin and C Nesson (eds *Borders in Cyberspace. Information Policy and the Global Information Infrastructure* (Cambridge, MA, MIT Press), at 3–7.

Latour, B (1994) *Der Berliner Schlüssel*, WZB Working Paper FS II 94-508 (Berlin, Wissenschaftszentrum Berlin für Sozialforschung).

Lessig, L (1999) *Code and other Laws of Cyberspace* (New York, NY, Basic Books).

Links & Law (2004) *Google's GMail: Privacy concerns* (http://www.linksandlaw.com/gmail-google-privacy-concerns.htm).

Lyon, D (2001) *Surveillance Society. Monitoring Everyday Life* (Buckingham and Philadelphia, MA, Open University Press).

Mayer-Schönberger, V (1998) 'Generational Development of Data Protection in Europe' in PE Agre and M Rotenberg (eds), *Technology and Privacy: The New Landscape* (Cambridge, MA, MIT Press) at 219–41.

—— (2003): 'The Shape of Governance: Analyzing the World of Internet Regulation', 43 *Virginia Journal of International Law* at 605–73.

OECD 1980: Organisation for Economic Cooperation and Development Recommendation of the Council Concerning Guidelines Governing the Protection of Privacy and Transborder Flows of Personal Data, Adopted by the Council 23 September 1980.

—— (1985) Declaration on Transborder Data Flows, adopted by the Governments of OECD Member Countries 11 April.

—— (1998a) Directorate for Science, Technology, and Industry, Committee for Information, Computer and Communications Policy, 'Group of Experts on Information Security and Privacy Practices to Implement the OECD Privacy Guidelines on Global Networks', OECD Doc No DSTI/ICCP/REG (98)6/FINAL, 23 December.

—— (1998b) Directorate for Science, Technology, and Industry, Committee for Information, Computer and Communications Policy 'Dismantling the Barriers to Global Electronic Commerce', An International Conference organised by the OECD and the Government of Finland in Cooperation with the European Commission, the Government of Japan and the Business and Industry Advisory Committee to the OECD, Turku, Finland, 19–21 November 1997, OECD Doc. No. DSTI/ICCP(98)13/FINAL, 3 July.

—— (1998c) Directorate for Science, Technology, and Industry, Committee for Information, Computer and Communications Policy, Working Party on Information Security and Privacy, Ministerial Declaration on the Protection of Privacy on Global Networks at the Conference 'Realising the Potential of Global Electronic Commerce', Ottawa, 7–9 October, OECD Doc No DSTI/ICCP/REG(98)10/FINAL, published 18 December 1998.

Perritt, HH (1997) 'Jurisdiction in Cyberspace: The Role of Intermediaries' in B Kahin and C Nesson (eds), *Borders in Cyberspace. Information Policy and the Global Information Infrastructure* (Cambridge, MA, MIT Press) 164–202.

Post, DG (1998) 'The "Unsettled Paradox": The Internet, the State, and the Consent of the Governed', 5 *Indiana Journal of Global Legal Studies* 521–39.

Power, M (2002) *The Audit Society. Rituals of Verification*, 3rd edition (Oxford, Oxford University Press).

Privacymark.org (2006) References (http://privacymark.org/ref).

Reidenberg, JR (1998) 'Lex Informatica: the Formulation of Information Policy Rules Through Technology', 76 *Texas Law Review* at 553–84.

—— (1999) 'The Globalization of Privacy Solutions. The Movement towards Obligatory Standards for Fair Information Practices' in CJ Bennett and R Grant (eds), *Visions of Privacy. Policy Choices for the Digital Age* (Toronto, University of Toronto Press).

—— (2000) 'Resolving Conflicting International Data Privacy Rules in Cyberspace', 52 *Stanford Law Review* 1315–71.

Richardson, L (2000) 'History of Self-Regulation Cast Doubt on its Effectiveness', *Privacy Times*, 12 July, 7–11.

Rosecrance, R (1996) 'The Rise of the Virtual State', 4 *Foreign Affairs* 45–61.

Rossnagel, A (2000) *Datenschutzaudit. Konzeption, Durchführung, gesetzliche Regelung* (Braunschweig/Wiesbaden, Fr Vieweg & Sohn).

Rössler, B (2001) *Der Wert des Privaten* (Frankfurt am Main, Suhrkamp).

Schwarz, PM and Reidenberg, JR (1996) *Data Privacy Law* (Charlottesville, VA, Michie Law Publisher).

Seltzer, W and Anderson, M (2001) 'The Dark Side of Numbers: The Role of Population Data Systems in Human Rights Abuses', 68 *Social Research* at 481–513.

Shaffer, G (1999) 'The Power of Collective Action: The Impact of EU Data Privacy Regulation on US Business Practice', 5 *European Law Journal* 419–37.

Shaffer, G (2000) 'Globalization and Social Protection: The Impact of EU and International Rules in the Ratcheting up of U.S. Data Privacy Standards' 25 *Yale Journal of International Law* at 1–88.

Sietmann, R (2004) 'Bundestag will Datenschutzreform anmahnen' in *Heise News* 1 December (http://www.heise.de/newsticker/meldung/53816).

Smith, B (2005) *Protecting Consumers and the Marketplace: The Need for Federal Privacy Legislation* (Redmond, Microsoft Corp).

Smith, MS (2006) *Internet Privacy: Overview and Legislation in the 109th Congress, 1st Session*, CRS Report to Congress RL31408 (Washington DC, Congressional Research Service).

Steiner, P (1993) Cartoon, 'On the Internet, nobody knows you're a Dog'61, *The New Yorker*, 5 July (http://www.cartoonbank.com/product_details.asp?sitetype=1&sid=22230003).

Swire, PP and Litan, RE (1998) *None of Your Business: World Data Flows, Electronic Commerce, and the European Privacy Directive* (Washington, DC, Brookings Institution Press)

Teubner, G (2003) 'Globale Zivilverfassungen: Alternativen zur staatszentrierten Verfassungstheorie', 63 *Zeitschrift für ausländisches öffentliches Recht und Völkerrecht* 1–28.

TRUSTe (2008) TRUSTe Fact Sheet, (http://www.truste.org/about/fact_sheet.php).

US DoC (United States Department of Commerce) (1997) 'Privacy and Self-Regulation in the Information Age', (http://www.ntia.doc.gov/reports/privacy/privacy_rpt.htm).

—— (2005) 'Safe Harbor Overview' (http://www.export.gov/safeharbor/sh_overview.htm).

—— (2007) 'Safe Harbor List' (http://web.ita.doc.gov/safeharbor/shlist.nsf/webPages/safe+harbor+list).

United States Internet Council (2000) *State of the Internet 2000* (Washington, DC., United States Internet Council).

Vogel, D (1995) Trading Up. Consumer and Environmental Regulation in a Global Economy (Cambridge, MA, Harvard University Press).

Warren, S and Brandeis, L (1890) 'The Right to Privacy' in 4 *Harvard Law Review* 193–220.

Weichert, T (2000) 'Zur Ökonomisierung des Rechts auf informationelle Selbstbestimmung' in H Bäumler (ed), *E-Privacy. Datenschutz im Internet* (Braunschweig and Wiesbaden, Vieweg) 158–84.

White House (1997) A Framework for Global Electronic Commerce, 1 July.

Winner, L (1986a) *The Whale and the Reactor. A Search for Limits in an Age of High Technology* (Chicago, IL University of Chicago Press).

Winner, L (1986b) 'Do artifacts have politics?' in L Winner, *The Whale and the Reactor. A Search for Limits in an Age of High Technology* (Chicago, IL: University of Chicago Press) 19–39.

WSIS (World Summit on the Information Society) (2003) 'Declaration of Principles. Building the Information Society: a global challenge in the new Millennium', Geneva, 12 December (http://www.itu.int/wsis/docs/geneva/official/dop.html).

WTO (1994) General Agreement on Trade in Services (GATS), Geneva, 15 April.

8

Transnational Consumer Law: Co-Regulation of B2C E-Commerce

GRALF-PETER CALLIESS*

A CENTRAL FUNCTION of private law is to facilitate market exchange by enabling economic actors to conciliate their mutual expectations and, thus, to cooperate. This *coordinative function* of private law becomes manifest in the definition of property rights and the enforcement of contractual obligations. Since the principle of party autonomy leaves the decision on substantive issues to contractual self-regulation, private law in this respect is merely a public framework for private ordering. In the modern welfare state, however, private law also fulfils a *regulatory function* in establishing certain constraints to party autonomy with respect to commutative justice and public policy. The legislation on the protection of consumers, as the weaker party in business transactions, figures as a prominent example (Grundmann *et al*, 2001).

While consumer protection within domestic markets is a well-established concept, the same does not hold for the international realm, where the enforcement of national protection regimes is hampered by a lack of international cooperation. Until recently this has not posed much of a problem, since consumers rarely engaged in international commerce directly. With the advent of the internet, however, matters have changed dramatically. In the networked economy, consumers increasingly shop online often without noticing that they get involved in cross-border situations, in which businesses are able to contract around national consumer rights by means of forum shopping and choice of law (Rothchild, 1999: 893; Calliess, 2006: chs 2–3).

It has been in this context that the issue of *consumer confidence* in business-to-consumer electronic commerce ('B2C e-commerce') entered the global agenda (European Commission, 1997; Federal Trade Commission, 2000;

* I wish to thank Harry Bauer for his help in translating substantial parts of this chapter into the English language and Martin Klamt for editorial work.

OECD, 2006a). While States remained reluctant to regulate cross-border consumer contracts by means of multilateral treaties, international organisations called for *co-regulatory* efforts in addressing the issue. Hence, the 1999 OECD Guidelines for Consumer Protection in the Context of Electronic Commerce (the 'OECD Guidelines') read:

> Part II, VI.B.: Businesses, consumer representatives and governments should work together to continue to use and develop fair, effective and transparent self-regulatory and other policies and procedures, including alternative dispute resolution mechanisms, to address consumer complaints and to resolve consumer disputes arising from business-to-consumer electronic commerce, with special attention to cross-border transactions.
>
> Part III: To achieve the purpose of this Recommendation, Member countries should ... encourage continued private sector leadership that includes the participation of consumer representatives in the development of effective self-regulatory mechanisms that contain specific, substantive rules for dispute resolution and compliance mechanisms.[1] (see also OECD, 2002)

It is widely accepted that international merchants are able to solve their coordination problems by means of private ordering and, therefore, that they should be allowed to opt out of the state's legal system by handing over disputes to arbitration and by choosing non-state rules as applicable law (Berger, 1999; Zumbansen, 2002; general critique at Cutler, 2003). This assumption's underlying rationale is that there is an absence of public interest in international commerce as merchants presumably meet on an equal footing. Regarding consumer contracts, in turn, private ordering is generally not thought to be an effective and legitimate means for achieving the regulatory functions of private law (Hadfield, 2001: 45; European Consumer Law Group, 2001). Thus, the interesting question arises as to what the concept of co-regulation promoted by the OECD exactly entails, and whether it could at all work in the context of B2C e-commerce.

In the following, I intend to examine the potential role of private ordering and co-regulation in the area of cross-border consumer contracts. I start with a survey of the different mechanisms of private ordering, which have developed in e-commerce (Section I). This illustrates that electronic market-places fulfil an essential role in bundling different means of private ordering into what I call *transnational civil regimes* for consumer protection (Section II). Finally, I aim at demonstrating how states, industry, and civil society actors can jointly contribute to the establishment of a *civil constitution* for such regimes with respect to the regulatory functions of private law (Section III).

[1] The Guidelines are available at: http://www.oecd.org/dataoecd/18/13/34023235.pdf. (All links to the internet in this text were last checked on 20 January 2007).

I. PRIVATE ORDERING IN B2C E-COMMERCE

There is a plethora of literature on private ordering in commercial relations, describing various governance mechanisms that merchants employ in order to reduce the likelihood of opportunistic behaviour among contractual parties (Bernstein, 1992; Benson, 1999; Aviram, 2004; Williamson, 2005; Greif, 2006). These mechanisms are generally applied 'in the shadow of the law', but their use is rendered essential in a situation of 'lawlessness', for example in low developed countries with inefficient legal systems (Dixit, 2004). The latter situation resembles the one in cross-border commerce in which businesses are confronted with constitutional uncertainties resulting from multi-jurisdictional litigation (Schmidtchen and Schmidt-Trenz, 1990; Streit and Mangels, 1996; Calliess *et al*, 2007). In this part of the chapter I intend to demonstrate, how the governance mechanisms employed by international merchants are increasingly adapted to B2C e-commerce transactions as well.

A. Online Reputation

One important mechanism of contractual governance is reputation: people do not engage in opportunistic behaviour in a certain transaction, because they fear that other parties might refrain from entering into future transactions with partners who, on the relevant market, have a reputation as bad co-operators (Posner, 2000). But the collection and processing of information on the past performance of potential contract partners is costly, since it is not usually spread in an organised manner but rather spontaneously. For this reason the reputation mechanism is categorised as 'informal third party control' (Panther, 2000). It follows that the reputation mechanism works most effectively for high volume transactions which legitimise the information costs involved, as well as on markets with a limited number of players who interact frequently and, thus, have a high probability of meeting repeatedly (Leeson, 2006). The interactive communication capabilities of the internet, however, have enabled the establishment of large-scale, 'word-of-mouth' networks at low cost. Online feedback mechanisms introduced by electronic market-places have led to an increasing formalisation of the reputation mechanism (Dellarocas, 2003). In the following, I shall discuss the eBay feedback system as an example of the adaptation of the reputation mechanism to the needs of large-scale and small-volume consumer markets with a low probability of repeated transactions (Baron, 2002; Resnick *et al*, 2006).

In order to enter eBay's electronic market-place, seller and buyer first have to become registered members. eBay offers different procedures for identity checking, where the appliance of the most rigorous check is indicated by a symbol attached to the member's name. In the aftermath of every transaction, buyer and seller can mutually assess each other—positively, neutral, or negatively—and can briefly justify their decision. Negative assessments can be commented on by the assessed and are allowed to be taken back by mutual agreement. In this way, multiple assessments constitute a rating profile of every member, the quality of which is indicated after the member's name by stars and shooting stars in different colours. This allows potential transaction partners to get information about each other before completion of a contract.[2] Furthermore, those vendors who on average have sold more than 300 items within the last three months or who have generated a turnover of 3,000 Euros and whose ratings are more than 98 per cent positive receive the status of 'PowerSeller'. Again, this is indicated by a particular symbol after the member's name. New members and those members who have changed their member name are also indicated by particular symbols. In sum, eBay provides a highly formalised reputation system, which offers its members a high degree of transparency through information about the trustworthiness of potential contractual partners. Shopping with a commercial 'PowerSeller' can be considered as safe as shopping with a traditional high street brand like Marks and Spencer, for example. Yet, occasional private sellers can also obtain an impeccable reputation over a longer period of time. In contrast, it is more risky to complete a contract with a new vendor lacking a distinct member profile. In such a case, every member has to consider whether he or she wants to take such a risk; especially if higher sums of money are involved, additional precautionary measures are available, such as an escrow service, which is further detailed below.

B. Trustmarks and Codes of Conduct

Following the principle 'caveat emptor', trustmarks offer a functional equivalent to trademarks in that both bundle information on a supplier in an easily accessible form and, thus, replace the need for individual investigations into its reputation. Trustmarks are of special importance to small and medium-sized enterprises (SMEs) which are unable to build up their own trademark on the global electronic market-place. They are awarded to vendors by a neutral third party, given that specific criteria prescribed in a code of conduct have been met (for the distinction of 'trust' in a vendor and 'reliance' on an independent third party see Pichler, 2000). Originally, trustmarks were awarded to products with regard to their technical standard. In principle, trustmarks can also be used to establish socio-ethical standards or to secure compliance with legal norms. Private, state, and hybrid institutions can play a crucial part in their award and monitoring. Businesses voluntarily submit themselves to such standards and monitoring

[2] In principle, this only applies to the buyer, as the vendor cannot know the winner of an auction in advance. Recently, however, eBay has provided sellers with the option of limiting their offer to buyers from a particular region or with a particular minimum rating profile.

as they hope to gain competitive advantages through the trustmark. The German 'blue angel' and the European 'eco-label' applied such a conception to environmental standards (compare Teubner *et al*, 1994; Pfaff and Sanchirico, 2000).[3] In the debate over internet governance, such trustmarks are discussed as a means for the protection of privacy, consumers, and children (Wagemans, 2003; Spletter, 2003).

Following the internet euphoria of the late 1990s, in B2C e-commerce numerous trustmark schemes have been established, but only a few of those have achieved some significance in the market-place (see GBDE, 2000; see also Nordquist *et al*, 2002). Particularly successful has been the BBBOnLine Reliability Seal which following an initiative by the Canadian and US-American Chambers of Commerce is used by almost 20,000 web pages.[4] In order to obtain the seal, internet vendors have among other things to become a member of the Better Business Bureau (BBB) located at the headquarters of their business, they have to follow the BBB Code of Online Business Practices[5] based on the OECD Guidelines and have to subject themselves to an alternative dispute resolution procedure that accords with BBB's fairness criteria.[6] To give an example, a pre-dispute binding arbitration clause in a contract is only admissible if the consumer has been fully informed about its consequences and costs, provided that the consumer signs the clause separately and that such acceptance is not a precondition for the transaction itself.[7]

With more than 1,500 certified traders, the private company Trusted Shops is one of the leading providers of trustmarks in Europe.[8] Participating traders have to meet certification criteria, which follow current German and European legal regulations in the field of distance selling and electronic commerce.[9] Furthermore, Trusted Shops' assessment encompasses credit ratings, safety technology, transparency of prices, customer services, and privacy issues. In collaboration with the credit insurer Atradius, Trusted

[3] *Cf* http://blauer-engel.de and http://www.eco-label.com/german/; for a survey of environmental trustmarks see www.label-online.de.

[4] See http://www.bbbonline.org/consumer.

[5] Available at: http://www.bbbonline.org/reliability/code/CodeEnglish.doc.

[6] 'To agree to participate in binding arbitration under BBB Rules of Arbitration (Binding) if the consumer also agrees, or in non-binding informal dispute settlement (IDS) under the BBB Rules for IDS for unresolved consumer complaints involving Participant's products or services. Alternatively, a company may pre-commit to a dispute settlement process through a provider other than the BBB, if the BBB determines the dispute settlement process substantially complies with BBB consumer dispute resolution criteria.', available at: http://www.bbbonline.org/reliability/dr.asp.

[7] 'In order to ensure that the consumer has knowingly chosen arbitration as the method of resolving disputes covered by the arbitration clause, binding arbitration clauses must contain the following: A separate signature line, appearing immediately below the arbitration clause, for the consumer to sign to acknowledge acceptance of the terms of the arbitration clause; and, a statement that the consumer will not be bound by the terms of the clause unless the consumer signs on the signature line': http://www.bbbonline.org/reliability/dr.asp.

[8] For the following see http://www.trustedshops.com/en/trustedshops/index.html.

[9] http://www.trustedshops.com/en/shops/obligations_en.html.

Shops additionally offers a money-back guarantee covering failed delivery, failed refund after return, and credit card fraud, which is free of cost to buyers. Moreover, Trusted Shops provides a central customer service and dispute resolution procedure. Customers can contact a multilingual service centre with any arising issue via telephone, email, or the internet. According to Trusted Shops, thus far there has been not a single court case filed between a customer and an online shop because of the mediation procedures in place. Certification criteria are continuously revised in collaboration with an advisory board encompassing, among others, members of consumer protection agencies and academics. Participating vendors are informed about new developments in law. All online shops can be accessed via a central portal, which consumers can use to search for particular goods. For all mentioned services vendors pay graded fees according to their turnover. Additionally, for their online shops and advertising campaigns vendors are offered pre-certified web-hosting and software solutions. Although big brands like Aral, Dell, Dorint and so on, have also joined; Trusted Shops remains committed to be a platform that especially allows SMEs to access e-commerce.

This example highlights that trustmark providers can generate a realm of private order, which rests not only on norms as part of codes of conduct but also on a combination of an insurance for filed payment and alternative dispute resolution procedures. Such an arrangement increases the security level to such an extent that e-shopping is rendered more reliable than traditional bricks-and-mortar business dealings, in which customers have to assert their legal rights in court and in which they carry the risk of insolvency. The withdrawal of the trustmark itself works as a powerful sanction mechanism. The severity of such a sanction as well as the credibility of its threat, however, depends on the success of the trustmark provider: only if the trustmark has gained some weight within the market-place can its withdrawal pose a serious competitive disadvantage to vendors. At the same time, only an economically successful trustmark provider can afford to lose vendors as clients. The success of trustmarks depends on three decisive factors usually termed as 'critical mass, financial sustainability, and branding' (Wagemans, 2003: 14). As mechanisms of private ordering, trustmarks are 'network goods' by nature (Aviram, 2003). This is the reason why international cooperation between trustmark schemes and both the interlinking with (for example market-places, alternative dispute resolution) and the embedding in (for example, Chamber of Commerce) already existing mechanisms of self-regulation seem particularly apposite.

C. Online Dispute Resolution

The notion that the internet's communicative potential can be used to establish alternative forms of dispute resolution procedures dates back to the mid

1990s (Post, 1995; Karamon, 1996; Cona, 1997; Eisen, 1998; Almaguer and Baggott, 1998; Bordone, 1998; Perritt, 2000). The term 'online dispute resolution' (ODR) covers on the one hand conflicts arising from the use of the internet itself, such as disputes over domain names or e-commerce transactions, and on the other hand services of alternative dispute resolution provided via the internet (eADR) (Hörnle, 2001; Teitz, 2001; Schultz, 2004; Ponte and Cavenagh, 2004). The latter includes the whole range of traditional ADR procedures—informal assisted negotiation, mediation, and formal arbitration—insofar as the involved parties and a neutral third party communicate via email or via password-protected web pages, they electronically exchange documents and photographs ('written proceedings'), and they even negotiate simultaneously in chat rooms, via the telephone or in videoconferences ('quasi hearings') (Krause, 2001: 457, 460). The kind and extent of the use of information and communication technology not only depends on its spread among potential users but also on the aim and kind of dispute resolution procedure. When, for example, in international commercial arbitration the formal requirements of the 1958 New York Convention are of concern, high technical standards are necessary, while in more informal dispute resolution procedures, easily accessible, timely, and inexpensive solutions are required (Hörnle, 2003).

Moreover, software-supported negotiation systems allow parties to settle disputes without the involvement of a neutral third party (Lodder and Thiessen, 2003). Thus, based on game theoretical premises, automatic negotiation systems are offered for those conflicts in which solely the amount of a sum is disputed, such as in insurance cases. Within a 'blind bidding'-procedure, the parties submit their offer for a settlement within a number of rounds; yet, their offer remains unknown to the opposite party. Then, computer software fixes a binding sum for the settlement based on the arithmetic mean of all offers, and given that the final sum remains within a certain range (see Tyler and Bretherton, 2003). Besides, systems exist that provide parties with a password-protected space for negotiation. Via menu-driven input masks, they allow parties to closer define the object of dispute, to fix their aims, to deduce the willingness to compromise, and to reach voluntary settlement by standardised information about possible ways to resolution.[10] Hence, ODR can be distinguished from more traditional procedures of ADR in that technology takes part as a 'fourth party' (Katsh and Rifkin, 2001: 93; Lodder and Thiessen, 2003).

A study by the Australian Ministry of Justice dating back to 2003 examined 76 ODR web pages worldwide; 42 of which were established in the years 1999/2000 and 19 of which had already ceased to provide their services (Tyler and Bretherton, 2003: updated; Tyler, 2004). Only 24 providers submitted information concerning the number of cases dealt with, and only

10 For www.smartsettle.com's service see Lodder and Thiessen, 2003: 5.

eight web pages contained statistical information about achieved results (Tyler and Bretherton, 2003: 9). One can assume that those providers that did not present any information were not particularly successful (Schultz *et al*, 2001: 67; Kaufmann-Kohler and Schultz, 2004). Among the more successful providers are especially those ODR pages which are linked to a market-place for e-commerce or which are run by a Chamber of Commerce or an industry association. The reason for such success may lie in the fact that those pages are easily accessible via the market-place or the vendor's web page, that they are partly advertised by a trustmark, and that they can be used for free or for a minimal charge due to subsidies by the operators of market-places or by subscription (Tyler and Bretherton, 2003: 11).

In the following paragraphs, I introduce the most successful ODR model in the area of B2C e-commerce (compare Hörnle, 2002). 'www.SquareTrade.com' is a private company with its headquarters in San Francisco. Since February 2000, it has dealt with over one million conflicts linked to 120 countries in five languages. This renders 'SquareTrade' the market leader for those ODR services dealing with transactions in electronic market-places. The dispute resolution procedure is arranged in two phases. At the first level, direct negotiations between the involved parties take place via a secure web page. Communication is organised via interactive input masks, which are constantly revised and improved in the face of new experiences (*software-facilitated direct negotiations*). In a majority of cases, the involved parties come to a settlement themselves. If this cannot be achieved, each party can call in a mediator at the second level of the procedure. Based on electronic documentation, the mediator is able to quickly gain an overview of the conflict and to support the parties in their quest for a settlement. On request, a party can even make a non-binding suggestion for a settlement (*online mediation*). Overall, 80 per cent of cases can be resolved by a settlement, which is obeyed in 98 per cent of cases. The average duration of a procedure is two weeks (Abernethy, 2003).

Based on a cooperation agreement with eBay, for eBay-members direct negotiations at SquareTrade are free of charge; the involvement of a mediator costs only 20 US dollars. The SquareTrade ODR service is easily accessible via links at the eBay web page. Furthermore, for an annual charge SquareTrade offers a trustmark that vendors can bear given that their identity and reliability has been established by SquareTrade and that they subscribe to the SquareTrade Selling and Customer Services Standards, which especially demand compromise-oriented participation in SquareTrade ODR procedures as well as strict compliance with settlements achieved thereby. The high levels of settlement and compliance achieved within eBay can be explained by the impending withdrawal of the trustmark and deterioration of eBay ratings. As eBay vendors heavily rely on their reputation via SquareTrade they can also render (unjustified) negative customer ratings the objects of dispute. If both parties agree to withdraw a negative rating within the SquareTrade procedure, the rating is not erased from the eBay-member profile, but it does not remain part of the PowerSeller rating, the highest category of which requires 98 per cent positive ratings.

One can record that the success of ODR procedures depends not only on the provision of easily accessible, quick, effective and low-cost dispute resolution, but also on *linkages* with heavily used market-places and with other providers of private ordering services. The example of SquareTrade proves that cost-effective ODR procedures—even covering cross-border transactions—can be organised and are affordable for low-volume mass market transactions. SquareTrade has succeeded in integrating its services in the primary markets for e-commerce, where online disputes arise. This integration is brought about by a cooperation agreement with the primary market-maker eBay, and by creating *socio-legal bonds* for potential dispute parties to commit to the process.[11] The SquareTrade mediation process is mandatory for those eBay-sellers who committed to the trustmark scheme. In addition, the commitment of parties to the process is streamlined by the potential repercussions from the eBay feedback system.

D. Method of Payment and Credit Security

In the context of private ordering in e-commerce, the role of payment service providers as *trusted third parties* is of interest. From international commerce it is known that mechanisms such as letters of credit, factoring, forfeiting, and credit insurance play a major role in the cushioning of those risks arising out of the consecutive exchange of goods and services (Häberle, 2002). In B2C e-commerce a number of models have been developed which facilitate consumers carrying the burden of the usually required advance payments. These models are introduced in the following paragraphs. More advanced 'real time e-payment' technologies aiming at the simultaneous exchange of services and payments in direct e-commerce with digitised goods remain very much in the future.[12]

In B2C e-commerce payment by credit card is most common (Federal Trade Commission, Bureau of Consumer Protection, 2003; compare OECD, 2006b).[13] Against widespread fear concerning credit card fraud on the internet, for consumers this method of payment is the most secure as

[11] The term 'legal bond' is used herein a very broad sense, including not only contractual design but also all kinds of 'private ordering' (see Mifsud Bonnici and de Vey Mestdagh, 2005: 31–42).

[12] For the transfer of a 'delivery vs payment'-system, well known from stock market clearings, to B2C e-commerce see European Central Bank, 2004.

[13] Visa is used more often than any other card for online shopping: see: http://www.visaeurope.com/personal/onlineshopping/main.jsp.

payments in e-commerce require credit card number and period of validity but not the signature of the credit card holder.[14] Hence, consumers can object to transactions with the bank issuing their credit card within six weeks after receipt of the credit card statement. According to the so-called 'credit card chargeback'-procedure, the vendor has to prove that the payment has taken place with consent of the credit card holder. Due to the lack of the consumer's signature, this can only be successful if the vendor can prove that he has delivered goods to the consumer and that the consumer has indeed ordered these goods. Failing such proof, for example because the consumer claims not to have taken the order, the paid purchase price is refunded and the vendor is subject to a hefty charge. In this way, banks have completely passed on the risks of online fraud to online vendors. Yet, due to possible abuse through unjustified complaints, in the meantime online vendors have been offered rating systems for credit card customers in order to identify in advance those consumers marked by numerous chargebacks. Somewhat misleadingly termed as consumer protection, yet indeed probably more used to protect vendors, Visa now offers 'Verified by Visa', a system that provides registered customers with an additional password and which allows identifying the customer via a secure Visa server. Hence, customers cannot claim any more that they have not ordered a particular good or service.[15]

In the debate on self-regulation in B2C e-commerce, credit card issuers have been discussed from early on as playing an important role in providing effective redress to consumers, since via the 'chargeback' procedure they could enforce decisions issued by ODR service providers (Perritt, 2000; ABA, 2002). Yet, this would mean that credit card suppliers either provide fair ODR procedures themselves or cooperate with an established ODR provider in this respect, neither of which is actually the case. In fact, current 'chargeback' procedures are relatively unfair since vendors are unlikely to succeed in a complaints procedure given the form of evidence necessary, plus they have to carry high costs. Moreover, a fair 'chargeback' procedure should not only cover the absence of card holder authorisation ('I did not do it') but also include other frequently raised complaints, such as 'item not received', 'item not as described', 'item defective', as well as 'refund for returned item'. In this regard, however, the legal situation differs from country to country: whereas such complaints are ruled out in France,

[14] *Cf* for the German legal situation Meder, 2002. Implementing Art 8 of the Distant Selling Directive (97/7/EC), § 676h BGB only provides a clarification. In praxis the allocation of the burden of proof is decisive. Apart from a given signature, prima facie evidence—that the consumer has handled the transaction personally or has not treated his PIN carefully—only exists in the case of the PIN procedure: see the German 'Bundesgerichtshof', Judgment of 5 October 2004 (XI ZR 210/03) (http://www.jurpc.de/rechtspr/20040285.htm).

[15] http://www.visaeurope.com/merchant/handlingvisapayments/cardnotpresent/verifiedbyvisa.jsp.

consumers in the United States enjoy such rights under the Fair Credit Billing Act. In other countries, the right to complain is stipulated by credit card agreements with the issuing bank; hence, it remains at the bank's discretion whether it further pursues complaints, which are foreseen in the international 'chargeback'-rules of credit card issuers (European Commission, 2000; OECD, 2006b: 19). Finally, the credit card system is unsuitable for small value transactions due to its tariff scale.

'E-payment' service providers like PayPal take advantage of this gap.[16] PayPal offers to its 56 million users a system of payment that allows transferring money to people in 45 countries provided they have an email address. The system requires opening a password-protected 'PayPal'-account, to which money can be transferred or for which a direct debit agreement can be authorised. In a protected procedure, money can then be transferred via email. The transferred amount is credited to the recipient's PayPal account, which can be opened free of charge even after receipt of the email transfer. Credit can be transferred to a bank account at any time. This standard service is free of charge for both parties, yet there is no payment of interest on credit. PayPal offers special accounts for companies that allow credit card payments via PayPal, even if the vendor does not participate in the credit card system. Since PayPal was acquired by eBay in 2002, PayPal offers a special service for eBay auctions. For eBay buyers who pay via PayPal, a money-back guarantee takes effect in cases where goods are 'not received or significantly not as described' up to a value of 1,000 US dollars; for transactions not covered, PayPal provides a Buyer Complaint Process in order to resolve complaints. Additionally, PayPal offers support for companies both in averting credit card chargebacks and by providing a seller protection policy, which covers losses up to 5,000 US dollars provided that the vendor carefully follows particular standards. In the context of settling disputed transactions, PayPal follows a rigid policy of freezing affected credit. Together with PayPal's partly limited attainability, this has led to criticism from companies and customers alike.[17]

Finally, comparable to a letter of credit Escrow.com offers an online escrow service, the use of which is recommended to customers by eBay for transactions involving higher sums and unknown contractual partners.[18] Buyer and seller register via Escrow.com's protected web page and specify their terms of trade, which include a description of the merchandise, sale price, number of days for the buyer's inspection, and any shipping information. Then the buyer deposits the purchase price in an escrow account,

16 See www.paypal.com.

17 See the critical web pages www.paypalsucks.com and www.paypalwarning.com, where vendors complain that PayPal would deliberately delay acting on complaints for months in order to benefit from the interest on blocked credits, whereas consumers claim that PayPal would like to withdraw their right to the credit card chargeback procedure.

18 See www.escrow.com; see also the Safe Trade programme offered by www.iloxx.de.

Escrow.com informs the vendor of payment receipt, which causes the vendor to dispatch the ordered good in a way that allows proof of delivery. If the time allowed for return of the good passes without complaint from the buyer, the purchase price is paid out to the vendor. In the case where the buyer does not want to keep the good, he or she returns it and gets back the purchase price (less 0.85 per cent as escrow charge) and dispatch costs according to previous agreement, provided that within a specified period the vendor has not objected to the return of the good. In the latter case, the purchase price remains with Escrow.com without interest payment until buyer and seller have come to a mutual agreement. According to Escrow.com's terms of trade, after 60 days the matter is passed on to the American Arbitration Association (AAA) in order to come to a binding decision. In the meantime, the involved parties are free to turn, for instance, to SquareTrade in order to find an amicable solution, although Escrow.com does not provide any binding rules concerning this procedure.

II. CONSUMER PROTECTING CIVIL REGIMES: THE ROLE OF VIRTUAL MARKET-PLACES

The above survey of self-regulation in the global electronic market-place has demonstrated that mechanisms of contractual governance ranging from reputation and the involvement of trustworthy third parties as intermediaries to alternative dispute resolution—all of which are well known from the debates on private ordering in international commerce—have been refined and adapted in order to be used in the field of B2C e-commerce as well. Yet, each of the introduced services alone leaves a number of problems unattended. If problems arise after a transaction has been entered into, it is hardly of use that the contractual partner has carefully been chosen on the basis of their reputation according to an individual rating system or participation in a trustmark scheme. The handling of payments by an escrow service leads to no solution where a dispute has arisen, and the parties involved are unable to agree on a particular dispute resolution procedure. Similarly, an ODR procedure is of no use if a settlement is not implemented by the parties involved.

Opportunistic behaviour can occur not only in the parties' direct contractual relationship, but also in the context of private ordering services offered by third parties. For example, a vendor might not only fail to perform as contractually promised, but might in addition fail to respond to a claim brought in an ODR procedure, or might fail to abide by a mutual agreement found in such ODR procedure. However, the efficacy of private ordering can be enhanced by combining different governance mechanisms, especially if it is agreed upon in advance which authority to turn to in case of a dispute, and if the parties' use of ODR procedures can be linked back to online reputation systems on the primary markets. Negative ratings are then not only given to sellers who deliver low-quality goods or to buyers who fail to pay, but also to those who behave uncooperatively in mediation, who do not follow settlements agreed on, or who evade an ongoing ODR procedure of an 'e-payment' provider via a parallel credit card chargeback, and so on.

In international commerce, the necessary *interlinkage* of different private ordering services regularly occurs in relation to an individual transaction. Of course one can find standardised contract clauses such as the 'Incoterms' of the International Chamber of Commerce, standard forms for different arrangements concerning letters of credit, and model arbitration clauses referencing the rules of certain arbitration institutions. Yet these are individually tailored by international law firms into a *contractual regime* as complete as possible (Calliess *et al*, 2007). In consumer markets, in turn, there is a higher need for standardisation, which is usually satisfied by companies' general business terms. Due to their unilateral imposition on customers, however, such terms and conditions are hardly suitable to achieve a satisfactory level of consumer protection. In the domestic context, this is the rationale of state intervention through coercive consumer protection laws and judicial review. Similarly, in global B2C e-commerce there exists a demand for a neutral third party that could standardise private ordering services and tie them into effective *civil regimes*.

In this context, operators of virtual market-places perform an important function. For even more than medieval harbours, fairs and market-places (Greif, 2006), operators of electronic market-places stand in international competition for suppliers and consumers. In order to attract turnover, it is not only necessary to provide an efficient technical infrastructure, but also to establish a 'safe harbour' policy, which strengthens the trust of potential customers in the fairness of transactions handled at the market-place. As international stock markets offer additional services for the handling of transactions (clearing) and try to establish standards of transparency and investor protection transcending legal minimum requirements (Adolff, 2003; Damrau, 2003), operators of virtual market-places make an effort to establish a market order that both fosters consumer trust and satisfies the needs of SMEs.

Founded 1995 in California, eBay has developed from an electronic advertisement section via a platform for online auctions into the currently most popular site for internet business between customers and, especially, small businesses. It encompasses more than 100 million registered users throughout the world and 24 localised web pages ('the world's online marketplace').[19] In order to increase the attractiveness of

[19] See http://pages.ebay.com/aboutebay/thecompany/companyoverview.html: currently, 'with millions of buyers and sellers worldwide, eBay offers localized sites in the following markets': Australia, Austria, Belgium, Canada, China, France, Germany, Hong Kong, India, Ireland, Italy, Malaysia, the Netherlands, New Zealand, the Philippines, Poland, Singapore, South Korea, Spain, Sweden, Switzerland, Taiwan, the United Kingdom, and the United States. 'In addition, eBay has a presence in Latin America through its investment MercadoLibre.com.'

the market-place, eBay fosters a public spirit among its users, which leads to the emergence of a private market order.[20] Since a virtual market-place is a 'network good'—ie, the benefit for existing users increases with each new user—the level of regulation has been increased only slowly in order to avoid a stagnation in growth triggered by over-regulation (Baron, 2002). As already discussed, at the core of this market order is a rating system, which has been developed further by the introduction of star ratings and trust symbols. Through cooperation with the ODR provider SquareTrade and escrow services as well as the take over of the payment service provider PayPal, it has been embedded in a *network* of private services providing order.[21] As an additional service eBay offers security tips to buyers and sellers with special attention given to international transactions.[22]

eBay's market order is based on the 'user agreement' and a number of additional 'policies', which regulate the behaviour of members in the market-place and their relationship with eBay itself.[23] These detailed rules are centrally laid down by eBay, yet they are rooted in closely observed customer habits in the market-place. They are constantly revised both in exchange with members of eBay fora and in reaction to arising issues becoming evident through the offered protection programmes for buyers and sellers. SquareTrade also contributes to norm development in the market-place. Although SquareTrade mediators issue no rulings the *ratio decidendi* of which could work as foundation for the precedent driven emergence of norms, they do not act arbitrarily but on the basis of those experiences gained in handling countless eBay disputes. From these standardised solutions for repeated conflicts, certain patterns develop that SquareTrade includes in its menu-driven software for direct negotiations between parties (Abernethy, 2003: 5). As sanction for norm violations, the online reputation mechanism is available (*informal third party control*). This mechanism is fostered by eBay via the introduction of a new option for sellers: buyer-requirements.[24] Accordingly, buyers who have a negative assessment, frequent 'item not paid' warnings,[25] or no PayPal account can

[20] See http://pages.ebay.com/aboutebay/community.html.

[21] See http://pages.ebay.com/securitycenter/.

[22] See http://offer.ebay.com/ws/eBayISAPI.dll?GlobalTradeHub&hubType=0.

[23] See http://pages.ebay.com/help/policies: 1. Rules for Buyers, 2. Rules for Sellers, 3. Rules for Everyone, 4. Prohibited and Restricted Items, 5. Rules about Intellectual Property, 6. Feedback, 7. Privacy, 8. Identity.

[24] As eBay rules provide for the binding nature of an offer (see Oberlandesgericht Hamm, Decision of 14 December 2000 (2 U 58/00), *Neue Juristische Wochenschrift* (NJW) 2001: 1142; Bundesgerichtshof, Decision of 7 November 2001 (VIII ZR 13/01), NJW 2002: 363; also summarised at http://www.lrz-muenchen.de/~Lorenz/urteile/njw02_363.htm), thus far sellers have not been able to select their buyer.

[25] See http://pages.ebay.de/help/tp/unpaid-item-process.html.

be excluded.[26] On the other hand, eBay itself may punish violations of the market order by imposing sanctions: from warnings or the temporary freezing of an account to the exclusion of an involved member (*formal third party control*).[27]

Against this backdrop, it is hardly surprising that the literature refers to the regime established by eBay as an autonomous legal order (Katsh *et al*, 2000: 705; Baron, 2002; Schultz, 2005: 27). Although the market-place is not located outside the state's legal order—especially in Germany numerous judgments concerning eBay transactions have been passed[28]—courts can only partially and indirectly impact on eBay's market order. Recently, the German Federal Court (the Bundesgerichtshof) decided that in the context of eBay auctions consumers have a right to cancel such transactions under the German distant selling provisions within a cooling-off period of two weeks.[29] The exercise of such a right, however, contradicts the eBay principle for auctions that a purchased good has to be paid for and that an unpaid item leads to a warning to the buyer due to his lack of reliability—all this independently of a right to return a good after receipt and inspection by the buyer.[30] Admittedly, eBay does not caution buyers for exercising their statutory right to cancel; yet, the latter's immanent possibility of misuse by its frequent and arbitrary exercise—producing high costs for vendors and eBay due to the necessary refund of commission-fees for auctions—can be tamed via negative feedback from the eBay community. Moreover, the effect of the judgment remains limited to those cases in which German law is applicable. Concerning cross-border transactions, German consumers can refer to the BGH, but they might find little understanding from the international eBay community for a behaviour that jeopardises the economic rationale and attraction of online auctions and which consequently questions the market order fundamentally. In the case of a cancellation of an auction with a US seller, the eBay 'private legal system' might hardly help a German consumer to get a refund.

[26] See http://pages.ebay.com/help/sell/buyer-requirements.html.

[27] See § 4 of the user agreement of eBay Germany: http://pages.ebay.de/help/policies/user-agreement.html?ssPageName=f:f:DE.

[28] An up-to-date collection of verdicts, including many full texts, can be found at http://www.internetrecht-rostock.de/ebay-und-internetauktionen.htm.

[29] Bundesgerichtshof, Decision of 3 November 2004 (VIII ZR 375/03), JurPC Web-Dok. 281/2004 (http://www.jurpc.de/rechtspr/20040281.htm); for critical remarks, see Janal, 2005; also Spindler, 2005.

[30] § 9 of the terms of trade of eBay.de (http://pages.ebay.de/help/policies/user-agreement.html?ssPageName=f:f:DE); see also http://pages.ebay.de/help/policies/unpaid-item-process.html. Interestingly, Amtsgericht Bremen, Decision of 20 October 2005 (16 C 168/O5) recently ruled, that a contractual penalty clause applying in case of an unwarranted exercise of a right to rescission (ie item not paid) is not an unfair business term under the European Unfair Contract Terms Directive (93/13/EEC). Thus, a buyer who refused to pay for a car he purchased at an auction on eBay was ordered to pay damages: http://www.internetrecht-rostock.de/ebayurteil29.htm.

III. CIVIL CONSTITUTION: REFLEXIVE CONSUMER PROTECTION LAW

Civil regimes protecting consumers in the field of global e-commerce have become independent from the legal order of States by linking private rule-making (codes of conduct) with online dispute resolution procedures (ODR), mechanisms of socio-economic sanctioning (reputation, loss of trustmark, exclusion), and private enforcement (money-back guarantee, charge back). Since a complex variety of such regimes has emerged, we can paint the picture of a *competition among civil regimes*, in which different providers of private order compete for the trust of vendors and consumers alike. With regard to the substantive consumer protection standards applied by such regimes, the Alternative Dispute Resolution Guidelines agreed on by the Global Business Dialogue on Electronic Commerce (GBDe) and Consumers International in November 2003 read:

> Applicable Rules: One of the principal reasons why business, consumers and governments consider the development of ADR systems to be of such strategic importance for the enhancement of consumer trust in electronic commerce is that such systems can settle disputes in an adequate fashion without necessarily engaging in cumbersome, costly, and difficult research on the detailed legal rules that would have to be applied in an official court procedure ... ADR dispute resolution officers may decide in equity and/or on the basis of codes of conduct. This flexibility as regards the grounds for ADR decisions provides an opportunity for the development of high standards of consumer protection worldwide.' (GBDe, 2003: 59)

If ADR providers do not resolve conflicts on the basis of state 'legal rules' but on the basis of 'codes of conduct', then substantive consumer contract law is privatised. This privatisation is triggered by a need for simple rules for international consumer contracts, where the application of state law including conflict of laws is 'cumbersome, costly, and difficult'. This combined internationalisation and privatisation leads to what I call 'transnational consumer contract law'.

As mentioned above, private law-making is subject to judicial control for fairness if a business imposes its terms and conditions unilaterally on the consumer in a contract of adhesion. In case of codes of conduct which are produced and applied by a consumer protecting civil regime, however, things are different. The bilateral contractual relationship between the business and the consumer is *triangularised*, since the civil regime comes in as a neutral third party. Here, the consumer is not only a recipient of goods but also a consumer of *private ordering services* supplied by an electronic marketplace like eBay or an ODR provider like SquareTrade, so that a trinity of contractual relationships arises (see Hacke, 2001: 31). On the level of the relationship between the immediate parties to a contract on the one hand

and the provider of private ordering services on the other hand, we deal with *reflexive consumer contract law* insofar as the procedural conditions are concerned which render the private generation of substantive consumer contract law rules as fair.

The thesis put forward here is that the establishment of effective consumer protecting civil regimes will factually displace state consumer contract law in particular areas of e-commerce, especially in the realm of formally organised virtual market-places. This is why the emerging transnational consumer contract law requires an embedding in a procedural constitution of freedom, which at the same time enables the *privatisation of civil law* and adds the necessary *civilisation to private law*. This is to say that state-backed regulation disappears on the substantive level of the primary contract law rules, but should reappear on the meta-level of the secondary rules which ensure that the competition of consumer protecting civil regimes will not lead to a so-called 'race to the bottom' in terms of substantive consumer rights.

In this respect, the necessary constitutionalisation of consumer protecting civil regimes has to distinguish between an interior and an exterior constitution: the emergence of transnational consumer contract law as a *system* is, on the one hand, characterised by *reflexivity*, that is, the application of a process to itself (for example, making norms on the making of norms, arbitrating over arbitration, self-regulation of self-regulation, and so on); hence, societal self-organisation constitutes a *spontaneous constitution* of private regimes quasi by itself (see Teubner, 2004). On the other hand, private regimes require embedding in a *public framework* that facilitates societal self-organisation as an exercise of party autonomy and at the same time limits it with respect to fairness, third party interests, and public policy. Here the phenomena of normative reflexivity entrenched in private regimes as well as their public framework work as mutually compensatory constitutional orders. In the context of global governance, this renders their boundaries fuzzy. Encompassing the collaboration of state, industry, and civil society actors, they appear as a *hybrid* order (Engel, 2001: 569), which shall be termed *civil constitution*.

The establishment of a global civil constitution for transnational consumer contract law mainly concerns the justification of reflexive institutions, which organise the described phenomena of self-regulation and private ordering in a way that, on the one hand, fosters effective redress through alternative mechanisms of consumer protection and, on the other hand, guarantees the fairness and justice of such procedures towards consumers and businesses. In the following paragraphs, different approaches for the constitutionalisation of consumer protecting civil regimes are introduced. Although both aspects cannot be sharply distinguished, the focus is on substantive contract law (*rights*) (in III.A) and on the procedural aspects of consumer law (*remedies*) (in III.B).

A. Reflexive Trustmarks: Contractual Standards of Hybrid Organisations

Trustmarks are awarded on the basis of a catalogue of criteria regularly consolidated in a code of conduct. For the internet and e-commerce, a plethora of trustmarks is available which, on the basis of different criteria, aim at enhancing the protection of consumers, children, and privacy, or any combination of these. In theory, the availability of competing trustmark schemes should lead, in the long run, to the most efficient level of regulation. In practice, however, consumers are often irritated by the complexity of the supply of trustmark schemes. Thus, the general trust in the industry could vanish.[31] Certainly, a sound regulatory competition between different trustmark schemes only works if consumers are not misled by trustmark providers who apply inferior standards which are not sufficiently monitored.

In order to increase transparency in the field of trustmarks, the notion has emerged that quality requirements should be developed in collaboration with states, industry, and consumer associations (Nordquist *et al*, 2002). Insofar as compliance with minimum requirements established by co-regulation is here rewarded with the award of a secondary trustmark (a *trustmark of trustmarks*), we deal with a reflexive form of self-regulation, which even regulates the conditions for its own possibility via self-regulation. Initial approaches to such civil constitutions have first been developed at the national level (III.A.1). From here they can be linked to supranational (III.A.2) and global civil constitutions (III.A.3) via cooperation.

1. *Secondary Trustmarks at the National Level*

On the suggestion of the British government, the Alliance for Electronic Business in collaboration with the Consumers' Association founded a consumer protection initiative in the field of self-regulation in e-commerce in 1999. Its aim was to fix minimum standards in the face of the proliferation of trustmark programmes.[32] To do this, the non-profit organisation TrustUK has been set up, the board of which consists of representatives of the Chambers of Commerce and of consumer associations. TrustUK established its own trustmark, which is, however, not directly awarded to vendors. As most companies are members of a Chamber of Commerce or of an association that binds its members to a code of practice, these 'code owners' are granted the licence for the distribution of the

[31] *Cf* the report of the Irish EU Presidency presented at the European Consumer Day 2004 Conference, 'Building Consumer Confidence in the European Online Marketplace, Dublin Castle, 15th March 2004', p 8, available at: http://register.consilium.eu.int/pdf/en/04/st09/st09466.en04.pdf.

[32] See www.trustuk.org.uk.

trustmark if their members' codes are in accordance with TrustUK's minimum requirements. Participating vendors bear the TrustUK label either alone or together with the trustmark of the 'code owner'; if issues arise, consumers have to contact the 'code owner' directly. Only if the consumer claims that the latter has not settled a dispute in accordance with TrustUK's guidelines is there the possibility to turn to TrustUK directly. Currently, four 'code owners' are accredited to TrustUK, covering more than 4,000 web traders.

The German initiative D21 is a network of political parties, enterprises, associations, and other institutions (a public–private partnership). Its aim is to improve the main conditions for Germany to quickly and successfully transit into the information and knowledge society.[33] In July 2002 members of the initiative have agreed on the D21 quality criteria for internet offers (D21-Qualitätskriterien für Internet-Angebote), which—as amended in 2005[34]—put the OECD Guidelines on the basis of European and German law in concrete terms; furthermore, the criteria explain and amend the latter. Currently, the D21 initiative recommends five trustmarks as meeting its quality criteria.[35] The monitoring and further development of these criteria have been transferred to a trustmark monitoring board, which apart from representatives of participating companies consists of a representative each of the Ministry of Economic Affairs, the Federal Data Protection Office, and a consumer association (Verbraucherzentrale Bundesverband eV) (Föhlisch, 2004). However, such initiatives at the national level enhance the transparency of the trustmark market to a certain extent, yet due to their gearing to national law they do not contribute much to solving issues involving cross-border consumer contracts (see also Nordquist *et al*, 2002).

2. *Supranational Standardisation via Co-regulation?*

With regard to cross-border situations inside the European internal market, the question as to which Member State's consumer protection standards shall apply, in principle, could be answered easily, as the minimum standards of consumer contract law are established in the European *acquis communautaire*, that is, a variety of EC Directives. Yet, attempts by the European Commission to unify the contract law of the Member States have so far failed, often due to the resistance of consumer associations and national governments, which agreed on a minimum harmonisation of consumer

[33] See www.initiatived21.de.

[34] Updated version available at http://www.internet-guetesiegel.de/docs/D21_Qualitaetskriterien_2005.pdf.

[35] See www.internet-guetesiegel.de: apart from Trusted Shops, among others, Euro-Label Deutschland of the EHI (www.shopinfo.net) and S@fer-Shopping (www.safer-shopping.de) run by the TÜV Süd are part of this initiative.

rights, but prevented the necessary combination of such measures with the 'country of origin'-principle (see also Calliess, 2003). Hence, one could ask whether it might not be a viable alternative to state-controlled legal harmonisation to generate substantive Principles of European Consumer Contracts via self-regulation, for instance by developing Europe-wide recommended general contract terms (European Commission, 2003: 21*ff*, at 4.2), or relating specifically to B2C e-commerce by elaborating a European code of conduct which could be applied in cross-border ADR procedures as institutionalised in the EEJ-NET.[36]

The European Commission, indeed, aims at such a project in the framework of its 'e-confidence' initiative. In its action plan concerning 'eEurope 2005', the following aims are introduced:

> Trust and confidence. By end 2003, the Commission, together with the private sector, consumer organisations and Member States will examine possibilities of establishing a European-wide online dispute resolution system. To facilitate cross-border electronic transactions for SMEs, the Commission will further support the establishment of online information systems on legal issues. The Commission will work with stakeholders on trustmarks requirements with a view to a recommendation on consumer confidence in electronic commerce. (European Commission, 2002a: 15)

In order to prepare such a recommendation, the Commission established an 'e-confidence forum' at the Joint Research Centre in 2000. In this context, a 'drafting group' comprising members of industry and consumer associations has drawn up 'principles for e-commerce codes of conduct'.[37] On this basis, the European industrial and consumer associations UNICE and BEUC have agreed on European trustmark requirements (ETR). For their implementation, a committee of association members shall be established and an 'e-confidence' web page shall be set up. Providers of trustmarks who want to join this portal have to pass an annual assessment of their compliance with the ETR by an independent third party (for example auditors) (see BEUC and UNICE, 2001). Since the announcement of the programme in October 2001, there have, however, been no recognisable steps towards the establishment of the system. In November 2004, the Commission finally accepted the failure of the initiative and blamed the industry for a lack of interest in the implementation of the ETR, especially with regard to the financing (see European Commission, 2004). This lack of interest may be rooted in the fact that the ETR have been developed by association officials who stand more for a traditional industrial society than a modern information society. In addition, it remains unclear how the ETR could contribute to the problems of cross-border B2C e-commerce.

[36] See http://ec.europa.eu/consumers/redress/out_of_court/eej_net/index_en.htm.
[37] On file with the author.

In this respect the ETR approach—praised by the Commission—is aiming for a race to the top:

> The ETR offer a basis for good online practice. They do not seek to override or replace any mandatory provisions at European level. They are supplementary to legal obligations and do not affect consumers' statutory rights. (BEUC and UNICE, 2001: 5)[38]

In this respect, the ETR accord with consumerists, who demand that soft law generated in the process of self-legislation should only lead to an increase in the level of protection, but under no circumstances to a softening or evasion of those obligatory consumer protection regulations in place in a consumer's home country (European Consumer Law Group, 2001). Yet, as the ETR refer to nationally applicable law on almost all important points, they appear strangely anaemic and neither guide SMEs to those regulations they should adopt for Europe-wide sales nor do they work as standard for ADR decisions in consequential conflicts. In order to facilitate EU-wide cross-border B2C e-commerce uniform legal standards which provide the necessary certainty are needed, and not just another code such as the ETR which merely adds to the existing regulatory chaos. One suspects that the protagonists involved with the ETR are too close to the European legislative process, which prevents the 'e-confidence' initiative from becoming an independent stimulus for the generation of legal certainty in the internal market.

At the European level, the 'Euro-Label' system, however, provides a functioning alternative, which has been established due to an initiative by the trade association EuroCommerce in 2002.[39] 'Euro-Label' is a network of national trustmark providers from Austria, Germany, France, Spain, Poland, and Italy that awards trustmarks on the basis of a common European code of conduct via co-branding. 'Euro-Label' also handles cross-border complaints against its 429 certified shops. If in this way issues cannot be resolved, the consumer is referred to the EEJ-Net. The European code of conduct is relatively detailed; instead of sweeping references to nationally applicable law, it details the concrete rules of the *acquis communautaire*. Concerning the right to cancel a contract, for instance, it repeats the EU Directive on distance contracts, which states that the cooling-off period is seven working days which does not commence before prior information and delivery and ceases after three months at latest. Certification, however, takes place with national authorities according to local standards. Thus, the European Codex beyond its function as a minimum standard for participating national trustmark providers will not be of crucial importance, for

[38] Appraisal of the European Commission, 2004: 9: 'The Commission Services are of the view that codes such as the ETR are most useful if they contain provisions that set an even higher standard of consumer protection than the protection offered by legislation.'

[39] See www.euro-label.com.

instance in the arbitration of cross-border disputes. Its wording, however, should render it more apposite than the ETR.

3. *Global Linkage*

As early as 2001, the GBDe published recommendations concerning trustmarks, including both guidelines for trustmark providers and minimum standards for the codes of conduct applicable to their online traders (GBDe, 2001). Also in 2001, the European umbrella organisation of the Chambers of Commerce 'Eurochambres', the mail order firm FEDMA and the US BBBOnLine' launched the Global Trustmark Alliance (GTA) as a common initiative in order to further develop and implement global standards. Its aim is to unite national and regional trustmark initiatives on the basis of common minimum standards under the umbrella of the global GTA trustmark, which is intended to be pursued as a co-branding endeavour.[40] In the meantime, GTA membership has been expanded especially by Asian organisations, and on the occasion of the annual meeting of the GBDe in November 2004, an organisational committee was installed and given the task of preparing 'best practices' (GTA, 2004). Given the global reach of the GTA initiative and based on OECD guidelines and the recommendations of the GBDe, it can be expected that the emerging code of conduct will set relevant standards for a transnational consumer contract law.

The organisations involved also intend to cooperate in the handling of cross-border disputes. A good example is the cooperation agreement on mutual cooperation in cross-border e-commerce complaints signed by ECOM ADR, a pilot project commissioned by the Japanese Ministry of Economy, Trade and Industry (METI) and operated by Next Generation Electronic Commerce Promotion Council of Japan (ECOM),[41] and the US Better Business Bureau in 2002, where complaints from consumers in one country against an e-trader situated in the other country are exchanged and both organisations work together, if necessary assisting with language problems. As of October 2004, 45 complaints from Japanese consumers against US-based companies had been forwarded from ECOM ADR to BBBOnLine, and 22 of these disputes had been settled. Twelve disputes came to Japan in turn, out of which only two could be settled, while the other cases involved fraud, where, for example, businesses turned out not to exist in Japan at all (Sawada, 2004). Although ECOM ADR ceased its operations as of March 2006, the quite impressive resolution rate of BBBOnLine may be taken as an outlook on how a seamless ODR network for cross-border B2C e-commerce might work in the future. Thus, similar cooperation agreements have been implemented between BBBOnLine and trustmark providers from the United

[40] See http://www.bbbonline.org/about/press/2001/042301.asp.

[41] See http://www.ecom.jp/adr/en/index.html; see also the outline in Sawada, 2004.

Kingdom, which jointly created a webpage for cross-border ADR,[42] and more recently with the Israel-based initiative Public Trust.[43]

B. Law-Consumer Protection: ODR Standards and their Implementation

A consumer who, in the case of a conflict with a business, seeks redress through an ODR scheme becomes a consumer of private legal services. Where the same consumer goes to court, she is not perceived as a 'consumer' of public legal services but as a 'citizen' with a 'right to a fair trial' as set down eg in Article 6(1) of the European Convention for the Protection of Human Rights and Fundamental Freedoms:

> In the determination of his civil rights and obligations ..., everyone is entitled to a fair and public hearing within a reasonable time by an independent and impartial tribunal established by law. Judgement shall be pronounced publicly.[44]

The inherent procedural guarantees are not only the kernel of the European civil procedure (Wolf, 2000), they also impact arbitration procedures provided that these are binding on the parties involved (Schiavetta, 2004). In this way, the European Court of Human Rights has acknowledged that one can give up one's right of access to court, yet such renunciation, for instance as part of a arbitration clause, is only effective if it is voluntary and explicitly expressed. Furthermore, by the judicial review of private arbitration tribunals the state remains obliged to guarantee the core of fundamental procedural rights, like the right to be heard, and the rights of judicial independence and procedural neutrality (*cf* Schiavetta, 2004). From the vantage point of ODR procedures in the field of B2C e-commerce, these principles do not only apply to consumer arbitration in a narrow sense, they can also become relevant on the side of companies which commit themselves to obligatory and binding ODR procedures, as it is the case with Online Confidence's arbitration procedure concerning amounts in dispute up to 5,000 Euros (Schiavetta, 2004).

Yet, even if the parties' right of access to court is not limited in any way, there is a demand for principles concerning the transparency and fairness of ODR procedures. Hence, companies, which have contractually committed themselves to participate in an online mediation procedure if demanded by a customer—like in the trustmark programmes of SquareTrade—have to be informed in advance about procedural conditions. In a similar way, the SquareTrade trustmark can only then enhance consumer trust in e-commerce if the consumer is able to form an impression of the course of the procedure

[42] See http://www.crossborderadr.org/.
[43] See http://www.bbb.org/alerts/article.asp?ID=658.
[44] http://conventions.coe.int/Treaty/en/Treaties/Html/005.htm.

and of whether it appears to be fair and reasonable with respect to the neutrality of mediators, to costs, to the promise of the implementation of negotiation results, and so on. On this matter, providers of ODR procedures can be subject to certain pre-contractual obligations to inform customers (Ponte, 2002b: 321).

In order to render the market for ODR services more transparent and to establish certain minimum standards of fairness, different public (state), private (industry), and hybrid (civil society) actors have released guidelines for ODR service providers (III.B.1), and a variety of measures were suggested in order to guarantee compliance with the principles contained in such guidelines (III.B.2).

1. *Guidelines for Providers of ODR Procedures*

Initially one has to keep in mind that there exist a number of principles for traditional ADR procedures in consumer affairs that special guidelines for B2C e-commerce can build upon: these include the 15 principles of the Due Process Protocol for Mediation and Arbitration of Consumer Disputes of 1998. The AAA has made compliance with these standards a precondition for consumer arbitration procedures (for the necessity to adopt the protocol to the internet see Ponte, 2002a: 441); similarly, it is a precondition for participation in the EEJ-Net to follow the European Commission's recommendations concerning dispute settlement (98/257/EG) and mediation (2001/310/EG) in consumer affairs.[45] A first outcome of the consultations on the European Commission's Green Paper on Alternative Dispute Settlement in Civil and Commercial Matters (2002b) is the European Code of Conduct for Mediators,[46] which contains a number of ethical principles and which can be adopted by single mediators or institutional providers of mediation procedures.

Based on extensive consultations, the Task Force on Electronic Commerce and Alternative Dispute Resolution of the American Bar Association (ABA) published 'Recommended Best Practices by Online Dispute Resolution Service Providers' in September 2002. These are meant as a non-binding point of orientation for ODR service providers, consumers and trustmark providers and suggest that an ODR service provider informs its users about all features of a procedure relevant to fairness in a transparent way (ABA, 2002). In November 2003 the Task Force on Consumer Policy for e-Business of the International Chamber of Commerce (ICC) published 'Best Practices for Online Dispute Resolution (ODR) in B2C and C2C transactions', which contain guidelines both for enterprises handling B2C e-commerce and for ODR service providers (ICC, 2003). At the same time, GBDe and Consumers

[45] See: http://ec.europa.eu/consumers/redress/out_of_court/adr_recommendations_en.htm.

[46] See http://www.cto.int/adr/adr_ec_code_conduct_en.pdf.

International (CI) have agreed on common 'Alternative Dispute Resolution Guidelines' for B2C e-commerce, which contain recommendations for enterprises, ODR service providers, and governments (GBDe, 2003).

2. *The Implementation of Global ODR Standards*

To implement the aforementioned standards for ODR service providers, a number of measures have been discussed reaching from self-regulation to national outline legislation. In this context, the role of the state tends to be more emphasised than is usually the case (Schultz, 2003). With respect to transnational consumer contract law, the suggested ODR standards touch upon the relationship between citizens and the state and, hence, they concern the kernel of the constitutional law set down in Article 6(1) of the European Convention for the Protection of Human Rights and Fundamental Freedoms. On the one side, such standards have to be developed and spread by institutions that leave no doubt about their neutrality in the face of conflicting interests and thus enjoy the unreserved trust of all involved (compare ABA, 2002: 32*ff*; Davis, 2002: 529). Initiatives for self-regulation led by industry and commerce such as those of the GBDe or the ICC do not meet these criteria on their own.[47] On the other side, ODR standards that have been developed with the support of States are advantageous as they can work as guidelines for judicial review in particular cases. The terms of trade of ODR service providers as well as terms of trade clauses concerning dispute settlement in consumer contracts cannot easily been declared ineffective if they stand in accordance with globally accepted ODR standards.

With the establishment of the European Extra-Judicial Network (EEJ-NET) as well as the above-mentioned EU recommendations, the European Commission in particular has demonstrated what a functioning state organisation at the supranational level could contribute. Following this model, the ABA Task Force has discussed the setting up of a 'Global Dispute Clearing House', which would deal with issues arising from cross-border consumer contracts, which consumers could turn to if problems emerged and which would be responsible for channelling conflicts to those ODR procedures accredited on the basis of global ODR standards. Furthermore, the establishment of an ODR trustmark was considered, which would be awarded to those ODR service providers following ODR standards developed by the Global Online Standards Commission (ABA, 2002: 27*ff*; compare Davis, 2002; Schultz, 2004).

[47] For this reason the GBDe developed its ADR Guidelines in cooperation with CI. The Guidelines call for governments to initiate 'government accreditation' and/or 'government-backed assessment rules' together with industry and consumer representatives, and on a global level only.

However, the ABA Task Force concludes that the ODR market is not mature enough yet to set up binding standards ('not one size fits all'). Moreover, an agreement about such standards in a Global Online Standards Commission under international law is unlikely due to the apparent divergences, for example between the United States and the EU concerning the authorisation of consumer arbitration jurisdiction. Additionally, the accreditation of ODR providers with a global ODR trustmark would require substantial financial and personal resources, which would be desirable, yet seem unachievable. In the current situation, for companies it is of prime importance to avoid dispute by setting up effective consumer complaints procedures ('customer satisfaction systems'). Furthermore, as a first step it is suggested that an 'i-ADR Centre' be established, which is given the task of consolidating information about available dispute resolution procedures on the web ('low cost, low profile'). Without being assessed, ODR providers can initially commit themselves to ODR standards such as the ABA Best Practices. At first financed by the state, such a centre for information could later function as a basis for the more advanced notion of a 'Dispute Clearinghouse' or 'ODR Trustmark Centres' (ABA, 2002: 31*ff*).

More than two years after the ABA recommendations were published, however, the suggested 'i-ADR Centre' has not been established; presumably no sponsor for the project could be found, despite the pursued approach ('low cost, low profile'). Taking the EEJ-NET as a blueprint, the UN would actually be the right point of contact. UNECE has indeed organised conferences concerning ODR in 2002 and 2003 in Geneva; in 2004, the third UN Forum on Online Dispute Resolution took place at the University of Melbourne in cooperation with UNESCA.[48] Due to its chronic lack of financing and efficacy, the UN is hardly able to contribute more than its name to the development of global ODR standards. The organisation of the conferences as well as the publication of the results was taken on by academic institutions. For instance, the Center for Information Technology and Dispute Resolution (CITDR) at the University of Massachusetts provides the website (www.odr.info), where not only the presentations of the UN ODR forum are published,[49] but also broad information is available about ODR providers, ODR standards, literature, and so on. This actually meets the described functions of the 'i-ADR Centre' suggested by the ABA Task Force.[50] Similar to the Transnational Law Database CENTRAL concerning the *lex mercatoria* at the University of Cologne, in the area of transnational

[48] See http://odrforum2004.themediationroom.com/.

[49] See http://www.odr.info/unece2003/index.htm.

[50] Although the information is not always comprehensive and up to date, since ODR information relies on voluntary contributions, mostly by academics.

consumer contract law, science can play an important part through the systematisation of information.[51]

Finally, I would like to introduce the model of state incentives that combines compliance with certain standards and the granting of legal privileges. Thus, the Act on ADR of North Rhine Westphalia couples the accreditation of a mediation institution with the advantage of executing a settlement comparable to a court ruling, provided there is compliance with the standards of transparency and fairness set forth in the Act.[52] During the political debate on the so-called 'Brussels I-Regulation', the responsible committee of the European Parliament suggested that, in deviation from Article 17 of the Regulation, enterprises should be allowed to introduce a choice of court clause into consumer contracts if in return they subject themselves to an acknowledged out-of-court dispute settlement body (Wallis, 2000). The notion that the state facilitates ADR provided there is compliance with certain minimum conditions of due process is well established in international commercial arbitration, where arbitral awards corresponding with the requirements outlined in the 1958 New York Convention and the 1985 UNCITRAL Model Law are recognised and enforced by the state (Redfern and Hunter, 2004). It seems logical, yet hardly realistic, to suggest that taking the juridical review of private arbitral awards as a model, compliance with globally accepted ODR standards could be guaranteed by setting up an international public online court, where appeals against outcomes of ODR-procedures could be lodged (see Schultz, 2003).

IV. CONCLUSION

In this chapter I have shown that the private governance mechanisms which have been developed in international commerce between merchants in order to tackle opportunism in cross-border economic exchange in a situation of constitutional uncertainty, that is, the absence of a world state effectively guaranteeing the protection of property rights and the enforcement of contracts, recently have successfully been adapted to the new phenomenon of cross-border electronic commerce between businesses and consumers. Thus, private ordering has proven to be a valuable alternative to state law not only in the apolitical domain of merchant law, where predominantly coordinative problems arise, but might also contribute to the solution of regulatory problems in the area of consumer law, where the protection of weaker parties is at stake.

[51] See eg the Transnational Law Database on the New Law Merchant established at the Center for Transnational Law (Professor KP Berger) of the University of Cologne (www.tldb.net).

[52] The 'GüSchlG NRW' is available through http://www.streitschlichtung.nrw.de/streit/gesetz.php.

One reason for this success is that the protection of consumers is in the rational self-interest of businesses which intend to engage in cross-border commerce with foreign consumers: In order to convince consumers to enter the borderless global retail market, businesses have to invest in building consumer confidence in electronic commerce by employing various consumer-protecting governance mechanisms. Another reason is the emergence of businesses which do not engage in the primary markets for consumer products and services themselves, but act as market-makers between other businesses and consumers, and, thus, in a secondary market for private legal services: These intermediaries are economically interested in attracting a maximum number of sellers as well as buyers to participate in their market places. Therefore, it lies in their rational self-interest to act as a neutral party towards both sides of the market, businesses as well as consumers. Electronic market-places are, thus, in a perfect position to effectively bundle different private governance mechanisms into what I call consumer protecting civil regimes.

As has been shown in Part III of this chapter, however, a variety of consumer protection concerns remain to be resolved. If consumers in the global electronic market-place are to be able to choose between different consumer protecting civil regimes, there is the need for transparency with regard to the level of protection offered as well as for the effectiveness and fairness of such regimes. In other words, there is a need for 'law-consumer protection', ie substantive as well as procedural minimum standards regarding the private provision of consumer-protecting services. Since such standards for the borderless character of B2C e-commerce must have a truly transnational character, they are developed outside the traditional international law sphere on the basis of co-regulatory efforts between States, industry, and civil society actors. There can be observed a variety of efforts to establish such global minimum standards, which contribute to the future establishment of a 'civil constitution' of transnational consumer contract law.

REFERENCES

ABA (American Bar Association), Task Force on Electronic Commerce and Alternative Dispute Resolution (2002) 'Final Report and Recommendations', reprinted as annex to Calliess (2006).

Abernethy, S (2003) 'Building Large-Scale Online Dispute Resolution & Trustmark Systems' in Katsh, E, and Choi, D (eds), *Online Dispute Resolution (ODR)*, Papers and Proceedings of the 2003 United Nations Forum on ODR (http://www.odr.info/unece2003/pdf/Abernethy.pdf).

Adolff, J (2003) 'Europäisches Gesellschaftsrecht: Vom Wettbewerb der nationalen Rechtsordnungen zum Systemwettbewerb der Börsen?' in CH Witt *et al* (eds), *Die Privatisierung des Privatrechts. Rechtliche Gestaltung ohne staatlichen Zwang, (Jahrbuch junger Zivilrechtswissenschaftler JJZ 2002)* (Stuttgart, Boorberg).

Almaguer, AE and Baggott, RW (1998) 'Shaping New Legal Frontiers: Dispute Resolution for the Internet' 13 *Ohio State Journal on Dispute Resolution* 711.

Aviram, A (2003) 'A Network Effects Analysis of Private Ordering', Berkeley Olin Program in Law & Economics Working Paper Series, Paper 80, University of California, Berkeley (http://repositories.cdlib.org/cgi/viewcontent.cgi?article=1079&context=blewp).

—— (2004) 'A Paradox of Spontaneous Formation: The Evolution of Private Legal Systems' 22 *Yale Law & Policy Review* 1.

Baron, DP (2002) 'Private Ordering on the Internet: The EBay Community of Traders' 4 *Business and Politics* 3, 1 (http://www.bepress.com/bap/vol4/iss3/art1).

Benson, BL (1999) 'An Economic Theory of the Evolution of Governance and the Emergence of the State' 12 *Review of Austrian Economics* 131.

Berger, KP (1999) *The Creeping Codification of the Lex Mercatoria* (The Hague, Kluwer Law International).

Bernstein, L (1992) 'Opting Out of the Legal System: Extralegal Contractual Relations in the Diamond Trade' 21 *Journal of Legal Studies* 115.

BEUC (Bureau Européen des Unions de Consommatuers/The European Consumers' Organisation) and UNICE (The Confederation of European Business) (2001) 'e-Confidence project' (http://ec.europa.eu/consumers/cons_int/e-commerce/e-conf_working_annexe.pdf).

Bordone, RC (1998) 'Electronic Online Dispute Resolution: A Systems Approach—Potential, Problems, and a Proposal' 3 *Harvard Negotiation Law Review* 175.

Calliess, GP (2003) 'Coherence and Consistency in European Consumer Contract Law: a Progress Report' 4(4) *German Law Journal* (http://www.germanlawjournal.com/article.php?id=265).

—— (2006) *Grenzüberschreitende Verbraucherverträge* (Tübingen, Mohr Siebeck).

Calliess, GP, Dietz, T, Konradi, W, Nieswandt, H, and Sosa, F (2007) 'Transformations of Commercial Law. New Forms of Legal Certainty for Globalised Exchange Processes?' in Hurrelmann, A, Leibfried, S, Martens, K, and Mayer, P (eds), *Transforming the Golden Age Nation State* (Houndmills, Basingstoke, Palgrave Macmillan).

Cona, FA (1997) 'Application of Online Systems in Alternative Dispute Resolution' 45 *Buffalo Law Review* 975.

Cutler, C (2003) *Private Power and Global Authority. Transnational Merchant Law in the Global Political Economy* (Cambridge, MA, Cambridge University Press).

Damrau, J (2003) *Selbstregulierung im Kapitalmarktrecht, Eine rechtsökonomische Analyse der Normsetzung der deutschen Börsen und ihrer Träger* (Berlin, Tenea).

Davis, BG (2002) 'Building the Seamless Dispute Resolution Web: A Status Report on The American Bar Association Task Force on E-Commerce and Alternative Dispute Resolution' 8 *Texas Wesleyan Law Review* 529.

Dellarocas, C (2003) 'The Digitization of Word-of-Mouth: Promise and Challenges of Online Reputation Systems' 49 *Management Science* 1407.

Dixit, A (2004) Lawlessness and Economics: Alternative Modes of Governance (Princeton, NJ, Princeton University Press).

Eisen, JB (1998) 'Are We Ready for Mediation in Cyberspace?' *Brigham Young University Law Review* 1305.

Engel, C (2001) 'Hybrid Governance Across National Jurisdictions as a Challenge to Constitutional Law' 2 *European Business Organisation Law Review* 569.

European Central Bank (2004) 'E-Payments without Frontiers', Issues Paper for the ECB Conference on 10 November (http://www.nbs.sk/PRESS/ECB/EPAY_2.PDF).

European Commission (1997) 'European Initiative for Electronic Commerce', COM(1997) 157 (http://www.icp.pt/template21.jsp?categoryId=96922&contentId=163212).

—— (2000) 'Payment card chargeback when paying over Internet' (http://europa.eu.int/comm/internal_market/en/ecommerce/chargeback.pdf).

—— (2002a) 'eEurope 2005: An information society for all, An Action Plan to be presented in view of the Sevilla European Council', 21/22 June, COM(2002) 263 final (http://eur-lex.europa.eu/LexUriServ/LexUriServ.do?uri=COM:2002:0263:FIN:EN:PDF).

—— (2002b) Green Paper on Alternative Dispute Settlement in Civil and Commercial Matters, COM(2002) 196 final (http://eur-lex.europa.eu/LexUriServ/LexUriServ.do?uri=COM:2002:0196:FIN:EN:PDF).

—— (2003) 'A More Coherent European Contract Law. An Action Plan', COM (2003) 68 final (http://eur-lex.europa.eu/LexUriServ/LexUriServ.do?uri=COM:2003:0068:FIN:EN:PDF).

—— (2004) 'Consumer Confidence in E-Commerce: lessons learned from the e-confidence initiative', Commission Staff Working Document, SEC(2004) 1390 (http://ec.europa.eu/consumers/cons_int/e-commerce/e-conf_working_doc.pdf).

European Consumer Law Group (2001) *Soft Law and the Consumer Interest*, ECLG/071/2001, March (http://europa.eu.int/comm/consumers/policy/eclg/rep03_en.pdf).

Federal Trade Commission (2000) 'Consumer Protection in the Global Electronic Marketplace, Looking Ahead', September 2000 (http://www.ftc.gov/bcp/icpw/lookingahead/electronicmkpl.pdf).

Federal Trade Commission, Bureau of Consumer Protection (2003) 'A Consumer's Guide to e-Payments' (http://www.ftc.gov/bcp/conline/pubs/online/payments.pdf).

Föhlisch, C (2004) 'Bedeutung der Gütesiegel im Internet für den Verbraucherschutz und Funktion des D21 Gütesiegel-Boards aus Sicht eines Anbieters', Presentation at the D21 Gütesiegelkongress, 27 September (http://www.initiatived21.de/news/aktuelles/doc/12701_1096616181.pdf).

GBDe (Global Business Dialogue on electronic commerce) (2000) 'Trustmark' (http://www.gbde.org/pdf/recommendations/trustmark00.pdf).

—— (2001) 'Consumer Confidence, Trustmarks' (http://www.gbde.org/pdf/recommendations/trustmarks01.pdf).

—— (2003) 'Alternative Dispute Resolution Guidelines', Agreement reached between Consumers International and the Global Business Dialogue on Electronic Commerce (http://www.gbde.org/agreements/adragreement03.pdf).

Greif, A (2006) Institutions and the Path to the Modern Economy. Lessons from Medieval Trade (Cambridge, MA, Cambridge University Press).

Grundmann, S, Kerber, W and Weatherill, S (eds) (2001) *Party Autonomy and the Role of Information in the Internal Market* (Berlin and New York, NY, de Gruyter).

GTA (Global Trustmark Alliance) (2004) 'Plans for global online consumer protection network take shape: Trustmark organizations in Asia, Europe and the Americas join global alliance' (http://www.globaltrustmarkalliance.org/press/113004.asp).

Häberle, SG (ed) (2002) *Handbuch für Kaufrecht, Rechtsdurchsetzung und Zahlungssicherung im Außenhandel* (München, Oldenbourg).

Hacke, A (2001) *Der ADR-Vertrag. Vertragsrecht und vertragliche Gestaltung der Mediation und anderer alternativer Konfliktlösungsverfahren* (Heidelberg, Recht und Wirtschaft).

Hadfield, GK (2001) 'Privatizing Commercial Law' *Regulation* (Spring 2001) 40.

Hörnle, J (2001) 'Disputes Solved in Cyberspace and the Rule of Law', *The Journal of Information, Law and Technology (JILT)* (http://www2.warwick.ac.uk/fac/soc/law/elj/jilt/2001_2/hornle/).

—— (2002) 'Online Dispute Resolution in Business to Consumer E-commerce Transactions', *The Journal of Information, Law and Technology (JILT)*: (http://www2.warwick.ac.uk/fac/soc/law/elj/jilt/2002_2/hornle/).

—— (2003) 'Online Dispute Resolution: More than the Emperor's New Clothes', in Katsh, E, and Choi, D (eds), *Online Dispute Resolution (ODR)*, Papers and Proceedings of the 2003 United Nations Forum on ODR, (http://www.odr.info/unece2003/pdf/Hornle.pdf).

ICC (International Chamber of Commerce) (2003) 'Tools for e-Business, Resolving disputes online—Best practices for Online Dispute Resolution (ODR) in B2C and C2C transactions': (http://www.iccwbo.org/uploadedFiles/ICC/policy/e-business/pages/ResolvingDisputesOnline.pdf).

Janal, R (2005) 'Anmerkung zu BGH, Urt v 3.11.2004—VIII ZR 375/03 (Widerrufsrecht bei Internet-Auktion)' *JurPC*, Web-Dok. 4/2005, Abs 1–29 (http://www.jurpc.de/aufsatz/20050004.htm).

Karamon, MC (1996) 'ADR on the Internet' 11 *Ohio State Journal on Dispute Resolution* 537.

Katsh, E, Rifkin, J and Gaitenby, A (2000) 'E-Commerce, E-Disputes, and E-Dispute Resolution: In the Shadow of "eBay Law"' 15 *Ohio State Journal on Dispute Resolution* 705.

Katsh, E and Rifkin, J (2001) *Online Dispute Resolution: Resolving Conflicts in Cyberspace* (San Francisco, CA, Jossey-Bass).

Kaufmann-Kohler, G and Schultz, T (2004) *Online Dispute Resolution: Challenges for Contemporary Justice* (The Hague, Kluwer Law International).

Krause, W (2001) 'Do You Want to Step Outside? An Overview of Online Alternative Dispute Resolution' 19 *The John Marshall Journal of Computer & Information Law* 457.

Leeson, PT (2006) 'Cooperation and Conflict. Evidence on Self-Enforcing Arrangements and Heterogeneous Groups' 65 (4) *American Journal of Economics and Sociology* 891.

Lodder, A and Thiessen, E (2003) 'The Role of Artificial Intelligence in Online Dispute Resolution' in Katsh, E, and Choi, D (eds), *Online Dispute Resolution (ODR)*, Papers and Proceedings of the 2003 United Nations Forum on ODR (http://www.odr.info/unece2003/pdf/lodder_thiessen.pdf).

Meder, S (2002) 'Die Kreditkartenzahlung im Internet und Mail-Order-Verfahren' 56 *Wertpapiermitteilungen, Zeitschrift für Wirtschafts- und Bankrecht* 1993.

Mifsud Bonnici, JP and de Vey Mestdagh, K (2005) 'On the use of legal measures to entice participation in Online Dispute Resolution systems for the settlement of online-related disputes' in J Zeleznikow and A Lodder (eds), *Second International ODR Workshop* (Tilburg, Wolf Legal Publishers) (http://odrworkshop.info/papers2005/odrworkshop2005BonnicideVey.pdf).

Nordquist, F, Andersson, F, and Dzepina, E (2002): 'Trusting the Trustmark?', Paper presented to the 17th BILETA Conference, April 2002, Free University, Amsterdam. (http://www.bileta.ac.uk/Document%20Library/1/Trusting%20the%20Trustmark.pdf).

OECD (2002) *Consumers in the Online Market Place. The OECD Guidelines Three Years Later*, DSTI/CP (2002)4/Final (http://www.olis.oecd.org/olis/2002doc.nsf/43bb6130e5e86e5fc12569fa005d004c/af6ec39d8631ca3ac1256cc2005c0edf/$FILE/JT00138646.PDF).

—— (2006a) 'Consumer Dispute Resolution and Redress in the Global Marketplace', Report of the Committee on Consumer Policy (http://www.oecd.org/dataoecd/26/61/36456184.pdf).

—— (2006b) 'Online Payment Systems for E-Commerce', DSTI/ICCP/IE(2004)18/FINAL, dated 18 April (http://www.oecd.org/dataoecd/37/19/36736056.pdf).

Panther, S (2000) 'Non-Legal Sanctions' in B Bouckaert and G de Geest (eds), *Encyclopedia of Law and Economics, Volume I. The History and Methodology of Law and Economics* (Cheltenham, Edward Elgar).

Pfaff, A and Sanchirico, CW (2000) 'Environmental self-auditing: setting the proper incentives for discovery and correction of environmental harm' 16 *The Journal of Law, Economics, and Organization* 189.

Perritt, HH (2000) 'Dispute Resolution in Cyberspace: Demand for New Forms of ADR' 15 *Ohio State Journal on Dispute Resolution* 675.

Pichler, R (2000) 'Trust and Reliance—Enforcement and Compliance: Enhancing Consumer Confidence in the Electronic Marketplace', Master of the Science of Law (JSM) Thesis, Stanford: (www.law.stanford.edu/publications/dissertations_theses/diss/PichlerRufus2000.pdf).

Ponte, LM (2002a) 'Boosting Consumer Confidence in E-Business: Recommendations for Establishing Fair and Effective Dispute Resolution Programs for B2c Online Transactions' 12 *Albany Law Journal of Science and Technology* 441.

—— (2002b) 'Broadening Traditional ADR Notions of Disclosure: Special Considerations for Posting Conflict Resolution Policies and Programs on E-Business Web Sites' 17 *Ohio State Journal on Dispute Resolution* 321.

Ponte, LM and Cavenagh, TD (2004) *Cyberjustice: Online Dispute Resolution* (New Jersey, Prentice Hall).

Posner, E (2000) *Law and Social Norms* (Harvard, MA, HarvardUniversity Press).

Post, DG (1995) 'Anarchy, State, and the Internet: An Essay on Law-Making in Cyberspace' *Journal of Online Law*: (http://www.temple.edu/lawschool/dpost/Anarchy.html).

Redfern, A and Hunter, M (2004) *Law and Practice of International* Commercial *Arbitration*, 4th edition (London, Sweet & Maxwell).

Resnick, P, Zeckhauser, R, Swanson, J, and Lockwood, K (2006) 'The Value of Reputation on eBay: A Controlled Experiment, 3 January 2006' (http://www.si.umich.edu/~presnick/papers/postcards/index.html).

Rothchild, J (1999) 'Protecting the Digital Consumer: The Limits of Cyberspace Utopianism' 74 *Indiana Law Journal* 893.

Sawada, T (2004) 'Cross-border Transactions on E-Commerce and the Role of ADR' (http://www.ecom.jp/adr/en/html/Full%20text%20incl.%20reference.pdf).
Schiavetta, S (2004) 'The Relationship Between e-ADR and Article 6 of the European Convention of Human Rights pursuant to the Case Law of the European Court of Human Rights' *The Journal of Information, Law and Technology (JILT)* 2004 Issue 1 (http://www2.warwick.ac.uk/fac/soc/law/elj/jilt/2004_1/schiavetta/).
Schmidtchen, D and Schmidt-Trenz, HJ (1990) 'The Division of Labour is limited by the extent of the Law' 1 *Constitutional Political Economy* 1.
Schultz, T (2003) 'An Essay on the Role of Government for ODR: Theoretical Considerations about the Future of ODR' in Katsh, E, and Choi, D (eds), *Online Dispute Resolution (ODR)*, Papers and Proceedings of the 2003 United Nations Forum on ODR (http://www.odr.info/unece2003/pdf/Schultz.pdf).
—— (2004) 'Does Online Dispute Resolution Need Governmental Intervention? The Case for Architectures of Control and Trust' 6 *North Carolina Journal of Law & Technology* 71.
—— (2005) 'eBay: un système juridique en formation?' 22 *Revue du Droit des Technologies et de l'Information* 27.
Schultz, T, Kaufmann-Kohler, G, Langer, D, and Bonnet, V (2001) 'Online Dispute Resolution: The State of the Art and the Issues', E-Com Research Project of the University of Geneva (http://www.online-adr.org/reports/TheBlueBook-2001.pdf).
Spindler, G (2005) 'Internet-Auctions versus Consumer Protection: The Case of the Distance Selling Directive', 6 *German Law Journal* (http://www.germanlawjournal.com/article.php?id=585).
Spletter, C (2003) *The Significance of Trustmarks in B2C E-Commerce*, LL.M.-thesis, University of Strathclyde (www.it-law.at/uploads/tx_publications/spletter_trustmarks.pdf).
Streit, ME and Mangels, A (1996) 'Privatautonomes Recht und grenzüberschreitende Transaktionen' 47 *ORDO Jahrbuch für die Ordnung von Wirtschaft und Gesellschaft* 73.
Teitz, EL (2001) 'The Promise and Challenge of On-Line Dispute Resolution' 70 *Fordham Law Review* 985.
Teubner, G (2004) 'Global Private Regimes: Neo-spontaneous Law and Dual Constitution of Autonomous Sectors in World Society?' in KH Ladeur (ed), *Public Governance in the Age of Globalisation* (Ashgate, Aldershot).
Teubner, G, Farmer, L, and Murphy, D (eds) (1994) Environmental Law and Ecological Responsibility: The Concept and Practice of Ecological Self-Organization (New York/Chichester, Wiley).
Tyler, MC (2004) '115 and Counting: The State of ODR 2004' in MC Tyler, E Katsh, and D Choi (eds). *Proceedings of the Third Annual Forum on Online Dispute Resolution* (http://www.odr.info/unforum2004/ConleyTyler.htm).
Tyler, MC and Bretherton, D (2003) 'Seventy-six and Counting: An Analysis of ODR Sites. A Report of Research Conducted for the Department of Justice, Victoria, Australia' in Katsh, E, and Choi, D (eds), *Online Dispute Resolution (ODR)*, Papers and Proceedings of the 2003 United Nations Forum on ODR (http://www.odr.info/unece2003/pdf/Tyler.pdf).
Wagemans, T (2003) 'An introduction to the labelling of websites, Conference Presentation' (www.selfregulation.info/iapcoda/qual_lab_bkgd-030225.pdf).

Wallis, D (2000) 'Report on the proposal for a Council regulation on jurisdiction and the recognition and enforcement of judgments in civil and commercial matters', Committee on Legal Affairs and the Internal Market, 18 September, PE A5-0253/2000 (http://www.europarl.europa.eu/sidesSearch/sipadeMapUrl.do?PROG=REPORT&SORT_ORDER=D&REF_A=A5-2000-0253&L=EN#).

Williamson, OE (2005) 'The Economics of Governance' 95 *American Economic Review* 1.

Wolf, M (2000) 'Zivilprozessuale Verfahrensgarantien in Art. 6 I EMRK als Grundlage eines europäischen Zivilprozessrechts' in G Köbler (ed) *Festschrift für Alfred Söllner* (München, Beck).

Zumbansen, P (2002) 'Piercing the Legal Veil: Commercial Arbitration and Transnational Law' 8 *European Law Journal* 400.

9

Multi-Interest Self-Governance through Global Product Certification Programmes[*]

ERROL MEIDINGER

I. INTRODUCTION

EMERGING GOVERNANCE SYSTEMS are overrunning several classical divisions of regulation, and indeed of law—between states, firms, and the public, and between national and international domains. Because these changes are effectuated through market-centered networks, it is sometimes said that modern transnational regulation is essentially a form of 'self-regulation' by economic actors. While there is truth in this depiction, it needs significant revision in order to comprehend the structure, dynamics, and implications of many emerging systems. First, the concept of 'self' must be expanded beyond a relatively narrow group of profit-maximising market participants to include a variety of other actors such as non-governmental environmental and social justice organisations and states. This has been done to some extent by adopting the term 'self-governance' in place of 'self-regulation', but again, the expanding and increasingly public nature of the regulatory communities involved merits notice and analysis. At the same time, the governance process is still implemented in large part by the traditional regulatory techniques of normatively based rules organised in terms of rights, duties, and carefully defined formal responsibilities. Second, the concept of regulation must be expanded beyond traditional 'public law' concerns to include 'private law' ones such as facilitating transactional predictability and efficiency. The new regulatory systems reach from negotiations about whether and how to control

[*] Earlier drafts were presented to workshops on 'Self-governance and the Law in Multinational Corporations and Transnational Networks' at the International Institute for Sociology of Law, Oñati, Spain, and 'Private Agreements and Regulation of the Global Environment' at Vanderbilt University Law School, Nashville, TN, USA.

social and environmental externalities of economic activities down through firms' routine organisational and management practices. Thus they are simultaneously broad and deep. Finally, the regulatory process appears to be growing increasingly dynamic, as negotiations among authorised actors transmute into competitions among contingently empowered regulators and their contested constituencies.

This Chapter examines these developments by reviewing transnational, supra-governmental regulatory systems that are taking shape in several sectors through the development of product certification programmes. These programmes set standards for proper management, assess compliance, and publicise results, typically by awarding rights to label products with their logos. The primary case is forestry, which has seen the most extensive and sharply defined institutional development over the past decade; examples from fisheries, agriculture, apparel, and other sectors are also noted. Section II begins by describing the evolution of certification institutions generally and their recent application to transnational social and environmental regulation. It also compares and contrasts some of the institutional arrangements that have emerged in different sectors. Section III examines the relationships and compatibility between the emergent certification institutions and state-based legal systems, with primary reference to the US legal system and the international trading regime. It preliminarily describes a complex set of relationships between certification programmes and active and passive state legal processes, which currently manifest both a high level of interpenetration and continuing partial autonomy among the different centres of legal activity. The final section considers some possible grounds for assessment of the emerging self-governance systems. It suggests, among other things, that the multi-sector certification systems have led to operational improvements in each area studied, and that they may be in the process of constituting a new non-principal agent accountability system whose most important capacity is to learn. It also describes distinctive legitimation strategies centred on the development of master metaphors while also relying on traditional standard-setting technologies and competitive testing.

II. CERTIFICATION PROGRAMMES

A. Forestry

Certification institutions enjoyed a major spike following the 1992 United Nations Conference on Environment and Development (UNCED) in Rio de Janeiro. Among the multiple reasons were both 'failures' and 'successes' of the Rio conference. On the negative side, UNCED failed to produce a binding forest convention to guide and harmonise forestry regulation across the various forested countries, leaving great disparities in forestry practices around the world and little hope of curbing accelerating forest destruction in many developing countries. On the positive side, UNCED consolidated the language and concepts of sustainable development and sustainable forest management, and ratified calls for a greater role for civil society organisations in setting and monitoring public policy (United Nations, 1992).

A consequential reaction to these developments was the 1993 establishment of the Forest Stewardship Council (FSC), a global non-governmental programme for certifying proper forest management. Founded by a coalition of environmental and social justice NGOs, progressive wood buyers, and forestry experts, the FSC quickly promulgated a set of globally applicable standards for forest management together with an institutional system for certifying complying forests and labelling products made of wood from them. Building on the sustainable development movement, the FSC standards combine environmental, social, and economic requirements in 10 'principles' and 56 'criteria' that further define the principles (FSC, 2006). These are given more detail in standards developed for specific countries and regions, as well as in assessment protocols used by certifiers. Certifiers are organisationally independent of both the FSC and the firms seeking certification, although they are chosen and paid by the firms and accredited by an FSC spin-off organisation.

The FSC has an elaborate stakeholder governance system organised in three chambers—environmental, economic, and social, each with equal voting power—and following increasingly participatory and transparent processes (Meidinger, 2006). Membership in the FSC is open to any person or organisation subscribing to its principles and endorsed by two existing members. Of the more than 600 current international members approximately 90 percent are organisations and 10 percent individuals. Membership is skewed towards developed countries, but voting principles give members from the developing world equal decisional power to those from the developed world.

While organisationally sophisticated, interesting, and important, the FSC is only one part of the larger transnational, supra-governmental regulatory system that has emerged in the forestry sector over the past decade. The founding and early success of the FSC triggered the establishment of competing forest certification programmes by coalitions of traditional forestry authorities including landowners, forest products companies, and governmental forestry agencies. The histories, details, similarities, and differences of the various programmes are discussed at length in many other publications (for example, Meidinger, 1999; Meidinger *et al*, 2003; Cashore *et al*, 2004; Humphreys, 2006). Here it suffices to make several fundamental observations. First, the programmes have coalesced into two competing alliances, one centred on the FSC and the other on traditional landowner and industry interests through the Programme for the Endorsement of Forest Certification (PEFC), which currently consists of 32 nationally-based programmes (PEFC,

2008). While some of the PEFC programmes were arguably established with the purpose of undermining the FSC and possibly forest certification as a whole, that has not been the result. Instead, a broader system has taken shape in which the programmes observe, mimic, compete, communicate, negotiate, and adapt to each other in various ways.

Second, the programmes do so within a larger social field that increasingly includes government agencies. Indeed, the founding of the PEFC inherently brought governments into closer involvement with forest certification, since traditional forestry interests had long enjoyed close relationships with government agencies. In most countries where land was largely privately owned, the professionalisation of forestry in the nineteenth and twentieth centuries also created close relationships between government forestry agencies, forest landowners, and forestry companies, catalysing new forest governance systems (for example, J Scott, 1998). Where forests were publicly owned (often developing countries with natural resources constitutionally assigned to the state but also with conflicting indigenous customary rights) (Goodman, 2002) the relationships were even tighter because government officials were directly in charge of forest management.

Third, the rapid globalisation of timber markets in the twentieth century, and the concurrent organisation of much of the world into exporting and importing countries, often reflecting their levels of economic development, also made forestry into an international policy arena. Forestry companies in countries with relatively demanding standards felt disadvantaged relative to those in countries with lenient or poorly enforced standards, while those from developing countries felt inherently disadvantaged in developed country markets. Moreover, new understandings of the importance of forests in controlling global climate change and preserving biodiversity converted local forest management practices into international environmental policy concerns. While international negotiations failed to resolve these conflicts, they helped define forestry as a transnational policy domain. Thus, the expanding global market effectively created a larger legal space in which legal pluralism was both compounded and seen as a problem. At the same time, however, international negotiations and discussions among forestry and environmental professionals, academics, and activists began to articulate broad possible principles of harmonisation, largely collected under the rubrics of sustainable development and sustainable forest management.

Finally, and perhaps most importantly, the adoption of forest certification was leveraged through existing international trading relationships. Transnational environmental and social justice organisations used the organisational and marketing interests of large transnational corporations, mostly brand-dependent retailers, to force the issue of global forestry standards (for example, Sasser, 2002). A decisive instance was the campaign by the Rainforest Action Network (RAN) to persuade Home Depot, the world's largest wood products retailer, to commit to buying FSC-certified products.

Although Home Depot originally refused, RAN conducted an intense campaign against the corporation designed to threaten the value of its brand. RAN activists staged many dramatic actions in Home Depot parking lots, such as setting up huge blimp-like inflated chainsaws painted with the Home Depot colours and logo and advertising a 'homedepotsucks.com' website. When customers were attracted to the spectacle RAN members enthusiastically thanked them for helping Home Depot destroy the world's rain forests and endangered species, but of course quickly verged into explanations of how Home Depot had the capacity to aid significantly in solving those problems but was in fact making them worse.

After dealing with hundreds of such actions, Home Depot came to see certification as desirable and agreed to buy as much FSC-certified wood as it could. When RAN turned its attention to the second largest wood product retailer, Lowes, agreement to the same terms came swiftly. Contemporaneous negotiations by other activist organisations also succeeded with European retailers such as British B&Q and German OBI. These decisions turned the considerable resources of several large wood product retailers and their supply chains to the favour of forest certification, helping to leverage certification programmes into the centre of the global forest policy arena and restructuring the regulatory community. It also gave transnational corporations as well as timber product importing and exporting states enduring interests in participating in and monitoring forest certification policy. As a result, the policy-making centre of the present forest governance system can be very roughly and abstractly portrayed as in Figure 1.

The reality is, of course, much more complicated than Figure 1 can indicate. Several significant types of actors, such as local landowner organisations, influential researchers, and local environmental organisations are not represented. Notably, lawyers, who often perform key roles in regulatory governance, are relatively rare in this arena, although the institutional arrangements take legal forms, and national and international legal frameworks are quite important. Relationships *among* the various types of actors in the diagram are highly complex and changeable. Relationships *within* all types of actors, particularly states, are complex and sometimes conflictual. Finally, the power of the system is directly tied to global trading relationships outside the diagram. Still, the diagram suggests the main contours of the policy-making system that appears to be emerging in the global forestry arena.

Such a system is potentially disorganised and ineffectual. The obvious question therefore is what phenomena might operate to structure both the governance system and the larger domain of forest management it seeks to organise. There seem to be several basic types of ordering mechanisms at work in the global forest self-governance system: (1) the increasingly detailed and elaborate discourse of sustainable forest management; (2) the increasingly formal and legalised institutional arrangements of forest

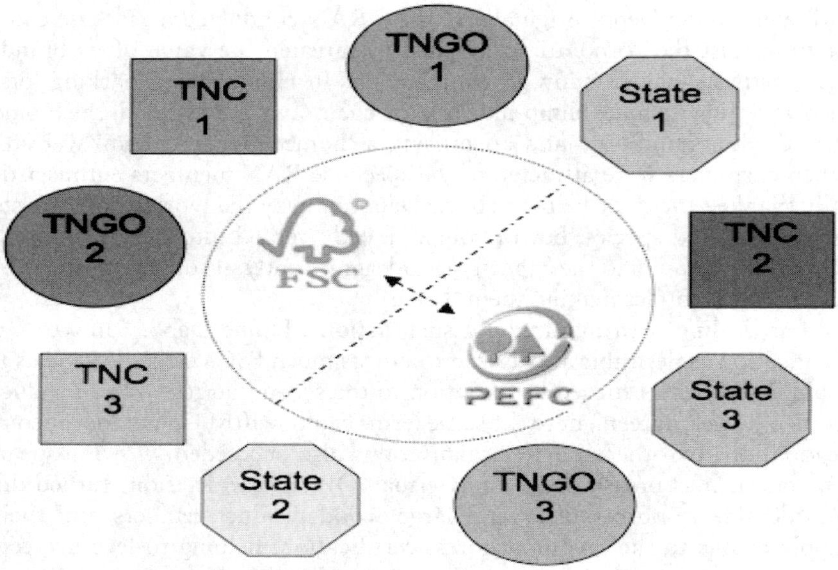

(TNC = transnational corporation; TNGO = transnational non-governmental organisation)[1]

[1] For suggestive conceptualisations see Scott, C (2001) and Sabatier and Jenkins-Smith (1993).

Figure 1 ***Emerging Structure of Transnational Forestry Policy-making.***

certification; and (3) the growing competition among certification programmes. In addition, all of these mechanisms operate in the framework of (4) elaborate state-based legal systems and global trade law. This Chapter concentrates on the second and fourth mechanisms, as discussed in sections II and III, but also outlines the first and third.

B. Institutional Components

When founded in 1993 the FSC was able to draw on a substantial fund of certification experience, some in forestry, but more in organic agriculture and the broader field of international standard-setting that had taken form through the International Organization for Standardisation (ISO). The ISO became very important with the rapid growth in international trade after World War II. Its primary work focused on 'technical' standard-setting, defining the characteristics of such things as metal bolts and magnetic credit card strips so that they would function reliably around the world. Although such work had long gone on in subject-specific national standard-setting bodies (Cheit, 1990; Krislov, 1997; Schepel, 2005), the ISO federated and largely unified them, thus constituting an extensive and important transnational governance system.

Along the way the ISO developed standardised approaches and methods for carrying out the main functions involved in certification programmes:

(1) setting standards,
(2) certifying compliance ('conformity assurance'),
(3) accrediting certifiers, and
(4) labelling products.

1. *Standard-setting*

The FSC was able to draw on both these ISO modalities and the experience of the International Federation of Organic Agriculture Movements (IFOAM), of which several FSC founders were veterans. It established the multi-stakeholder mechanism for setting standards outlined above, together with protocols for accrediting and auditing certifiers. Although these were somewhat different from the standard ISO approaches, carefully building in multi-stakeholder structures and non-economic criteria such as environmental and community protection, they were still clearly recognisable adaptations of the ISO models.

In the 1980s the ISO also began setting standards for organisational management. The premise was that globalisation created demand for a mechanism whereby firms considering transactions with new partners could ascertain that they were well managed, and therefore good business prospects. Positing that good management could be systematised and certified like any other commodity, ISO developed its 9000 series of standards, the hallmark requirements of which were that (1) a well-managed organisation must continuously seek ways to improve its performance and (2) that specific officials in the organisation must be made responsible for planning, monitoring, evaluating, and improving performance. It was thus a form of organisational governance that sought to institute organisational dynamism in tandem with predictability.

In response to UNCED, ISO committed to developing an environmental management standard as well, issuing the ISO 14000 series in 1996. The importance of this series was that it offered an alternative model of forest certification to that promoted by the FSC. While the FSC model relied on general performance standards in much the same way as many of the traditional ISO technical standards, the new ISO standards focused on internal management systems that would themselves define environmental goals and then monitor their success in meeting them and developing new ones. The ISO approach thus vested much policy-making discretion in firms, whereas the FSC vested it primarily in external multi-stakeholder groups.

The industry-based forest certification programmes generally favoured the management standard approach, although a few incorporated substantive requirements. Over time most appear to have incorporated a slowly growing number of substantive standards, although this is difficult to gauge accurately and there are uncertainties about how binding they are in many cases. A sense of the variation can be gained by comparing the FSC and the American Forest & Paper Association's (AF&PA) Sustainable Forestry Initiative (SFI) standards regarding biodiversity.

FSC Principle 6 provides (FSC, 2006):

> Forest management shall conserve biological diversity and its associated values, water resources, soils, and unique and fragile ecosystems and landscapes, and, by so doing, maintain the ecological functions and the integrity of the forest.
>
> Criteria: …
>
> 6.2 Safeguards shall exist which protect rare, threatened and endangered species and their habitats (eg, nesting and feeding areas). Conservation zones and protection areas shall be established, appropriate to the scale and intensity of forest management and the uniqueness of the affected resources. Inappropriate hunting, fishing, trapping and collecting shall be controlled.
>
> 6.3 Ecological functions and values shall be maintained intact, enhanced, or restored, including: a) Forest regeneration and succession. b) Genetic, species, and ecosystem diversity. c) Natural cycles that affect the productivity of the forest ecosystem.
>
> 6.4 Representative samples of existing ecosystems within the landscape shall be protected in their natural state and recorded on maps, appropriate to the scale and intensity of operations and the uniqueness of the affected resources.

The analogous portion of the SFI standard provides (SFI, 2005–09):

> Objective 4. To manage the quality and distribution of wildlife habitats and contribute to the conservation of biological diversity by developing and implementing stand- and landscape-level measures that promote habitat diversity and the conservation of forest plants and animals, including aquatic fauna.
>
> Performance Measure 4.1. Program Participants shall have programs to promote biological diversity at stand and landscape levels.
>
> Indicators:
>
> 1. Program to promote the conservation of native biological diversity, including species, wildlife habitats, and ecological or natural community types, at stand and landscape levels.
> 2. Program to protect threatened and endangered species.
> 3. Plans to locate and protect known sites associated with viable occurrences of critically imperiled and imperiled species and communities …
> 4. Development and implementation of criteria, as guided by regionally appropriate science, for retention of stand-level wildlife habitat elements (eg, snags, mast trees, down woody debris, den trees, nest trees).

While both standards contain prescriptive language, the FSC standard contains a great deal more, and the SFI standard requires simply that a firm has programmes to promote a goal, rather than necessarily achieves that goal or any other outcome. What constitutes an adequate programme in the SFI framework is therefore likely to depend to a greater degree on the certifier, and it may be difficult for any certifier to find that a company fails to meet the requirement of having a programme merely because the programme is not very effective.

2. *Implementation*

As with law generally, the real meaning of any standard depends on its implementation. Much attention has gone into defining appropriate protocols for certification, qualifications of certifiers, and use of labels. It is neither possible nor important to discuss these in detail in this short Chapter, but several basic institutional patterns deserve note.

The first falls slightly outside the traditional categories of legal analysis. It is that the new governance systems reach well into the internal organisation of certified firms and seek to turn them into affirmative legal actors. This is most obvious in the ISO standards, which rely on installation of detailed internal management systems to ascertain current performance, set goals, monitor achievement, and make corrections and improvements. If implemented well, this method has the potential to significantly enhance a firm's performance. The continuous improvement mandate creates a standard beyond simple 'compliance'. It implies a dynamic learning and adaptation process. And the whole approach seeks to enrol the firm in the process of policy formulation and improvement. It is not clear how far this potential will actually be realised. Neither the PEFC nor the FSC has placed heavy stress on continuous improvement. Still, empirical research on environmental management systems suggests that they can catalyse significantly improved environmental performance (for example, Parker, 2000; Coglianese and Nash, 2001; Potoski and Prakash, 2005).

A central actor in implementing multi-interest self-governance is the certifier, who is conceived as a trustworthy expert who can verify for outsiders that a firm is performing to standard. The certifier is analogous to a government inspector or hearing officer in a traditional regulatory scheme, except that the firm, rather than the state, chooses and pays the certifier. Although this compensation scheme seems to pose significant corruption risks, it apparently has worked well in traditional certification schemes. There may be various reasons for this, but probably a key one is that the certifier typically works to ascertain quality in a product that, if absent, will affect its performance. Therefore poor certification work is likely to be discovered by a product user.

Certification programmes focused on production processes, such as environmental or worker protection, do not enjoy such a quality check, since they do not have a direct effect on the functionality of the product. Forest certification programmes do not seem to have focused very carefully on this risk thus far, preferring to deal with it primarily by relying on professionalism in accreditation standards and, in some cases, random external auditing. Since programmes compete with each other, however, and since outside critics of various kinds have considerable capacity to uncover substandard certifications, it is possible that quality controls are adequate. As discussed in section III, there is even some possibility that risks of legal liability for substandard certifications will create incentives for quality work.

Because certification programmes rely heavily on governance through economic transactions, product labelling is an important implementation mechanism in most certification programmes (although not all). Labels serve as signals of economic reliability and social probity, in principle allowing customers to distinguish properly from improperly produced products. To function well, labels must be perceived as meaningful and accurate. The proliferation of certification programmes in some sectors has made this problematic, in turn leading the programmes to concentrate more heavily on 'brand' management through use of intellectual property laws. The forest certification programmes have also engaged in an intensive and interesting dialogue about how much certified fibre a given product must contain to be certified. The FSC originally required every piece of wood in a certified product to be directly traceable to a certified forest. The necessary tracking and wood flow management can be very expensive, particularly in complex product chains with many small producers, and the PEFC challenged this practice frontally by instituting a 'per cent in, per cent out' policy, making it much easier to use their label. FSC has responded by revising its policy several times to make use of its label more feasible in complex product chains. Thus labelling requirements, rather than being mere technical matters, also are forums for policy debate and competition.

Enforcement systems in certification programmes differ somewhat from traditional government regulatory systems in that the sanctions involved tend to be more diffuse and their administration less procedurally rigorous. While one form of sanction is revocation of certification, which is relatively formalised, this sanction is not very important in its own right. Its significance, as suggested in the section I, has to do with potential loss of access to markets and the value of brands. These can be imposed in a variety of ways, such as negative publicity campaigns, and by a variety of actors, including important customers and NGOs. For the system to work reliably, more regularity and reliability will probably have to be achieved in the processes by which NGOs laud and shame firms.

3. *Public Law*

As suggested above, certification institutions can be understood as supra-governmental legal systems. They perform the legislative function of setting standards, the adjudicatory function of certifying compliance, and the administrative functions of monitoring performance and sanctioning non-compliance. They are organised in terms of rules, rights, and duties. They rely on normative justifications for their decisions and have enjoyed considerable uptake in practice. Moreover, their needs to make good policies and implement them reliably are quite similar to those of governments. It is therefore not surprising that certification programmes have been using and elaborating a kind of administrative law to organise their activities. While there is much variation among programmes, several broad tendencies are evident in the competing forest certification programmes (Meidinger, 2006).

First, driven by the FSC example, forest certification programmes have gradually expanded and improved their provisions for public participation, both structural and procedural. On the procedural side, most certification programmes now provide for public notice and comment processes in rule-makings and sometimes in adjudications. They also appear to be moving toward publicly explaining their responses to the comments. Structurally, again driven by the FSC model, even the industry-based programmes have sought to include participation by representatives of diverse interests. This participation is often controlled to a significant extent, for example by choosing who can represent which outside interests, but there nevertheless seems to be a widely felt imperative to be able to demonstrate multi-interest participation in policy-making. The definition of who should be allowed to participate increasingly extends beyond directly affected interests.

Second, the certification programmes have also been moving towards greater transparency, even in individual certifications. While one of the attractions of certification for firms could be that the certifier can stand between the firm and outsiders to assure them that all is well in the firm, thereby preserving the private and confidential nature of management operations, there is growing pressure to provide as much public information as possible regarding the quality and content of the certification decision. Even the industry-based programmes are moving in this direction, albeit haltingly.

In sum, although it would be easy to overstate the participatory and transparent nature of the forest certification programmes, they do seem to be moving slowly but broadly in the direction of more openness and deliberative regularity, which also seems to be a trend throughout the world of private standard-setting (Schepel, 2005: 6). This improves at least their potential for responsiveness and adaptability over time, and seems to put them in a favourable position vis-à-vis governments to produce high quality and effective governance. Of course, it is not an either/or situation, and certification institutions must be understood as acting in tandem with governments. Section III discusses some of the actual and possible relationships between certification programmes and state-based law. But first it is helpful to note some of the variations evident in supra-state governance systems sectors other than forestry.

C. Other Sectors

As noted above, the basic methods of extra-governmental standard-setting and certification have been applied in a number of sectors and to a number of problems over the years. They seem to have originated in cases where their primary function was to facilitate the predictability and efficiency of economic transactions. Although they undoubtedly produced winners and losers, they were thought to have relatively little overtly political import, at least in the sense of making important choices about fairness and justice. Of course, in some cases this has been a kind of subterfuge. Defining questions as largely technical and managerial makes them seem apolitical and therefore more controllable by interests with access to expertise (Wood, 2002–3). Even in the technocratic types of cases, however, recent years have brought an expanding commitment to increased public participation and transparency. The more interesting and harder cases are those in which the interests involved are not directly included in production chains. Forest certification provides a key example in which the standard-setting and certification mechanisms are used to pursue environmental protection and social justice. This subsection briefly notes some potentially significant similarities and differences in other sectors that also involve overtly political concerns, although a more careful analysis will have to await future work.

1. *Organic Agriculture*

Organic agriculture appears to be a transitional case. While organic agriculture is an ethical and political movement, it also is premised on the assumption that organic food products are in fact healthier and safer than non-organic ones and that consumers should be able to make accurate distinctions between organic and non-organic foods. Thus, it must have seemed quite logical, if a bit forward-looking, to develop organic agriculture certification programmes, the first of which was established in Germany in 1928, but the rest of which began after the late 1960s (Coleman and Reed, forthcoming). In 1972 the International Federation of Organic Agriculture Movements (IFOAM) was founded to develop global standards. IFOAM's membership is open, and it generally subjects draft standards to broad public criticism, but voting rights are restricted to organisations that qualify as 'predominantly organic'.

In 1980 IFOAM published a set of 'Basic Standards' seeking to harmonise criteria among then-existing nationally based organic certification programmes. Perhaps even more than forest certification, organic agriculture certification has sought to define and revise standards by reasoning in terms of basic principles. The principles have gradually broadened from relatively focused goals (for example, 'to maintain the long term fertility of soils' in 1980) to broad precepts (for example, 'Organic Agriculture should sustain and enhance the health of soil, plant, animal, human and planet as one and indivisible' in 2006) (IFOAM, 2006). The discussion of principles in turn appears to be closely tied to a more fundamental discussion of basic concepts. IFOAM's operational standards have been revised several times, and are currently undergoing a major revision that has lasted for several years.

Broadly speaking, IFOAM standards have sometimes been used as the basis for government-enforced organic food standards. But perhaps more importantly, as many as 60 governments have promulgated their own, often less stringent standards. Moreover, the US, Japan, and to a lesser extent Europe, appear to have developed their organic agriculture regulations with relatively little reference or deference either to the IFOAM standards or to each other (Courville and Crucefix, 2003; Bolster 2006). The US, for example, conducted its own legislative and rule-making processes starting in about 1990, which ultimately defined 'organic' in a way considerably narrower than its meaning in the IFOAM system. The IFOAM standards certainly had an influence on that process, but were not determinative.

While the US relies mainly on private certifiers to enforce the system, it requires that they be accredited through a division of the US Department of Agriculture (USDA),[1] spurning the IFOAM-affiliated International Organic Accreditation Service. Approximately two dozen accredited certifiers are state agencies (usually departments of agriculture). Approximately one-third are located in foreign countries, effectively leveraging the size of the US domestic market to extend US standards into foreign countries.[2] Finally, although the USDA does not preclude the use of other standards in the field, it does preclude their using the label 'organic' for products not meeting the federal standards. It thus remains possible to develop other, more stringent food labelling systems that might serve as either as add-ons or alternatives to the USDA system, but the government's monopolisation of the term 'organic' makes that difficult in practice. Overall, then, the case of organic agriculture suggests caution in assessing the potential of supragovernmental regulatory programmes to foster consistent transnational governance frameworks.

[1] National Organic Program, Final Rule, Agricultural Marketing Service, US Department of Agriculture. 7 CFR Part 205 (http://www.ams.usda.gov/nop/NOP/standards/FullText.pdf).

[2] The international trade law dimensions of this process are beyond the scope of this chapter.

2. *Apparel*

The transnational apparel industry[3] poses profoundly difficult problems of worker protection and parity. Since the early 1980s activists have sought to use developed countries' market power to force improved labour conditions in developing country factories that supply those markets. The first major flurry of initiatives involved promulgation of corporate codes of conduct. These were typically prepared by individual corporations seeking to protect their brands from activist attacks, but soon began to show broad common patterns (see, for example, Webb, 2005). In the late 1990s three separate apparel certification programmes were founded, all with the express goal of improving the consistency and implementation of codes of conduct. Two of them, Social Accountability International (SAI) and the Fair Labor Association (FLA), were primarily the offspring of NGOs and governments, while the third, Worldwide Responsible Apparel Production (WRAP), was a creature of industry (see generally Bartley, 2003). SAI and WRAP certify individual factories, whereas FLA certifies entire supply chains.

Competition among the programmes has been intense and contentious at times. Efforts to put brand integrity at issue have occasionally brought backlashes that have challenged the legitimacy of the certification programmes. Perhaps more than in forest certification and organic agriculture, apparel certification programmes have been able to draw on labour standards developed by intergovernmental organisations, mainly the ILO. Yet labour standards remain contested, both in principle and in practice. Governments have been quite engaged in apparel certification debates, but in highly varying ways. The biggest challenge of the programmes has been to achieve effective and credible control of labour conditions in far-flung countries where production is shifted rapidly among factories (O'Rourke, 2000). With many exporting and importing governments holding inconsistent views about appropriate labour standards, the problem of achieving transnational consistency seems even more difficult than in forestry and organic agriculture, and the overall governance arena more disorganised and contentious. Still, despite the structural difficulty of the situation, one school of thought strongly argues that the presence of apparel certification programmes has helped to 'ratchet up' worldwide labour standards (Fung *et al*, 2001).

3. *Fisheries*

As in the forestry and apparel sectors, a fisheries certification programme has been created to curb stresses created by the expansion of global markets. Modelled partly on the FSC, the Marine Stewardship Council (MSC)

[3] This chapter does not distinguish between the clothing and footwear industries, although there would be reason to do so in a more extended discussion.

is an independent, non-profit organisation seeking to promote sustainable fisheries and fishing practices worldwide. It was founded in 1997 as a joint initiative between the World-Wide Fund for Nature (WWF) and Unilever (owner of the Birds Eye brand among others, and one of the world's largest buyers of fish), eschewing the FSC's open membership system. As in the other sectors, the MSC has a broad set of principles and criteria. These are largely biological and operational, however, and do not extend to social issues (MSC, 2006a). The MSC has also focused on stakeholder processes, although they seem to have been somewhat narrower and more targeted to date than those of the other sectors discussed above.

Certification under the MSC principles and criteria is carried out by a small group of independent, MSC-accredited certification bodies. Twenty-two fisheries have received MSC certification to date, with an almost equal number presently undergoing assessment (MSC, 2006b). Government cooperation is essential to fisheries certification, since governments are primarily responsible for controlling access and take in most fisheries. Governments, thus, are among the main actors being certified. To date the uptake of MSC-certified products seems to be limited to Europe and North America. There are grounds for believing that the MSC has contributed to improved fisheries management in many locales, but the challenges of over-fishing and of achieving effective control over open waters remain severe (see, for example, Gulbrandsen, 2005).

III. CERTIFICATION AND THE STATE

With the partial exception of organic agriculture, all of the certification programmes described above build upon and often require compliance with state-promulgated statutes and regulations. Even organic agriculture certification must accommodate state regulation of organic labelling. Moreover, certification programmes often set stricter or different requirements than do state programmes, thereby adding a layer of regulatory and normative complexity to the legal environment. This legal imbrication of certification programmes with state policy and law raises important questions about how state legal systems relate to certification programmes. In principle, the possibilities are nearly infinite, since states can choose to react or not to react, to incorporate, regulate, or repudiate certification standards, and to do so either immediately through direct action or from a distance through general legal standards. The sections below describe both active modes of state engagement and more passive ones, where certification institutions come into play with general bodies of established law. The discussion is provisional, however, and must be treated as a first approximation because the questions posed are quite open-ended and subject to multiple possible resolutions.

A. Direct Engagement

As the prior subsections indicate, governments interact with certification programmes in a bewildering and sometimes contradictory variety of ways. In forest certification, while seemingly somewhat distant from developments at first, governments produced much of the information and management criteria that were drawn upon from the beginning. Moreover, several European governments provided crucial initial early funding to help to get FSC off the ground. Over time governments became more involved, with government land managers and regulators participating in a number of FSC national and regional standard-setting initiatives, as well as in PEFC programmes.

1. *Proprietary*

Even more strikingly, many government agencies, operating in their proprietary roles at the national, provincial, and local levels, have chosen to subject the forests they manage to certification under one or more programmes (see, for example, Cashore *et al*, 2006). Thus they have acknowledged the presumptive legitimacy and applicability of certification standards to their activities, which are already carried out under elaborate state laws. This rapidly growing trend by itself may indicate the growing authority of certification programmes.

A number of governments, mainly in Europe,[4] have adopted procurement policies either directly or effectively requiring that wood products purchased by government be certified. There is an ongoing EU debate about what criteria may legitimately be included (Tarasovsky *et al*, 2005). Such procurement policies also seem somewhat at odds with the effort of international trade law to discourage regulations of extra-territorial production processes and methods (PPMs) as potential non-tariff barriers to trade, as noted below, but they are generally exempted from the GATT treaties.[5] Government purchasing policies are covered in a supplementary treaty that includes most industrialised and a few developing countries, but the status under that treaty of procurement policies requiring or promoting certification remains to be adjudicated.[6] A reasonable prediction is that it

[4] The UK timber procurement policy, for example, requires governmental bodies to purchase timber from legal and sustainable sources (http://www.proforest.net/cpet/uk-government-timber-procurement-policy). For a definition of legal and sustainable, see http://www.proforest.net/cpet/pdf/definition-of-legal-and-sustainable-e1-final.doc. This policy was developed through ISO 9001 and 14001 processes undertaken by the government (http://www.environment-agency.gov.uk/business/444217/444285/317943/514774/?lang=_e&theme=&region=&subject=&searchfor=sustainable+procurement).

[5] Article 1.4 of the TBT General Provisions (http://www.wto.org/English/docs_e/legal_e/17-tbt.pdf) and Article III:8(a) of the General Agreement

[6] The Agreement on Government Procurement precludes signatories (the United States, Canada, Aruba, the EU countries, Iceland, Norway, Liechtenstein, Switzerland, Japan, Korea,

would follow an analysis parallel to that discussed in the next section on state-mandated standards in international trade law, and treat as reasonable such requirements as conforming to international standards. In any event, the adoption of government procurement policies has already been a major force both in promoting certification generally and in raising standards for participation and transparency in PEFC policies.

2. *Regulatory*

In addition to proprietary powers, states can exercise regulatory powers with regard to certification programmes. For analytical purposes it is helpful to distinguish regulation of activities within the state's territory (discussed in this section) from activities outside it (discussed under 'Trade and Competition Law' below), although the distinction can be quite difficult to maintain in practice. Overall, the picture is quite mixed, especially when multiple sectors are taken into account. In forestry, with a few exceptions, governments initially stood aside and observed the rise of certification. A few have adopted requirements that forestry enterprises operating within their jurisdictions obtain certification (see, for example, Carrera et al, 2006). This does not seem to have occurred in the United States, but if it did it would face several legal questions. The first entails the 'non-delegation doctrine', which is generally understood to prohibit legislatures from delegating their legislative powers to private organisations.[7] This has long been an issue with non-governmental standard-setting bodies. The orthodox solution has been for legislatures simply to adopt as their own the privately developed standards.[8] Legislatures in the United States have often adopted private standards for housing construction, plumbing, electrical wiring, fire safety, and many other areas. But such adoption does not appear to have occurred for the kind of transnational, multi-interest environmental and social standards discussed in this Chapter, although legislatures in some other countries have indeed mandated conformance to standards developed by forest certification programmes (see, for example, Quevedo, 2006; Derani, chapter ten, this volume). At this stage, however, a more limited alternative seems possible. Rather than wholesale adoption of certification standards, particular provisions might be adopted to make state laws conform more closely to

Hong Kong, and Singapore) from using technical specifications, including those defining processes or methods of production, so as to create 'unnecessary obstacles to international trade'. Technical specifications adopting recognised international standards seem likely to enjoy a presumption of not being unnecessary trade obstacles, as discussed below.

[7] Following *Carter v Carter Coal Company*, 298 US 238 (1936).

[8] See, eg, *State v Crawford*, 177 P 360 (Kansas, 1919), in which the Kansas Supreme Court held that state fire inspectors could be authorised to enforce an electrical code promulgated by the National Fire Protection Association, but only if the Kansas Legislature first adopted that code word for word through its standard legislative process.

certification standards. This is currently under discussion with regard to forestry in at least one US state (Pinchot Institute for Conservation, 2006), and a number of state fisheries laws probably have needed to be adapted to achieve certification under the MSC standard as discussed above.

At the administrative level, US agencies have a long history of incorporating privately generated standards in all kinds of public regulations (Hamilton, 1978). Moreover, to help US law to conform to World Trade Organization (WTO) requirements discussed below, the National Technology Transfer and Advancement Act of 1995 (NTTAA) mandates federal agencies to 'use technical standards that are developed or adopted by voluntary consensus bodies' if feasible and also to participate in their development when possible.[9] Again, however, to date there seem to be no examples of adoption of multi-interest transnational regulatory standards of the kind discussed in this Chapter. The most relevant example is organic agriculture, where the US Department of Agriculture adopted regulations that are partly inconsistent with IFOAM criteria. This is possible under the NTTAA because it allows agencies to reject voluntary standards when it would be 'inconsistent with law or otherwise impractical' to adopt them.

Certification could also be used as a simple enforcement tool, a way of demonstrating compliance with accepted standards. This kind of delegation of inspection and adjudication responsibilities to certification programmes would seem to be less problematic, since the standards to be applied would be authorised by state legislation, and a number of administrative implementation functions have been privatised over the past two decades. However, the constitutional arguments also are less developed. The central question at the federal level would probably be whether the certifier should be classified as an 'officer of the United States', in which case the delegation would most likely be invalid, or a 'contractor', in which case there would not be an inherent constitutional problem. The certification process would still probably have to meet constitutional due process requirements. There are at least some cases of states using non-governmental certification programmes to implement state law. Colorado, for example, requires wildlife sanctuaries to be certified by the American Zoological Association,[10] and there are doubtless many other such requirements.

Even when governments do not require certification, they may offer certified firms preferential treatment. The EPA 'Performance Track' programme, for example, gives special treatment to firms meeting certification-like

[9] National Technology Transfer and Advancement Act of 1995, 15 USC § 3701 (1996).

[10] Colorado Wildlife Commission Regulations. Chapter 11—Wildlife Parks and Unregulated Wildlife, s 1104-C (http://wildlife.state.co.us/NR/rdonlyres/BDD5AB1C-D572-4458-AA3C-F7CF3BCA00AE/0/Ch11.pdf).

requirements.[11] In addition to displaying the Performance Track logo, qualified companies enjoy streamlined monitoring, record-keeping, and reporting under the Clean Air and Water Acts, and increased flexibility in installing 'best available control technology' under the Clean Air Act. Approximately 17 states have similar programmes (US EPA, 2006). Even in the absence of such official policies, it seems likely that governmental regulators will be prone to view certified firms more positively than uncertified ones. Thus, over time, absorption or incorporation of certification standards and routines into state law seems likely to occur informally, through infusion into the general expectations and conventional assumptions of regulatory communities.

B. Indirect Engagement

The preceding subsection discussed states as affirmative actors in the way that the governance literature typically views them—as policy makers, regulators, conveners, facilitators, resource managers, subjects of regulation, and so on. However, states also act on certification programmes in more passive ways, through general legal systems with which certification programmes must be compatible and through which they must work. This section examines some of those more passive forms of engagement. It is necessarily incomplete and preliminary. An infinite amount of general law is potentially applicable to certification systems. Moreover, the results of legal interactions in the future are inherently difficult to predict, both because key legal provisions are unsettled and because state legal systems embody conflicting values. Thus, this section is intended to suggest general patterns of interaction, rather than describe the entire set of relationships or convey detailed results.

1. *International Trade Law*

One of the most important legal factors shaping certification programmes to date has been the international trade law regime. Most of the certification programmes discussed in this Chapter have formed in significant part as a response to it. They made sense in the short term because governments were retreating from active regulation in favour of market liberalism and in the longer term because recognised international voluntary standards enjoy a special status in the international trading regime. Thus the FSC, for example, was purposely designed as a voluntary non-governmental standard.

[11] To qualify, companies must: (1) adopt and implement an environmental management system, (2) have a record of sustained compliance, (3) demonstrate continuous improvement, (4) conduct community outreach programmes, and (5) complete annual performance reports: US EPA National Environmental Performance Track (http://www.epa.gov/performancetrack/partners/comptools.htm).

Yet the status of the certification programmes in international trade law remains somewhat ambiguous. This ambiguity depends to some extent on the particular relationship of certification programmes to states, since the international trade regime focuses primarily on the activities of states in promoting and regulating trade. So long as certification programmes are seen as completely independent of states, their status under international trade law appears relatively unproblematic. They are 'purely voluntary' standards, and traders can conform to them or not as they choose. As seen above, however, certification programmes tend to be entangled with states in various ways, and to become more so over time. The question thus naturally arises whether they should be viewed as truly independent of states, or rather as attributable to them and therefore covered by the WTO agreements.

The question is easiest to answer in those few cases where states effectively mandate certification of imported goods. States can do this either by requiring certification under a named programme of all goods of a certain type sold in their territories, or by requiring importers to prove that their goods meet standards identical to those of the programme. These requirements are subject to scrutiny because they can constitute 'technical barriers to trade' by effectively disadvantaging foreign goods and services in local markets. Such requirements may focus either on characteristics of the product itself or on the processes and methods by which it was produced (PPMs), which is likely to be the case for the kinds of certification programmes discussed in this Chapter.

Where conformance is mandatory, PPM certification standards seem likely to be treated as 'technical regulations' under the TBT Agreement[12] and hence subject to the requirements that they must not create 'unnecessary obstacles to trade' or 'be more trade-restrictive than necessary to fulfill a legitimate objective'.[13] Legitimate objectives are indicated, but not clearly defined by the Agreement.[14] While they include the protection of human health and the environment, it seems likely that the goal of protecting environmental or social conditions in another state would be subject to vigorous challenge should it be raised. Nonetheless, the Agreement does grant a rebuttable presumption of acceptability to regulations 'in accordance with relevant

[12] 'Technical regulation' is defined by the Agreement as a 'document which lays down product characteristics or their related processes and production methods, including the applicable administrative provisions, with which compliance is mandatory. It may also include or deal exclusively with terminology, symbols, packaging, marking or labelling requirements as they apply to a product, process or production method': Annex 1, TBT Agreement.

[13] Article 2.2, TBT Agreement.

[14] 'Such legitimate objectives are, *inter alia:* national security requirements; the prevention of deceptive practices; protection of human health or safety, animal or plant life or health, or the environment': *ibid.*

international standards'[15] so long as they pursue one of the enumerated objectives.

Where certification standards are not mandatory they might still qualify as 'standards'[16] under the TBT, which are subject to additional, somewhat vague requirements involving coordinating with other relevant standards.[17] Certification standards are only standards for TBT purposes if they are approved by a 'recognised body', a term not defined in the Treaty.[18] However, the WTO Committee on Technical Barriers to Trade has listed criteria for assessing the acceptability of an international standard, including transparency, openness, impartiality and consensus, effectiveness and relevance, coherence, and accessibility to developing countries. In principle, many of the standards processes discussed in this Chapter might meet these criteria. The problem is that the document also notes that membership in the standard-setting body should be 'open to all relevant bodies of all WTO members'. The underlying model appears to be the ISO, with its designated national standards bodies. Whether this model can be extended to embrace organisations such as the FSC is problematic. Some commentators argue that they should not be viewed as a recognised bodies, in part because they operate with a much more ambiguous status in the eyes of states (Webb, 1999). This argument is bolstered where certification domains are inhabited by competing programmes. Yet the practical question will still have to be answered whether there is a sufficient nexus between the certification programmes and governments to bring them under the TBT agreement. The answer could also change over time if the imbrication of state and non-state requirements continues to expand.

Certification programmes operate under a complex set of legal incentives here. Internationally recognised standards are valued by the trade law regime as a way of facilitating international trade. States are enjoined to use 'relevant' ones in developing technical regulations, except when they would be ineffective or inappropriate—and these conditions must be

[15] 'Whenever a technical regulation is prepared, adopted or applied for one of the legitimate objectives explicitly mentioned in paragraph 2, and is in accordance with relevant international standards, it shall be rebuttably presumed not to create an unnecessary obstacle to international trade': Article 2.5, TBT Agreement.

[16] 'Standard' is defined as a 'document approved by a recognized body, that provides, for common and repeated use, rules, guidelines or characteristics for products or related processes and production methods, with which compliance is not mandatory. It may also include or deal exclusively with terminology, symbols, packaging, marking or labelling requirements as they apply to a product, process or production method:' Annex 1, para 2, TBT Agreement.

[17] Article 4.1, TBT Agreement.

[18] WTO Committee on Technical Barriers to Trade, Second Triennial Review of the Operation and Implementation of the Agreement on Technical Barriers to Trade, G/TBT/9, 13 November 2000.

'fundamental' to justify departures.[19] The WTO appellate body, moreover, has defined 'relevant' fairly broadly as 'bearing upon or relating to the matter in hand; pertinent'.[20] To date, this approach does not seem to have brought any of the non-ISO certification programmes discussed in this Chapter into the embrace of states.

Yet the programmes are operating as if this may eventually happen, and they have worked hard to qualify as recognised standardising bodies. They presumably hope that doing so will allow them not only to survive possible legal attacks, but also ultimately to amplify their effectiveness through state regulatory systems conforming to international trade law. The FSC, for example, has systematically reviewed and revised its structure and procedures so as to meet international criteria for standard-setting and certification, and recently succeeded in getting itself added to the World Standards Services Network (WSSN) list of standardising bodies (WSSN, 2006). Success in this arena will allow it to continue competing in the certification arena and over time possibly to draw states into acceptance and enforcement of its standards, at least those that survive its competition with the PEFC.

In sum, then, international trade law has performed two large key roles regarding certification systems. First, it has defined some of the key conditions under which they have evolved—particularly their careful distance from nation states in the early stages. Second, it has offered a possible vehicle through which they could greatly extend their reach, by endorsing international standards as the basis for state regulations and standards. Ultimately, of course, the rise of certification programmes may also call for some clarification or revision of international trade law, as their full capacities and implications become more apparent.

2. *National Competition Law*

National and regional competition laws have also played important roles in the formation and operation of certification programmes, but these appear to be both highly variable and poorly researched. At present two limited points can be made with reference to US law.

[19] 'Where technical regulations are required and relevant international standards exist or their completion is imminent, Members shall use them, or the relevant parts of them, as a basis for their technical regulations except when [they] ... would be an ineffective or inappropriate means for the fulfillment of the legitimate objectives pursued, for instance because of fundamental climatic or geographical factors or fundamental technological problems': Art 2.4, TBT Agreement.

[20] *EC-Sardines Case European Communities—Trade Description of Sardines*, Report of the Appellate Body, WT/DS231/AB/R, 26 September 2002 (http://www.worldtradelaw.net/reports/wtoab/ec-sardines(ab).pdf), para. 110.

First, US anti-trust law seems to have shadowed many efforts to develop and extend certification programmes, and to have often been used as a tactical device in programme competition. The AF&PA, for example, argued vehemently that if a buyer's group explicitly limited its purchasing strategy to FSC products it would violate US anti-trust law. This appears to have led many purchasing programmes to articulate more generic standards, which the SFI could possibly meet (Cashore *et al*, 2003). Similar events occurred under UK competition law. Second, US anti-trust law does potentially constrain self-regulatory programmes like those discussed in this Chapter, but only under relatively unusual circumstances where they have clearly anti-competitive effects (for example, artificially raising prices), reduce choices to consumers, or are rigged so as to unfairly disadvantage products of equal quality (Pitofsky, 1998).

Finally, it is worth noting that the US Constitution creates an added barrier to the uptake of certification requirements by individual states. Although they are free to require certification of activities conducted within their jurisdictions, they would be challenged if they required it of imported products. Under the 'dormant commerce clause', state regulations affecting interstate commerce are sustained only if the burden they place on interstate commerce is justified by the local interest they protect, and simply protecting local producers from less costly out-of-state products is unlikely to meet the test.

3. *Regulatory Law*

As noted above, some of the most important and difficult-to-trace forms of legal change unfold in informal processes. These processes include broad discussions in industrial, professional, and policy circles, as well specific transactions among firms, regulators, and sometimes community organisations. It seems quite likely that certification programmes will affect regulatory programmes through these almost invisible channels, beyond whatever changes are promulgated as official policy. Some tacit changes are likely to occur as inspectors evaluate practices at production facilities and question whether firms are following best practices. Others may come into play when permits go through revision cycles, and regulators or public interest groups push for up-to-date standards reflecting best available technologies and management practices, which are themselves likely to be reshaped through the dynamic adaptations of certification programmes.

Regulatory officials can also promote certification standards in their choices of which firms to inspect and monitor. Thus, as suggested above, they might tend to treat certification by a rigorous programme as an indicator of strong performance, and to concentrate their enforcement efforts on other firms. As it became apparent in an industry that certified firms were likely to suffer fewer or less intensive inspections, or to find it easier to get necessary regulatory approvals, the standard of practice in the industry would tend to converge with that of certification programmes.[21] Moreover, US law tends to presume the validity of administrative decisions. The burden is on challengers to show that administrative actions are 'arbitrary and capricious' or clearly beyond the legal capacity of the agency, and this becomes steadily more difficult as conventional assumptions in a field converge with certification standards.

4. *Tort Law*

Tort law might also be a channel for the legal expansion of certification standards over time. In general, US tort law requires parties to exercise reasonable care under the circumstances. Those who fail to do so must compensate those who are foreseeably injured as a result. Standards set by private associations have often been the measure of reasonable care in US tort law. It is hard to predict how important tort law will be in the types of environmental and social justice standards considered here, since it typically requires some sort of direct injury. One can imagine possible examples, such as a worker being injured due to the absence of protective gear that, while not specifically required by state regulatory law, is required by a certification standard. And it is conceivable that negligence would be found, whether the particular firm involved was certified or not.

Similar results are possible under nuisance law, which generally prohibits uses of land that 'substantially' and 'unreasonably' interfere with the use and enjoyment of land by others. Although what is unreasonable is hard to define, and depends on many factors, certification standards could be used to define some land uses as unreasonable. For example, stream pollution resulting from a clear-felled area larger or nearer a stream than would be allowed by a certification programme, which substantially affects downstream water quality could potentially be cited as unreasonable and enjoined by a court. Thus, in both types of cases, the state legal system could operate to extend voluntary certification standards to non-participants. But no examples of such liability have turned up in research thus far.

Finally, tort law can also be a source of liability for certification organisations. Several cases have held standard-setting organisations liable for injuries proximately caused by practices which conformed to their standards

[21] International environmental law could also become an important source of indirect incorporation of certification standards. Discussions about how to implement the Kyoto Protocol for the Reduction of Greenhouse Gases, for example, include the possibility of using forest certification to verify the maintenance of carbon retention 'sinks', as well as using ISO 14000 management systems to achieve reductions in greenhouse gas emissions.

but were found by courts not to constitute due care—the most evocative examples being injuries in swimming pools meeting private standards.[22] It is also possible that a certifying organisation could be sued for failing to detect a substandard practice in a firm that it inspects. Certification programs and organisations are aware of these risks, and it is possible that these concerns occasionally lead them to be more careful in their standard-setting and certification activities. Interview information indicates that they seek to carry appropriate insurance and to work out the terms of liability contractually, but thus far no evidence has come to light that tort law is a significant factor in shaping social and environmental certification programmes.

5. *Information Law*

Much US law focuses on what kinds of information are, or may be, required from market participants. Certification programmes exist for the purpose of conveying reliable information to consumers and others that certified organisations operate properly. As suggested in Sections I and II, there is often disagreement as to what are appropriate standards. Many environmentalists, for example, argue that the SFI certifies some practices that do not in fact qualify as sustainable forestry. There is at least some potential for lawsuits about such issues under the US 'Lanham Act', which creates general liability for commercial misrepresentation of goods or services. This potential seems limited at present, however, because, although the Act's terms create liability to 'any person who believes that he or she is or is likely to be damaged' by a misrepresentation,[23] American courts have thus far limited standing to competitors and rejected suits by consumers (Winders, 2006). There has been some discussion among activists of bringing Lanham Act suits against certified firms with substandard practices, but to date no such suits appear to have been filed, and it would probably take an unusual set of circumstances for a timber company to bring such a suit against another such company.[24]

On the other hand, some major corporations have brought legal actions to constrain the information published by certification programmes. The Monsanto Corporation, for example, recently sued a Maine dairy certified

[22] Eg, *King v National Spa and Pool Institute, Inc*, 70 So. 2d 612 (Alabama 1990), holding that the Institute had a duty to exercise reasonable care in the interests of consumers when setting voluntary standards for swimming pools.

[23] 15 USC §1125(a)(1) (1994)

[24] The Federal Trade Commission and various state attorneys-general also have the authority to bring suits against companies for commercial misrepresentation, and have done so in other cases, but have shown little interest in certification programmes to date. The Federal Trade Commission also has authority under other statutes to issue guidelines for certification programmes, but again has shown little interest in doing so.

under a voluntary programme for milk producers who do not use bovine growth hormone. Wielding the Lanham Act as a sword, Monsanto argued that the product label—'Our Farmers Pledge: No Artificial Growth Hormones'—was a misleading representation of fact harming its interests, since 'there is no known way to tell the difference between milk from cows supplemented with [bovine growth hormone] and milk from other cows'. The case was settled when the dairy agreed to add a disclaimer that the Food and Drug Administration saw no difference between certified and uncertified milk (Kysar, 2004). While this case may appear as an isolated incident at present, other examples seem likely to occur as certification programmes become important. For now, however, while participants in certification programmes may be aware of the possibility of suits for misrepresentation, there is little evidence that this has had a significant influence on certification practices.

Finally, it is also possible that US securities laws, which require disclosure of 'material' information on publicly held corporations, could eventually raise the profile of a corporation's certification status, but any such requirement appears to be well in the future. Present regulations are limited to legal liabilities, and certification status, while connected, is only one, relatively indirect way of getting at the question of potential liability. Thus, while many firms choose to disclose their certification status in securities filings, the securities laws seem to have little to do with those disclosures and it is too early to predict whether a 'common law' pattern is emerging.

6. *Summary*

The above analysis is inherently schematic and partial. It leaves out many potentially important areas of law, such as contract, corporate, and intellectual property law among others, and many legal systems. Nonetheless, if accurate, it indicates a significant and growing interpenetration among self-regulatory certification systems and state-based legal systems and a strong potential for mutual influence. Clearly some of the initiative in setting and implementing governing rules has shifted to non-state forums, and that trend seems likely to continue. Yet their dynamics are also shaped by, directed towards, and potentially reconstitutive of state legal systems. In evaluating emerging self-governance arrangements, therefore, it will be important to pay attention to both their state and non-state dimensions and to further describe the ways in which they shape and reshape each other.

IV. ASSESSMENT

For many readers the value of this research depends on what it can tell us about the implications of multi-interest self-governance for society and law. Unfortunately, the answer at present is limited. The institutions are still too preliminary and the research too partial to offer strong conclusions. In one form, the fundamental question is empirical: how well do these institutions work? But answering it is also deeply normative, since it is necessary to define what working well means. The contemporary discussion focuses primarily on three concerns: effectiveness, accountability, and legitimacy. The following subsections briefly indicate what can be said about each of these concerns and, perhaps more importantly, what further questions should be asked.

A. Effectiveness: Racing with Problems?

Most debate about multi-interest self-governance systems has centred on their effectiveness, or presumed lack thereof. Not wielding the formal coercive power of states, multi-interest self-governance systems have had to rely on other forces—primarily the kind of market leveraging described above—to create pressures for compliance. These pressures seem inherently episodic and transitory, lacking the persistence of a state agency. Still, research to date supports the proposition that several of the new regimes have been remarkably effective. FSC certification, for example, clearly has shifted a multitude of practices in many places around the world. These include not only the environmental practices of forestry firms, but also their dealings with local communities, labour, and other stakeholder groups (Bass *et al*, 2001; Cashore *et al*, 2006). The increased consultation and participation spurred by certification also seems to have rippled out into other local institutions in many cases (see, for example, Tysiachniouk and Meidinger, 2004). Although less is known about the other sectors discussed in this Chapter, there are reasons to expect that emerging multi-interest self-governance systems have also had significant effects on practices and relationships.

At this stage we have relatively little detailed research about the channels and mechanisms through which certification institutions effectuate these changes, but the analysis above suggests some likely ones. These include the leveraging of existing supply chains and economic relationships, establishment of competitive programmes that observe and critique each other, institutional modifications that extend far along commodity chains (see, for example, Vandenbergh, forthcoming) and deep into organisational management routines (see, for example, Edelman *et al*, 1999), gradual interweaving of certification systems with state regulatory and legal systems, and, ultimately, changes in cultural understandings and expectations of appropriate behavior (see, for example, Haufler, 2001).

While evidence that multi-interest self-governance systems are effectuating behavioural change is growing, it does not follow that they are 'solving' the problems they seek to address. The latter question may be impossible to answer with any confidence (Young, 1999), particularly since the problems that regulatory systems seek to address evolve continually and are always understood only partially. Yet it is hard to assess a governance system without some sense of whether it has the capacity to carry out its mission. Here two limited points can be made. First, there do not seem to be any plausible competitor governance systems in the fields examined. The image of states articulating strong, intelligent, adaptive treaties and reliably enforcing them remains a distant dream at present—although ironically, it could turn out that the systems described here lay the groundwork for such treaties. Second, the great strength of these systems is their dynamism—their continual competition and contestation in an effort to gain adherents and legitimacy. Thus, their strongest promise of effectiveness may be their searching adaptability. Accordingly, we may be best off viewing and evaluating them in terms of their ability to 'race' with the problems they confront—rather than to 'solve' them per se (see, for example, Sabel, 2004). Whether they will be dynamic enough, and whether they will continue to be dynamic over the long term is necessarily speculative. Effective dynamism requires the ability to formulate strategies, implement them, assess them, and change strategies relatively easily. At the same time, strategies must be seriously implemented and widely adopted even though change is expected. This is a demanding standard. The evidence to date is not inconsistent with this possibility, but considerable optimism is required to predict that the emerging systems will realise it. Tropical forests, for example, are still declining rapidly, and will require a very effective governance system to arrest that decline.

B. Accountability: Learning for Cosmopolitan Society?

Even if multi-interest self-governance through product certification systems proves reasonably effective, that does not necessarily make it a good thing. The question naturally arises, effective for *what purposes*? And embedded in that question is, for *whose purposes*? Here the emergent systems present serious conceptual challenges. They are fundamentally transnational, and do not match up with territorial polities. Thus, no claim can be made that they are fully accountable to territorial citizenries. Yet, as noted above, certification systems are at least partly accountable to territorial polities in that they must be compatible with state laws and seem to be growing increasingly intertwined with state legal systems. At the same time, global self-governance systems may seek to foster and respond to an incipient global citizenry. The actual nature of this global citizenry is a mystery at this time, and is likely to be formed more by global market and information flows than by certification programmes per se. One of the great challenges of certification systems will be to incorporate the enormous global diversity of local communities and yet respond to and support them (Archibugi and Held, 1995; Santos *et al*, 2005).

At present, it is impossible to tie the accountability systems of the multi-interest self-governance systems described in this Chapter to one social entity. There is no single 'principal' whose will can serve as the measure of their accountability. Rather, they are best understood as *compound* accountability systems, resting on a mix of national and international law, familiar institutions for standard-setting and certification, increasingly (but far from completely) open and transparent decisional procedures, and dynamic competition among certification programmes for business and public acceptance. Commentators with a critical cast of mind may see this either as no accountability system at all, or alternatively as such a confused and potentially gridlocked one as to amount to the same thing. Those with a stronger belief in the functionality of emerging governance systems may see it as a desirable mix of responsiveness and stability in a complicated and highly changeable world (for example, Cohen and Sabel, 1997; Sabel, 2004). What can be said to both sides of this divide, however, is that at present we are only at the most rudimentary stage of understanding or assessing accountability in these governance systems.

Nonetheless, one fundamental point is becoming clear. Whatever the utility of principal-agent models for understanding and rationalising state-centered governance systems, they will not suffice for the new ones discussed here. Instead, it will be necessary to carry out serious empirical research on which interests the new systems answer to, and how. It may turn out that they are evolving a new accountability system based on learning and adaptability, and possibly answering to a newly emerging transnational citizenry by fitting regulatory requirements to hard found areas of overlapping consensus (Rawls, 2001) while effectively addressing problems. Or it may turn out that the sceptics are correct, and that the new systems effectively answer to no one, or only to already privileged social interests. We will only be able to answer these questions through creative and theoretically sophisticated empirical research. Traditional principal–agent models of accountability are likely to be of limited value in this effort.

C. Legitimacy: Principled Experimental Mimicry?

Ultimately multi-interest self-governance systems must prove themselves legitimate—that is, socially accepted and expected—if they are to persist. While it is little use guessing whether they will succeed, it is worth describing the main strategies they seem to be pursuing. First, the certification systems described in this Chapter manifest a strong commitment to the power of ideas. The fields are all highly conceptual and seem to centre on continuing conceptual development over time. This is especially evident in organic certification, the oldest of the fields, but also strongly present in the others. This focus on conceptual development does not seem to be simply a matter of sloganeering—for example, 'fair trade' or 'sustainable forestry'—but rather of finding a powerful idea or charismatic metaphor and giving it meaning through iterative experimental practices and adaptable rules. Arguments about how to define standards and criteria, moreover, frequently rely heavily on central concepts and principles.

While certification systems thus manifest a strong 'logic of appropriateness', this is not to the exclusion of a 'logic of consequences' (March and Olsen, 2004). As noted above, the competition among certification programmes is conditioned to a considerable degree on how well they 'work'. Rules and routines are under constant pressure to adjust to conditions and experience. Achievements and failures rub elbows with costs and practicality on a daily basis.

Finally, it seems clear that multi-interest self-governance systems rely heavily on mimicking well-established institutions—primarily those of standard-setting and certification discussed above, but also the best practices of government regulatory institutions. While it is quite possible that they do this in part out of a belief that these institutions will function well in performing the tasks assigned to them, it also seems clear that they are chosen in part because of their well-established public acceptability. As David Szablowski (2006) notes, however, while this may work for purposes of fostering public acceptance and confidence, it is very difficult to tell at this time whether such acceptance is well founded in any given case. That will ultimately require persuasive showings of persistent effectiveness and broad accountability as well.

REFERENCES

Archibugi, D and Held, D (1995) *Cosmopolitan Democracy: An Agenda for a New World Order* (London: Polity Press).

Bartley, T (2003) 'Certifying Forests and Factories: States, Social Movements, and the Rise of Private Regulation in the Apparel and Forest Products Fields' 31 *Politics & Society* 433.

Bass, S, Thornber, K, Markopoulos, M, Roberts, S, and Grieg-Gran, M (2001) *Certification's Impacts on Forests, Stakeholders, and Supply Chains* (London: International Institute for Environment and Development).

Bolster, T. (2006) 'Governing Organic', SUNY Buffalo Law School Independent Study, 23 January (copy on file with author).

Carrera, F, Stoian, D, Campos, JJ, Morales J, and Pinelo, G (2006) 'Forest Certification in Guatemala', in B Cashore, F Gale, E Meidinger, and D Newsom (eds) *Confronting Sustainability: Forest Certification in Developing and Transitioning Countries* (New Haven, CT, Yale Forestry School).

Cashore, B, Auld, G, and Newsom, D (2003) 'The United States' Race to Certify Sustainable Forestry: Non-State Environmental Governance and the Competition for Policy-Making Authority' 5 *Business and Politics* 219.

—— (2004) *Governing Through Markets: Forest Certification and the Emergence of Non-State Authority* (New Haven, CT, Yale University Press).

Cashore, B, Gale, F, Meidinger, E and Newsom D (eds) (2006) *Confronting Sustainability: Forest Certification in Developing and Transitioning Countries* (New Haven, CT, Yale Forestry School).

Cheit, RE (1990) *Setting Safety Standards: Regulation in the Public and Private Sectors* (Berkeley, CA, University of California Press).

Coglianese C and Nash, J (eds) (2001) *Regulating from the Inside: Can Environmental Management Systems Achieve Policy Goals?* (Washington, DC, Resources for the Future).

Cohen J and Sabel, C (1997) 'Directly-Deliberative Polyarchy' 3 *European Law Journal* 313.

Coleman, WD and Reed, AJ (2007) 'Legalisation, Transnationalism and the Global Organic Movement', in C Brütsch and D Lehmkuhl (eds) *Law and Legalization in Transnational Relations* (Routledge).

Courville, S and Crucefix, D (2003) 'Existing and Potential Models and Mechanisms for Harmonisation, Equivalency And Mutual Recognition, Discussion Paper for the International Task Force on Harmonisation' (copy on file with author).

Edelman, LB, Uggen, C, and Erlanger, HS (1999) 'The Endogeneity of Legal Regulation: Grievance Procedures as Rational Myth' 105 *American Journal of Sociology* 406.

FSC (2006) 'Forest Stewardship Council Principles and Criteria' (http://www.fsc.org/en/about/policy_standards/princ_criteria/8).

Fung, A, O'Rourke, D, and Sabel, S (2001) *Can We Put an End to Sweatshops? A New Democracy Forum on Raising Global Labor Standards* (Boston, MA: Beacon Press).

Goodman, E (2002) 'Nontimber Forest Products Customary Claims' in ET Jones, RJ McLain, and J Weigand (eds), *Nontimber Forest Products in the United States* (Lawrence, KA: University of Kansas Press).

Gulbrandsen, LH (2005) 'Mark of Sustainability? Challenges for Fishery and Forestry Eco-Labeling' 47 *Environment* 8.

Hamilton, RW (1978) 'The Role of Nongovernmental Standards in the Development of Mandatory Federal Standards Affecting Safety or Health', 56 *Texas Law Review* 1329.

Haufler, V (2001) *A Public Role for the Private Sector: Industry Self-Regulation in a Global Economy* (Washington, DC, Carnegie Endowment).

Humphries, DR (2006) 'The Certification Wars'. in DR Humphreys, *Logjam: Deforestation and the Crisis of Global Governance* (London: Earthscan).

IFOAM (2006) 'Principles of Organic Agriculture' (http://www.ifoam.org/about_ifoam/principles/index.html).

Krislov, S (1997) *How Nations Choose Product Standards and Standards Change Nations* (Pittsburgh, University of Pittsburgh Press).

Kysar, DA (2004) 'Preferences for Processes: the Process/Product Distinction and the Regulation of Consumer Choice' 118 *Harvard Law Review* 525.

March, JG and Olsen, JP (2004) 'The Logic of Appropriateness', Arena Working Paper 04/09, Center for European Studies, University of Oslo (http://www.arena.uio.no/publications/working-papers2004/papers/wp04_9.pdf).

Meidinger, E (1999) 'Human Rights, "Private" Environmental Regulation, and Community' 6 *Buffalo Environmental Law Journal* 123

—— (2006) 'The Administrative Law of Global Private-Public Regulation: the Case of Forestry' 17 *European Journal of International Law* 47.

Meidinger, E, Elliott, C, and Oesten, G (2003) 'The Fundamentals of Forest Certification', in E. Meidinger, C. Elliott, and G. Oesten (eds) *Social and Political Dimensions of Forest Certification* (Remagen-Oberwinter, Germany: Forstbuch).

MSC (2006a) 'Marine Stewardship Council Principles and Criteria' (http://www.msc.org/assets/docs/fishery_certification/MSCPrinciples&Criteria.doc).

—— (2006b) 'Marine Stewardship Council Fisheries List' (http://www.msc.org/html/content_463.htm).

O'Rourke, D (2000) 'Monitoring the Monitors: A Critique of Price Water House Coopers (PwC) Labor Monitoring, Independent Whitepaper' (http://nature.berkeley.edu/orourke/PDF/pwc.pdf).

Parker, C (2000) 'Reinventing Regulation Within the Corporation: Compliance-Oriented Regulatory Innovation' 32 *Administration and Society* 529.

PEFC (2008) Programme for the Endorsement of Forest Certification member schemes (http://www.pefc.org/internet/html/members_schemes/4_1120_59.htm).

Pinchot Institute for Conservation (2006) 'Oregon Forestlands and the Programme for the Endorsement of Forest Certification (PEFC): An Assessment of the Process & Basis for Eligibility' Final Report to the Oregon Department of Forestry, 11 April, Washington, DC (http://www.oregon.gov/ODF/RESOURCE_PLANNING/docs/PEFC_Study.pdf).

Pitofsky, R (1998) 'Self Regulation and Antitrust', Speech of the FTC Chairman (http://www.ftc.gov/speeches/pitofsky/self4.htm#N_21_).

Potoski M and Prakash, A (2005) 'Covenants with Weak Swords: ISO 14001 and Facilities' Environmental Performance' 24 *Journal of Policy Analysis and Management* 745.

Quevedo, L (2006) 'Forest Certification in Bolivia' in B Cashore, F Gale, E Meidinger, and D Newsom (eds), *Confronting Sustainability: Forest Certification in Developing and Transitioning Countries*, (New Haven, CT, Yale Forestry School).

Rawls, J (2001) *The Law of Peoples* (Cambridge. MA: Harvard University Press).

Sabatier, PA and Jenkins-Smith, H (eds) (1993) *Policy Learning and Policy Change: An Advocacy Coalition Approach*. (Boulder, CO: Westview Press).

Sabel, C (2004) 'Beyond Principle-Agent Governance: Experimentalist Organizations, Learning, and Accountability', in E Engelen and M Sie Dhian Ho (eds) *De Staat van de Democratie. Democratie voorbij de Staat*, WRR Verkenning 3 (Amsterdam, Amsterdam University Press) 173–95.

Santos, B, Rodríguez-Garavito, C, Arup, C, and Chanock, M (2005) *Law and Globalization from Below: Towards a Cosmopolitan Legality* (Cambridge, Cambridge University Press).

Sasser, E (2002) 'Gaining Leverage: NGO Influence on Certification Institutions in the Forest Products Sector', in L Teeter, B Cashore, and D Zhang (eds) *Forest Policy for Private Forestry* (Oxford, CABI Press).

Schepel, H (2005) *The Constitution of Private Governance: Product Standards in the Regulation of Integrating Markets* (Oxford: Hart Publishing).

Scott, C (2001) 'Analysing Regulatory Space: Fragmented Resources and Institutional Design', *Public Law* 329.

Scott, J (1998) *Seeing Like a State: How Certain Schemes to Improve the Human Condition Have Failed* (New Haven, CT, Yale University Press).

SFI (2005–09) 'Sustainable Forestry Initiative Standard' http://www.aboutsfb.org/generalPDFs/SFBStandard2005-2009.pdf

Szablowski, D (2006) 'Of Models and Mimics: Legitimation Strategies and the Constitution of Transnational Legal Authority', Paper prepared for presentation at the International Studies Association Conference, San Diego, 22–25 March (copy on file with author).

Tarasofsky, RG, Mechel, F, and Sprang, P (2005) 'Public Procurement and Forest Certification: Assessing the Implications for Policy, Law, and International Trade', Draft report to Chatham House and Ecologic (http://www.ecologic.de/download/projekte/900-949/933/draft_report_050602.pdf).

Tysiachniouk M and Meidinger, E (2004) 'Using Forest Certification to Strengthen Rural Communities: Cases from Northwest Russia', Paper presented to the American Sociological Association Mini-conference on Community and Ecology: The Intersection of Community Sociology and Environmental Sociology, 12–13 August 2004, San Francisco (http://www.law.buffalo.edu/eemeid/scholarship/FCNWRussia.pdf).

United Nations (1992) 'Non-legally Binding Authoritative Statement of Principles for a Global Consensus on the Management, Conservation and Sustainable Development of All Types of Forests,' A/Conf.151/26 (http://www.un.org/documents/ga/conf151/aconf15126-3annex3.htm).

US EPA (2006) 'National Environmental Performance Track' (http://www.epa.gov/performancetrack/partners/comptools.htm).

Vandenbergh, M (forthcoming) 'The New Wal-Mart Effect: The Role of Private Contracting in Global Governance, *UCLA Law Review*.

Webb, K (2005) 'Understanding the Voluntary Codes Phenomenon', in K Webb (ed) *Voluntary Codes, the Public Interest, and Innovation* (Ottawa: Carleton University).

—— (1999) 'Voluntary Initiatives and the Law', in R Gibson (ed) *Voluntary Initiatives: The New Politics of Corporate Greening* (Peterborough, Ontario: Broadview Press).

Winders, DJ (2006) 'Note: Combining Reflexive Law and False Advertising Law to Standardize "Cruelty Free" Labeling of Cosmetics' 81 *NYU Law Review* 454.

Wood, S (2002–03) 'Environmental Management Systems and Public Authority in Canada: Rethinking Environmental Governance,' 10 *Buffalo Environmental Law Journal* 129–210.

WSSN (2006) 'World Standards Services Network, International Standardizing Bodies', http://www.wssn.net/WSSN/listings/links_international.html.

Young, OR (1999) *Governance in World Affairs* (Ithaca: Cornell University Press).

10

State and Private Sector in a Cooperative Regulation: The Forest Stewardship Council and other Product Labels in Brazil

CRISTIANE DERANI AND JOSÉ AUGUSTO FONTOURA COSTA

I. INTRODUCTION

FOREST CERTIFICATION PLAYS an important role in the Brazilian regulatory system, both filling gaps in the formal legal system and partially compensating for inadequate or corrupt implementation mechanisms. Increasingly, the Brazilian state has found ways to incorporate and to coordinate with the kind of private regulation evidenced by forest certification.

II. THE FOREST STEWARDSHIP COUNCIL

Certification has emerged as a private initiative from a series of international events, mainly the United Nations Conference on Environment and Development in 1992 at Rio de Janeiro and the UN-based Intergovernmental Panel on Forests (IPF). In 2000,[1] the UN created a subsidiary body, the United Nations Forum on Forests (UNFF), which resulted from a five-year period (1995–2000) of policy dialogue, facilitated by the IPF and the Intergovernmental Forum on Forests. As an intergovernmental policy forum, all UN members, as well as specialised agencies, have a seat in the UNFF during the UN's annual sessions.

UNFF's main goal is to promote the management, conservation, and sustainable development of all types of forests and to strengthen a long-term political commitment towards this objective. Among the principal actions established to achieve this objective, UNEF will enhance the cooperation and

[1] Resolution no 35, October 2000, of the Economic and Social Council (ECOSOC).

policies, and programme coordination with international and regional organisations, institutions, and instruments on related issues, as well as stimulating synergy amongst them. In 2005, UNFF considered recommending parameters of a mandate to develop a legal framework on all types of forests, which would allow the establishment of approaches focusing on the appropriate financial and technological transfer support in order to enable the implementation of sustainable management.

Besides these government-based activities, initiatives based on civil society were developed in the early 1990s. A major step was the foundation of the Forest Stewardship Council (FSC) in 1993.

The World Wildlife Fund (WWF, now Worldwide Fund for Nature) and Greenpeace supported the creation of the FSC. In its first five years of existence, it was composed only of environmentalists and civil society representatives, without the participation of the producers. It later became a tripartite council, which today includes representatives from the timber industry, environmentalists, civil society and indigenous peoples' organisations, multinational enterprises committed to environmental protection, and product certification organisations.

As an international network, the FSC promotes responsible management of the world's forests, defining itself (on its website[2]) as a stakeholder-owned system. Its 10 goals are to foster:

(1) Compliance with laws and FSC principles
(2) Tenure and use rights and responsibilities
(3) Indigenous people's rights
(4) Community relations and workers' rights
(5) Benefits from the forest
(6) Environmental impact studies
(7) Management plans
(8) Monitoring and assessment
(9) Maintenance of high conservation values
(10) Plantations.[3]

The FSC's actions are guided by international standards for responsible management. These standards are created through a consultative process developed by FSC members. The FSC General Assembly adopts the decision about certification criteria. Having established these rules, FSC accredits independent third party organisations (certification bodies—CBs) that can certify managers and producers according to FSC standards. FSC certification standards and methods are disseminated among producing countries.

[2] www.fsc.org.

[3] http://www.fsc.org/plantations/docs/FSC-STD-01-001%20FSC%20Principles%20and%20Criteria%20for%20Forest%20Stewardship%202004-04.pdf.

Forests which are managed according to these standards can receive FSC certification after assessment by CBs, thus becoming authorised to use the FSC label. This trademark provides international recognition to organisations that support the growth of responsible management, allowing consumers worldwide to recognise the use of those standards.

In order to promote the FSC label and its contents—that is, to allow the consumer to recognise compliance with FSC standards—the organisation undertakes marketing programmes and information services. With these, it tries to increase the consumption of certified products, which in turn contributes to the mission of promoting responsibility worldwide. The label gains legitimacy through its social recognition. An important step in promoting FSC labelling as the consumer's buying choice is its acceptance by large chains of US and European wood products retailers, such as Home Depot, B&Q, and IKEA.

Over the past 10 years, 50 million hectares in more than 60 countries have been certified according to FSC standards, and several thousand products are produced using FSC-certified wood and carrying the FSC's trademark. The FSC operates through its network of national initiatives in more than 34 countries.[4] Although certification was originally designed for tropical countries, it has had its greatest uptake in moderate or boreal climate zone countries, such as Finland, the United States, Canada, and Germany.

III. CONTENTS OF CERTIFICATION

FSC certification can be achieved in two ways:

1. Forest Management (FM) Certificate:

This involves the assessment of the management unit by an independent FSC-accredited CB to ascertain whether its management complies with the internationally agreed FSC principles and criteria of responsible management. When the management complies with FSC standards, the FSC-accredited CB may issue a certificate for the operation. Certified operations can thus claim that the products they produce come from responsibly managed forests.

Before a certified operation can sell its products as FSC-certified, it must also obtain chain of custody (COC) certification (FM/COC).

[4] FSC National Initiatives: Argentina, Belgium, Bolivia, Brazil, Bulgaria, Cameroon, Canada, Chile, Colombia, Croatia, Czech Republic, Denmark, Ecuador, Estonia, Finland, Germany, Ghana, Hungary, Italy, Japan, Mexico, Mozambique, Papua New Guinea, Peru, Poland, Romania, Russia, Slovakia, Spain, Sweden, United Kingdom, United States, and Vietnam.

2. Chain of Custody Certificate

While the FM certificate is related to production processes, the COC certificate is attached to forest products. Chain of custody is the path taken by raw materials from the forest site to the consumer, including all successive stages of processing, transformation, manufacturing, and distribution.

Nowadays, products other than wood, known as 'non-timber forest products' (NTFPs), such as essential oils, resins, fruits, and seeds of trees may also receive FSC certification when they are produced according to specific standards prepared by the local National FSC Initiative (NI) and approved by FSC International (FSC-IC). In Brazil, IMAFLORA (Institute for Agricultural and Forest Management Certification), a subsidiary of Rain Forest Alliance, which is a US certifier accredited by FSC, has carried out a number of certification processes for NTFPs. This type of certification allows the consumer to buy products, other than wood, from a well managed forest, thus contributing to the sustainability of resources.

IV. BRAZILIAN FOREST RESOURCES

Brazil has about 5.5 million km^2 of forests (65% of its territory), which represents 10% of the total forests of the world and the second largest continuous forested area. In 2002, the total value of its forest products, such as pulp and paper, sawn wood from plantations and from natural forests (mainly in the Amazon Region), NTFPs and other products, represented 4% of Brazil's GDP and 8% of its exports, generating about two million jobs. About half of this production comes from unsustainable, non-certified sources, mostly logs obtained from clearing natural forests to create land for agriculture.

In the beginning of 2005, Brazil had approximately 3 million hectares of certified forests, certified under 52 separate certificates. About 1.7 million hectares are plantations, distributed in 33 private areas, and 1.3 million hectares are natural forests, in 19 private areas. This represents a robust increase over the previous four years, since in 2001 there were only 875 thousand hectares of certified forests, divided between 15 certified areas, 10 areas of plantations and five areas of natural forests.

It is important to note that about 30% of the private area referred to above regarding certified plantations, in fact, consists of natural forests set aside for preservation purposes. Most of the certified plantations are found in the Atlantic ecosystem, which today covers little more than 7% of its original area.

The certification can also be applied to community management of forests. This kind of certification has also shown good growth in recent years. In the beginning of 2002, there was no certified community management in the Amazon Region. In the beginning of 2005, there were already six community projects with FSC certification. Through FSC, products from these projects have fetched better prices, sometimes in the vicinity of 200 per cent more than before certification.

As mentioned earlier, the production and sales of certified NTFPs have also experienced a fast-paced growth, predominantly to meet the demand of cosmetics industry companies, such as Natura, Croda, and Beraca. These companies realise that certification enhances their corporate image; in addition to providing a guarantee that the raw material they use comes from sustainable sources.[5]

V. THE CERFLOR LABEL AND THE NATIONAL INSTITUTE FOR METROLOGY AND INDUSTRIAL QUALITY

Brazil took its first step towards certification with the creation of its national certification entity, CERFLOR,[6] an initiative of the Sociedade Brasileira de Silvicultura (Brazilian Society for Silviculture—SBS). CERFLOR was presented at the World Congress of the Food and Agriculture Organisation (FAO) in Paris in 1991. Due to the absence of an effective public policy to promote sustainable management, Brazil adopted certification first inspired by a private initiative of CERFLOR, which itself is a private organisation. Later on, this initiative was encompassed by a public institution, the National Institute for Metrology and Industrial Quality (INMETRO), which is now responsible for the CERFLOR certification system. It is worth mentioning that the Pluriannual Government Plan 2004–2007 includes certification as one of its goals, with special emphasis on NTFPs.

CERFLOR, which was formally established in 1996 with the participation of timber producers, researchers, and NGOs, nowadays has a structure that also includes representatives of the public administration. CERFLOR's Technical Subcommittee on Certification (TSC) is part of INMETRO's structure and is composed of four groups of representatives, each one with four members: producers, consumers, representatives of the Brazilian Technical Normalisation Association (ABNT), and scientists from the National Research Centre of EMBRAPA (Brazilian Enterprise for Agropecuary Research). As representatives of the regulatory agencies, there are five ministries (Agriculture, Environment, Labour; Development, Industry and Commerce, and Foreign Affairs) and representatives of INMETRO itself.

The TSC sets the rules, which have the power of law. It is remarkable, in our point of view, that the TSC's concern about egalitarian representation has been well observed. Many times, Brazil has shown itself capable of organising a great number of representative meetings, many of which are mere formalities. It is important to point out, however, that the results

[5] IMAFLORA, *Brasil certificado: a história da certificação florestal no Brasil/Imaflora* (Piracicaba, SP, Imaflora, 2005).

[6] Portuguese initials for Forest Certification.

of these forums are not satisfactory, due to a number of political, structural, and personal reasons. For instance, Brazilian national environmental policy relies on a regulatory agency, the National Council on Environment (CONAMA), composed of representatives of civil society, the judiciary and administrative spheres, scientific organisations and universities. This agency has the legal power to elaborate on rules relating to environmental issues, but the efficacy and even the constitutionality of its work is debatable.

Certification introduces new subjects and new values into the market. The certification in 2001 of the Chico Mendes's Federal Reserve Settlement Project Association in Seringal Cachoeira, Xapuri County, in Acre State, is considered a milestone. It was certified by FSC, for its logging operations, and it was the first certification given to an association of officially settled former rubber gatherers.

It is hoped that, with certification, the group of 19 families living in the Seringal Cachoeira, located at Assentamento Agroextrativista Chico Mendes, will achieve three times their current annual income of less than US$450 (R$1,000) from subsistence agriculture and gathering of Brazil nuts, due to change in their main economic activity. In addition, by relying less on agriculture, these families will avoid the destruction of many hectares of forest that are converted to land for pasture and annual crops every year. This was the reason why Chico Mendes, a prominent community union leader, was murdered in 1988.

The price premium to be paid to these families for the certified wood they will sell to the emerging furniture industry of Xapuri is 10 per cent. It may seem very little, but when the daily wage of R$30 obtained from wood sales is compared to the R$5.50 obtained from agricultural activities, the change is very worthwhile considering also that the workers will not be subjected to the hot tropical sun.[7]

INMETRO specifically deals with the quality and safety of materials and products, as well as with processes and products related to the quality of the environment. INMETRO is a public agency and is Brazil's official accreditation organisation. It is a scientific institute where engineers and technicians test materials and process and propose norms and standardisations. These proposals are approved by a council with representatives from the productive sector, consumers, and scientists, referred to as the National Council for Metrology, Standardisation and Industrial Quality (CONMETRO).

The standards created by INMETRO have the same enforcement level as Brazilian legal norms, and the Brazilian Consumer Code recognises these standards as legal regulation. As an example, Article 39, item VI states:

> it is forbidden to market any product or service that does not fulfil the rules and requirements set out by official institutions or, if those do not exist,

[7] http://www.herbario.com.br/dataherb08/seloac.htm.

without fulfilling the requirements set out by the Brazilian Association for Standardisation—ABNT—or by any other institution accredited by the National Council for Metrology, Standards, and Industrial Quality—CONMETRO.

Standardisation agencies are a good example of the participation of private agents whose authority is tantamount to that of public agents, which is a significant accomplishment. In terms of liability and inspection, the rules of these agencies have the same effect as domestic regulations, bonding and commanding citizens' actions. The state power is completed by more specific private regulations, recognised by the domestic legal system as complementary. In fact, the state, by statute, gives legal value to private standardisation processes, as is set forth in Article 12, item IX, of the Decree 2181/97:

> The following practices are considered infractions to the law: … IX. To market any product or service: a) not according to the rules set forth by official institutions or, if those do not exist, by the Brazilian Association for Standardisation—ABNT—or by any other institution accredited by the National Council for Metrology, Standards, and Industrial Quality—CONMETRO.

The Brazilian Programme of Certification—CERFLOR—now belongs to INMETRO. This programme was created and improved through the initiative of timber producers, who wanted a certification system because they were concerned with the conservation of natural resources.

Since 22 November 2002, INMETRO has been a member of the Programme for the Endorsement of Certification Schemes (PEFC), the largest programme of certification in the world, which incorporates 27 independent national systems in five continents. INMETRO has already developed six standards for certification and two for the accreditation of certification bodies.

These standards, which are equivalent to the legal norm, are the following:

— Principles, Criteria and Standards for Plantations (NBR 14789)
— Chain of Custody (NBR 14790)
— Guidelines for Audits—General Aspects (NBR 14791)
— Auditing Procedures—Management Audits(NBR 14792)
— Auditing Procedures—Qualification Criteria for Auditors (NBR 14793)
— Principles, Criteria and Standards for Native Forests (NBR15789).

It is undeniable that the certification movement—which was born from a non-governmental organisation, without any political representation—fills the gap left by the normative power of the public administration. This occurs because the state does not dedicate itself to more effective action in the regulatory field and also because the terms of regulatory definitions are intentionally unclear and too general and there is no guarantee of proper auditing.

VI. THE BRAZILIAN LEGAL SYSTEM REMAINS THE 'OLD-FASHIONED WAY'

Brazilian law does establish a command and control regime aiming at supervising the utilisation of forest resources. The regime is—at least in theory—applicable, regardless of the voluntary adoption of certification programmes by timber producers.

For instance, there is the Forest Product Transportation Authorisation (FPTA), granted by the IBAMA (Instituto Brasileiro para o Meio Ambientee Recursos Naturais Renováveis—the Brazilian Institute for the Environment and Renewable Natural Resources). This authorisation is required for the transportation and sale of forest products. However, it controls only one third of the wood effectively marketed in Brazil; the other two thirds are logged and sold illegally. In fact, the main problem is the lack of effective control measures. This lack of effectiveness is due to an administration which is characterised by a long history of corruption and privatisation of the public sphere, where personal interest and arbitrariness determine the award of log permits and the efficacy of control.

Besides authorisation for transportation and sales, current legislation seeks to promote sustainability by requiring authorisation for logging activities and imposing forest restoration. Decree 1282/94, in Article 1, paragraph 2, establishes that sustainable management means the administration of forests in order to obtain economic, social, and environmental benefits, in a way that respects the mechanisms of ecosystem maintenance and promotes the use of multiple timber species, non-timber products, and other goods or services of the forest. In other words, management is to be understood as fulfilling goals related to economic, social, and environmental sustainability, while a set of possible devices to achieve such goals are the use of a wider range of timber species, as well as the development of several by-products in order to increase the productivity of an exploited area.

Certainly, management is a fundamental instrument for forest sustainability. The challenge however is its administrative details and effective control measures to ensure the fulfilment of its goal.

The Decree specifies more general rules contained in Articles 15, 19, 20 and 21 of the Brazilian Forestry Code in providing that:

> The person that harvests, uses, transforms or consumes forest raw material is obliged to replace it.
>
> *Sole Paragraph:* The replacement referred above will be done in the natural state of the raw material, by planting the proper species, especially native ones, in order to produce wood in the amount that is at least equal to the annual volume necessary to fully sustain the activity, according to parameters set forth by IBAMA.

This Article shows that the state is not inactive with respect to the sustainable use of natural resources, establishing duties, ways to accomplish them, and defining who is responsible for fulfilling them.

Interestingly, the Decree, which also states exceptions to the replacement obligation, contains one exception for areas under 'sustainable forest management' (Decree 1284/94, Article 10, paragraph I).

It is reasonable to infer that once one private area produces certificated timber, it follows the standards set by the FSC. This means that the area is exploited in a sustainable way and will be exempt from the law-enforced replacement, since the area is supposedly already committed to sustainable use. Hence, Article 10 states:

> An individual or corporation that is able to prove that the forest residue or raw material he (it) uses is of the type mentioned below is exempt of replenishing its forest supplies:
>
> *I—raw material coming from areas under sustainable forest management*
>
> *Sole paragraph:* This exemption does not mean that the interested party does not have to prove to the competent authority the origin of the forest residue or raw material.

Although there is no clear normative statement about the meaning of 'sustainable forest management', or a jurisdictional precedent, the administrative practices of IBAMA usually accept the FSC-COC as evidence of sustainable management. The link between the legal system and the private certificate regulations is, as a consequence, established by the administrative instances, and no further evidence is needed to waive the the burden of proof for the individual or corporation. It is necessary to stress that evidence issues are factual ones. Nevertheless, the use of FSC certificates also demonstrates that the procedures adopted by the private organisation are accepted by the state on reliance that the exploitation procedures under audit automatically comply with the administrative imposition of replacement. It means, necessarily, that the standards and procedures adopted fulfil the regulatory needs.

In this specific case, national law relinquishes its sovereign regulatory power, acknowledging that self-regulation of sustainable use of resources would comply with an administrative imposition of replacement.

Another instrument foreseen by the Decree is the Forest Integrated Plan (FIP), which is to be submitted to IBAMA by large users of forest raw material. These consumers, individuals, or corporation, have an obligation to establish plantations—or subcontract this task with third parties—that will assure their raw material self-sufficiency, according to parameters set forth by IBAMA.

The responsibility for defining specific criteria in regards to the replacement of forest raw materials belongs to state agencies, since they depend on particular local conditions. However, IBAMA remains the federal agency responsible for controlling the implementation of such replacement. Articles 11 to 13 of Decree 1282/94 state this as follows:

> *Article* 11: Taking into consideration the particular state or regional conditions, the individual or corporation that needs a large amount of forest raw material, shall maintain—by himself (itself) or in partnership with third parties—the forests required to the full sustainability of his (its) economic activity, according to criteria and parameters to be determined by IBAMA.
>
> *Article* 12: The Forest Integrated Plan (FIP), to be presented by the individual or corporation to IBAMA, as mentioned in Article 11 of this Decree must include the programme for the annual supply of the forest raw material, in order to ensure the full sustainability of the industrial activity.
>
> §1 the programme for the annual supply of the forest raw material may encompass one or more of the following sources:
> (a) own sustainable forest management or from third parties;
> (b) native forests, according to regulations to be established by IBAMA;
> (c) forestation by land owner or by others (third parties);
> (d) forestation and reforestation based on company-sponsored tree-planting programmes;
> (e) residues as mentioned in Article 10 of this Decree;
>
> §2 the supply of forest raw material mentioned in §1 shall have its origin, volume, and destination proved to IBAMA.
>
> *Article* 13: IBAMA has the power to audit enterprises mentioned in the Integrated Forest Plan, established in Article 12 of this Decree, in order to decide about its approval, as well as to make non-scheduled audits or carry out inspections deemed necessary to the full compliance of the obligations assumed in the programme of raw material self-sufficiency.

The above provisions are set out to demonstrate that there is no gap concerning the sustainable use of timber resources by Brazilian law. Nevertheless, this regulation is insufficient and its control measures are precarious and cannot stop deforestation or prevent illegal wood from reaching national and international markets. The weakness of Brazilian institutions enhances corruption, and local governors tend to favour exploitation. Impunity and lack of resources and personnel have encouraged IBAMA staff to participate in corruption schemes, which are, for the most part, punished only by administrative fines.

In June 2005, the Brazilian federal police dismantled the largest scheme of illegal logging in the history of the Amazon Region, valued at more than $370 million. Arrested IBAMA staff members were accused of forging official documents authorising the transportation of illegal wood, a frequent practice in the Amazon Region according to environmentalists.[8]

[8] http://noticias.terra.com.br/brasil/interna/0,,OI544087-EI714,00.html.

There is however also some criticism with respect to the state's reliance on independent certification. In a report IMAFLORA suggested the following:

> Certification costs money, efforts, dedication, and hope. Changing paradigms involves a huge cost. Effective market and official recognition are necessary and require great effort on the part of producers. Some enterprises are facing more difficulties with regulatory agencies today than they did before they became certified.[9]

In fact the engagement in certification procedures implies the disclosure of the necessary information, which later becomes 'at the disposal' of governmental authorities. Sometimes it is easier to cheat control agencies working in shadows.

VII. LIMITS TO THE EFFICACY OF CERTIFICATION

Certification is emerging in Brazil, mostly induced by the weakness of state institutions and control mechanisms. Brazil laid down some good rules a long time ago. However, they have not been enforced until now. On the other hand, certification evokes a voluntary process, which is less expensive to the state, since the costs are supported by producers and consumers. Considering that competition could be the most persuasive instrument for the adoption of certification in a poor and oligarchic country, this new approach of pursuing environmental protection faces market barriers and the forestry industry's complaints that they will lose competitiveness if they choose the path of environment protection.

In fact, there are economic limits to the operation of the system of certification, since the prices of timber are determined by the black market and taking into consideration that the foreign trade is also fed by illegal products. An entrepreneur who wants to undertake environmentally and socially sustainable management 'must invest his financial resources for at least two years in planning, training programs and equipment etc before a single cubic meter of wood can be sold. He must spend considerable time and effort to have his project ready for certification and, when the wood is sold, his costs will be higher because he will have to pay all taxes',[10] and therefore face the cruel, unfair competition from outlaws.

Legal and responsible producers also complain about the lack of supportive public policies, since the Brazilian state does not offer any aid, legal or financial, to fund certification schemes. On the one hand, the FSC furthers the acceptance of its certificates through the provision of information on marketing and environmental benefits. On the other hand, there are no public funds available to improve forest management. The official banks

[9] Brasil certificado : a história da certificação florestal no Brasil/Imaflora 2005.

[10] Reinoldo Poembacher, Forest and Supply Chain Director, Klabin SA, the largest paper exporter in Brazil.

have no 'special loans' offered to enterprises that hold environmental and social accountability. Particularly in the timber industry, it would be necessary to provide long-term loans, since the forest growth cycle takes about 25 to 30 years. The lack of synergy between the certification of private organisations and public legal and financial policies has been a barrier to the widening of sustainable areas of timber exploitation.

VIII. OTHER EXAMPLES OF CERTIFICATION AS AN ENCOURAGEMENT TO REGULATION BY THE STATE

The Brazilian implementation of cattle traceability chains and the growth of the organic food industry are good examples of private initiatives which are helping to increase standards of environmental protection. In both industries, private self-regulation increases the uniformity of production and marketing procedures, which encourages public environmental policies. Improvement of business and the conquest of new market niches are important initial pushes to private actors in promoting environmental protection and human health. This wider offer of public goods is, consequently, followed by the state's agencies and policies which apply these standards to other economic actors as well, spreading the original pattern throughout all other industries.

To allow the traceability process, a commitment must be adopted by the operators acting vertically in the production chain. Therefore, supermarkets, producers, and distributors operate jointly, binding their product chains and satisfying consumer demand. INMETRO has received intense pressure to assume the regulation of this traceability system, thereby expanding the participation of the public sector in this private initiative.

'Carrefour's Certificate of Origin' label is an attempt by the Carrefour supermarket chain to get closer to the agents involved in the production chain in order to fulfil the demands of consumers. This label has guided cattle producers and qualified meat-processing industries in improving their production systems and the quality of slaughtered animals.[11]

Despite this initiative, the bovine production chain is characterised by strong competition and lack of trust among cattle breeders and other sectors of the industry,[12] which bars the enrollment of several producers in the traceability system.

In addition, another motive which avoids a wider adoption of the traceability system is the high costs and lack of financing faced by primary producers. There are also problems in finding qualified laboratories that have the expertise necessary for identifying biological and chemical risks.[13]

[11] Edison Fernando Pompemeyer, in *Revista de Direito Ambiental Econômico*, Sérgio Fabris, 2005.

[12] *Ibid.*

[13] *Ibid.*

Nonetheless, this procedure is becoming imperative to producers who wish to export to the European Union. Following the 'mad cow disease' episode, European health authorities are imposing various bovine meat traceability rules.

Another example is the production of organic foods, which has grown by about 300% in the last two years. There are 19,000 farms across the country, harvesting 300,000 tons of food a year. The main reason behind this growth is the demand from international markets and, above all, the guaranteed purchasing contracts offered to producers by large supermarket chains. These supermarkets are reacting to consumer demand that is growing, even though certified organic products cost 30% more than regular products.

In Brazil, there is a private association that grants certification to organic agriculture operations and organic food processors. The Biodynamic Institute (BDI) (Instituto Biodinâmico) is a private certification association that carries out assessments of agricultural and cattle farm enterprises, food producers, and processors for the purpose of certification, both organic and biodynamic. It began its certification work in 1990 and has since expanded its operations throughout the whole of Brazil and into other South American countries. In 1995, the Institute gained accreditation by the International Federation of Organic Agriculture Movement (INFOAM). In 1990, it also obtained accreditation from the International Standardisation Organisation under ISO Standard 65. This standard governs the procedures of certification organisations of all types of products, including organic products. Its equivalent in the European Union is the standard NUU 45.011.[14] In 2002, the BDI also received the approval of the US Department of Agriculture, allowing products carrying its certification to be sold as 'organic' in the United States.

Among other products, organic production certified by the BDI includes agricultural projects, food processing, and raising cattle for meat production, fisheries, and silviculture. The BDI today covers about 700 certified projects, or projects in the process of certification, involving more than 4,000 producers.

The BDI largely acts without interference from official regulation. The first law to regulate organic agriculture (Law 10.831) only appeared in December 2003. This law does not affect private practices, because it is of a general character, without establishing specific performance standards. It only introduces concepts, objectives, and principles. However, the Brazilian Ministry of Agriculture has adopted an internal administrative instruction establishing the procedures to be followed with respect to organic certification. These procedures describe in a legal format the steps that are already followed in practice by the BDI in its certification scheme. However, nothing is mentioned about control measures for the certification process.

[14] http://www.iso.ch/iso/en/ISOOnline.openerpage.

Therefore, it is possible to affirm that the certification system fills the vacuum left by both the national legislation and the lack of effectiveness of those laws already in existence.

Given the fact, that national legislation is unable to effectively regulate Brazilian production processes, and recognising the potential of what were traditionally known as *private* structures in taking over the role played by public agencies, as shown in the case of certification, we can speak about a change from a hierarchical model to a coordination model between the state and social actors. Consequently, the role of civil society is greatly expanded.

The private sector, moved by private interests, creates new regulatory structures with respect to health, safety, and environmental protection. Companies belonging to a given industry organise themselves into an association in order to develop a concerted effort to regulate the quality of their products and their production processes with respect to the environment, consumer health, and general social welfare. We agree with Rehbinder, who prefers the expression *private regulation* to *self-regulation* (Rehbinder, 2003: 333).

So, it is possible to say that the administrative field opens itself to another form of social construction, coming from non-state actions, but recognised by law in its representation procedures, decision-making criteria, producer and consumer information and possibly legitimated by accepted social results. The social acceptance mainly emerges in the field of consumption relations. In a final analysis, the social subject will accept and ratify the new regulation in its consumption practice.

It is possible to conclude that the assumption by private institutions of the power of regulatory functions, which is recognised and strengthened by the acceptance by the market of higher practices, is directly linked to the lowering of the credibility of the state effectiveness in the fulfilment of public interests.

IX. REFLECTIONS ON THE POTENTIAL AND LIMITS OF PRIVATE REGULATION

Eco-labelling implies an assessment of environmental impacts present in a product, a production process, or the full life cycle of the product. Its quality, of course, depends on the rigour of the criteria of the certification process (sustainability and safety) (Rehbinder, 2003: 339).

Certification is a soft and flexible instrument of environmental policy in that it uses consumer preferences in order to encourage forest owners to employ sound management methods with regard to their forests. For instance, product labelling must in some way define its vision of sustainable development. Ideally, this would require accurate information and the most perfect and responsible intention from the consumer. Neither of these are possible. Choices, besides being guided by ideals, are also made because of necessity and advantages, and through balancing the sustainable development value with other values. Nothing can guarantee that sustainable development will be the only goal of consumers and that by their informed choices they will build an ecologically balanced environment.

All collective action is subject to failure in regards to reaching the results originally expected. Uncertainty and fear of failure on the part of the intervening parties are sufficient to block the collective action or to make it ineffective Underlying this is the classical problem of the incompatibility between individual rationality and reaching the collective well-being (Salais, 1998: 58). State action has insistently attempted to solve the problem of the gap between the rush for private advantage and the range of collective interests.

When speaking about private certification, even with the participation of representatives of various social sectors, we cannot ignore the interests of the individual groups trying to obtain some advantage, either private (timber producers) or sectorial (environmental and/or social organisations). One might argue here that the 'public choice' theory can be applied to phenomena outside of the state's reach, with the difference being that each decision represents a choice of preferences of a certain sector or group of stakeholders turned public.

Public action, that is action imposed by the state, is expected to be action that comes into effect in the absence of possible satisfactory coordination among the various private actors. However, it is currently the coordination of social sectors that emerges in the absence of satisfactory public action.

This development reveals the change in the state and the law, because social relations have also changed: they have become more complex, wider in geographic terms, more flexible in their interests and strategies, which makes bipolarisation more difficult, a situation typical of that in the first centuries of capitalism. A whole juridical universe organises itself around a skeleton of repeated dichotomies, never to be overcome (such as fact or law, legality or opportunity, public or private, content or format, *de lege lata* or *de lege ferenda*, natural law or positive law) (Ost and van de Kerchove, 2002: 12).

The legal system for simplifying the reality of the situation that included and excluded certain elements as a way to organise itself has been shaken by the advancements of the last 50 years. Social relations have changed in many dimensions. In terms of geography, time, and relations, many things have changed significantly and rapidly. Issues of distance are not the same as before, and the means of communication facilitate a network of knowledge and interrelationships between people located in most of the different regions of the world like never seen before. The time required to establish relations has diminished, and their stability and continuity have gained another dimension.

Relationships have become more diverse and complex. For instance, in the field of international law we can find, aside from the classical agents of international law, the presence of civil organisations which act as institutions allowing a more detailed and permanent relationship in a way that was once exclusive to that of municipal law. Production, distribution, and consumption relations underwent these geographic changes in time and behaviour in the extreme. In this perspective, thinking in terms of complexity is necessary where dualisms are not sufficient to encompass the whole meaning and antagonism generated within these relations.

Ost and van de Kerchove write about a migration from the idea of a juridical pyramid to one of a network, and propose a change from such principles as coherence, security, stability, and obedience, to values such as creativity, lightness, pluralism, and permanent learning (Ost and van de Kerchove, 2002: 18). They remind us that 'if historical experience taught us that law could disappear due a change into a pyramidal model, reminding us of the authoritarian gesture of a dictator, prudence should guide us to think that law could also disappear in another form of power'.

In fact, so influential is the consumer's will that it attracts agents to abide by certification rules. The certification system of the FSC, unlike the juridical system of the state, is characterised by voluntary submission, as an instrumental alternative to that of traditional law. In spite of this, social agents strongly commit themselves to it, moved by economic interests (Rehbinder, 2000: 240). By this self-submission, it is possible to change the whole existing economic processes and introduce new procedures and techniques (Rehbinder, 2000: 241). These procedures will gain more power as more agents self-submit to their rules; therefore, the greater the regulatory capacity of the system in mobilising producers, the better its results will be.

Despite its achievements, this kind of self-regulation cannot, however, be taken as a panacea to the integration of production activities with environmental protection (Rehbinder, 2000: 246). Rehbinder remains doubtful as to whether it is a realistic possibility for certification to achieve real environment protection and a sustainable use of natural resources. It is certainly a useful instrument but has its limits and must be completed by other policies and regulations.

With all the efforts for equal representation and publicity in criteria development in the operation of these regulatory and control organisations, such as the FSC, there are still problems with accountability and representative capacity. The process is not controlled by the kind of checks and balances provided for in the state decision-making process through periodic elections.

Midway between state regulation and regulation established by quasi-official agencies, there is sectoral regulation established within administrative boundaries. Regulation should therefore not be left up to market forces alone, but kept under the umbrella of the public sector, even if it is only according to broad guidelines. Sectoral regulation has gained acknowledgement, even if at first glance it denies the basic principles of state law: stability, security, legislative formation, and generality. Dynamic regulation directed at specific actions of specific sectors is increasingly accepted as the concerns experienced by society, due to lack of public action, grow deeper and deeper.

We may say that the organisation of market actions by non-state institutions responds to a governance imperative essential to social life. (Ost and van de Kerchove, 2002: 22). The conversion of public space as a governmental space of the state is a fact which originates in the changing of the human existence reproduction relations. It does not mean the 'end of the state'. What one should describe is the different paths taken by society, with specific forms of organisation.

Among these interests, the market interest is the most 'organised' in the way that it has a strong field of interconnections, and also because it holds its place in the institutional forms of the government that are changed to better serve it.The market is the field for seeking individual advantages. If in this environment it is possible to satisfy different interests other than those linked to individual profit, it should be seen as an adequate field for the production of a coordinated regulation of interests. If this is true, alternative forms of state regulation that have the market as their implementation field should be stimulated to demonstrate their capacity to achieve social objectives, such as environmental protection and guarantee of social rights.

However, if the answer is negative, or if we realise that regulation by market agents (producers, consumers) fulfils poorly or partially the social and environmental objective, we have to live with state regulation, at least to coordinate the rules set forth and applied to market dynamics. A regulation that has the market as its environment and is able to use its own implementation instruments will be efficient, as long as it can contribute to the development of those relations, independently of the degree of satisfaction and the extension of the results that its actions could bring to society.

The Brazilian experience shows that the state's action has become intertwined with private action. This implies a significant change in the role of the state as a regulatory power. The state absorbs self-regulatory rules translating them into formal law, elects a public forum for coordination, but has an extremely weak performance in the creation of new procedures in the interconnection of these rules with other public activities and is incapable of creating a public control agency.

Brazil should more rigorously use its command and control competence by exercising its power to establish policies and, above all, by integrating private regulation in the other fields of state policy, coordinating sectoral rules with the rest of general state laws and with social interests. In other words, the state has a wide field to accomplish its commitments.

Nevertheless, in the command and control field, Brazil has not been able to do much. The attempts to minimise this weakness call for new structures in the administration. We may mention the example of the organisation of the certification process of materials and the procedures involved in the construction sector. The law recognises the construction companies' associations as being able to carry out self-inspection and define quality goals. This same law creates a management centre in the federal executive power to organise, give publicity to this self-regulation procedure. Companies and private institutions agreed to act toward achieving these goals, and once the agreement is made, it becomes obligatory. Those forest companies involved contribute to this association by preparing the assessment procedures, since all of them are interested in a uniform level of procedure and quality standards; otherwise unfair competition will prevail.

This state structure contributes to the argument in this chapter that action parallel to the state's definition of quality standards is important, as well as the use of consumer power to stimulate more sustainable production.

Even though this mechanism needs coordinated state activity to enjoy better publicity, as well as to ensure its integration in the checks and balances system, it is essential to build a democratic society.

X. A NEW LEGAL RIGHT?

Ost and Kerchove write about the constant erosion of the law. This erosion has two different expressions. On the one hand, erosion that results from the spread of international regulation into sovereign countries, which transfers regulatory power from the State to international institutions, is evidence of the inability of the State to maintain and control all human relationships. On the other hand, on the domestic front, erosion results from the different pace of law making and social complexity, which encompasses the reproduction of social relationships. State law, as a consequence of both aspects of legal erosion, cannot deal with all the antagonisms that emerge from a single relation anymore, since this single relation is always embedded in a mass of complex structures.

In one way or another, due to international action or to the position of the market agents' self-regulatory sector, there is always a void to be filled. While, in the state's sphere, *lege ferenda* discussion spaces grow, and *lege lata* frequently is questioned because of its lack of sensibility to the facts and the poor regulation given to them, the international sphere and production sectors work separately from the state; of the state can only act as a coordinator.

With an organised system such as the FSC, can we speak in terms of juridical pluralism? Could the state's recognition of its validity bring another juridical source under the wrap of the state's juridical system? By realising the permeability of the certification system in relation to state's law, which embodies it, we should not speak in terms of juridical pluralism, but we should insist on the idea of coordination. The state's recognition of the validity of this regulation recognises another form of normative production, which must, however, be submitted to permanent control mechanisms to ensure compatibility with the constitution and with the rest of the existing legal rules, adopting Meidinger's assertion that 'certification programs may also have broader external effects by stimulating improvements in governmental environmental regulation and increasing consistency among jurisdictions' (Meidinger, 2002: 315).

In synthesis, we may conclude in a preliminary way that environmental protection, with the maintenance of economic practices of intensive use of natural resources to produce goods and services demanded by the market, should not do away with the diverse regulation mechanisms that need to work in an integrated way.

In conclusion, despite the problems related to social representation mechanisms that intend to ensure a democratic system, the FSC and other similar private associations represent an important policy for environmental conservation in a country where administrative institutions suffer from many diseases, such as corruption and lack of efficacy.

However, those mechanisms demand coordinated action on the part of the state in order to promote better publicity of its actions, enforce the information principle, and guarantee its involvement in the checks and balances system, which is vital for building a democratic society.

The problems of integrating private rules into other State's spheres and policies, and of coordinating sectoral rules with the rest of the legal system and social interests, are far from being solved. This difficulty exposes a state's crucial problem in times of governance and regulation: if, on one hand, those are characteristic phenomena of a time of both political and social integration by market forces, or on the other hand, it is necessary to achieve and develop instruments that neutralise the uncountable perverse effects generated by the conduct of the rules of social life by market mechanisms of changes and consumption. Theoretically this is quite evident, but the weakness of the Brazilian state calls for more accurate mechanisms of integration and checks and balances in the relationship between producers, consumers, civil society, workers in the sector, administration and whatever representation is important to make a democracy more real in times of dissolution of the subject in the name of a flowing globalisation.

REFERENCES

Meidinger, E (2002) 'Forest Certification as Environmental Law Making by Global Civil Society', in E Meidinger, C Elliott and G Oesten (eds), *Social and Political Dimensions of Forest Certification* (Remagen-Oberwinter, Verlag Dr Norbert Kessel).

Ost, F and van de Kerchove, M (2002) *De la pyramide au réseau? Pour une théorie dialectique du droit* (Bruxelles, Publications des Facultés Universitaires Saint-Louis).

Rehbinder, E (2000) 'Integrierte Umweltschutzschutztechnologien—Definition, umweltpolitische Bewertung und Hemmnisse für ihre Einführung im Unternehmen', in G Winter (ed) *Produktionsintegrierter Umweltschutz und Eigenverantwortung der Unternehmen* (Frankfurt, Peter Lang).
—— (2003) 'Certification and environmental law', in E Meidinger, C Elliott, and G Oesten (eds), *Social and Political Dimensions of Forest Certification* (Remagen-Oberwinter, Verlag Dr Norbert Kessel).
Salais, R (1998) 'Action Publique et Conventions: Etat des Lieux', in J Commaille and B Jobert (eds), *Les Metamorphoses de la Regulation Politique* (Paris, Librairie Générale de Droit et de Jurisprudence).

Part IV

Transnational Self-Governance in Perspective

11

Regulatory Networks and Multi-Level Global Governance

SOL PICCIOTTO

THE CENTRAL THEME of this chapter is that private economic regulation is not a matter of autonomous self-organisation, nor is it purely private. The privatisation of state-owned assets and the reduction of direct state economic intervention have not led to a reduced role for the state but to changes in its form, involving new types of formalised regulation, the fragmentation of the public sphere, the decentring of the state and the emergence of multi-level governance. This has been complemented by the increased salience of 'private' regulation, so that in many ways the apparently private sphere of economic activity has become more public. In fact, there has been a complex process of interaction with a blurring of the divisions between apparently private and public regulation. Despite talk of deregulation there has been extensive reregulation, or formalisation of regulation, and the emergence of global regulatory networks, intermingling the public and the private. The transition from government to governance means a lack of a clear hierarchy of norms, a blurring of distinctions between hard and soft law, and a fragmentation of public functions entailing a resurgence of technocracy. The increasingly important role for regulation in global governance undermines the formalist view of law's legitimacy as deriving from national state political structures, and requires new approaches to articulating normative interactions that are more conducive to democratic deliberation, in order to establish the public interest firmly as the prime concern in all forms of management of economic activity.

I. INTRODUCTION: FROM GOVERNMENT TO GOVERNANCE

The term 'governance' has come into increased use, generally to describe changes in governing processes from hierarchy to polyarchy. In international relations theory, it denotes the management of world affairs in the absence of a global government (Rosenau and Czempiel, 1992), hence the term 'global governance' has become commonplace. For theorists of the state it refers to the 'hollowing out' of the unitary state, or the decentring of government, and the shift to 'governing without government' (Rhodes, 1997).

Two interrelated processes seem to have been involved, over the past 30 years. First, there have been major changes in both the political or 'public' sphere of the state and the 'private' sphere of firms, industry, and other social institutions, as well as in the relationships between the two.

The most visible aspect has been the privatisation of much of what was previously regarded as the public or political sphere, resulting from the sale of state-owned firms and assets, the introduction of contracting into public arenas, and the delegation of a range of activities (from waste disposal to the running of prisons) to service providers. Conversely, however, there has been a parallel and complementary trend, much less noticed or analysed, in which the apparently 'private' sphere of economic activity has become more public. The corporations and business networks which dominate the so-called 'market', even as they urge a reduction in intrusive state controls, find their activities governed by an increasing plethora of various types of regulation. Indeed, the biggest paradox has been the growth of industry and corporate codes of conduct, the private sector adopting public standards for itself, although this has generally been in response to pressures from their customers, workers, and suppliers, and sometimes in order to forestall the imposition of legal obligations (Haufler, 2001; Picciotto, 2003).

The second and interrelated process has entailed transformations in the international coordination of governance. In the classical liberal model of the international system, states were recognised as interdependent, but coordination was primarily through governments, which had exclusive legitimate powers internally, and were allowed considerable scope to decide how to use those powers to fulfil their international obligations. In this system, national law was the primary form of governing private economic activity, and governments managed the national economy to a great extent by controlling cross-border flows of money and commodities. However, as the demands on government have become greater, national economic management has become more difficult and complex. International economic liberalisation since the mid 1970s has entailed the substantial removal of border barriers (tariffs and currency controls), greatly reinforcing the movement towards deeper international economic integration. But this shift towards more 'open' national economies did not create a unified and free world market. Instead, like an outgoing tide, it revealed a craggy landscape of diverse national and local regulations. Trying to deal with these differences has generated an exponential growth of networks of regulatory cooperation, coordination, and harmonisation. These are no longer primarily of an international character, but also supranational and infranational, frequently by-passing central government. They also reflect and reinforce changing public–private forms, since these regulatory networks are very often neither clearly state nor private but of a hybrid nature. Indeed, a major reason for the growth of corporate and industry codes has been concerns that state-based regulation is ineffective and leaves too many gaps (Haufler, 2001: 114–15).

Thus, there has been a movement from the classical liberal international state system towards one that is often denounced as neo-liberal, but is perhaps better described as post-liberal. The next section will sketch out some of the main elements of these changes. The third section will analyse three main problematic features of the new landscape: the destabilisation of normative hierarchies, the blurring of distinctions between normative forms, and the political problems caused by the fragmentation of statehood accompanied by the growth of technocratic governance. The final section will consider the role of the law and lawyers in managing global regulatory networks, based on a brief overview of some of the main recent theoretical contributions to this question.

II. DILEMMAS OF THE POST-LIBERAL STATE SYSTEM

A. Changing Public–Private Forms and Relations

The thrust of privatisation since the 1980s, led in Europe by the United Kingdom followed by others such as Germany and France, entailed the withdrawal of States from direct involvement in economic activity, in particular by sales of state-owned firms and assets. Privatisation appeared to be part of a wider move away from state-centred direction of the economy, especially as it was powered by anti-statist ideas and accompanied by much talk of deregulation and free markets. There were indeed pressures and proposals to restructure administrative arrangements in many States, aiming to dismantle state intervention. In practice, however, privatisation often tended to produce little if any reduction of state activity, but instead changes in its form, with a shift to indirect provision of services within a regulatory framework (Feigenbaum *et al*, 1998; Prosser, 2000).

At the same time, as many authors have argued, the character of regulation has significantly changed, away from the top-down hierarchical model of state command, towards more fluid, often fragmented, and interactive or 'reflexive' processes (Ayres and Braithwaite, 1992; Scott, 2001; Parker, 2002; Jordana and Levi-Faur, 2004). This involves a mixture of legal forms, both public and private, and an interplay between state and private ordering (Ayres and Braithwaite, 1992). Thus, a private legal form such as contract can be used as a tool to achieve both managerial and policy objectives, either when private firms are entrusted to deliver public services, such as refuse collection or hospital cleaning (Vincent-Jones, 1998), or even entirely within the public sector if quasi-markets are introduced (Vincent-Jones, 1999). This is not to say that such adaptations are always successful. Contracts provide flexibility, but private contract law does not easily accommodate and may undermine the public interest safeguards developed by public or administrative law, for example by shielding service providers from public accountability, perhaps even from legislative changes, and from liability to intended beneficiaries who are not parties to the service contract (Collins, 1999; Freeman, 2000). On the other hand, public bureaucracies find it hard to achieve genuine responsiveness to individual citizens, although they have tried to do so by adopting a managerial culture of service delivery (corporate plans, customer charters, performance targets, etc).

Furthermore, the increased demands being made on the state have resulted in its fragmentation, as regulatory functions have increasingly been delegated to public bodies or agencies with a status semi-autonomous from central government. Such entities are generally not formally part of the government, and may be constituted as private organisations (Aquina and Bekke, in Kooiman, 1992), with a mandate either laid down by public law or by private legal forms such as contract, or a mixture of the two. They themselves may deploy a greater variety of forms and techniques of regulation. In the United States, which had almost no state ownership and a long tradition of regulation by independent agencies, there was criticism of 'command and control' forms of regulation for being excessively legalistic and adversarial (Bardach and Kagan, 1982), leading to new debates and theories about regulation and its design (for example, Noll, 1985). This has spread to other countries (notably Australia), and generated debates about new approaches to 'smart regulation' (Gunningham and Grabovsky, 1998). These build on the seminal work of Ayres and Braithwaite, who argued that business regulation should be viewed as an interactive process, involving both firms themselves and civil society actors, with the 'big stick' of the state being kept very much in reserve (Ayres and Braithwaite, 1992).

Indeed, from this broader perspective of regulation it can be seen that 'private' economic actors also may take on a regulatory role. As Colin Scott has pointed out, this may result from the state adopting a policy of 'deregulation', leaving a void which may be filled by a non-state actor: he cites an official inquiry into New Zealand's telecommunications regime which concluded that 'in the absence of state authority, the privatized company, Telecom New Zealand, had, in effect, become the regulator of the market' (Scott, 2001: 337). Thus, private bodies may themselves assume tasks which are of a public character, or entail provision of 'public goods'. The role of private entities may even extend to controlling public as well as private activities, for example bond rating agencies, and technical standards compliance certification (Scott, 2002).

B. Deregulation, Reregulation, and Formalisation

Thus, the so-called 'retreat of the state' left a gap which was quickly filled by new institutions and techniques of regulation. In place of administration based on social ties within closed corporate-state bureaucracies, new types of formalised regulation have emerged. These developments were seen as a shift from the Keynesian welfare state to a 'new regulatory state' better able to deal with the 'risk society' (Braithwaite, 2000). Thus, the state, having failed to deliver on expectations raised by state-centric models, now has a new role of trying to maintain coherence via steering, since roles previously considered as those of government have been recast as societal problems concerning a variety of actors (Pierre, 2000). Influential ideologists have argued for a redefinition of the role of government, to separate 'steering' from 'rowing': politicians should define aims and targets but subcontract delivery, which should be competitive and aim to meet the needs of customers (Osborne and Gabler, 1992). More critically, followers of Foucault have argued that the state is a 'mythical abstraction', without either the unity or functionality attributed to it, and suggested a broader understanding of 'governmentality' as involving 'a proliferation of a whole range of apparatuses pertaining to government and a complex body of knowledges and "know-how" about government' (Rose and Miller, 1992: 175). In this light, the shift from welfarism to neo-liberalism means, according to Rose and Miller, that 'private enterprise is opened, in so many ways, to the action at a distance mechanisms that have proliferated in advanced liberal democracies, with the rise of managers as an intermediary between expert knowledge, economic policy and business decisions' (*ibid*: 200).

More broadly, the shift towards new forms of governance may be seen as rooted in the transition from the 'Fordist' model of industrial capitalism, to a post-industrial knowledge economy and learning society. In many ways this entails new processes of socialisation of economic activity and decommodification, as valorisation involves far more than the sale of physical commodities. Thus, there has been a shift to 'lifestyle' products and the 'services' economy. At the same time, this has entailed pressures towards recommodification, as seen in the very concept of the sale of 'services', as well as the increased emphasis on intangible property, or intellectual property rights (IPRs), ranging through trademarks, copyright, patents, and confidential information. While this recommodification and re-individualisation may re-establish the conditions for production and circulation based on exchange, it also requires dense institutional networks to manage the flows of information and remuneration. These institutions and networks are generally of a hybrid public–private character, for example the Rights Remuneration Organisations (RROs) that license the public playing of music.

The emergence of a multiplicity of forms of regulation, and the constant variation and adaptation of, and experimentation with them, may be seen to reflect the basic modernist dilemma of attempting to govern an increasingly complex lifeworld. This is the conclusion of Michael Moran's study of the emergence of the new British regulatory state, which he describes as a roller-coaster ride of hyper-innovation and policy disasters, 'from stagnation to fiasco' (Moran, 2003: 155*ff*). He analyses in detail the sharp transition from the stagnating traditional British system of government which he characterises as 'club rule', developed in the nineteenth century essentially 'to protect elites from democratic threats' (*ibid*: 41). This culture of cooperation resting on the gentlemanly ideal legitimised a high degree of independence from state control, based on self-regulation throughout the world of corporate business, banking and finance, and the professions, which became institutionally embedded in 1880–1918, and endured for two thirds of the twentieth century. However, the class compromises which underpinned this system were weakened by the end of empire and the collapse of social cultures of deference to authority in the 1960s; its transformation was then precipitated by the economic crisis of the 1970s and the ensuing renewed burst of globalisation.

Thus, the British story, convincingly analysed by Moran, is one of the transformation of closed communities of self-regulation, in which privatisation and the reduction of direct state management have been counterpointed by a strong shift to the formalisation and codification of regulation. His trenchant analysis of privatisation argues that the new forms of management of infrastructure services emerged due to the exhaustion both of the traditional modes of public operation and of the regulation of private corporations, neither of which provided adequate accountability of managers. Government nevertheless stumbled into and through privatisation. Some form of regulation was clearly needed since the utilities were monopolies, but the Office of Fair Trading (the competition authority) found the task too daunting, and the US regulatory commission model of 'juridified constitutionalism' was rejected as unduly bureaucratic. Resistance to change ensured the persistence of many elements of the club model, and the individual regulators were initially given broad discretion with little public accountability, shielded from politics behind their status as experts. However, this 'expert' decision-making depended on access to information, which the industry managers could control and contest, resulting in conflicts which inevitably became politicised.

This has led to an increasingly formalised regulatory system, with a fragmented but loosely coordinated epistemic community of regulators, whose mainly private negotiations with corporate managers are periodically brought to public attention by a drama or crisis. It has proved very difficult to design an adequate institutional framework enabling public debate of key issues such as the extent of public service obligations and the proper scope of competition, due to the substantial reliance on technocratic legitimation. In telecommunications the public regulator has been criticised for slowness in requiring the privatised telephone company BT to give its competitors access to its fixed-line network. In the case of the railways, the public regulator/private operator split broke down due to the crisis over safety standards dramatised by successive rail crashes in 2000–01, leading to the establishment of a new type of body in Network Rail. This is a 'public interest company' supposed to 'operate on a sound commercial basis' with, instead of shareholders, members representing both the rail industry and the public interest (Darling, 2002). Postal services are regulated by the Postal Services Commission, which tries to maintain a balance between the Royal Mail (still state-owned) and private operators, through licensing, price controls, quality standards, and network access obligations.

C. Global Regulatory Networks

As Moran also emphasises, the difficulties facing the transformation of the British state have been exacerbated since it also resulted from the pressures of renewed globalisation. Thus, the very machine which was used to push through the drastic restructurings, the strong parliamentary central government, was itself becoming 'hollowed out', with the transfer of significant powers upwards to Brussels, and downwards to Edinburgh and Cardiff. Similarly in other countries, various types of national corporate-state arrangements have also been undermined, although they have followed different trajectories. The relatively formal neo-corporatist institutions which in some countries, especially in continental Europe, tied governments, business, and trade unions together in bargaining over wage rates and macroeconomic policy could not easily be maintained in a more competitive and fluid world economy.

The attempt to recreate institutions to represent 'organised interests' at the regional level in Europe also failed (Schmitter and Streek, 1991; Greenwood *et al*, 1992). Instead, the EU has evolved into a paradigm of networked governance. From the 1980s, the earlier impetus to supranationalism and integration gave way to the 'new approach' to harmonisation of technical regulations (Joerges, 1990; Dehousse, 1992; Woolcock, 1996). This aimed to reduce the role of European legislation to the setting of minimum essential requirements, based as far as possible on performance, leaving it to technical organisations (public, private, or hybrid, but anyway usually dominated by industry experts) to specify detailed standards. To complement this, the European Court of Justice developed the principles of mutual recognition and equivalence of standards, to prevent national regulations from acting as a barrier to imports. Nevertheless, the management of the complex interaction of regulation has spawned the growth of comitology (Joerges and Vos, 1999), leading to what has been described as the networked state (Castells, 1998) or networked governance (Kohler-Koch and Eising, 1999).

Hence, as suggested at the beginning of this section, the changes in the public and private spheres and in their interaction also have an international dimension. Economic liberalisation has further exacerbated the pressures on the political sphere, which have led to its increased fragmentation and the growth of new regulatory forms. Indeed, the new types of hybrid public–private regulatory networks often develop in response to the need to govern economic activities that are increasingly internationally integrated and yet take place in very dispersed and diverse geographic and cultural contexts.

Indeed, public functions may more easily be provided in the global sphere by private bodies. They nevertheless face the dual difficulties of partiality towards specific private interests and power-political interference by governments. Two paradigmatic instances may serve as illustrations: international financial markets, and the internet.

The liberalisation of financial flows has certainly created an internationally integrated financial system, but it consists of a maze of networks involving banks and other financial firms, organisations such as exchanges and clearing houses, specialist traders of many kinds, and professionals such as lawyers, with both private associations and public bodies playing regulatory and supervisory roles. Financial markets and transactions are in fact highly regulated, but a large amount of this regulation is generated by and among market participants themselves (Abolafia, 1985). For example, the terms of complex transactions in financial derivatives are governed by the standard agreements drawn up by the International Swaps and Derivatives Association (ISDA).[1] Perhaps better known is the important role of rating agencies such as Moody's and Standard & Poors in evaluating the creditworthiness of bond issuers, not only private firms but governments (Sinclair, 1999).[2]

Of course, such private regulation is not autonomous, but intersects with more public forms of supervision and control. However, as Tony Porter has argued, international public institutional arrangements have generally been developed only when private governance is absent or weak (Porter, 1993).[3] Even then, it often takes the form of 'meta-regulation', or the supervision of the adequacy of private regulation.[4] Thus, for example, the capital adequacy standards developed by the Basel Committee on Banking Supervision (BCBS) have been refined in the so-called Basel II Capital

[1] See www.isda.org.

[2] A good example of private regulation of the public analysed by Scott (2002), as discussed above.

[3] This is the reverse side of Colin Scott's point, referred to above, that private governance may emerge when the state retreats.

[4] The term 'meta-regulation' has been applied to national state laws which lay down overarching requirements or standards (for example, for environmental protection) with which more specific industry or corporate codes are expected to comply (Gunningham and Grabosky, 1998; Parker, 2002). This term has been extended to describe the 'disciplines' laid down by WTO law on national states by Bronwen Morgan (2003), who has described WTO rules as 'global meta-regulation', or rules prescribing how States should regulate.

Adequacy Framework which is now being introduced. The BCBS still maintains its basic rule of an 8 per cent ratio of capital to risk-weighted assets, as well as its general standards on definition of capital. However, the new approach in Basel II allows each bank to decide its own risk management system (generally based on well-known models), provided it meets specified minimum requirements, and subject to review by the local supervisor of the bank's systems and controls (BCBS, 2005: 2). Thus, the BCBS essentially acts as a node of coordination in a network of public–private regulatory arrangements.

Like financial markets, the internet, although highly decentralised and apparently anarchic, is in fact a highly ordered system. Also in somewhat similar fashion to finance, the development of the internet has been substantially driven by the formulation of norms and standards by non-official groups, networks, and institutions.[5] Probably most successful has been the Internet Engineering Task Force (IETF), which has been responsible for developing the technical standards that enable the internet to function and grow. The IETF itself developed in an entirely unplanned way, as a network of specialists, who evolved very non-bureaucratic methods of cooperation, based on principles which later became clarified as: open process, volunteer participation, technical competence, consensual and practical decision-making, and responsibility.[6]

Of course, this work has been greatly facilitated because its subject-matter is specialist and the participants may be said to share a common commitment and understandings and hence form an 'epistemic community' (Haas, 1992). However, as Michael Froomkin points out in his fascinating analysis of the IETF and internet regulation (Froomkin, 2003), the commitment of the IETF community is not to a closed apolitical technicist task, but to the much broader normative value of ubiquitous global communication (*ibid*: 810–11). He contrasts the IETF with another key body, ICANN (the Internet Corporation for Assigned Names and Numbers). ICANN was also set up as a private entity, although at the suggestion of the US government, to take over from the IETF the task of managing internet domain names, and it claimed to model its procedures on those of the IETF. However, Froomkin demonstrates that in practice ICANN's methods have been closed and secretive rather than open, and its decisions made by fiat rather than consensus (*ibid*: 838*ff*, especially 852–3), resulting in severe legitimation problems. This he attributes to the greater political and especially economic contentiousness of the subject-matter, as well as ICANN's institutional design failures.

[5] Even though, as is well known, the internet began as a US military project: for further details see Leiner *et al*, 2003.

[6] See 'A Mission Statement for the IETF', Request for Comments 3935, October 2004, (http://www.ietf.org/rfc/rfc3935.txt, accessed 15 February 2005).

III. REGULATORY INTERACTIONS IN MULTI-LAYERED NETWORK GOVERNANCE

The previous section has sketched out the tensions in the classical liberal state system which have led to its fragmentation, involving both changes in the nature and interaction of the private and public, and the shift towards networked international coordination. This section will look more closely at three major features of these international regulatory networks.

A. The Destabilisation of Regulatory Hierarchy

The 'network' metaphor attempts to capture this central feature of governance, which distinguishes the post-liberal from the classical liberal system. In the latter, legal rules fell into relatively clear categories and hierarchies, with international law binding states, and national or local law governing legal persons. This made it possible, at least in principle, to determine the validity of rules and to decide which should apply to a particular transaction or activity. In networked governance, the determination of the legitimacy of an activity under any one system of norms is rarely definitive; it can usually be challenged by reference to another system. Indeed, normative systems overlap and interpenetrate. Also, the fragmentation of the public sphere sometimes involves the creation of largely private arenas to which only the more privileged or powerful economic actors have access, resulting in a kind of privatisation of justice.

Thus, international law now includes supranational law, which may have direct applicability to legal persons. However, this possibility is not definitive, since the interaction is often indeterminate or problematic. The most developed supranational law is EC law, which was greatly expanded by the European Court of Justice's development of the jurisprudence of 'direct effect' of some treaty provisions and Directives (which formally are addressed to States not legal persons). Yet managing these interactions depends on accommodations between the national-level authorities and courts and those at the EU level, as shown, for example, in the German Constitutional Court's reservation of Kompetenz-Kompetenz (the ultimate right to determine the jurisdictional validity of EU as against national law) in its famous *Maastrichturteil* (MacCormick, 1995; Weiler, 1995). Importantly, the supranational character of EC law gives private parties (especially firms) a legal basis to challenge national laws and administrative practices which might limit the market freedoms enshrined in EC law.

Supranational law is much less developed globally, at least from the formal viewpoint. Notably, States have taken care to insist that WTO law does not have direct applicability as part of national law.[7] Nevertheless, the WTO's rules impose sweeping obligations (or, in WTO-speak, 'disciplines') with which national measures must comply. This compliance is ensured both by elaborate monitoring procedures through the WTO's committees, and in the final resort by binding adjudication through the WTO's powerful dispute-settlement procedure. Although this is formally a state–state procedure, the two most powerful trade blocs have established procedures to give (some) private entities procedural rights to invoke WTO law at national level: in the United States under section 301 of the Trade Act, and in the EC under the Trade Barrier Regulation. These create what has been described as a system of public–private partnerships, so that 'WTO law, while formally a domain of *public* international law, profits and prejudices *private* parties' (Shaffer, 2003: 3).

An even starker example of the carving-out of a specific and privileged jurisdictional arena is provided by international investment or market liberalisation agreements.[8] These give 'investors' (essentially transnational corporations, TNCs) a direct right of access to international arbitration if they consider that national laws or administration have contravened the broad non-discrimination and property protection provisions of the treaty. This basically enables the private rights of a legal person to be used to challenge the public policy decisions of government and state bodies, using secretive procedures modelled on private commercial arbitration. The effect is to destabilise the legitimacy of national laws, even if the outcomes of such arbitrations rarely override national law in any definitive way. The threat of such a claim, which could lead to an award which may run to hundreds of millions of dollars, as well as the cost of defending it, gives foreign investors a powerful weapon especially against poor States.[9] This grant by States

[7] The WTO Agreement, Art XVI.4, requires each Member State 'to ensure the conformity of its laws, regulations and administrative procedures with its [WTO] obligations'. However, WTO rules are not generally considered to be 'supranational', ie to have direct effect as national law (Matsushita *et al*, ch 5).

[8] The main type are Bilateral Investment Agreements (BITs), which have been used since 1959, but have developed into a much more widespread network since the 1990s (UNCTAD, 2000). The North American Free Trade Agreement (NAFTA), a multilateral agreement between Canada, Mexico, and the United States, includes a strong version of such a treaty as its Ch XI. An attempt to negotiate an ambitious Multilateral Agreement on Investment (MAI) through the OECD collapsed in 1998 (Picciotto and Mayne, 1999).

[9] From 1987 to the end of 2005 some 219 such cases are reported to have been formally initiated, although the number is likely to be understated since there is no obligation to publish complaints. Over 40 of these have been against Argentina, mostly claiming compensation for losses resulting from its decision to abandon the link of the peso with the dollar; so far one of these has been successful, resulting in an award of $133m, although the Argentine government is attempting to block the award (UNCTAD, 2005). On the other hand, a private tribunal rejected a $970m claim brought against the United States by Methanex, a Canadian company, alleging that Californian gasoline regulations discriminated against methanol, which it produced. Cases may be affected by political controversy: for example, Aguas del Tunari, a majority

to private parties of a right to international arbitration acts in effect as a governance mechanism, in which private rights, enforced by an extension of the private procedure of commercial arbitration, may override formal state law (Van Harten, 2007).

There has also been a growth of what may be called infra-state regulation, legal and quasi-legal regulatory arrangements, involving both public and private, as well as hybrid, bodies. For example, tax authorities in the main OECD countries have developed procedures for the coordination of taxation of related members of corporate groups (TNCs). These operate under provisions in bilateral tax treaties which authorise information exchange, as well as consultations between the 'competent authorities', for the purposes of ensuring that taxation is in accordance with the treaty. These procedures enable international consultations between the two (or sometimes more) tax authorities and the TNC (or its advisers, usually the large accountancy firms), in particular to debate and negotiate the methodology each firm uses for setting transfer prices for goods and services supplied between its constituent parts. Agreements between the competent authorities, which may relate to individual cases or to more general issues of interpretation of the treaty, have an ambiguous legal status: they may be treated as no more than a statement of intent by and between administrative authorities, although a good argument can be made that they are binding international agreements (Picciotto, 1992: 297–9). They clearly have a very hybrid character, with elements of public and private, national and international law.

A major destabilising factor is the creation of jurisdictions of convenience or 'havens'. These entail a kind of privatisation of sovereignty (Palan, 2002), in which a legal enclave offering privileges for certain types of private business is created, often designed by lawyers acting as intermediaries between government and private interests. These aim to provide the beneficiaries with a legal refuge or protection from the laws of other states, without needing to relocate in any real sense since they can use the legal fictions of corporations or trusts. Thus, 'flags of convenience', which originated in

foreign-owned firm which had been awarded a concession to run privatised water services in Cochabamba, Bolivia, brought a claim for compensation for cancellation of the concession due to strong local opposition to the privatisation and the consequent sharp increases in water charges; in January 2006 the claim was reported to have been withdrawn, although the firm had won the initial jurisdictional stage of the dispute. This was a controversial decision, since by a 2:1 majority the tribunal accepted that the complaint could be brought under the Bolivia–Netherlands investment treaty, even though the main investor was the US firm Bechtel, which created a Netherlands holding company as part of a financial restructuring and for tax reasons following the grant of the concession. This decision, in common with others brought through the World Bank's International Centre for the Settlement of Investment Disputes (ICSID) can be found at http://www.worldbank.org/icsid/cases/. An excellent source is *Investment Treaty News* produced by the International Institute for Sustainable Development (IISD), available at http://www.iisd.org/investment/itn/.

the 1920s to avoid US liquor prohibition laws, have enabled a large proportion of international shipping to avoid many types of regulation (especially taxation), and to choose the jurisdiction they consider most favourable. The flag states essentially offer a ship registration service, the administration of which may have little or no physical contact with the state itself, being subcontracted to private firms. Notably, the Liberian International Ship and Corporate Registry is run from Vienna, Virginia, USA, which made it possible to continue operation uninterrupted, despite the turbulence and civil war in Liberia which incapacitated the government of that country for a long period. The actual surveys and the issuing of safety certificates for ships are done by recognised private classification societies, including the American Bureau of Shipping and Lloyd's Register of Shipping.[10]

Due to long-standing concerns about the safety standards of such 'open registries', led by a long-running campaign by the International Transport Federation (ITF) of trade unions, regulatory networks have emerged to try to deal with low-standard ships and registries, or 'flags of convenience'. A key development has been cooperation between the maritime authorities of Port States. They now deploy sophisticated inspection systems, based on checklists of internationally agreed standards, deficiency reporting, a computerised database, and the possibility of detention.[11] Thus, the seaworthiness and employment conditions of ships are governed by a variety of regulatory bodies, both public and private, national and international. None of them have definitive jurisdiction, although port authorities can apply the ultimate sanction of detention (Couper *et al*, 1999; Gerstenberger, 2002).

As these examples show, networked governance disrupts the channels of democratic accountability, which in the classical liberal system are through national constitutional structures, ideally parliamentary representative democracy. A number of suggestions have been made to help structure global governance arenas in ways that can facilitate democratic deliberation, insulated as far as possible from private or special interests, and based on principles of accountability, transparency, responsibility, and above all empowerment (Picciotto, 2001). This does not mean abandoning existing democratic structures, but suggests that they must be complemented by ensuring transparency and accountability of all arenas and actors playing a regulatory role.

[10] See http://www.liscr.com/. Ten such bodies have formed the International Association of Classification Societies (IACS), which in December 2005 adopted a set of Common Structural Rules for ship classification and approval: see http://www.iacs.org.uk/csr/index.html.

[11] The first was established by 20 maritime authorities covering Europe and the North Atlantic, based on the Paris MOU (Memorandum of Understanding): for details see http://www.parismou.org. This has been followed by Asia–Pacific, Caribbean, and Latin American groups.

B. The Blurring of Distinctions between Normative Forms

A corollary of the erosion of the hierarchical norm structure of classical liberalism has been both the erosion of the public–private law distinction (discussed earlier), and a shift from formal law to quasi-legal forms of regulation in global arenas. These are generally referred to as 'soft law', as opposed to formal 'hard law', and include a wide range of types, such as codes, guidelines, declarations, sets of principles, and memorandums of understanding (MOUs).[12] Although not binding law, in practice they often have considerable normative force, as much or more than does 'hard' international law, which in any case mainly relies on consensual rather than coerced compliance.

Such soft law forms may be used in interstate agreements, which often take the form of declarations or 'proclamations', for example the principles of sustainable development, announced at the conclusion of major international conferences from Stockholm in 1972, to Rio de Janeiro in 1992, and Johannesburg in 2002. From a formal lawyer's viewpoint they may seem to consist of no more than fine-sounding rhetoric. However, they are linked to action programmes (in particular 'Agenda 21', adopted at Rio), and their principles may be given substantive effect,[13] or lead to more specific hard law instruments.[14] Sometimes, this type of instrument is chosen to emphasise the aspirational character of the norms, as with the ILO's 1998 Declaration on Fundamental Principles and Rights at Work, the adoption of which was strongly resisted by the governments of some developing countries. Its impact therefore greatly depends on the effectiveness of the procedures for encouraging and monitoring compliance (Hepple, 1999). These may be quite rigorous: for example the implementation of the Recommendations of the Financial Action Task Force (FATF) has been very closely monitored, through 'peer review' procedures, and 'naming and shaming' jurisdictions which fail to meet the standards.

Second, codes and guidelines have been developed since the late 1960s to establish standards at the international level addressed directly to firms. Here again, a non-binding form is often deliberately chosen, yet the implementation in practice could be rigorous (although often has not been), and could involve adoption or transformation of the soft law norms into hard law. For example, the Baby-Milk Marketing Code adopted as a Recommendation by the WHO in 1981 has been used as a basis for national legislation in a number of countries, although the main pressure

12 See generally Shelton, 2000.

13 Thus, the Appellate Body of the WTO, in its important decision in the *Shrimp-Turtle* case (1998), in interpreting the provisions of the WTO agreements, took account of the reference to the principle of sustainable development and to the Rio Declaration and Agenda 21 in the WTO Agreement and the WTO Council's Decision on Trade and Environment.

14 For example, the Montreal Protocol on Substances Depleting the Ozone Layer, and the Convention on Biological Diversity.

for compliance has come from a sustained and vigorous international campaign.[15] In the 1990s, following a decade or more of pressures by business on States to reduce regulation and dismantle barriers to market access, TNCs themselves began to introduce corporate codes of conduct in order to reassure customers and other stakeholders of their adherence to international standards of social and environmental responsibility (Haufler, 2001; Jenkins *et al*, 2002). Firms have generally preferred 'voluntary' codes, stressing the need for flexibility to adapt the norms to the specific characteristics of the business, and the desirability of raising standards by encouragement and self-generated commitment, as opposed to the rigidity and instrumentalism of externally imposed and bureaucratically enforced law. Corporate critics and sceptics have countered by challenging the effectiveness of self-selected and self-monitored standards, and have argued that competitive equality requires generally applicable rules rather than self-selected codes. However, on closer examination it becomes clear that the sharp distinction between voluntary codes and binding law is inaccurate: codes entail a degree of formalisation of normative expectations and practices, and may be linked to formal law, both public and private, in various complex ways which may be described as a 'tangled web' (Webb and Morrison, 2004), so the question is how they should be articulated (Picciotto, 2003).

Finally, the growth of international regulatory networks linking public bodies at 'sub-state' level has involved the use of novel forms of agreement, especially the MOU. These are often very specific and establish detailed arrangements: for example, there is a network of MOUs between regulators of financial markets and exchanges for cooperation in information exchange and other enforcement activities.[16] These also may be stated to be 'non-binding' although in practice compliance may be very effective. In this case, the formally non-binding character is because it is often not clear whether they fall under national or international, public or private law. Under international law, sub-state or non-state bodies are not considered to have the capacity to bind the state or government concerned.[17] In some

15 A key role has been played by the International Baby Food Action Network (IBFAN) which is a grassroots-based non-governmental organisation (NGO), although it has received substantial support from UNICEF. Details on the monitoring of compliance with the Code may be found on its website (www.ibfan.org). The early history of this Code was recounted by Chetley, 1986, and a more recent account of corporate codes which deals with it in detail is Richter, 2001.

16 These grew on a bilateral basis in the 1980s, but became coordinated through the International Organization of Securities Commissions (IOSCO), in which the public supervisory authorities agreed the Boca Declaration of 1996, which is intended to augment the MOUs agreed between the (private) exchanges themselves; the Boca Declaration and the lists of MOUs between supervisory authorities are available on the IOSCO website (http://www.iosco.org/library/index.cfm?section=mou).

17 As noted in a leading text on the law of treaties (McNair, 1961: 21), the proliferation of agreements between subordinate state agencies, and the great variation in the relationship of such bodies to the central government, makes it hard to determine when such an agreement could be considered to be internationally binding.

cases they may be regarded simply as 'private' contracts, if the parties are legal persons: for example, agreements between stock exchanges or futures markets to enable reciprocal trading of products or cooperate in market monitoring and enforcement. Yet they may have a very hybrid character, as with the international tax 'competent authority agreements' discussed above. Equally, agreements which take the form of private contracts may be more appropriately regarded as quasi-public, such as the international construction contracts analysed by Oren Perez (Perez, 2002, 2004).

Generally, the growth of soft law and the blurring of the public–private law divide indicates that the range and depth of international normative coordination no longer fits within the classical liberal model of agreements negotiated by central governments on behalf of States (Reinicke and Witt, 2000). Soft law allows regulatory regimes to be developed and applied directly by those involved, rather than through diplomatic channels and foreign offices,[18] and for them to involve a wider range of participants regardless of their formal status as state, public, or private entities. Soft law is not necessarily fuzzy or vague, it is often specialised and detailed;[19] but it does provide greater flexibility for adaptation to change. Equally, it may be ad hoc or particularistic, and lack independent mechanisms for ensuring and monitoring compliance.

C. Functional Fragmentation, Technicisation, and Legitimacy

The fragmentation of statehood and the transfer of specific functions to relatively autonomous public bodies is also a further extension of the process of technicisation in the modern state. In the traditional Weberian perspective, technocracy is seen as a means merely of implementing policies which have been formulated through political processes. From this viewpoint, the growth of delegation to specialist regulators is a response to the problems of governing increasingly complex societies, by giving greater autonomy to technocratic decision-makers within a policy framework set by government. However, the new forms of governance are more decentralised and interactive, which further exacerbates the legitimacy problems which Weber already identified with the 'iron cage' of bureaucracy when it loses its accountability to social values.

Indeed, functional fragmentation may also be seen as reflecting the broader changes in the nature and relationship of the 'public' and the 'private' sphere which we have been discussing. The transfer of specific public

[18] However, foreign offices also recognise the need for soft law such as MOUs, to provide a less formal and more flexible means of dealing with detailed and technical matters, or perhaps to provide confidentiality, for example in defence matters (Aust, 2000: ch 3).

[19] I disagree on this point with Abbott and Snidal (2000), who suggest that soft law tends to be less detailed; this rests on their initial definition of 'legalisation' with which I also disagree (see further below).

functions to what have been described as 'non-majoritarian' regulators (Coen and Thatcher, 2005) is often justified in terms of the need to insulate some areas of decision-making from influence by private special interests and the short-term considerations which dominate electoral politics. Hence, it also reflects changes in political processes, with the breakdown of representative government, which 'public choice' theorists have argued is prone to capture by private interests (Buchanan and Tollison, 1984). In place of party-democracy there has been the emergence of what Bernard Manin has called 'audience democracy' (Manin, 1997), increasingly based on populist forms of political mobilisation. This in turn poses the question of whether the decentralisation or fragmentation of hierarchical government based on formal or instrumental rationality, and the shift to networked governance requiring reflexive interactions and based on communicative rationality, may offer a basis for new forms of deliberative or discursive democracy (Dryzek, 1990, 1999). The changes in public–private interactions discussed above make it vital to find ways to remodel the sphere of political debate and decision-making. Central to this are questions about the nature of technocratic governance and the basis of its legitimacy.

This is especially relevant to global governance, since much of the activity of international regulatory networks has been generated by technical specialists or 'epistemic communities'. This concept was developed within a neo-functionalist paradigm, to suggest that a stronger basis for international cooperation may be provided by delegating specific issues to be dealt with in a depoliticised manner by specialists deploying scientific, managerial, or professional techniques and working within shared universal discourses (Haas, 1992). This concept seemed to maintain the Weberian assumption that broad policy goals should be decided politically, so that the delegation should be of practical details of implementation, facilitating the resolution of global policy issues by 'narrowing the range within which political bargains could be struck' (Haas, 1992: 378). From this perspective governance networks could be said to strengthen the liberal state system, since they simply entail cooperation between government officials, who can be held accountable by citizens through national state mechanisms (Slaughter, 1997).

There is certainly evidence that global expert action networks have been extremely effective in mobilising and sustaining global governance regimes: for example, Canan and Reichman's sociological study of the 'global community' of environmental experts and activists which formed around the Montreal Protocol on Substances Depleting the Ozone Layer (2002). Far from being depoliticised, however, such networks often include activists as well as technical specialists; and even if the issues are specialised, the participants share common social values. This seems to be the case, for example, with the computer scientists of the IETF who have developed and maintained internet standards, discussed above. The contribution of technical specialists to international diplomacy is often to help gain acceptance for proposals which are put forward as objective and scientific, although actually carefully calibrated for political acceptability. Indeed, even some liberals such as Anne-Marie Slaughter now seem to concede that global governance networks do raise some accountability problems, which perhaps require them to operate as 'a kind of disaggregated global democracy based on individual and group self-governance' (Slaughter, 2004: 240).

In this context, the importance of expertise suggests that the dangers of technicism must be addressed. This is especially the case since so many decisions now entail inputs often from different specialist or expert fields, as well as an evaluation from the general public perspective. Technical rationality can operate in an autocratic way, if it seeks to claim a spurious authority. This can be counter-productive, as has been the case in the frequent episodes when it has resulted in a spiral of public mistrust of science, and scientists' despair at public ignorance. To avoid technicism, specialists need to acknowledge the ways in which their techniques rest on formal models based on assumptions which allow them to abstract the specific aspects of an issue or the data with which they are concerned from the entirety and complexity of the issue in the real world. Since the conclusions they can reach based on such assumptions can only have a partial or conditional validity, they should not be treated as determinative of the issue as a whole, but as an important contribution towards more general public debates. Scientific responsibility should therefore include cognitive openness and reflexivity (Dryzek, 1990, 1999).[20]

IV. THE ROLE OF LAW AND LAWYERS IN GLOBAL REGULATORY NETWORKS

The law and lawyers have played a major role in the construction and management of these globalised regulatory networks. However, this has been analysed in very different ways.

One influential group of US commentators have discussed the legalisation of world politics from an essentially Weberian perspective. They assess the extent of legalisation along a spectrum according to three criteria: being based on rules which are regarded as binding, which are precise, and the

[20] Michael Froomkin has provided an interesting account and analysis of the governance of the internet (mentioned earlier), suggesting that the success of the IETF in terms of both efficacy and legitimacy was due largely to its essentially democratic participative procedures, which he argues is an exemplar of Habermasian practical discourse ethics; in contrast, ICANN suffered a legitimation crisis, because its operations were secretive and claimed legitimacy from a rigid corporatist representation system (Froomkin, 2003).

interpretation of which has been delegated to a third party adjudicator (Abbott *et al*, 404–6). This essentially limits law to formal state law, excluding any hybrid or private forms of governance, and has been criticised as taking a narrow view of law (Finnemore and Toope, 2001). As already mentioned above, the view that 'hard' law provides precise rules, while quasi-legal 'soft' law is more vague or imprecise, does not stand up to empirical analysis. For example, financial market regulations discussed above, whether developed by private bodies such as the ISDA or public ones such as the BCBS, are as detailed as any legislation, but they are formally 'soft' law. On the other hand, from the formalist viewpoint, the WTO agreements rate highly as exemplars of legalisation, since they lay down an enormous quantity of formally binding rules, the interpretation of which has been delegated to the WTO's Appellate Body (AB) as an adjudicator. However, the suggestion that these rules are precise and unambiguous is highly dubious, and it can be shown that both the general structure and many of the specific provisions of the WTO agreements raise issues of interpretation which were known to be highly contestable, and indeed were being contested, in the period when the texts were negotiated and agreed (Alter, 2003, Picciotto, 2005). Furthermore, this perspective fails to capture the multiple forms and roles of law in the multi-level system described and analysed above, nor the mode of the interaction.

In contrast, the heterarchical character of regulatory networks has led some theorists to revive concepts of legal pluralism (for example, Snyder, 2000), building on the challenge by earlier versions of legal pluralism to the privileging of state law in the classical liberal paradigm. However, while pluralism may help in drawing attention to the existence and interactions of multiple legal orders, it is prone to the criticism advanced by von Benda-Beckmann that 'talking of intertwining, interaction or mutual constitution presupposes distinguishing what is being intertwined' (cited in Melissaris, 2004: 61).

The most sophisticated and complex attempt to establish a conceptual analysis which incorporates a pluralist approach has been that of Santos (1987, 1995). He distinguishes his perspective from that of traditional legal anthropology which conceived different legal orders as 'separate entities coexisting in the same political space', and cogently argues that: 'We live in a time of porous legality or legal porosity, of multiple networks of legal orders forcing us to constant transitions and trespassings. Our legal life is constituted by an intersection of different legal orders, that is by *interlegality*' (Santos, 1995: 473). He suggests that the new legal pluralism is concerned with 'the identification of the three time-spaces of the legal field—the local, the national, and the transnational' (*ibid*: 117), and uses the metaphor of cartography to suggest that different types of laws are based on different scales, projections, and symbolisations, and that social groups become more adept in the types of action suited to the legal order within which they are predominantly socialised (*ibid*: 465–6). However, his analysis tends to be structural: he conceives of different legal orders as overlapping but mutually exclusive and that 'each legal construction has an internal coherence' (*ibid*: 473), rather than being internally contradictory. In particular, he argues that the new *lex mercatoria* and the proliferation of business and corporate codes constitute 'the emergence of new legal particularisms' which 'create a transnational legal space that often conflicts with national state legal space' (*ibid*: 469). Thus, Santos perhaps does not fully exploit the concepts of porosity and interlegality, nor does he explore how legal techniques can be used strategically, and can help to manage the interactions of different arenas and forms of law.

Analysts of regulation have attempted to capture the characteristics of different layers of regulation and their interaction, notably with the concept of 'meta-regulation', discussed above. This kind of approach to regulatory interactions is based in concepts of responsive or reflexive law. As part of the response to the crises of the welfare state, Nonet and Selznick put forward a new modernist paradigm of responsive law, as an evolution from the repressive and autonomous phases of law, and envisaging regulation as an interactive process of developing methods to realize purposes expressed through law and thereby clarifying the public interest (Nonet and Selznick, 1978/2001). The concept was taken up in regulation theory notably by Ayres and Braithwaite (1992), seeking to reassert a civic republican tradition in which the layers of social institutions, from the state through industry associations and down to individual corporations, play their different parts in social regulation,[21] lubricated by a two-way flow of public discourse.

An alternative analysis was offered by Gunther Teubner, who argued that the emergence of reflexivity in modern law resulted from the 'trilemma' created by the increased legalisation or juridification of the social sphere (Teubner, 1983, 1987). For Teubner it is the autonomy of the legal field that generates its autopoeitic self-referentiality, but the politicisation resulting from increased application of law into social fields creates expectations which require instrumentalisation, perhaps through new forms of self-regulation. The pressure for legal regulation to go beyond the limits possible through the autonomous logics of self-reproduction means that it either lapses into irrelevance, or results in disintegration either of the social field to which it is applied or of the law itself, so that regulatory failure is the rule rather than the exception. More recently Teubner has suggested that new forms of 'global law without a state', of which he instances *lex mercatoria*, have been generated self-referentially, although he argues that

[21] Subtitled *Transcending the Deregulation Debate*, the book sought to reconcile the growth of regulation with a reduced role for the state by arguing for an 'enforcement pyramid' (a concept which Braithwaite has consistently championed across many fields of regulation), in which the state should speak softly and carry a variety of both big and smaller sticks.

their depoliticised origin and apolitical character would not protect them from repoliticisation (Teubner, 1997).

However, the extensive sociological research of Dezalay and Garth demonstrates that the concept of *lex mercatoria* was a strategic move in the competitive struggles between arbitration centres, in which lawyers mediated skilfully between the spheres of political and corporate power to create the new arena of international commercial arbitration (Dezalay and Garth, 1995, 1996). Certainly, the learned doctrine of *lex mercatoria*, backed by the neutral authority of the grand European professors which validated it in the eyes of their disciples in the Third World, helped to provide a 'middle way' in the post-colonial clashes over the scope of state sovereignty, especially concerning the control of oil; but in practice the legal arbitrations were only one strand (and a minor one) in the broader political negotiations (Dezalay and Garth, 1995: 83–91, 313). Rather than creating a purely private legal sphere outside the realm of state law, the two have been deeply entangled, and the authority of law, especially legal concepts of private rights, has been used to counter political notions of state sovereignty in the struggles to reconfigure economic and political power. Thus, as suggested above, it is essential to understand these shifting forms of governance as resulting from strategic moves in contests of power.

A more actor-oriented approach is take by Bourdieu, who criticises the confusion in systems theory between the symbolic structures of the law and the objective orders of the legal and other professional fields, in which agents and institutions compete for the right to formulate the rules, 'le droit de dire le droit' (Bourdieu, 1986). This is perhaps especially valuable in providing a basis for empirical and sociological studies of the actual practices of lawyering, centring on the practices of interpretation of legal texts, which involves the appropriation of the 'symbolic power which is potentially contained within the text', in terms of competitive struggles to 'control' the legal text (Bourdieu, 1987: 818).[22]

I suggest that a clearer understanding of regulatory networks, and of the role of law in them, comes from dislodging positivist and instrumentalist views of law. Legalisation has certainly been an important feature of the management of economic globalisation. Under a formalist view of law, legitimacy is thought to be provided by law because it offers a process for decision-making which is technical–rational: a logical application of precise or unambiguous rules prescribing obligatory conduct, to implement

[22] He suggests that coherence emerges partly through the social organisation of the field, and partly because to succeed competing interpretations must be presented 'as the necessary result of a principled interpretation of unanimously accepted texts' (*ibid*). This explains the apparent paradox that, while lawyers spend much of their time disagreeing about the meaning of texts, they often do so from an objectivist perspective. They generally deny that indeterminacy is inherent, and tend to attribute disagreements to bad drafting and lack of clarity in the texts, which are said to create 'loopholes' in the logical fabric of the law.

politically determined aims (Abbott *et al*, 2000). Yet the interpretation and application of legal rules is not a mechanistic but a flexible process, which allows scope for the overt or covert consideration of social, political, and cultural factors, and adaptation to circumstances.

Law therefore plays a key role in global governance not because of its precision, but its flexibility. This provides a possibility to help to accommodate the diversity of local and national social and cultural particularities to the increasingly globally integrated world market, and to manage conflicts resulting from power disparities (Picciotto, 1997: 266). However, its failures and crises, of which there are many, result from the design failures which attempt to substitute the legitimacy of formal legal rationality for the political and social legitimacy (and efficacity), which can only come from a broader democratic structures.

V. CONCLUSIONS

This chapter has argued that the far-reaching changes in both the sphere of politics and that of the economy have further eroded the distinction between the public and private. The transition to a new form of statehood, described as networked governance, certainly poses new political challenges. However, it would be illusory once again to attempt the separation of public and private. What is needed is to develop modes of interaction which can more effectively ensure the primacy of public over private interests in the management of economic activities generally.

Law has an important part to play, but it should not be regarded as a separate sphere through which public standards are applied to control private interests in otherwise closed arenas. Lawyers operate at the interface between state and market, and play a crucial role in accommodating public concerns to private interests. Lawyering entails interpretive practices which mediate between the public standards and values expressed in the wide variety of norms, and the particular activities and operations of economic actors, offering the hope that economic power should be exercised ultimately for the general good. However, this expectation is illusory unless law operates within a broader democratic framework, in which legal practices themselves are also subject to high standards of transparency, accountability, and responsibility.

REFERENCES

Abbott, K *et al* (2000) 'The Concept of Legalization', 54(3) *International Organization* 401–19.

Abbott, KW and Snidal, D (2000) 'Hard and Soft Law in International Governance', 54(3) *International Organization* 421–56.

Abolafia, MY (1985) 'Self-Regulation as Market Maintenance', in RG Noll (ed), *Regulatory Policy and the Social Sciences* (Berkeley, CA, University of California Press) 312–43.

Alter, KJ (2003) 'Resolving or exacerbating disputes? The WTO's new dispute resolution system', 79(4) *International Affairs* 783–800.
Aquina, H and Bekke, H (1993) 'Governance in Interaction: Public Tasks and Private Organisations', in J Kooiman (ed) *Modern Governance. New Government-Society Interactions* (London, Sage) 159–170.
Aust, A (1986) 'The Theory and Practice of Informal International Agreements', 35 *International and Comparative Law Quarterly* 787.
Ayres, I and Braithwaite, J (1992) *Responsive Regulation. Transcending the Deregulation Debate* (New York, Oxford University Press).
Bardach, E and Kagan, RA (1982) *Going by the book: The problem of regulatory unreasonableness* (Philadelphia, Temple University Press).
BCBS (Basel Committee on Banking Supervision) (2005) 'International Convergence of Capital Measurement and Capital Standards. A Revised Framework', (http://www.bis.org/publ/bcbs118.htm, accessed 15 February 2006).
Bourdieu, P (1986) 'La Force du Droit. Eléments pour une sociologie du champ juridique' 64 (sept) *Actes de la Recherche en Sciences Sociales* 3–19.
—— (1987) 'The Force of Law: Toward a Sociology of the Juridical Field', 38 *Hastings Law Journal* 805.
Braithwaite, J (2000) 'The New Regulatory State and the Transformation of Criminology', 40 *British Journal of Criminology* 222–38.
Buchanan, J and Tollison, RD (1984) *The Theory of Public Choice* (Ann Arbor, MI, University of Michigan Press).
Canan, P and Reichman, N (2002) *Ozone Connections. Expert Networks in Global Environmental Governance* (Sheffield, Greenleaf).
Castells, M (1998) *The Information Age: Economy, Society and Culture* (Malden, MA, Blackwell Publishers).
Chetley, A (1986) *The Politics of Baby Foods. Successful challenges to an international marketing strategy* (London, Pinter).
Coen, D and Thatcher, M (2005) 'The New Governance of Markets and Non-Majoritarian Regulators', 18(3) *Governance* 329–46.
Collins, H (1999) *Regulating Contracts* (Oxford, OUP).
Couper, AD, Walsh, CJ, Stanberry, BA, and Boerne, GL (1999) *Voyages of Abuse. Seafarers, Human Rights and International Shipping* (London, Pluto Press).
Darling, A (2002) 'Statement to Parliament by Transport Secretary, Darling, A, on Network Rail', 27 June (http://www.dft.gov.uk/stellent/groups/dft_railways/documents/pdf/dft_railways_pdf_503197.pdf, accessed 11 April 2006).
Dehousse, R (1992) 'Integration v Regulation? On the Dynamics of Regulation in the European Community', 30(4) *Journal of Common Market Studies* 383–402.
Dezalay, Y and Garth, B (1995) 'Merchants of Law as Moral Entrepreneurs: Constructing International Justice from the Competition for Transnational Business Disputes', 29(1) *Law and Society Review* 27–64.
Dezalay, Y and Bryant G (1996) *Dealing in Virtue. International Commercial Arbitration and the Construction of a Transnational Legal Order* (Chicago, IL: Chicago University Press).
Dryzek, JS (1990) *Discursive Democracy* (Cambridge, Cambridge University Press).
—— (1999) 'Transnational Democracy', 7(1) *Journal of Political Philosophy* 30–51.

Feigenbaum, HB, Henig, JR, and Hamnett, C (1998) *Shrinking the state: The political underpinnings of privatization* (Cambridge, UK/New York, Cambridge University Press).
Finnemore, M and Toope, SJ (2001) 'Alternatives to 'Legalization': Richer Views of Law and Politics', 55(3) *International Organization* 743–58.
Freeman, J (2000) 'The Contracting State', 28 *Florida State University Law Review* 155–214.
Froomkin, AM (2003) 'Habermas@Discourse.Net: Towards a Critical Theory of Cyberspace', 116 (3) *Harvard Law Review* 749–873.
Gerstenberger, H and Welke, U (eds) (2002) *Seefahrt im Zeichen der Globalisierung* (Munster, Westfalisches Dampfboot).
Greenwood, J, Grote, JR, and Ronit, K (eds) (1992) *Organized Interests and the European Community* (London, Sage).
Gunningham, N and Grabovsky, P (1998) *Smart Regulation: Designing Environmental Policy* (Oxford, Clarendon Press).
Haas, PM (1992) 'Introduction: Epistemic Communities and International Policy Coordination', 46(1) *International Organization* (Special Issue on Knowledge, Power and International Policy Coordination) 1–36.
Haufler, V (2001) *A Public Role for the Private Sector. Industry Self-Regulation in a Global Economy* (Washington DC, Carnegie Endowment for International Peace).
Hepple, B (1999) 'A Race to the Top? International Investment Guidelines and Corporate Codes of Conduct', 20(3) *Comparative Labor Law and Policy Journal*) 347–63.
Jenkins, R, Pearson, R and Seyfang, G (eds) (2002) *Corporate Responsibility and Labour Rights* (London, Earthscan).
Joerges, C (1990) 'Paradoxes of Deregulatory Strategies at Community Level: the Example of Product Safety Policy' in G Majone (ed), *Deregulation or Re-regulation? Regulatory Reform in Europe and the United States* (London, Pinter) 176–97.
Joerges, C and Vos, E (eds) (1999) *EU Committees: Social Regulation, Law and Politics* (Oxford, Hart).
Jordana, J, and Levi-Faur, D (eds) (2004) *The Politics of Regulation. Institutions and Regulatory Reforms for the Age of Governance* (Cheltenham, Edward Elgar).
Kohler-Koch, B and Eising, R (eds) (1999) *The Transformation of Governance in the European Union* (London, Routledge).
Leiner, BM et al (2003) 'A Brief History of the Internet', (http://www.isoc.org/internet/history/brief.shtml, accessed 15 January 2006).
MacCormick, N (1995) 'The Maastricht-Urteil: Sovereignty Now', 1(3) *European Law Journal* 259–66.
Manin, B (1997) *The Principles of Representative Government* (Cambridge, Cambridge University Press).
McNair, L (1961) *The Law of Treaties* (Oxford and London: Oxford University Press).
Matsushita, M, Schoenbaum, TJ, and Mavroidis, P (2003) *The World Trade Organization. Law, Practice, and Policy* (Oxford, OUP).
Melissaris, E (2004) 'The More the Merrier? A New Take on Legal Pluralism', 13(1) *Social & Legal Studies* 57–79.

Moran, M (2003) *The British regulatory state: High modernism and hyper-innovation* (Oxford/New York, Oxford University Press).

Morgan, B (2003) 'The Economization of Politics: Meta-Regulation as a Form of Nonjudicial Legality', 12(4) *Social & Legal Studies* 489–523.

Noll, RG (ed) (1985) *Regulatory Policy and the Social Sciences* (Berkeley, CA, University of California Press).

Nonet, P and Selznick, P (1978; 1st edition; 2001, 2nd edition) *Law & society in transition: toward responsive law* (New Brunswick, NJ, Transaction Publishers).

Osborne, D and Gaebler, T (1992) *Reinventing Government. How the Entrepreneurial Spirit is Transforming the Public Sector* (Reading, MA, Addison-Wesley).

Palan, R (2002) 'Tax havens and the commercialization of state sovereignty', 56(1) *International Organization,* 151–76.

Parker, C (2002) *The Open Corporation: Effective Self-regulation and Democracy* (Cambridge, Cambridge University Press).

Perez, O (2002) 'Using Private–Public Linkages to Regulate Environmental Conflicts: The Case of International Construction Contracts', 29(1) *Journal of Law & Society* 77–110.

—— (2004) *Ecological sensitivity and global legal pluralism: Rethinking the trade and environment debate* (Oxford: Hart).

Picciotto, S (1992) *International Business Taxation* (London, Weidenfeld & Nicolson).

—— (1997) 'Fragmented States and International Rules of Law', 6(2) *Social and Legal Studies* 259–279.

—— (2001) 'Democratizing Globalism', in D Drache (ed), *The Market or the Public Domain? Global Governance and the Asymmetry of Power* (London, Routledge) 335–59.

—— (2003) 'Rights, Responsibilities and Regulation of International Business', 42(1) *Columbia Journal of Transnational Law* 131–52.

—— (2005) 'The WTO's Appellate Body: Formalism as a Legitimation of Global Governance' 18(3) *Governance* 477–503.

Picciotto, S and Mayne, R (eds) (1999) *Regulating International Business. Beyond Liberalization* (Basingstoke: Macmillan).

Pierre, J (ed) (2000) *Debating Governance* (Oxford, Oxford University Press).

Porter, T (1993) *States, Markets, and Regimes in Global Finance* (Basingstoke, Macmillan).

Prosser, T (2000) 'Public Service Law: Privatization's Unexpected Offspring', 63 *Law & Contemporary Problems* 63–82.

Reinicke, W and Witte, JM (2000) 'Interdependence, Globalization and Sovereignty: The Role of Non-Binding International Legal Accords', in D Shelton (ed), *Commitment and Compliance. The Role of Non-Binding Norms in the International Legal System* (Oxford, Oxford University Press) 75–100.

Rhodes, RAW (ed) (1997) *Understanding Governance: Policy Networks, Governance, Reflexivity, Accountability* (Milton Keynes, Open University Press).

Richter, J (2001) *Holding Corporations Accountable. Corporate Conduct, International Codes and Citizen Action* (London, Zed Books).

Rose, N and Miller, P (1992) 'Political power beyond the State: problematics of government', 43(2) *British Journal of Sociology* 173–205.

Rosenau, J and Czempiel, E-O (eds) (1992) *Governance without Government* (Cambridge: Cambridge University Press).
Santos, BdS (1987) 'Law, a Map of Misreading: Towards a Postmodern Conception of Law', 14 *Journal of Law & Society* 279–302.
—— (1995) *Toward a New Common Sense. Law, Science and Politics in the Paradigmatic Transition* (London, Routledge).
Schmitter, PC and Streeck, W (1991) 'From National Corporatism to Transnational Pluralism: Organized Interests in the Single European Market', 19(2) *Politics & Society* 133–64.
Scott, C (2001) 'Analysing Regulatory Space: Fragmented Resources and Institutional Design', (Summer) *Public Law* 329–53.
—— (2002) 'Private Regulation of the Public Sector: A Neglected Facet of Contemporary Governance', 29(1) *Journal of Law & Society* 56–76.
Shaffer, GC (2003) *Defending Interests: Public-Private Partnerships in WTO Litigation* (Washington DC, Brookings Institution Press).
Shelton, D (ed) (2000) *Commitment and Compliance. The Role of Non-Binding Norms in the International Legal System* (Oxford, Oxford University Press).
Sinclair, TJ (1999) 'Bond-Rating Agencies and Coordination in the Global Political Economy', in AC Cutler, V Haufler, and T Porter (eds), *Private authority and international affairs*, SUNY Series in Global Politics (Albany, NY, State University of New York Press) 153–67.
Slaughter, A-M (1997) 'The Real New World Order', 76(5) *Foreign Affairs*: 183–97.
—— (2004) *A New World Order* (Princeton, NJ/Oxford, Princeton University Press).
Snyder, F (2000) 'Global economic networks and global legal pluralism', in GA Bermann, M Herdegen, and PL Lindseth (eds), *Transatlantic Regulatory Cooperation* (Oxford, Oxford University Press) 99–115.
Teubner, G (1983) 'Substantive and Reflexive Elements in Modern Law', 17 *Law & Society Review* 239.
—— (1987) 'Juridification—Concepts, Aspects, Limits, Solutions', in G Teubner (ed) *Juridification of Social Spheres: A Comparative Analysis in the Areas of Labor, Corporate, Antitrust and Social Welfare Law* (Berlin, de Gruyter) 3–49.
—— (ed) (1997) *Global Law Without a State* (Aldershot, Dartmouth).
UNCTAD (United Nations Conference on Trade and Development) (2000) *Bilateral Investment Treaties 1959–1999* (Geneva, UNCTAD).
—— (2005) 'Latest Developments in Investor-State Dispute-Settlement', *IIA Monitor No 4* (Geneva, United Nations).
Van Harten, HHA (2007) *Investment Treaty Arbitration and Public Law* (Oxford, Oxford University Press).
Vincent-Jones, P (1998) 'Responsive Law and Governance in Public Services Provision: A Future for the Local Contracting State', 61 *Modern Law Review* 362–81.
—— (1999) 'The Regulation of Contractualisation in Quasi-Markets for Public Services', (Summer) *Public Law* 1–31.
Webb, K and Morrison, A (2004) 'The Law and Voluntary Codes: Examining the "Tangled Web"', in K Webb (ed) *Voluntary codes: Private governance, the public interest and innovation* (Ottawa: Carleton Research Unit for Innovation Science and Environment, Carleton University).

Weiler, JHH (1995) 'Does Europe Need a New Constitution? Demos, Telos and the German Maastricht Decision' 1(3) *European Law Journal* 219–58.

Woolcock, S (1996) 'Competition Among Rules in the Single European Market', in W Bratton, J McCahery, S Picciotto and C Scott, (eds) *International Regulatory Competition and Coordination. Perspectives on Economic Regulation in Europe and the United States*, (Oxford, Oxford University Press) 289–321.

Index